vault

PUBLISHER
DAMIAN A. WASSEL

EDITOR IN CHIEF
ADRIAN F. WASSEL

ART DIRECTOR
NATHAN C. GOODEN

MANAGING EDITOR
REBECCA TAYLOR

SALES & MARKETING, DIRECT MARKET
DAVID DISSANAYAKE

SALES & MARKETING, BOOK TRADE
SYNDEE BARWICK

PRODUCTION MANAGER
IAN BALDESSARI

EVP BRANDING & DESIGN
TIM DANIEL

PRINCIPAL
DAMIAN A. WASSEL SR.

DANIEL
KRAUS
WRITER

CHRIS
SHEHAN
ARTIST

JASON
WORDIE
COLORIST

JIM
CAMPBELL
LETTERER

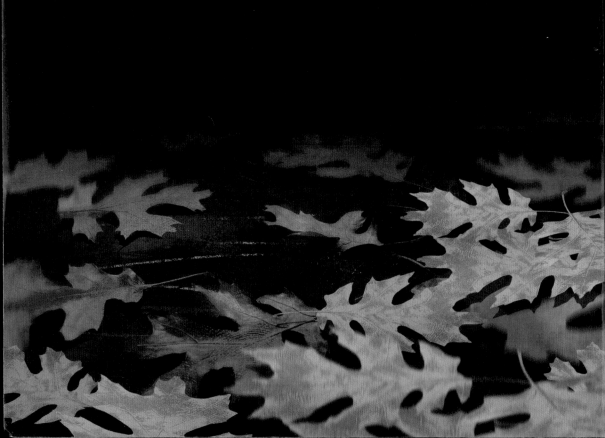

AUTUMNAL

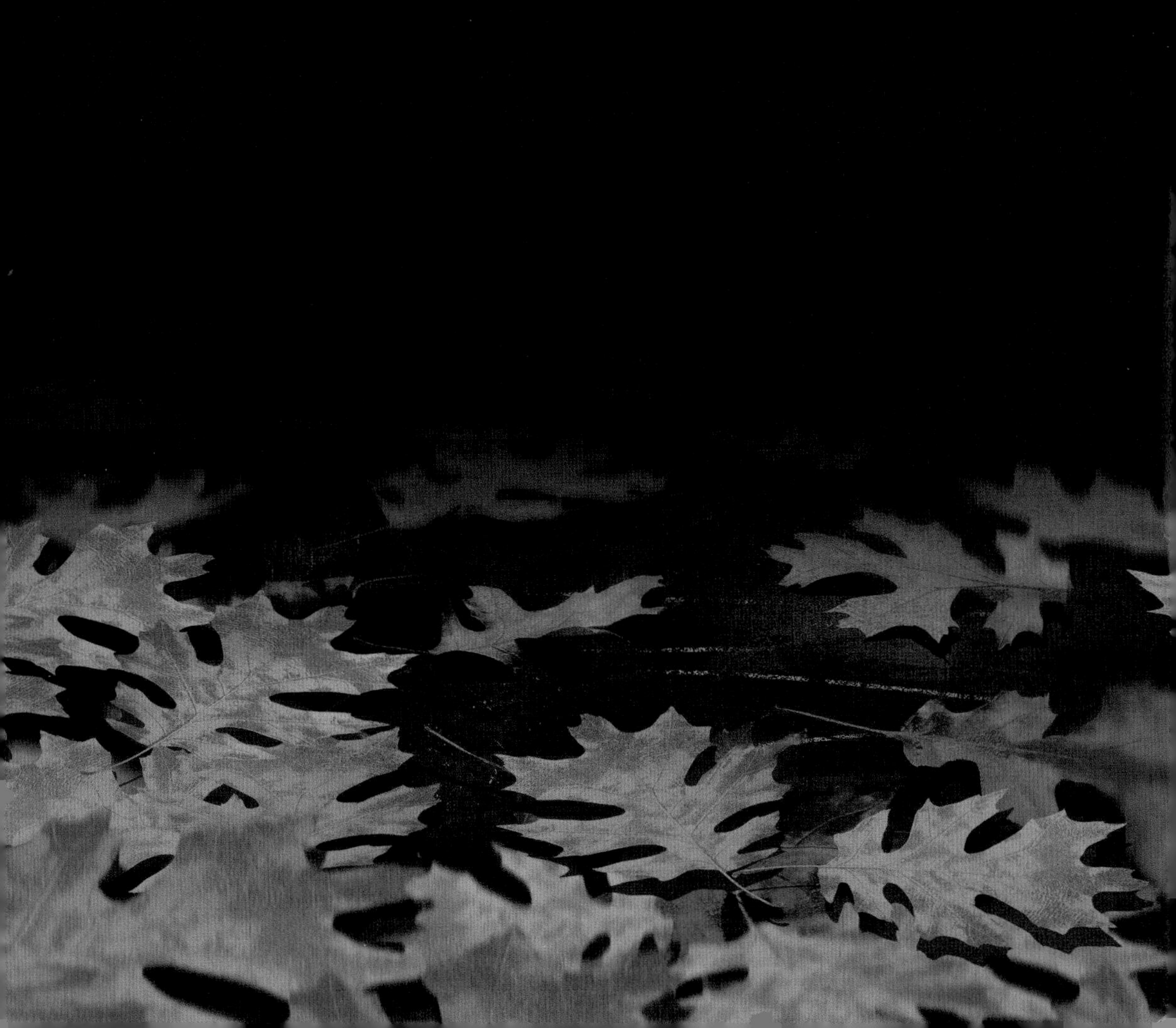

CHAPTER
ONE

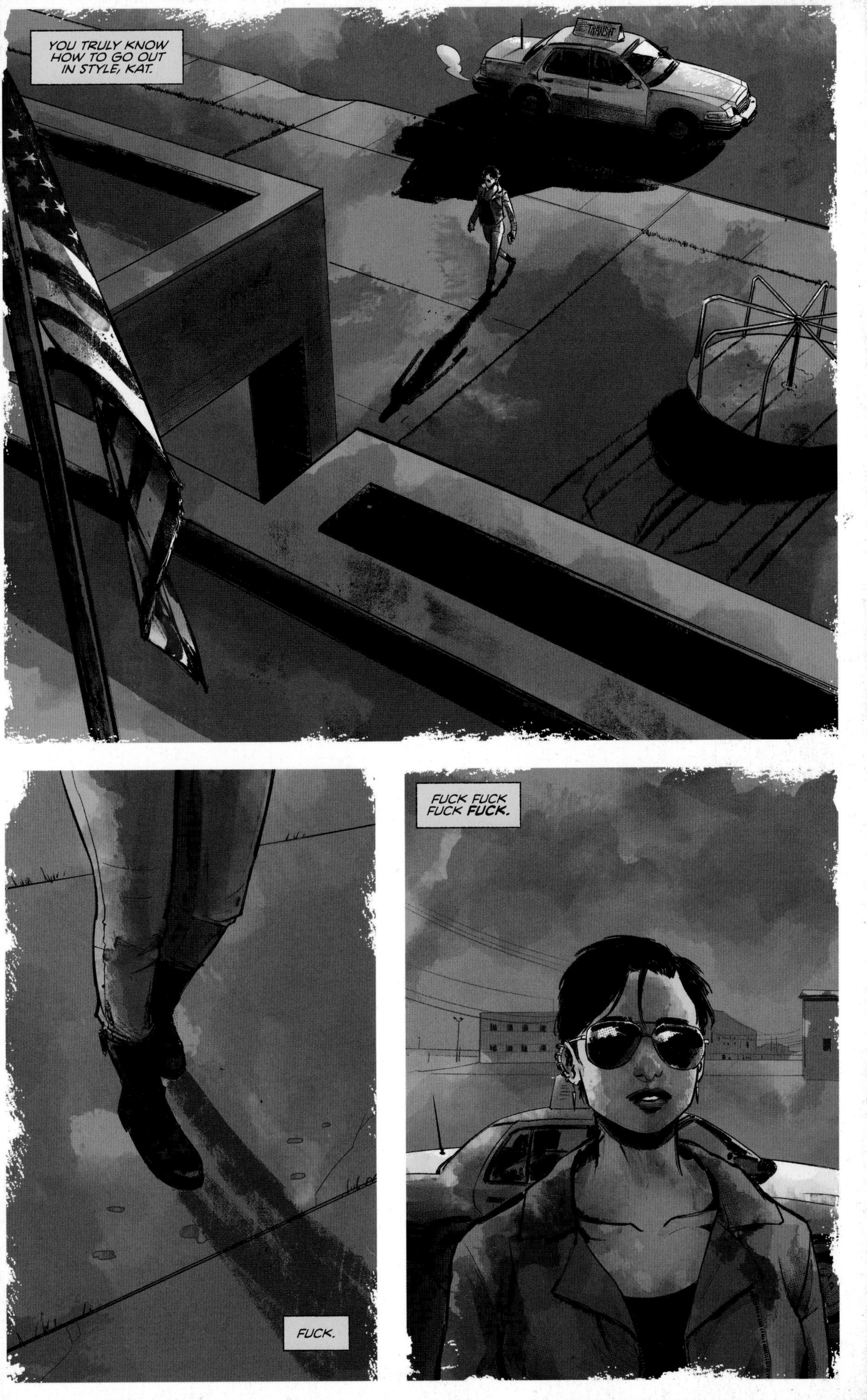
YOU TRULY KNOW HOW TO GO OUT IN STYLE, KAT.
FUCK.
FUCK FUCK FUCK **FUCK.**

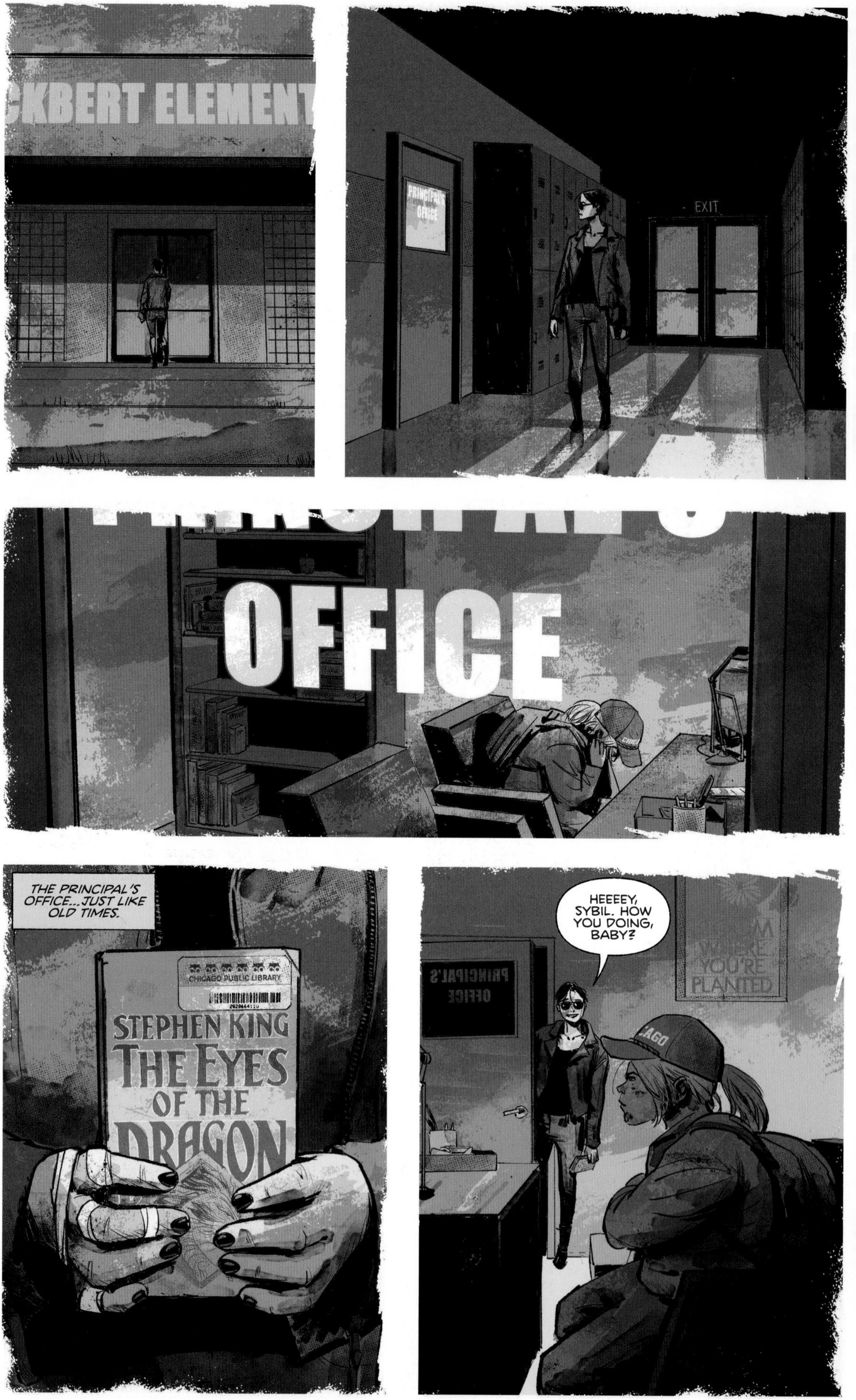
CKBERT ELEMENT
PRINCIPAL'S OFFICE
EXIT
OFFICE
THE PRINCIPAL'S OFFICE... JUST LIKE OLD TIMES.
CHICAGO PUBLIC LIBRARY
STEPHEN KING
THE EYES OF THE DRAGON
HEEEEY, SYBIL. HOW YOU DOING, BABY?
YOU'RE PLANTED

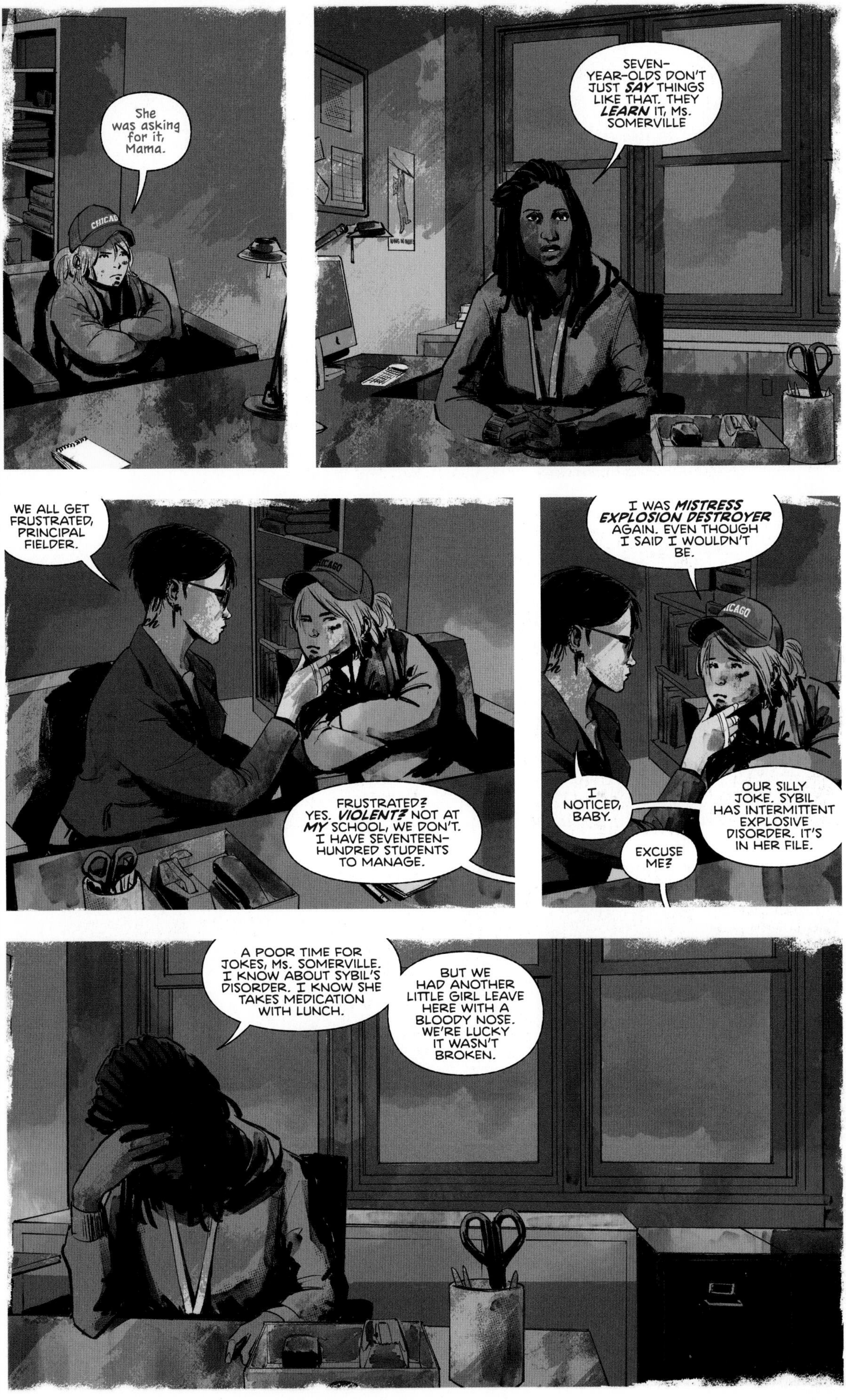
She was asking for it, Mama.
SEVEN-YEAR-OLDS DON'T JUST SAY THINGS LIKE THAT. THEY LEARN IT, Ms. SOMERVILLE
WE ALL GET FRUSTRATED, PRINCIPAL FIELDER.
FRUSTRATED? YES. VIOLENT? NOT AT MY SCHOOL, WE DON'T. I HAVE SEVENTEEN-HUNDRED STUDENTS TO MANAGE.
I WAS MISTRESS EXPLOSION DESTROYER AGAIN. EVEN THOUGH I SAID I WOULDN'T BE.
I NOTICED, BABY.
OUR SILLY JOKE. SYBIL HAS INTERMITTENT EXPLOSIVE DISORDER. IT'S IN HER FILE.
EXCUSE ME?
A POOR TIME FOR JOKES, Ms. SOMERVILLE. I KNOW ABOUT SYBIL'S DISORDER. I KNOW SHE TAKES MEDICATION WITH LUNCH.
BUT WE HAD ANOTHER LITTLE GIRL LEAVE HERE WITH A BLOODY NOSE. WE'RE LUCKY IT WASN'T BROKEN.

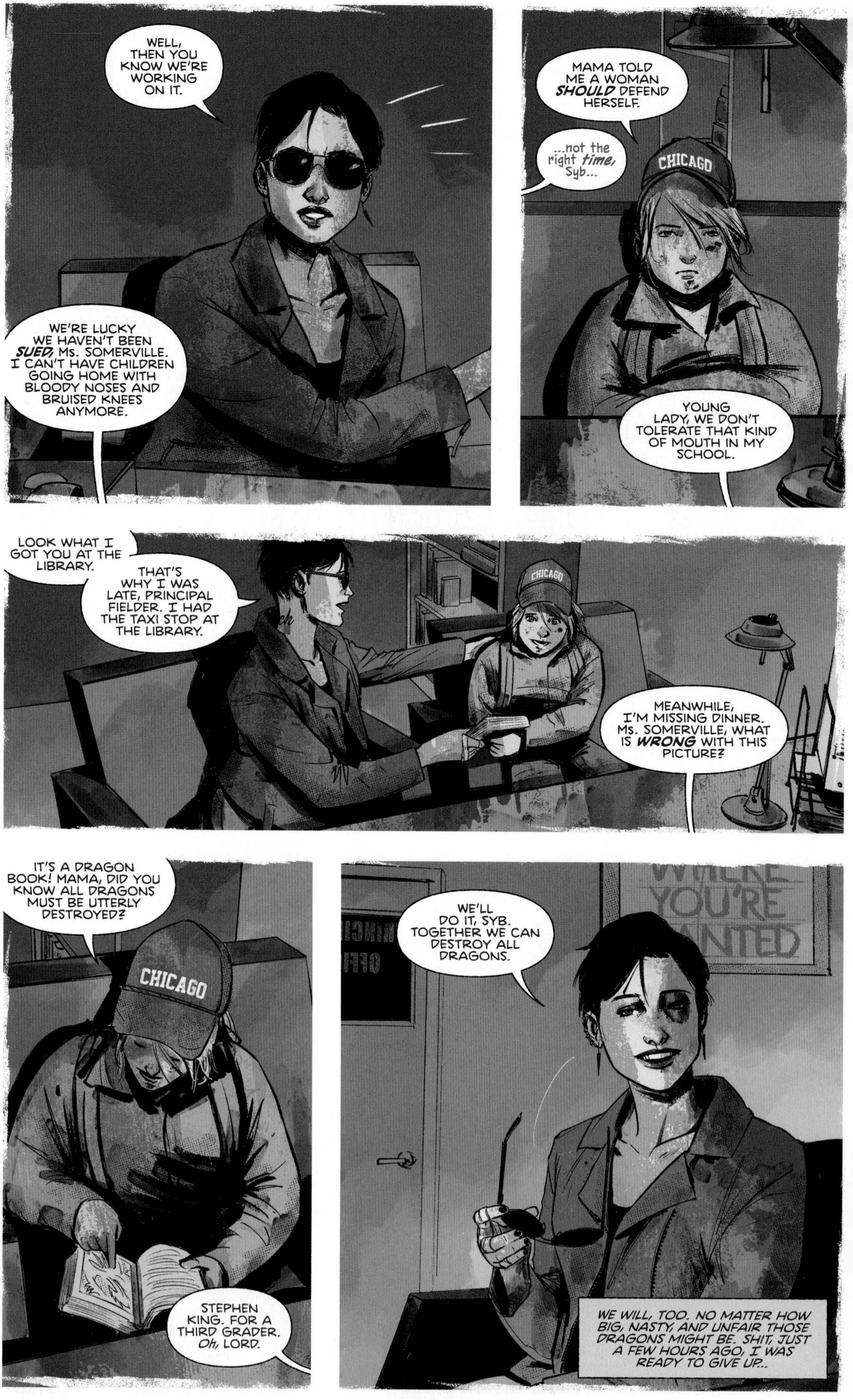
WELL, THEN YOU KNOW WE'RE WORKING ON IT.
WE'RE LUCKY WE HAVEN'T BEEN *SUED*, Ms. SOMERVILLE. I CAN'T HAVE CHILDREN GOING HOME WITH BLOODY NOSES AND BRUISED KNEES ANYMORE.
MAMA TOLD ME A WOMAN *SHOULD* DEFEND HERSELF.
...not the right *time*, Syb...
CHICAGO
YOUNG LADY, WE DON'T TOLERATE THAT KIND OF MOUTH IN MY SCHOOL.
LOOK WHAT I GOT YOU AT THE LIBRARY.
THAT'S WHY I WAS LATE, PRINCIPAL FIELDER. I HAD THE TAXI STOP AT THE LIBRARY.
CHICAGO
MEANWHILE, I'M MISSING DINNER. Ms. SOMERVILLE, WHAT IS *WRONG* WITH THIS PICTURE?
IT'S A DRAGON BOOK! MAMA, DID YOU KNOW ALL DRAGONS MUST BE UTTERLY DESTROYED?
CHICAGO
STEPHEN KING. FOR A THIRD GRADER. *Oh*, LORD.
WE'LL DO IT, SYB. TOGETHER WE CAN DESTROY ALL DRAGONS.
YOU'RE
WE WILL, TOO. NO MATTER HOW BIG, NASTY, AND UNFAIR THOSE DRAGONS MIGHT BE. SHIT, JUST A FEW HOURS AGO, I WAS READY TO GIVE UP...

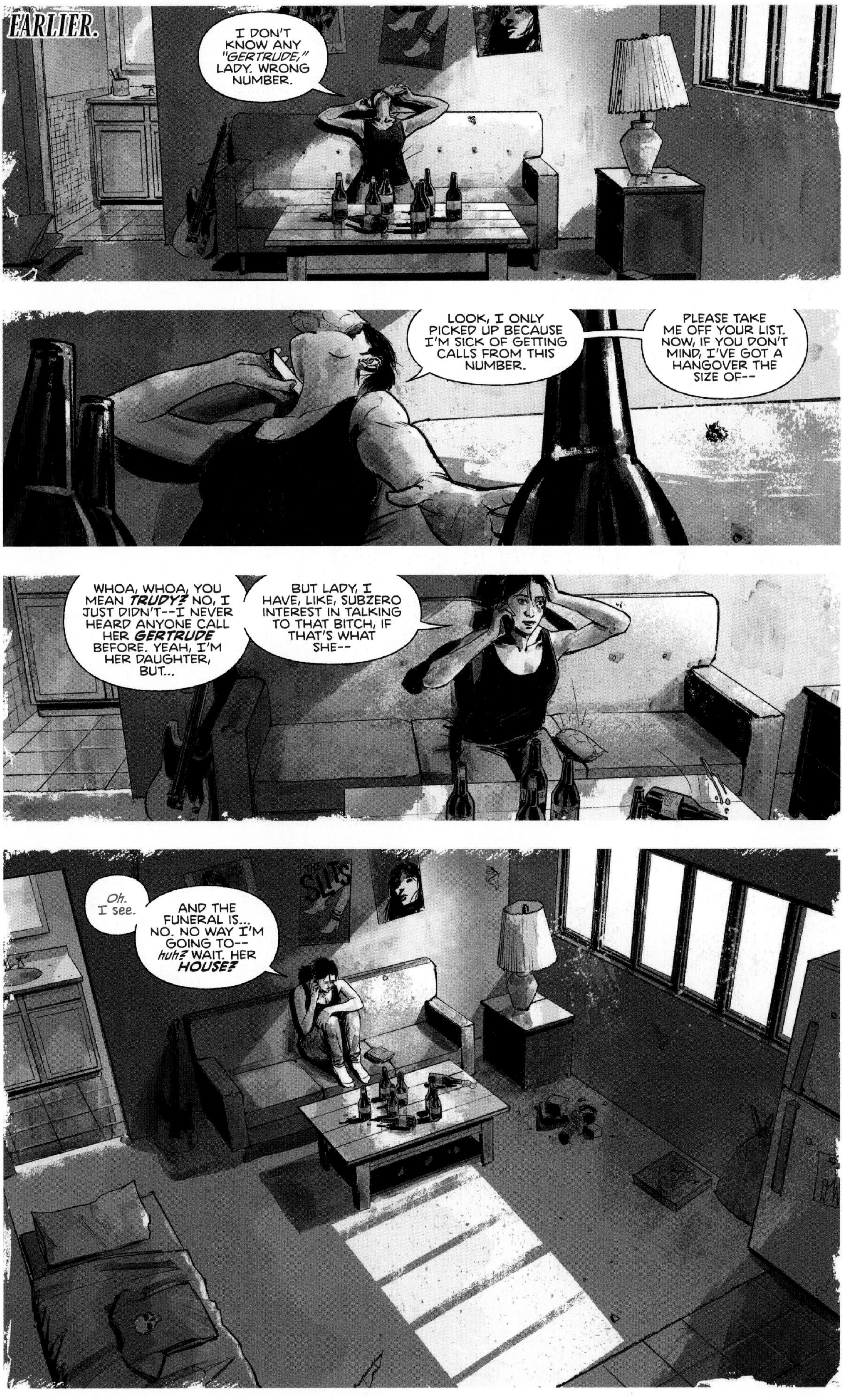
EARLIER.
I DON'T KNOW ANY "GERTRUDE," LADY. WRONG NUMBER.
LOOK, I ONLY PICKED UP BECAUSE I'M SICK OF GETTING CALLS FROM THIS NUMBER.
PLEASE TAKE ME OFF YOUR LIST. NOW, IF YOU DON'T MIND, I'VE GOT A HANGOVER THE SIZE OF--
WHOA, WHOA, YOU MEAN *TRUDY?* NO, I JUST DIDN'T--I NEVER HEARD ANYONE CALL HER *GERTRUDE* BEFORE. YEAH, I'M HER DAUGHTER, BUT...
BUT LADY, I HAVE, LIKE, SUBZERO INTEREST IN TALKING TO THAT BITCH, IF THAT'S WHAT SHE--
Oh. *I see.*
AND THE FUNERAL IS... NO. NO WAY I'M GOING TO-- *huh?* WAIT. HER *HOUSE?*
THE SLITS

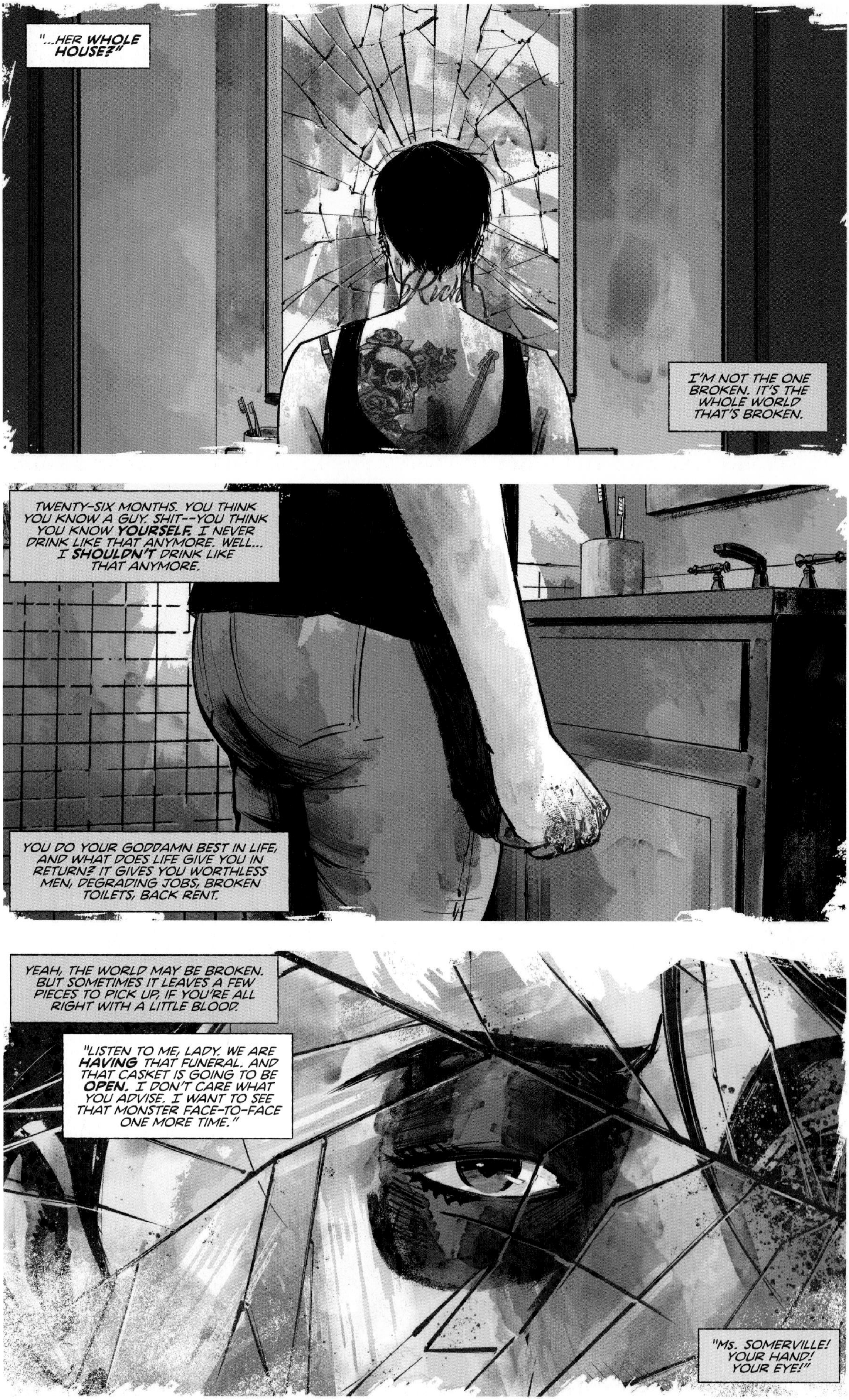
"...HER WHOLE HOUSE?"
I'M NOT THE ONE BROKEN. IT'S THE WHOLE WORLD THAT'S BROKEN.
TWENTY-SIX MONTHS. YOU THINK YOU KNOW A GUY. SHIT--YOU THINK YOU KNOW YOURSELF. I NEVER DRINK LIKE THAT ANYMORE. WELL... I SHOULDN'T DRINK LIKE THAT ANYMORE.
YOU DO YOUR GODDAMN BEST IN LIFE, AND WHAT DOES LIFE GIVE YOU IN RETURN? IT GIVES YOU WORTHLESS MEN, DEGRADING JOBS, BROKEN TOILETS, BACK RENT.
YEAH, THE WORLD MAY BE BROKEN. BUT SOMETIMES IT LEAVES A FEW PIECES TO PICK UP, IF YOU'RE ALL RIGHT WITH A LITTLE BLOOD.
"LISTEN TO ME, LADY. WE ARE HAVING THAT FUNERAL. AND THAT CASKET IS GOING TO BE OPEN. I DON'T CARE WHAT YOU ADVISE. I WANT TO SEE THAT MONSTER FACE-TO-FACE ONE MORE TIME."
"MS. SOMERVILLE! YOUR HAND! YOUR EYE!"

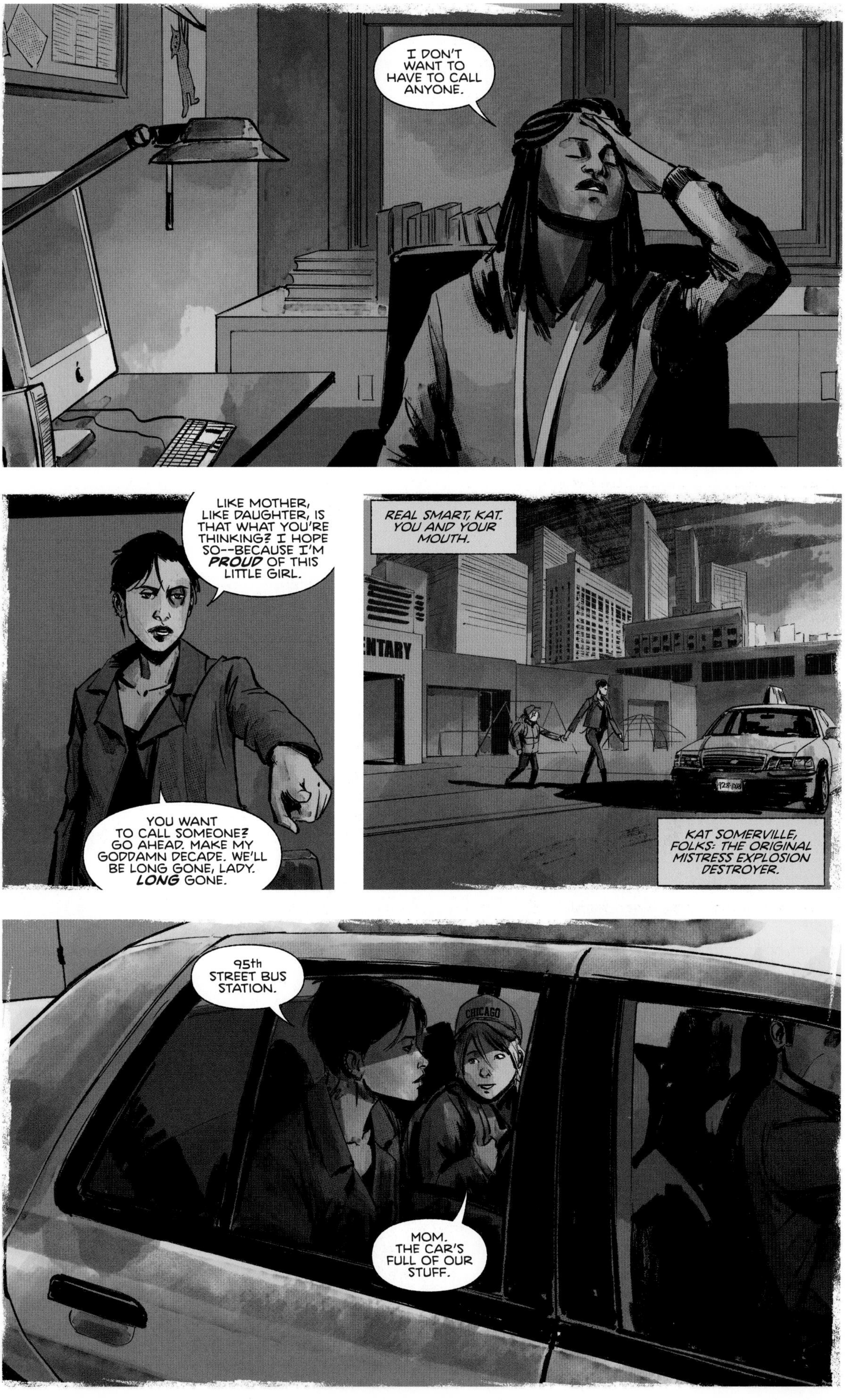
I DON'T WANT TO HAVE TO CALL ANYONE.
LIKE MOTHER, LIKE DAUGHTER, IS THAT WHAT YOU'RE THINKING? I HOPE SO--BECAUSE I'M *PROUD* OF THIS LITTLE GIRL.
YOU WANT TO CALL SOMEONE? GO AHEAD. MAKE MY GODDAMN DECADE. WE'LL BE LONG GONE, LADY. *LONG* GONE.
REAL SMART, KAT. YOU AND YOUR MOUTH.
ENTARY
KAT SOMERVILLE, FOLKS: THE ORIGINAL MISTRESS EXPLOSION DESTROYER.
95th STREET BUS STATION.
CHICAGO
MOM. THE CAR'S FULL OF OUR STUFF.

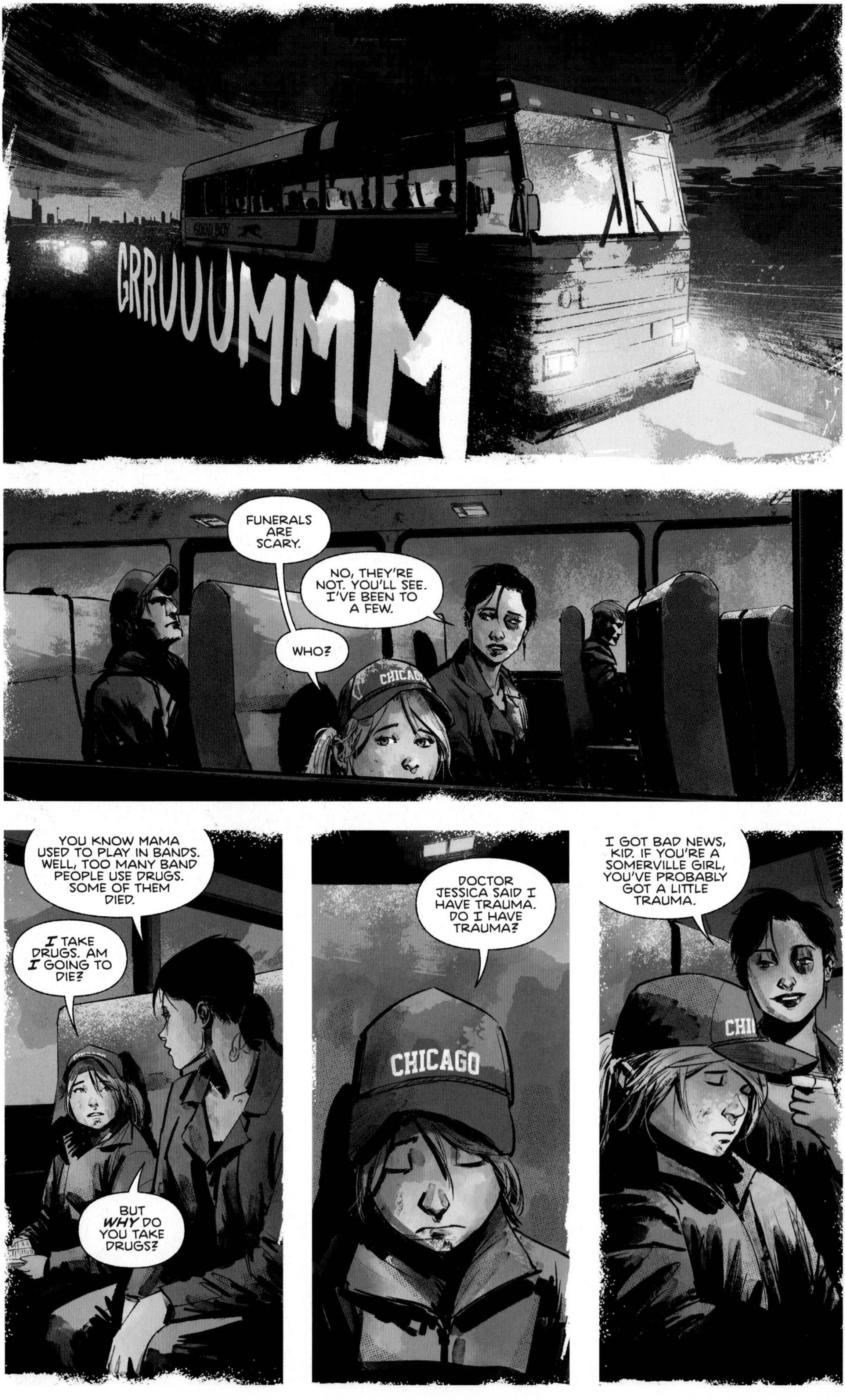
GRRUUUMMM
FUNERALS ARE SCARY.
NO, THEY'RE NOT. YOU'LL SEE. I'VE BEEN TO A FEW.
WHO?
CHICAGO
YOU KNOW MAMA USED TO PLAY IN BANDS. WELL, TOO MANY BAND PEOPLE USE DRUGS. SOME OF THEM DIED.
I TAKE DRUGS. AM *I* GOING TO DIE?
BUT *WHY* DO YOU TAKE DRUGS?
DOCTOR JESSICA SAID I HAVE TRAUMA. DO I HAVE TRAUMA?
CHICAGO
I GOT BAD NEWS, KID. IF YOU'RE A SOMERVILLE GIRL, YOU'VE PROBABLY GOT A LITTLE TRAUMA.

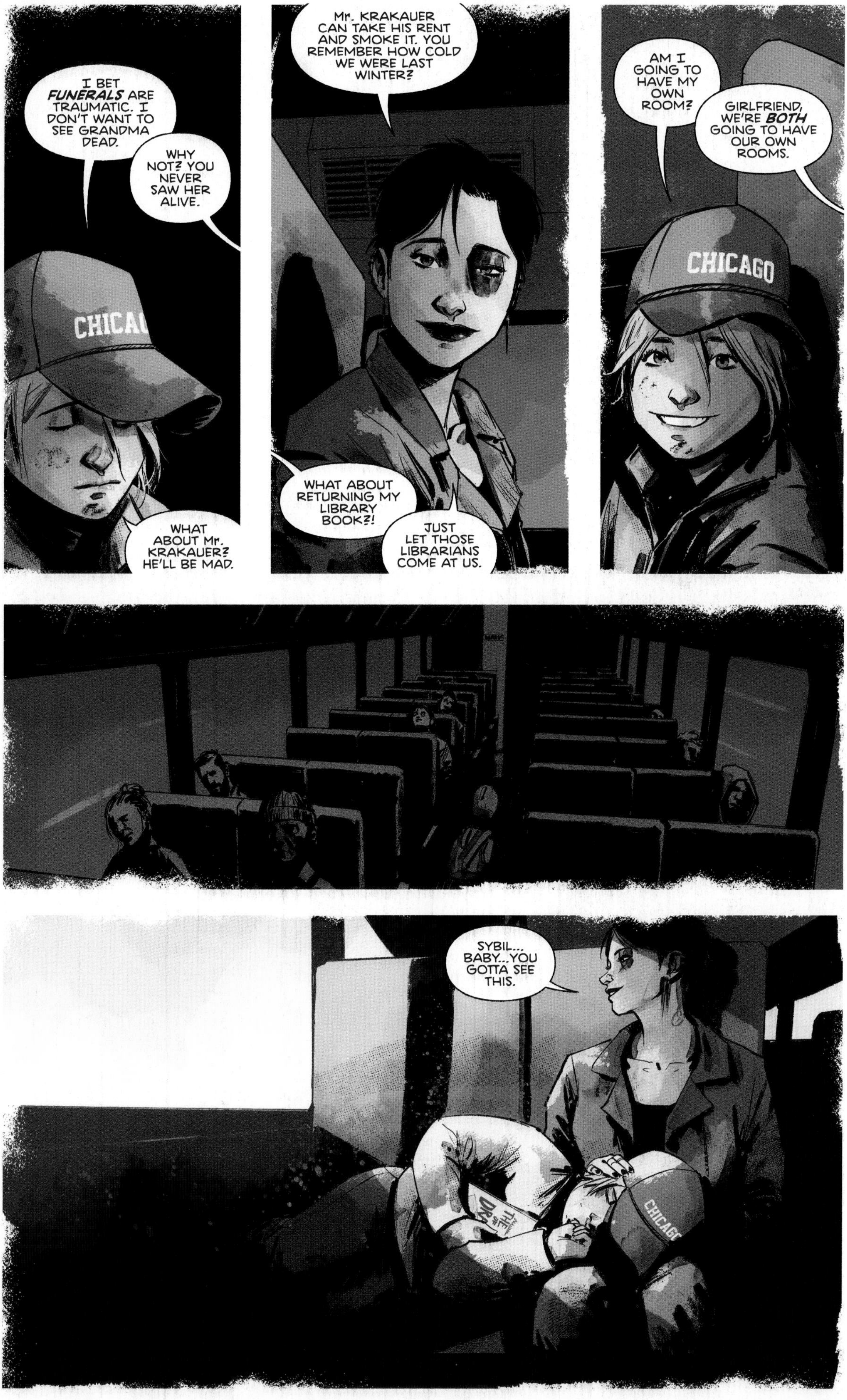
I BET *FUNERALS* ARE TRAUMATIC. I DON'T WANT TO SEE GRANDMA DEAD.
WHY NOT? YOU NEVER SAW HER ALIVE.
WHAT ABOUT Mr. KRAKAUER? HE'LL BE MAD.
Mr. KRAKAUER CAN TAKE HIS RENT AND SMOKE IT. YOU REMEMBER HOW COLD WE WERE LAST WINTER?
WHAT ABOUT RETURNING MY LIBRARY BOOK?!
JUST LET THOSE LIBRARIANS COME AT US.
AM I GOING TO HAVE MY OWN ROOM?
GIRLFRIEND, WE'RE *BOTH* GOING TO HAVE OUR OWN ROOMS.
CHICAGO
SYBIL... BABY... YOU GOTTA SEE THIS.

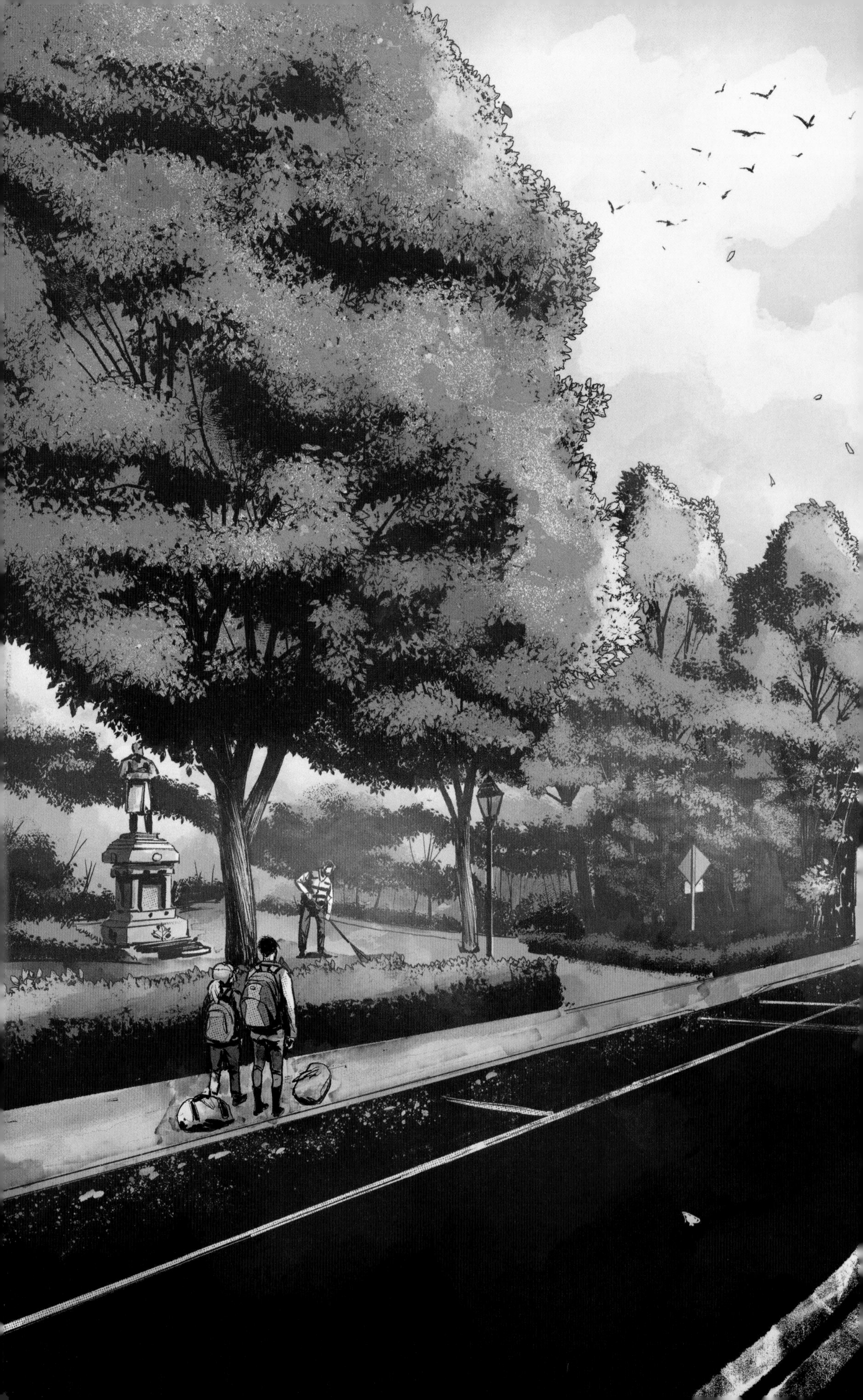

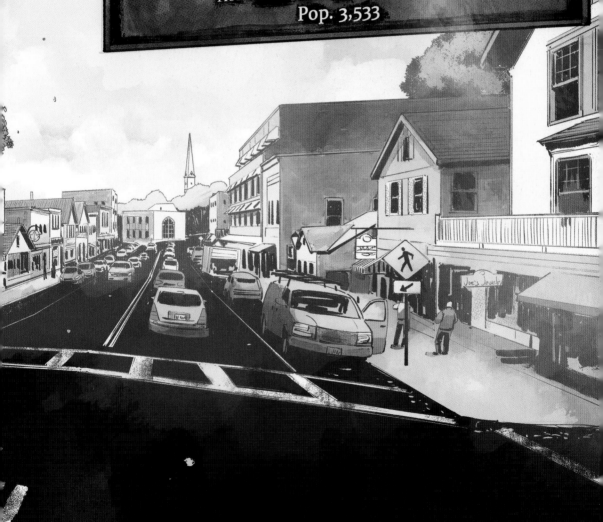

Welcome To
Comfort Notch

Home of America's Prettiest Autumn
Pop. 3,533

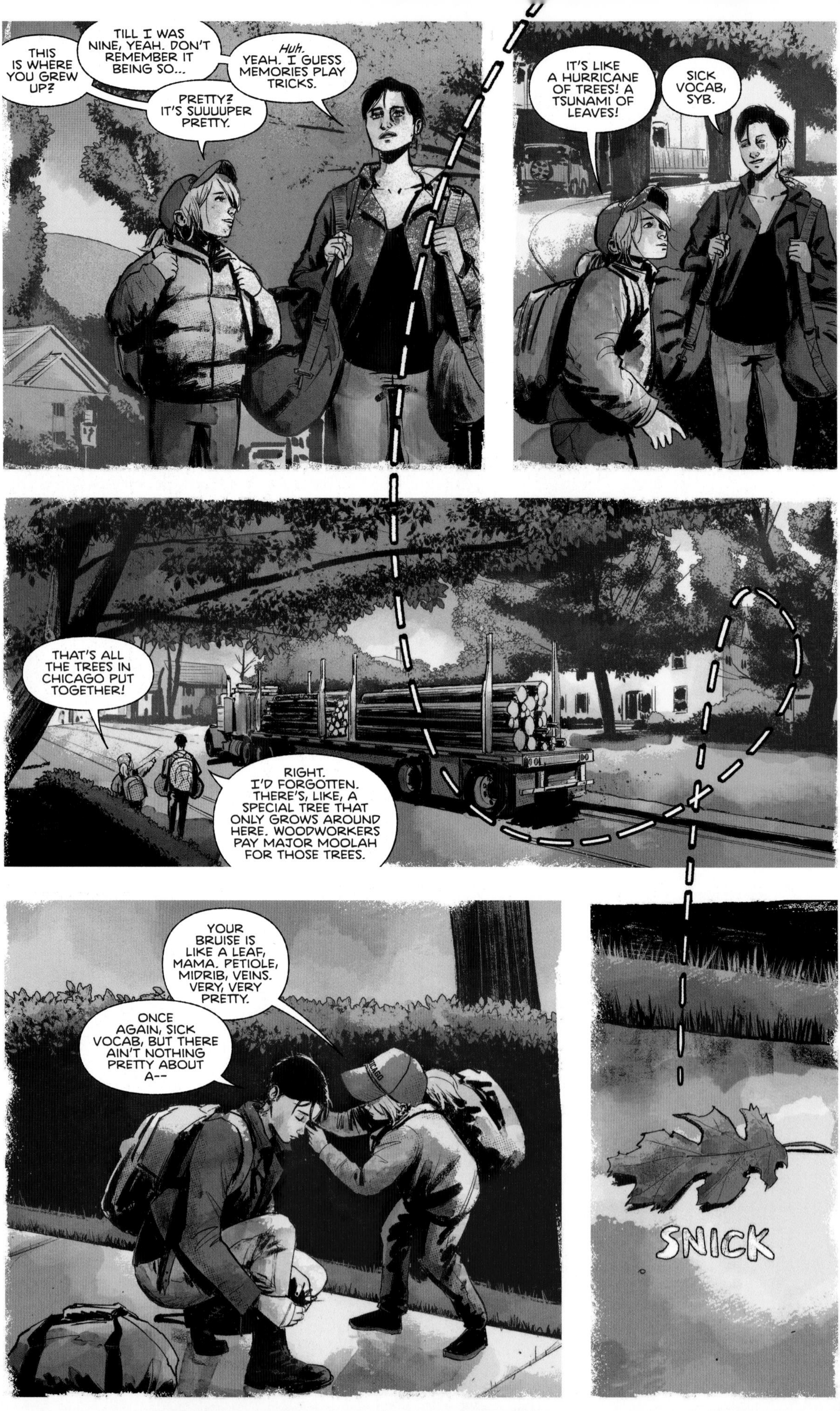
THIS IS WHERE YOU GREW UP?
TILL I WAS NINE, YEAH. DON'T REMEMBER IT BEING SO...
PRETTY? IT'S SUUUUPER PRETTY.
Huh. YEAH. I GUESS MEMORIES PLAY TRICKS.
IT'S LIKE A HURRICANE OF TREES! A TSUNAMI OF LEAVES!
SICK VOCAB, SYB.
THAT'S ALL THE TREES IN CHICAGO PUT TOGETHER!
RIGHT. I'D FORGOTTEN. THERE'S, LIKE, A SPECIAL TREE THAT ONLY GROWS AROUND HERE. WOODWORKERS PAY MAJOR MOOLAH FOR THOSE TREES.
YOUR BRUISE IS LIKE A LEAF, MAMA. PETIOLE, MIDRIB, VEINS. VERY, VERY PRETTY.
ONCE AGAIN, SICK VOCAB, BUT THERE AIN'T NOTHING PRETTY ABOUT A--
SNICK

I DON'T WANT YOU LOOKING LIKE ME.
I CAN'T HELP IT. WE HAVE THE SAME CHLOROPHYLL.

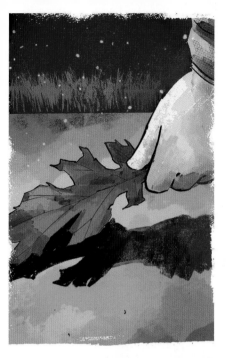

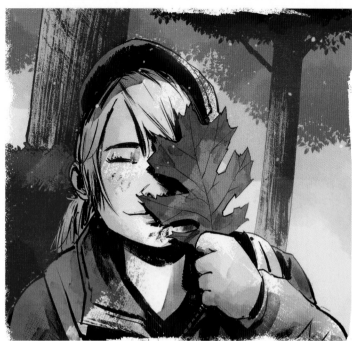

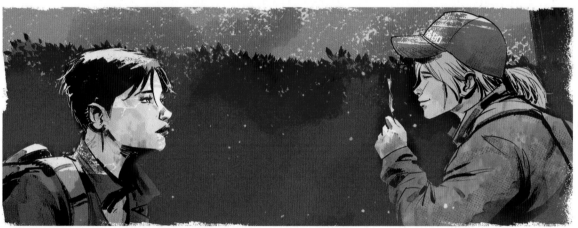

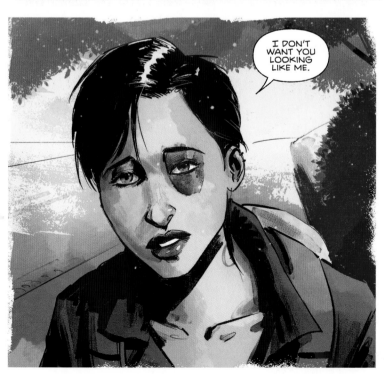

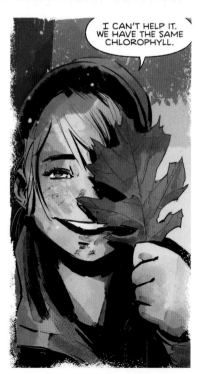

DON'T DO THAT!

I'M SORRY, MA'AM. I'M SORRY, LITTLE LADY. IT'S JUST, YOU NEVER CAN TELL WHAT'S ON THESE SIDEWALKS, YOU KNOW? PESTICIDE RUNOFF, DOG PEE.

IT'S OKAY. SHE'S JUST NOT USED TO SEEING SO MUCH NATURE. ARE YOU, SYB?

CITY FOLK, *eh?* SORRY TO SAY, COMFORT NOTCH DOESN'T HAVE A WHOLE LOT TO OFFER IN TERMS OF EXCITEMENT. ESPECIALLY WITH THE FALL EQUINOX COMING OUR WAY.

YOUR SIGN SAYS "AMERICA'S PRETTIEST AUTUMN." YOU MUST GET FOLIAGE TOURISTS.

LEAF PEEPERS? *Nah.* WE'RE GROWERS, NOT SHOWERS. NOW LOOK, THAT BUS OF YOURS ONLY CHUGS BY ONCE A WEEK. BUT I KNOW A GOOD KID WHO'D DRIVE YOU TO ROCHESTER FOR TEN BUCKS, I BET--

WE'RE HERE TO SEE MY DEAD GRANDMA.

JESUS, SYB, A LITTLE TACT, HOW ABOUT?

YOU'RE NOT...RELATED TO OL'...

GRANDMA.

TRUDY.

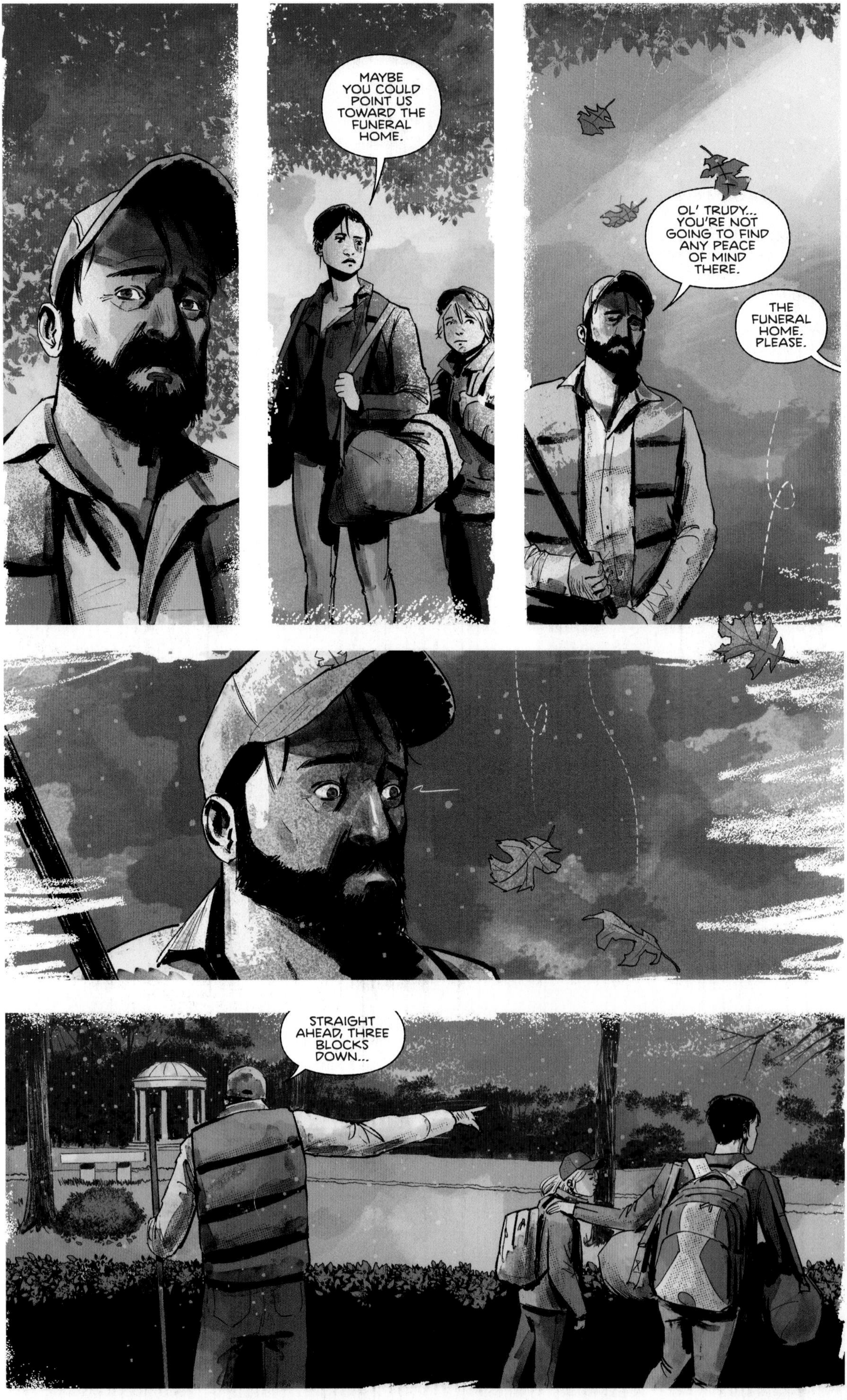
MAYBE YOU COULD POINT US TOWARD THE FUNERAL HOME.
OL' TRUDY... YOU'RE NOT GOING TO FIND ANY PEACE OF MIND THERE.
THE FUNERAL HOME. PLEASE.
STRAIGHT AHEAD, THREE BLOCKS DOWN...

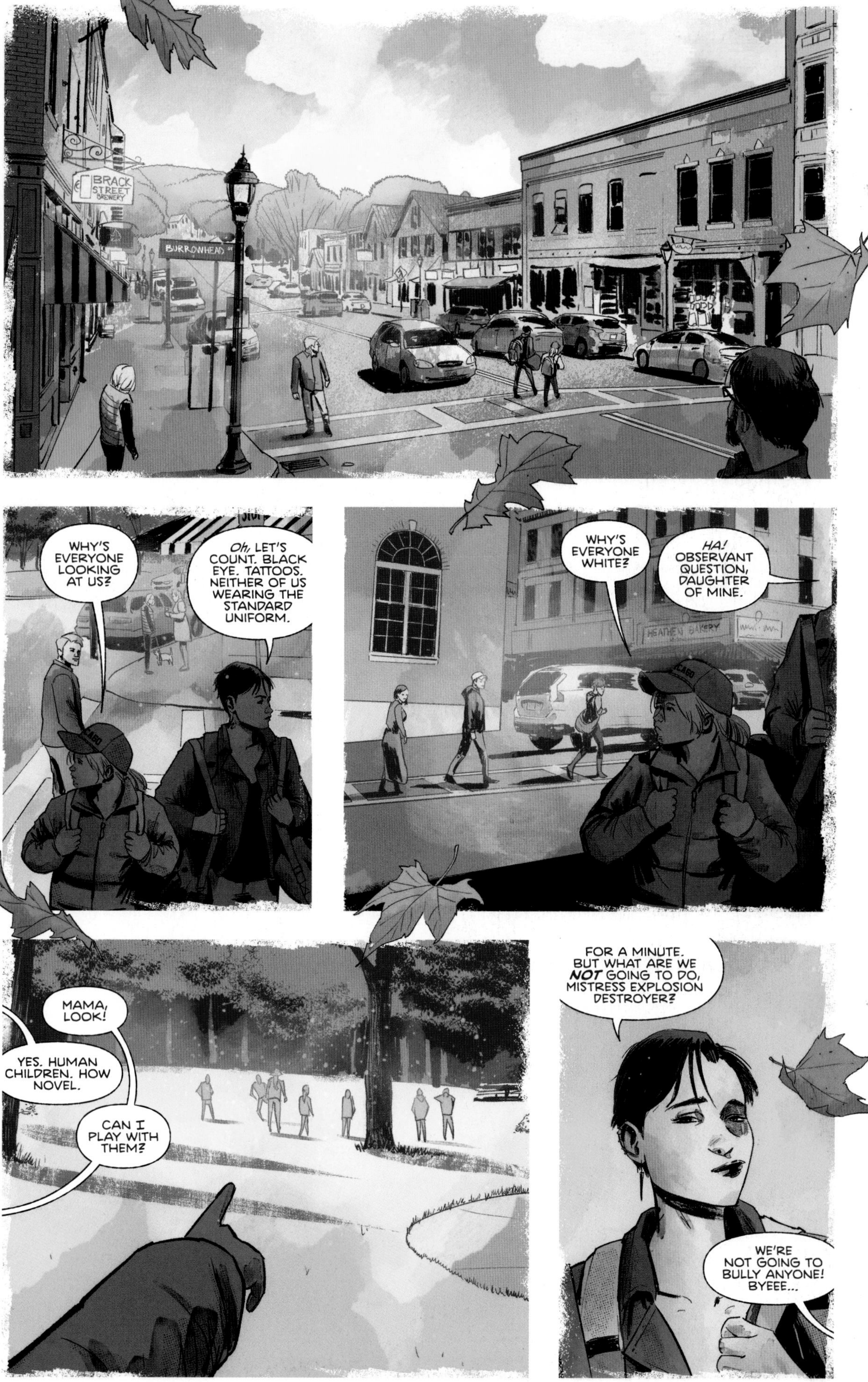
BRACK STREET BREWERY
BURROWHEAD
WHY'S EVERYONE LOOKING AT US?
Oh, LET'S COUNT. BLACK EYE. TATTOOS. NEITHER OF US WEARING THE STANDARD UNIFORM.
WHY'S EVERYONE WHITE?
HA! OBSERVANT QUESTION, DAUGHTER OF MINE.
HEATHEN BAKERY
MAMA, LOOK!
YES. HUMAN CHILDREN. HOW NOVEL.
CAN I PLAY WITH THEM?
FOR A MINUTE. BUT WHAT ARE WE ***NOT*** GOING TO DO, MISTRESS EXPLOSION DESTROYER?
WE'RE NOT GOING TO BULLY ANYONE! BYEEE...

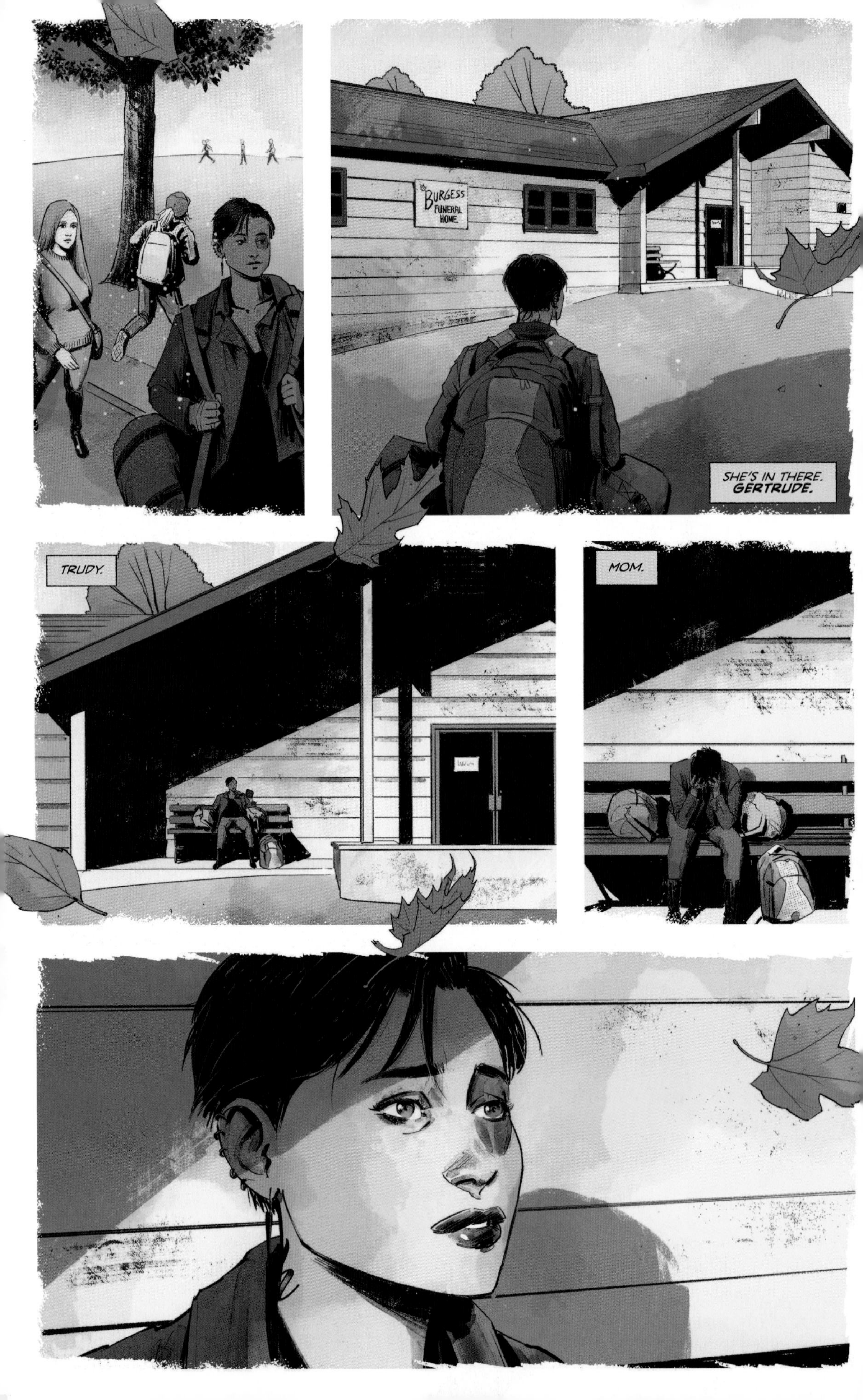
BURGESS
FUNERAL
HOME
SHE'S IN THERE.
GERTRUDE.
TRUDY.
MOM.

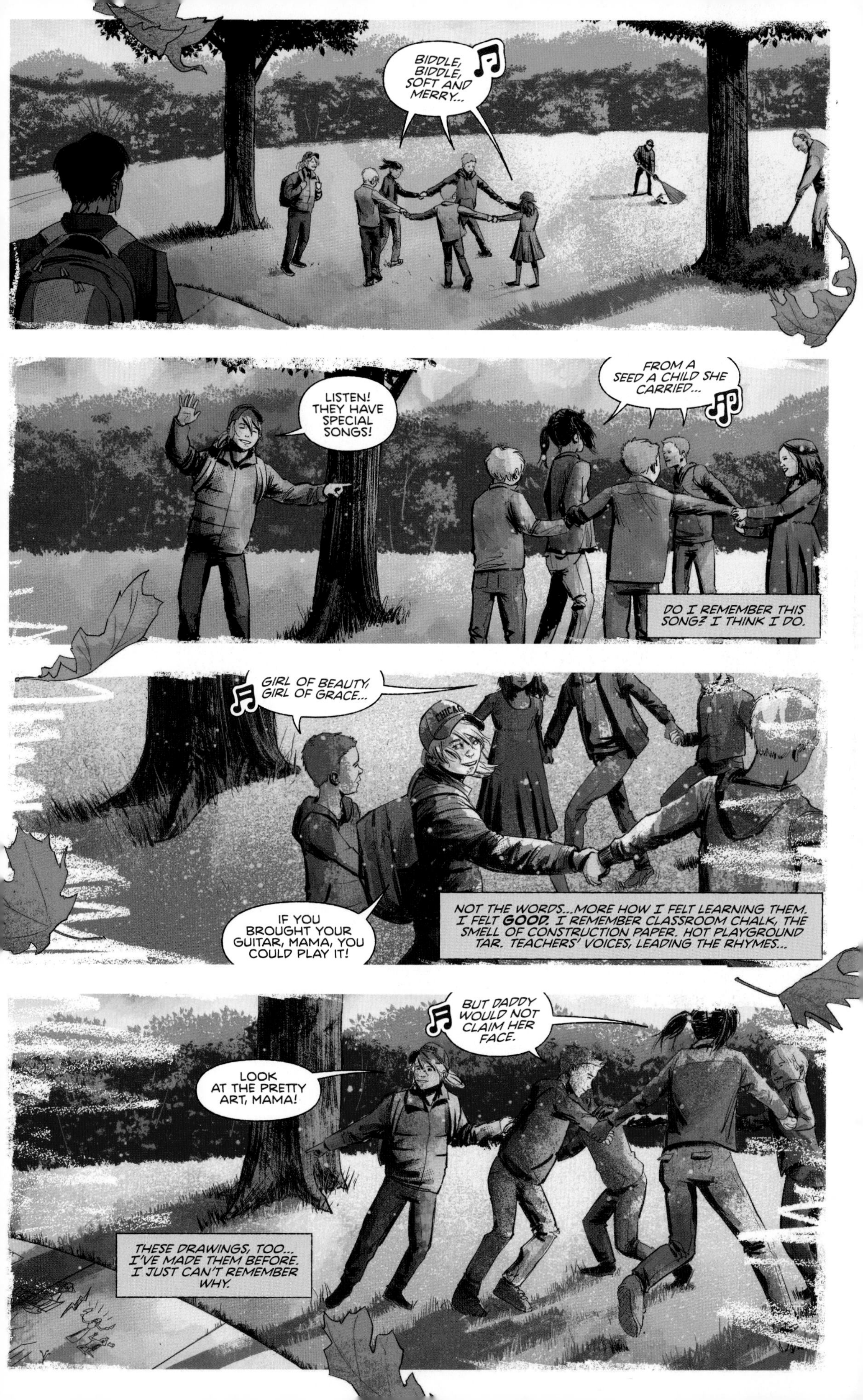
BIDDLE, BIDDLE, SOFT AND MERRY...
LISTEN! THEY HAVE SPECIAL SONGS!
FROM A SEED A CHILD SHE CARRIED...
DO I REMEMBER THIS SONG? I THINK I DO.
GIRL OF BEAUTY, GIRL OF GRACE...
IF YOU BROUGHT YOUR GUITAR, MAMA, YOU COULD PLAY IT!
NOT THE WORDS...MORE HOW I FELT LEARNING THEM. I FELT GOOD. I REMEMBER CLASSROOM CHALK, THE SMELL OF CONSTRUCTION PAPER. HOT PLAYGROUND TAR. TEACHERS' VOICES, LEADING THE RHYMES...
BUT DADDY WOULD NOT CLAIM HER FACE.
LOOK AT THE PRETTY ART, MAMA!
THESE DRAWINGS, TOO... I'VE MADE THEM BEFORE. I JUST CAN'T REMEMBER WHY.

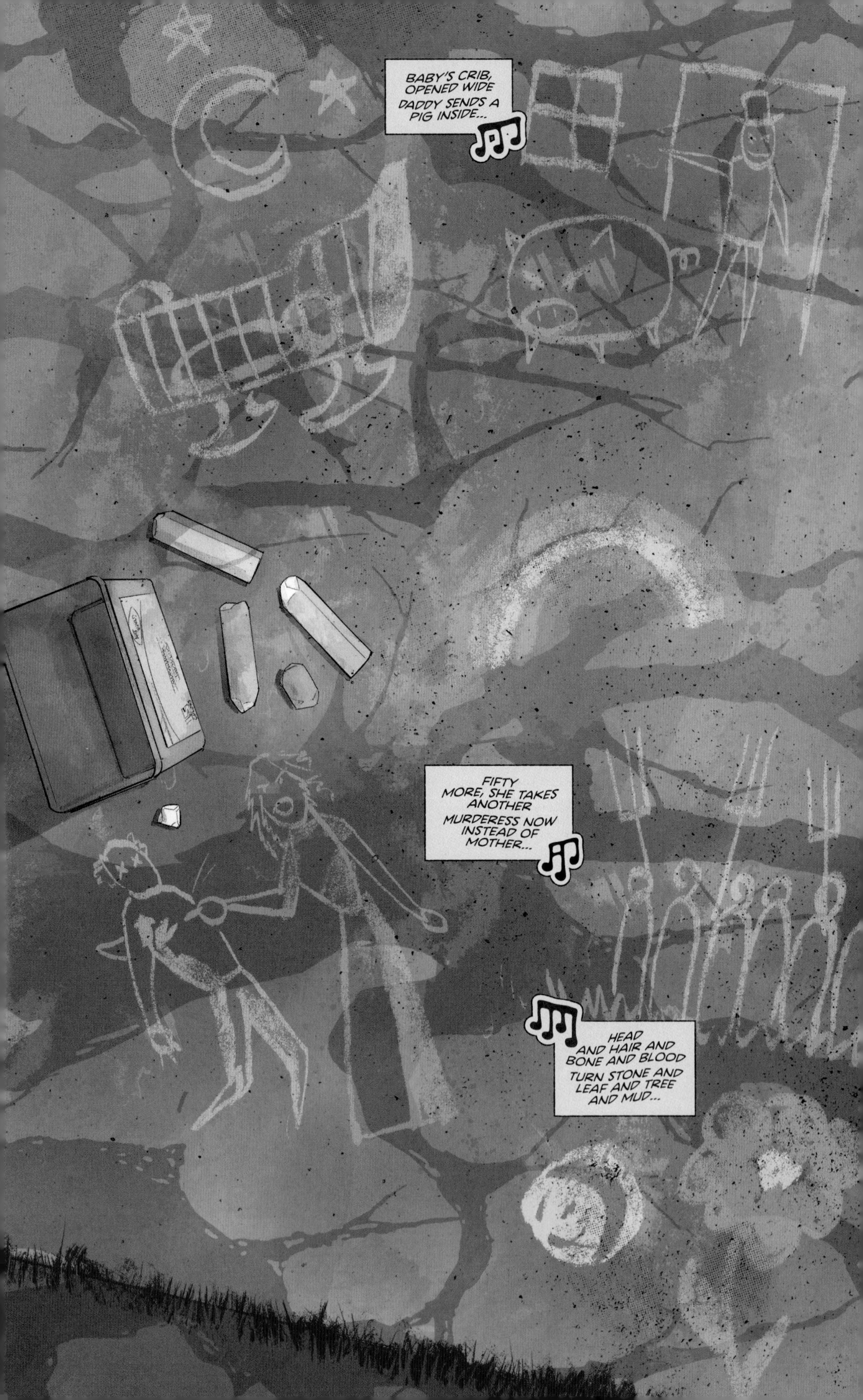
BABY'S CRIB, OPENED WIDE
DADDY SENDS A PIG INSIDE...
FIFTY MORE, SHE TAKES ANOTHER
MURDERESS NOW INSTEAD OF MOTHER...
HEAD AND HAIR AND BONE AND BLOOD
TURN STONE AND LEAF AND TREE AND MUD...

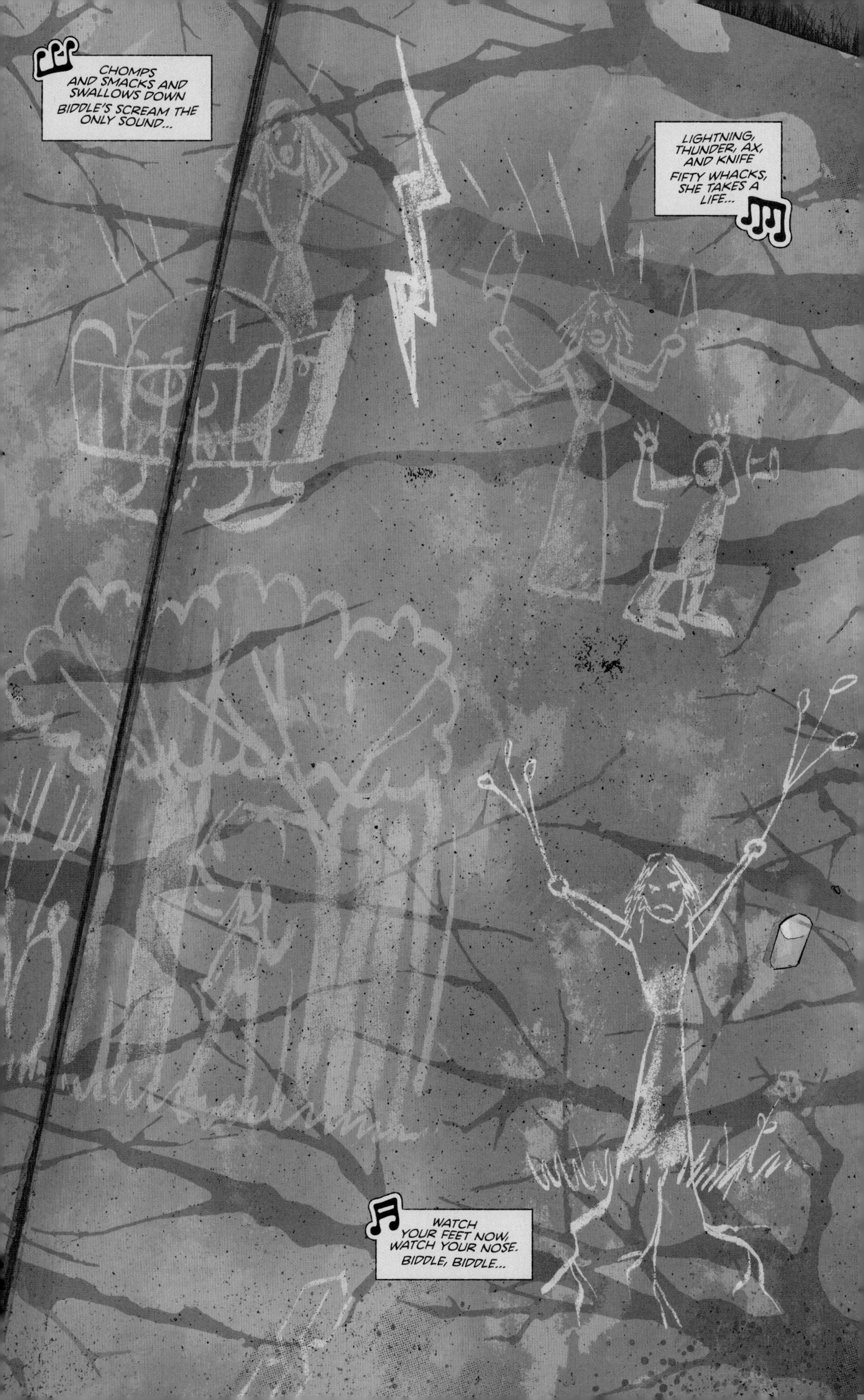
CHOMPS AND SMACKS AND SWALLOWS DOWN BIDDLE'S SCREAM THE ONLY SOUND...
LIGHTNING, THUNDER, AX, AND KNIFE FIFTY WHACKS, SHE TAKES A LIFE...
WATCH YOUR FEET NOW, WATCH YOUR NOSE. BIDDLE, BIDDLE...

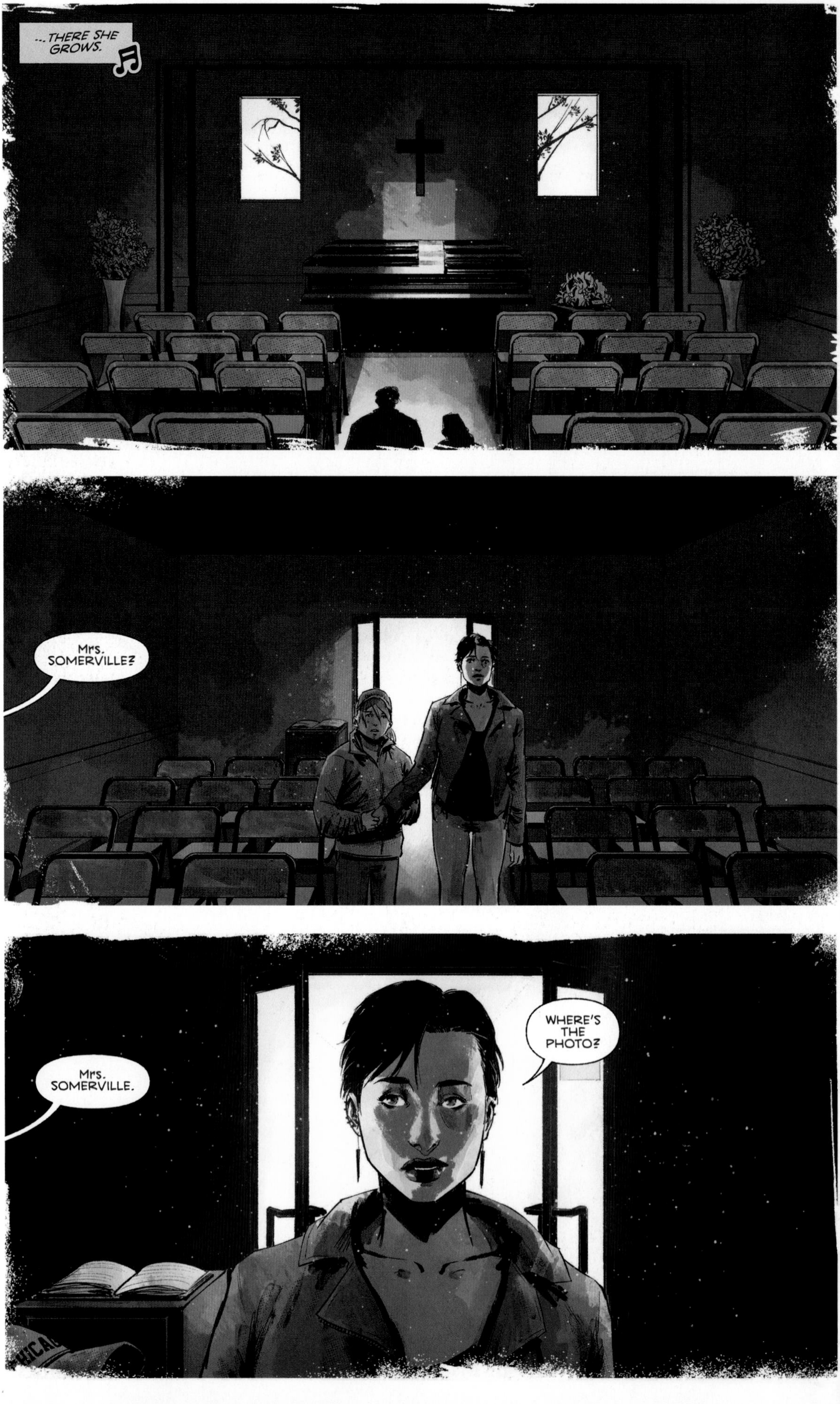
...THERE SHE GROWS.
Mrs. SOMERVILLE?
Mrs. SOMERVILLE.
WHERE'S THE PHOTO?

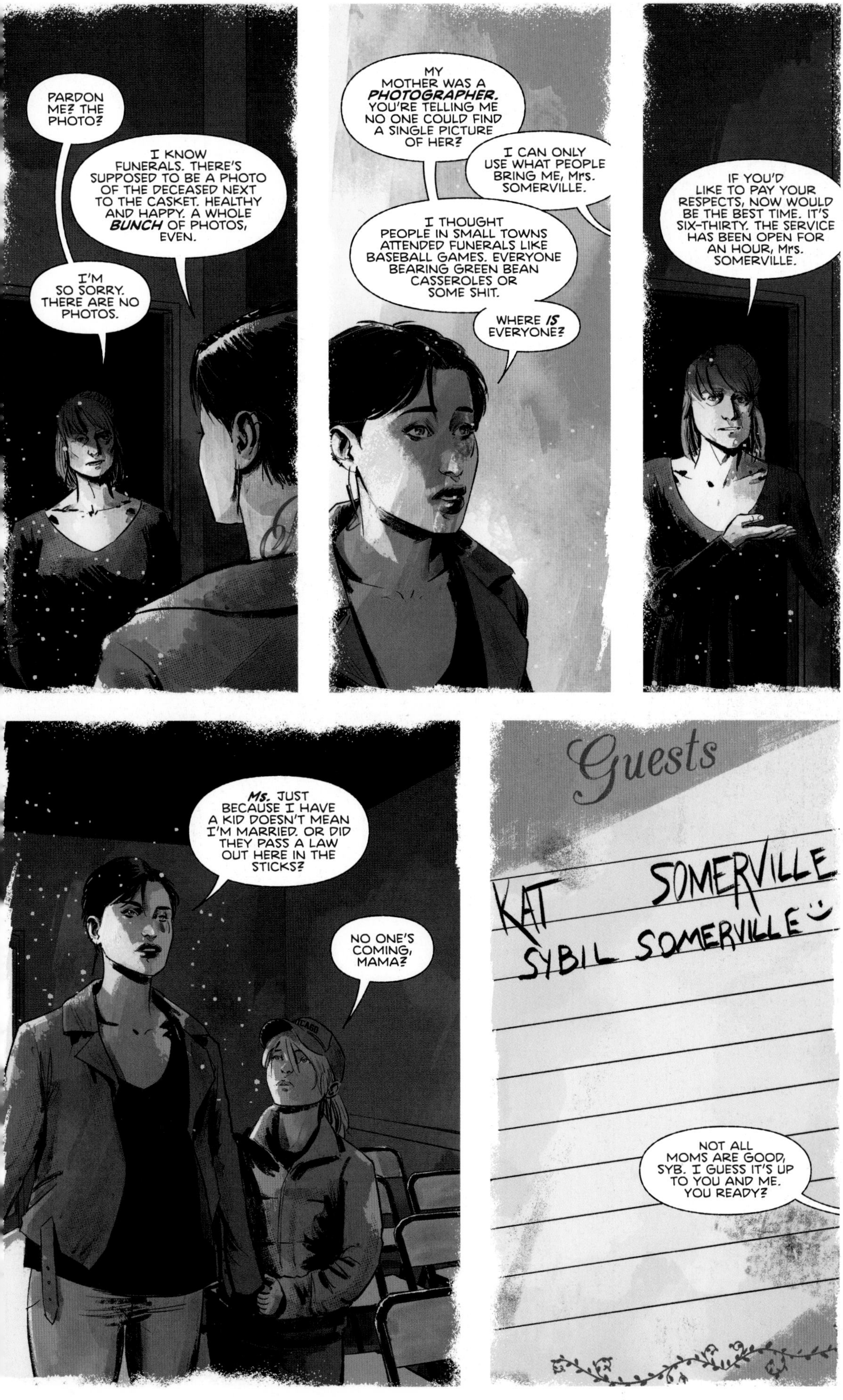
PARDON ME? THE PHOTO?
I KNOW FUNERALS. THERE'S SUPPOSED TO BE A PHOTO OF THE DECEASED NEXT TO THE CASKET. HEALTHY AND HAPPY. A WHOLE BUNCH OF PHOTOS, EVEN.
I'M SO SORRY. THERE ARE NO PHOTOS.
MY MOTHER WAS A PHOTOGRAPHER. YOU'RE TELLING ME NO ONE COULD FIND A SINGLE PICTURE OF HER?
I CAN ONLY USE WHAT PEOPLE BRING ME, Mrs. SOMERVILLE.
I THOUGHT PEOPLE IN SMALL TOWNS ATTENDED FUNERALS LIKE BASEBALL GAMES. EVERYONE BEARING GREEN BEAN CASSEROLES OR SOME SHIT.
WHERE IS EVERYONE?
IF YOU'D LIKE TO PAY YOUR RESPECTS, NOW WOULD BE THE BEST TIME. IT'S SIX-THIRTY. THE SERVICE HAS BEEN OPEN FOR AN HOUR, Mrs. SOMERVILLE.
Ms. JUST BECAUSE I HAVE A KID DOESN'T MEAN I'M MARRIED. OR DID THEY PASS A LAW OUT HERE IN THE STICKS?
NO ONE'S COMING, MAMA?
Guests
KAT SOMERVILLE
SYBIL SOMERVILLE
NOT ALL MOMS ARE GOOD, SYB. I GUESS IT'S UP TO YOU AND ME. YOU READY?

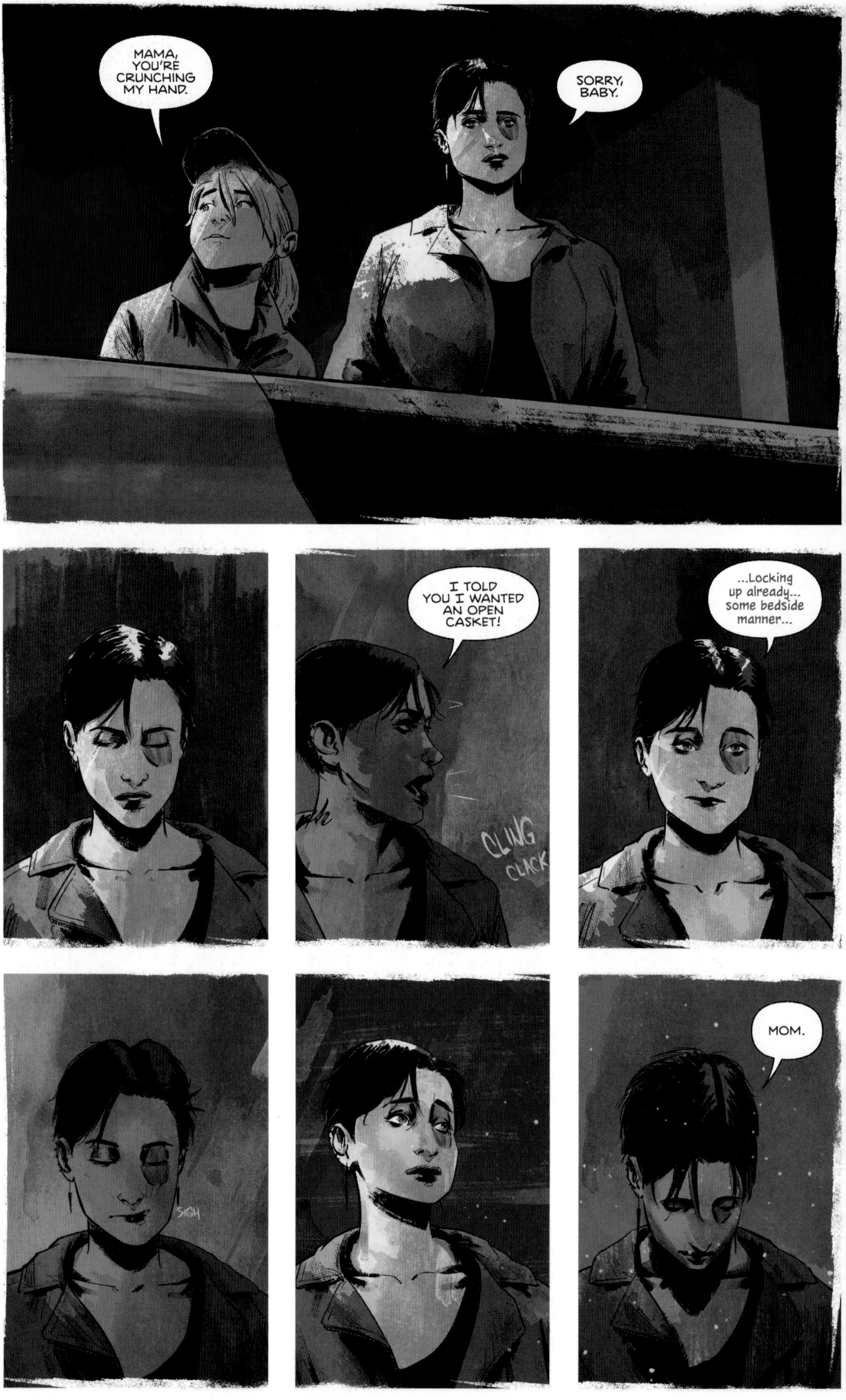
MAMA, YOU'RE CRUNCHING MY HAND.
SORRY, BABY.
I TOLD YOU I WANTED AN OPEN CASKET!
CLING
CLACK
...Locking up already... some bedside manner...
SIGH
MOM.

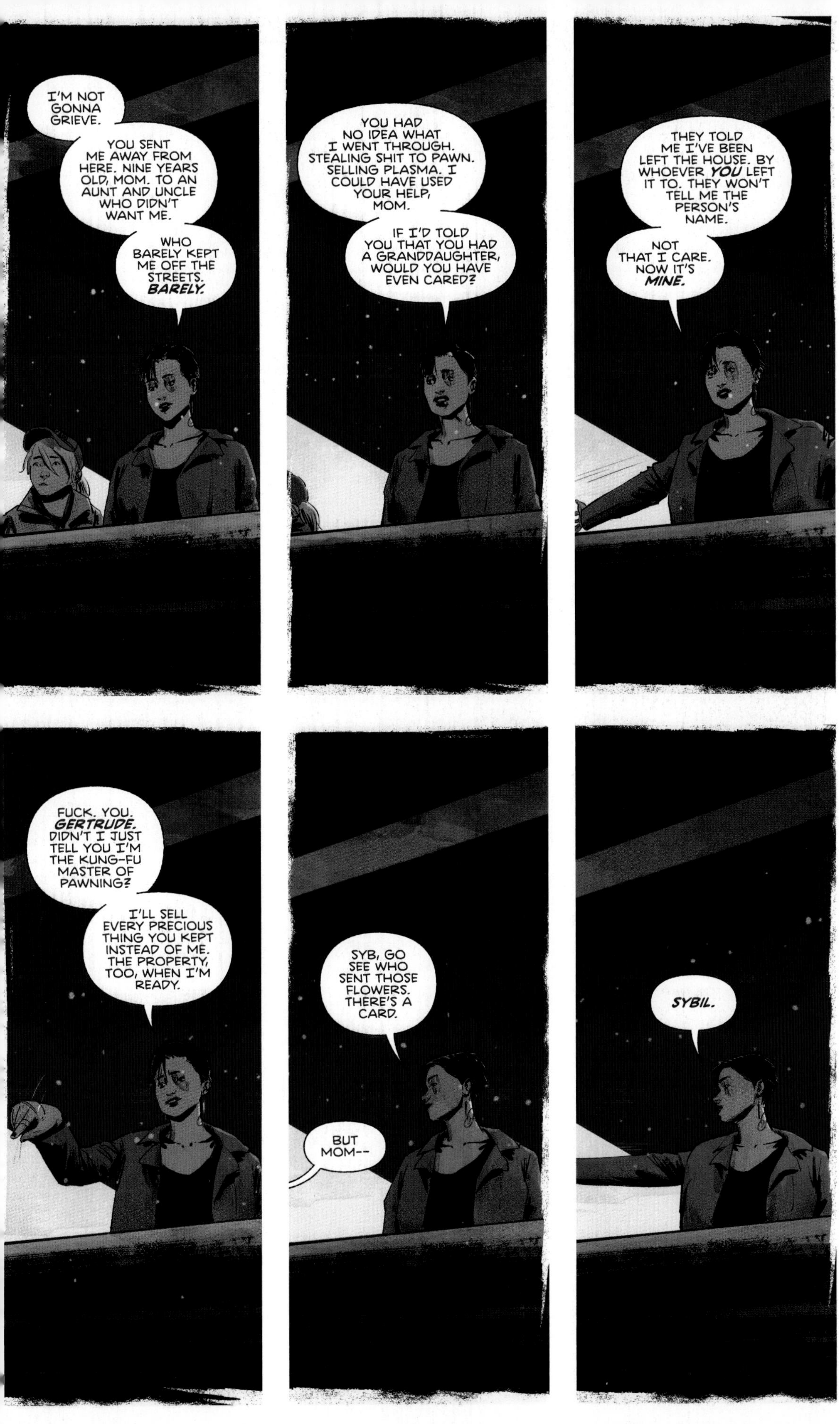
I'M NOT GONNA GRIEVE.
YOU SENT ME AWAY FROM HERE. NINE YEARS OLD, MOM. TO AN AUNT AND UNCLE WHO DIDN'T WANT ME.
WHO BARELY KEPT ME OFF THE STREETS. BARELY.
YOU HAD NO IDEA WHAT I WENT THROUGH. STEALING SHIT TO PAWN. SELLING PLASMA. I COULD HAVE USED YOUR HELP, MOM.
IF I'D TOLD YOU THAT YOU HAD A GRANDDAUGHTER, WOULD YOU HAVE EVEN CARED?
THEY TOLD ME I'VE BEEN LEFT THE HOUSE. BY WHOEVER YOU LEFT IT TO. THEY WON'T TELL ME THE PERSON'S NAME.
NOT THAT I CARE. NOW IT'S MINE.
FUCK. YOU. GERTRUDE. DIDN'T I JUST TELL YOU I'M THE KUNG-FU MASTER OF PAWNING?
I'LL SELL EVERY PRECIOUS THING YOU KEPT INSTEAD OF ME. THE PROPERTY, TOO, WHEN I'M READY.
SYB, GO SEE WHO SENT THOSE FLOWERS. THERE'S A CARD.
BUT MOM--
SYBIL.

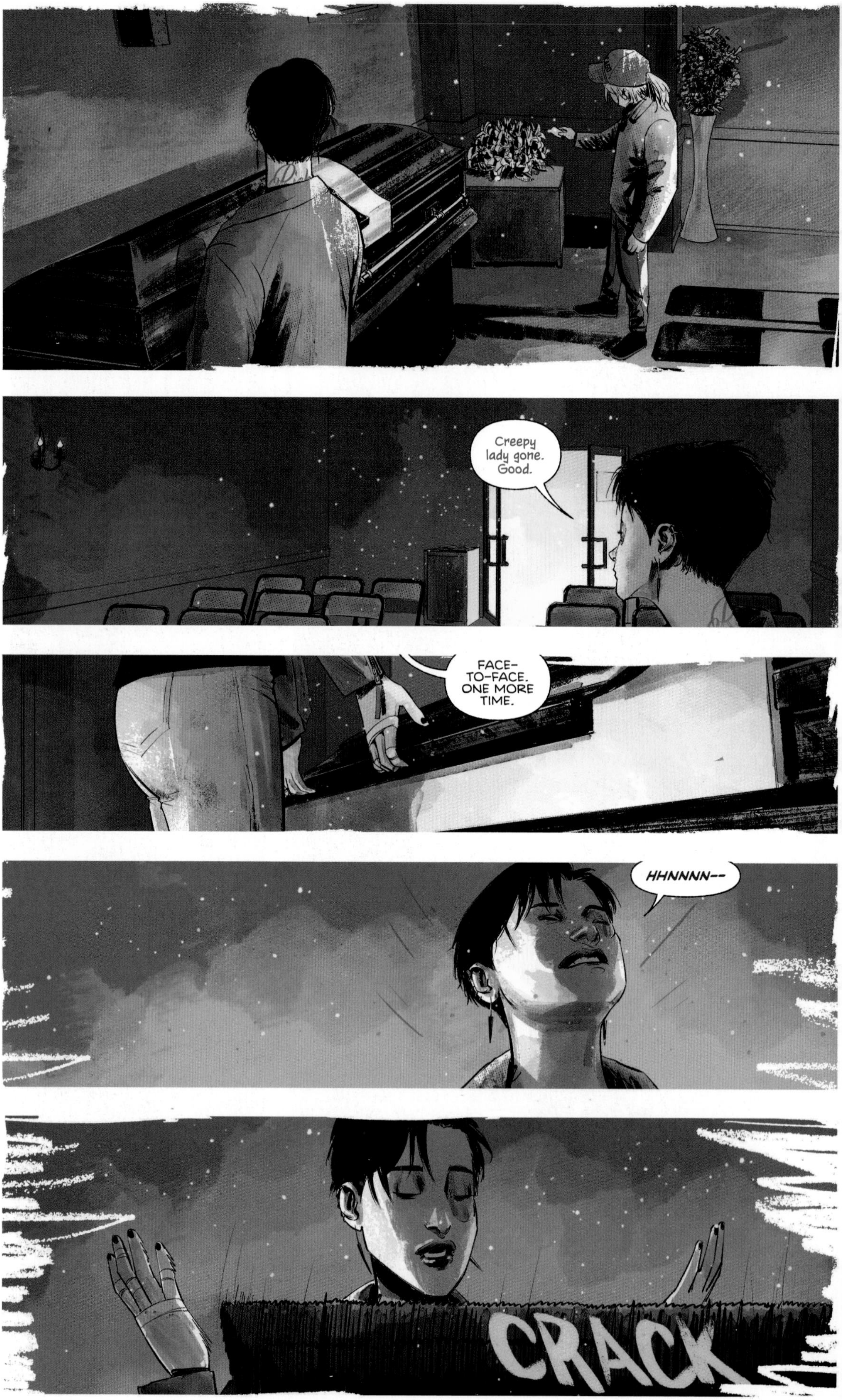
Creepy lady gone. Good.
FACE-TO-FACE. ONE MORE TIME.
HHNNNN--
CRACK

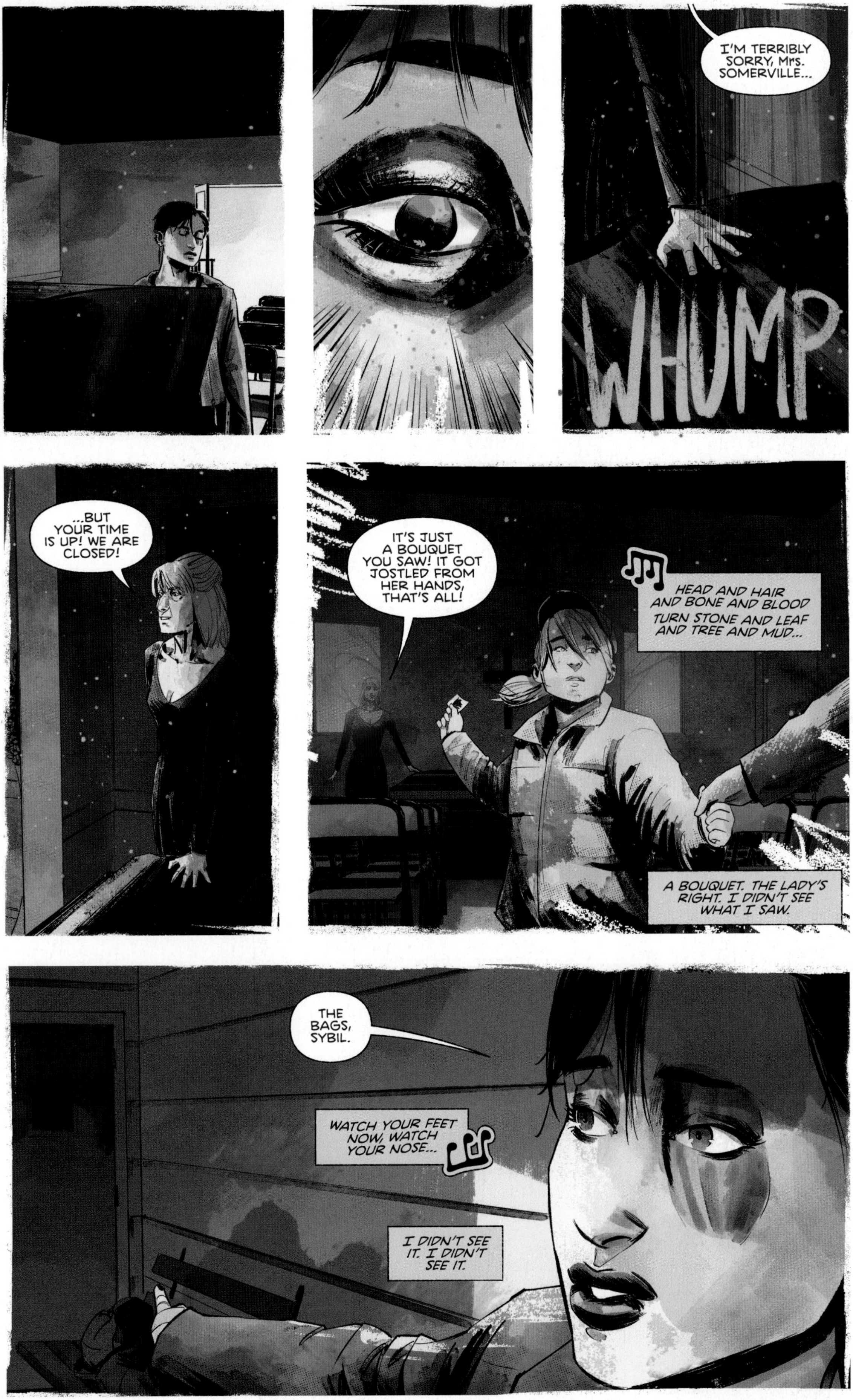
I'M TERRIBLY SORRY, Mrs. SOMERVILLE...
WHUMP
...BUT YOUR TIME IS UP! WE ARE CLOSED!
IT'S JUST A BOUQUET YOU SAW! IT GOT JOSTLED FROM HER HANDS, THAT'S ALL!
HEAD AND HAIR AND BONE AND BLOOD TURN STONE AND LEAF AND TREE AND MUD...
A BOUQUET. THE LADY'S RIGHT. I DIDN'T SEE WHAT I SAW.
THE BAGS, SYBIL.
WATCH YOUR FEET NOW, WATCH YOUR NOSE...
I DIDN'T SEE IT. I DIDN'T SEE IT.

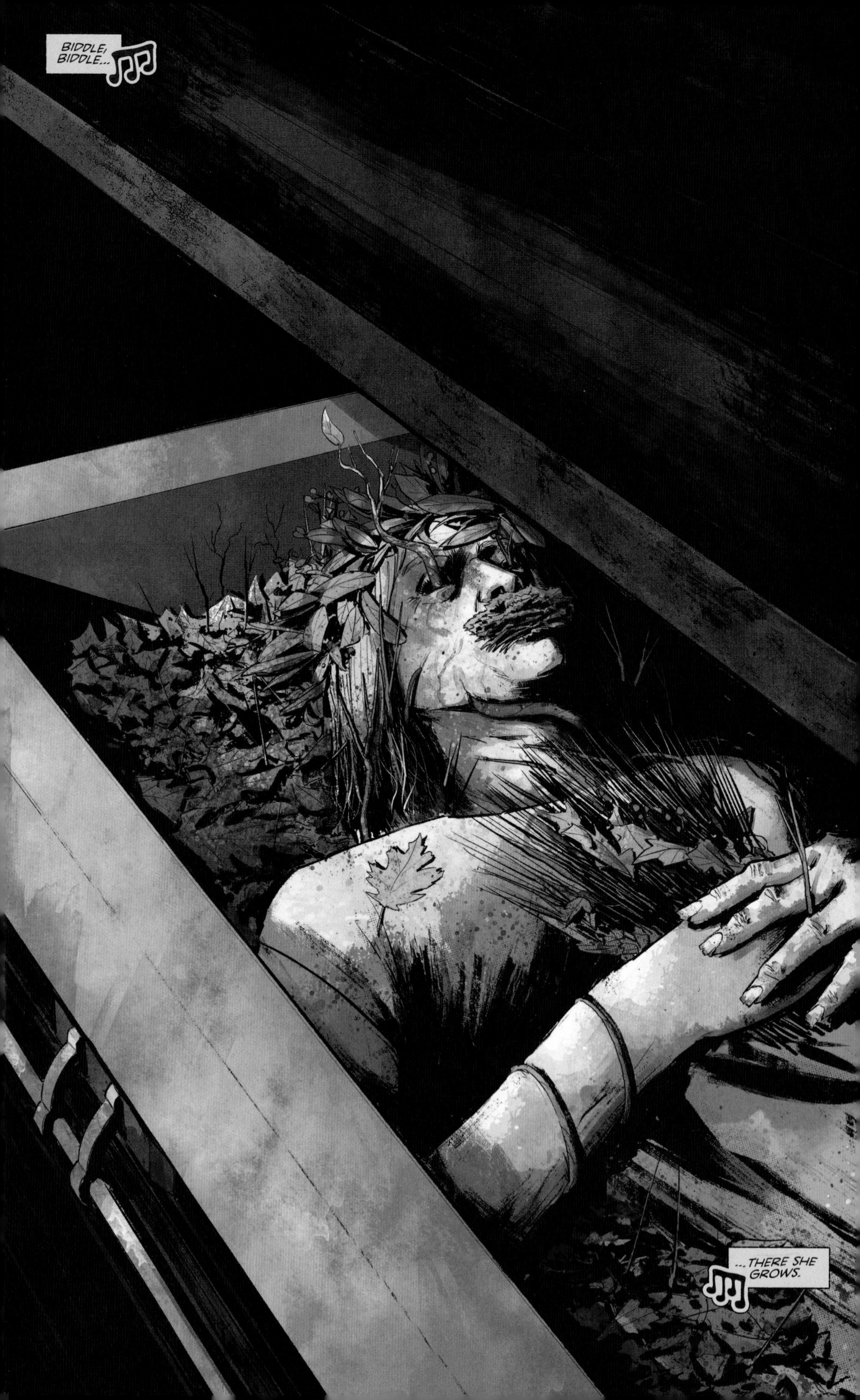
BIDDLE, BIDDLE...
...THERE SHE GROWS.

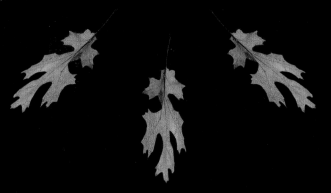

Head and hair and bone and blood

CHAPTER

TWO

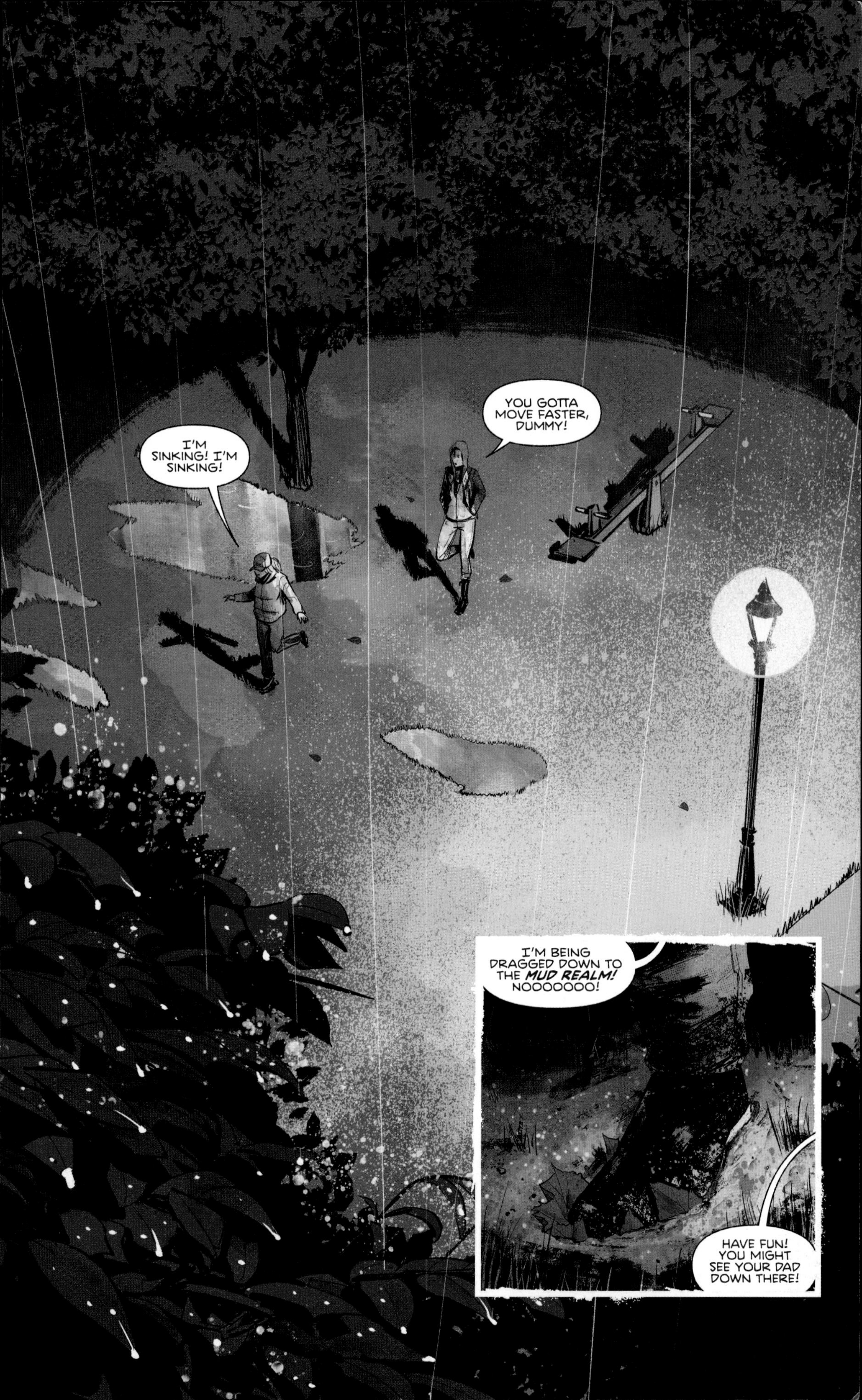
YOU GOTTA MOVE FASTER, DUMMY!
I'M SINKING! I'M SINKING!
I'M BEING DRAGGED DOWN TO THE MUD REALM! NOOOOOOO!
HAVE FUN! YOU MIGHT SEE YOUR DAD DOWN THERE!

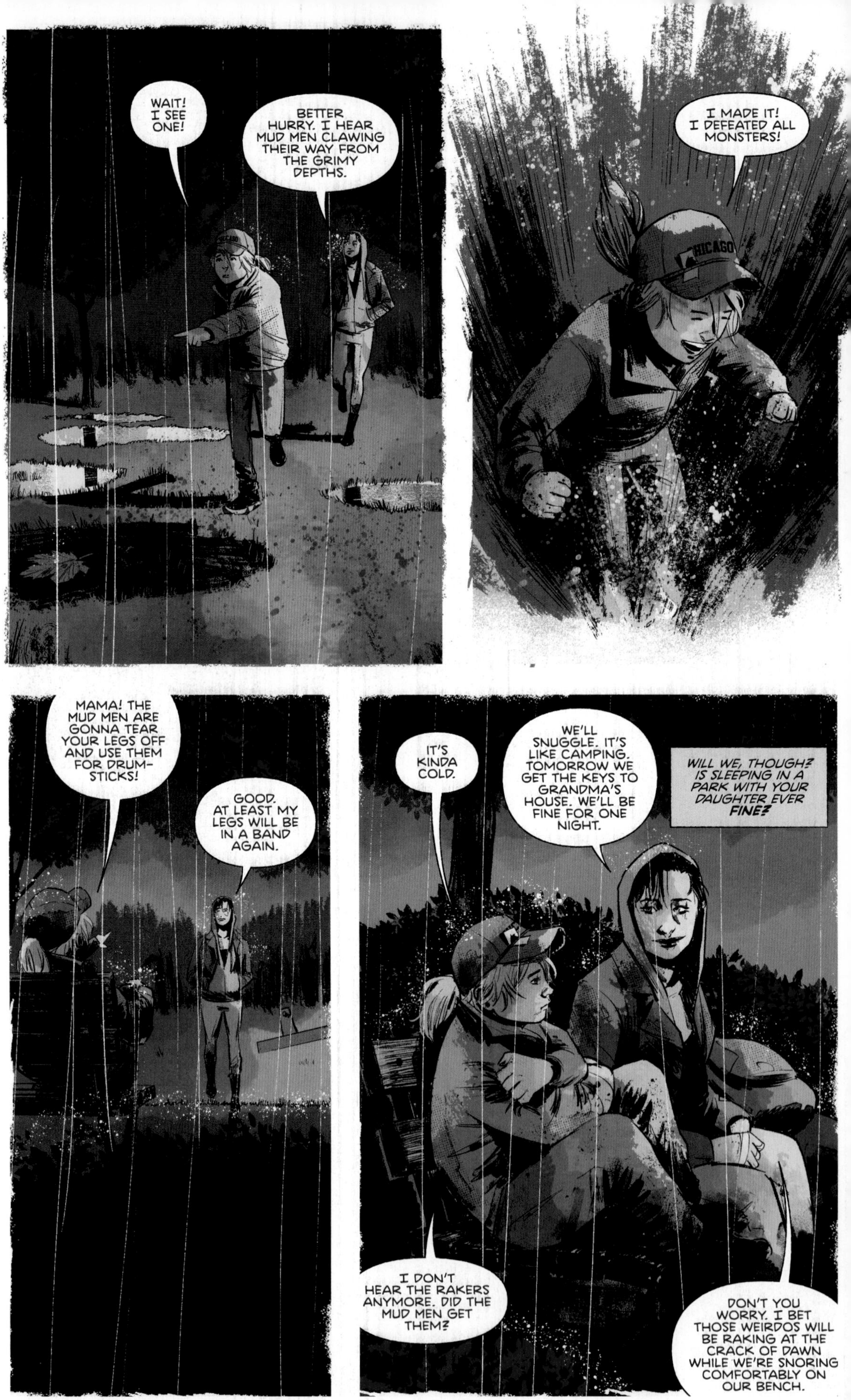
WAIT! I SEE ONE!
BETTER HURRY. I HEAR MUD MEN CLAWING THEIR WAY FROM THE GRIMY DEPTHS.
I MADE IT! I DEFEATED ALL MONSTERS!
CHICAGO
MAMA! THE MUD MEN ARE GONNA TEAR YOUR LEGS OFF AND USE THEM FOR DRUM-STICKS!
GOOD. AT LEAST MY LEGS WILL BE IN A BAND AGAIN.
IT'S KINDA COLD.
WE'LL SNUGGLE. IT'S LIKE CAMPING. TOMORROW WE GET THE KEYS TO GRANDMA'S HOUSE. WE'LL BE FINE FOR ONE NIGHT.
WILL WE, THOUGH? IS SLEEPING IN A PARK WITH YOUR DAUGHTER EVER ***FINE?***
I DON'T HEAR THE RAKERS ANYMORE. DID THE MUD MEN GET THEM?
DON'T YOU WORRY. I BET THOSE WEIRDOS WILL BE RAKING AT THE CRACK OF DAWN WHILE WE'RE SNORING COMFORTABLY ON OUR BENCH.

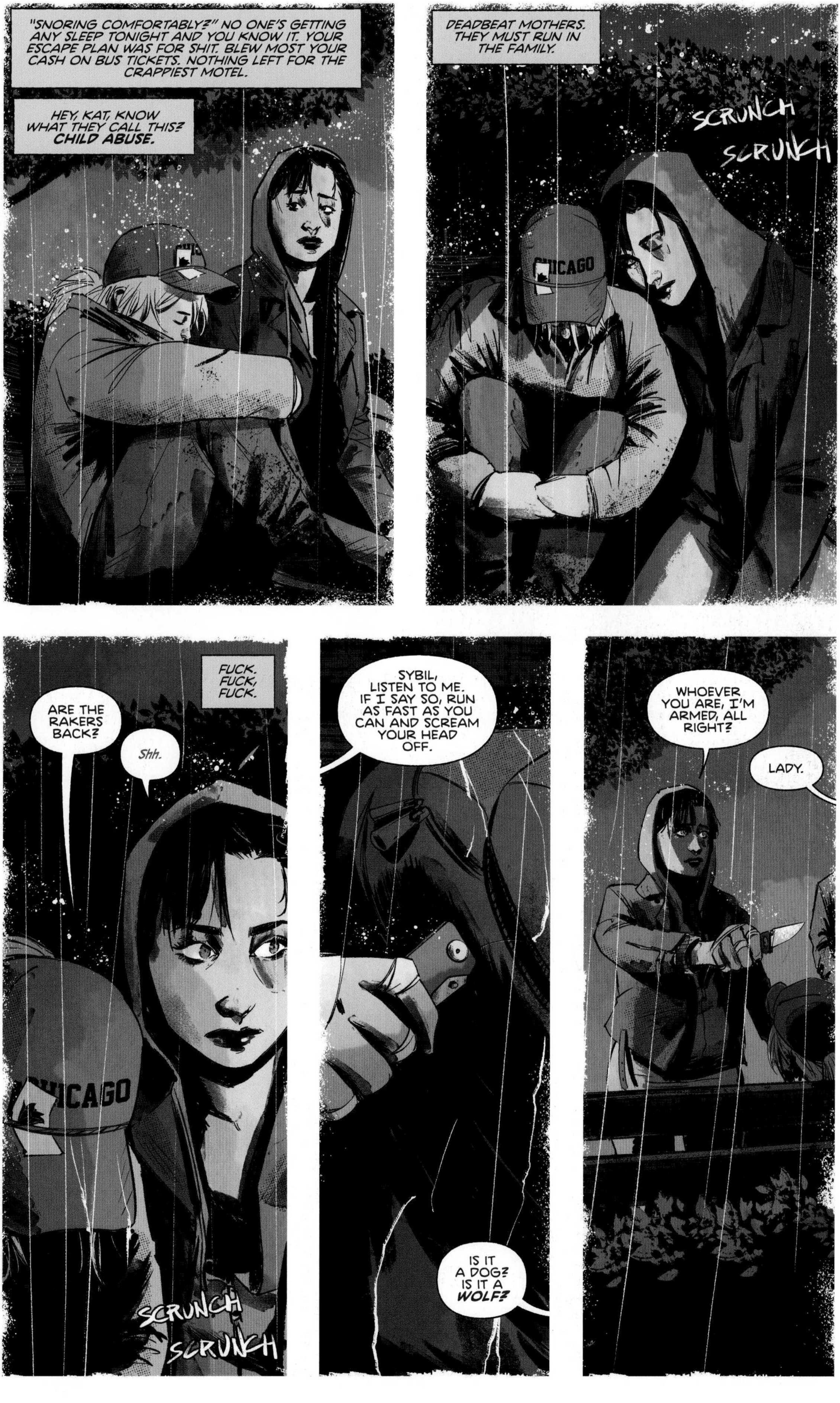
"SNORING COMFORTABLY?" NO ONE'S GETTING ANY SLEEP TONIGHT AND YOU KNOW IT. YOUR ESCAPE PLAN WAS FOR SHIT. BLEW MOST YOUR CASH ON BUS TICKETS. NOTHING LEFT FOR THE CRAPPIEST MOTEL.
HEY, KAT, KNOW WHAT THEY CALL THIS? CHILD ABUSE.
DEADBEAT MOTHERS. THEY MUST RUN IN THE FAMILY.
SCRUNCH
SCRUNCH
CHICAGO
FUCK. FUCK, FUCK.
ARE THE RAKERS BACK?
Shh.
CHICAGO
SCRUNCH
SCRUNCH
SYBIL, LISTEN TO ME. IF I SAY SO, RUN AS FAST AS YOU CAN AND SCREAM YOUR HEAD OFF.
IS IT A DOG? IS IT A WOLF?
WHOEVER YOU ARE, I'M ARMED, ALL RIGHT?
LADY.

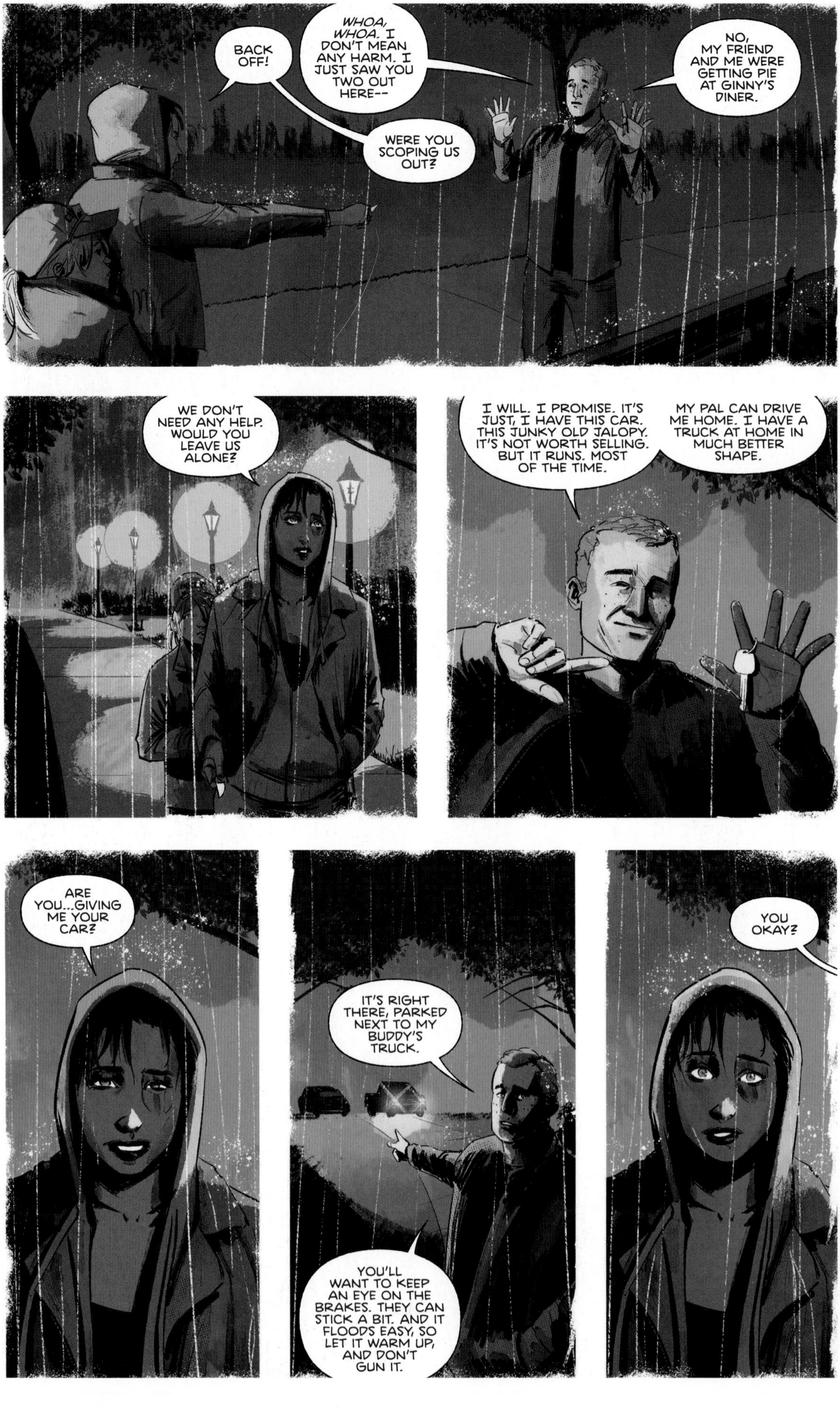
BACK OFF!
WHOA, WHOA. I DON'T MEAN ANY HARM. I JUST SAW YOU TWO OUT HERE--
WERE YOU SCOPING US OUT?
NO, MY FRIEND AND ME WERE GETTING PIE AT GINNY'S DINER.
WE DON'T NEED ANY HELP. WOULD YOU LEAVE US ALONE?
I WILL. I PROMISE. IT'S JUST, I HAVE THIS CAR. THIS JUNKY OLD JALOPY. IT'S NOT WORTH SELLING. BUT IT RUNS. MOST OF THE TIME.
MY PAL CAN DRIVE ME HOME. I HAVE A TRUCK AT HOME IN MUCH BETTER SHAPE.
ARE YOU...GIVING ME YOUR CAR?
IT'S RIGHT THERE, PARKED NEXT TO MY BUDDY'S TRUCK.
YOU'LL WANT TO KEEP AN EYE ON THE BRAKES. THEY CAN STICK A BIT. AND IT FLOODS EASY, SO LET IT WARM UP, AND DON'T GUN IT.
YOU OKAY?

NOW, LOOK, I'M JUST GOING TO TUCK THE KEYS INTO THIS BAG HERE, ALL RIGHT?

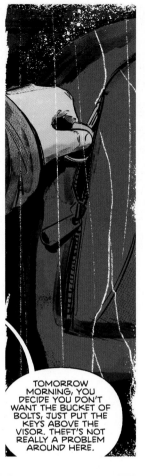

TOMORROW MORNING, YOU DECIDE YOU DON'T WANT THE BUCKET OF BOLTS, JUST PUT THE KEYS ABOVE THE VISOR. THEFT'S NOT REALLY A PROBLEM AROUND HERE.

WHY... WHY WOULD YOU DO THIS?

BECAUSE IT'S COLD. AND WET. AND THE LEAVES--WELL, IT'S JUST NOT SAFE.

I TOLD YOU, MAMA. THE MUD MEN.

I'M NOT SURE YOU COULD GET MUCH MUDDIER, YOUNG LADY.

OKAY. G'NIGHT, FOLKS.

I'M KAT. THIS IS SYBIL. THANKS, ALL RIGHT?

I'M AUBREY. YOU'RE TERRIBLE AT APOLOGIZING, KAT. BUT HEY--YOU TWO STAY WARM TONIGHT.

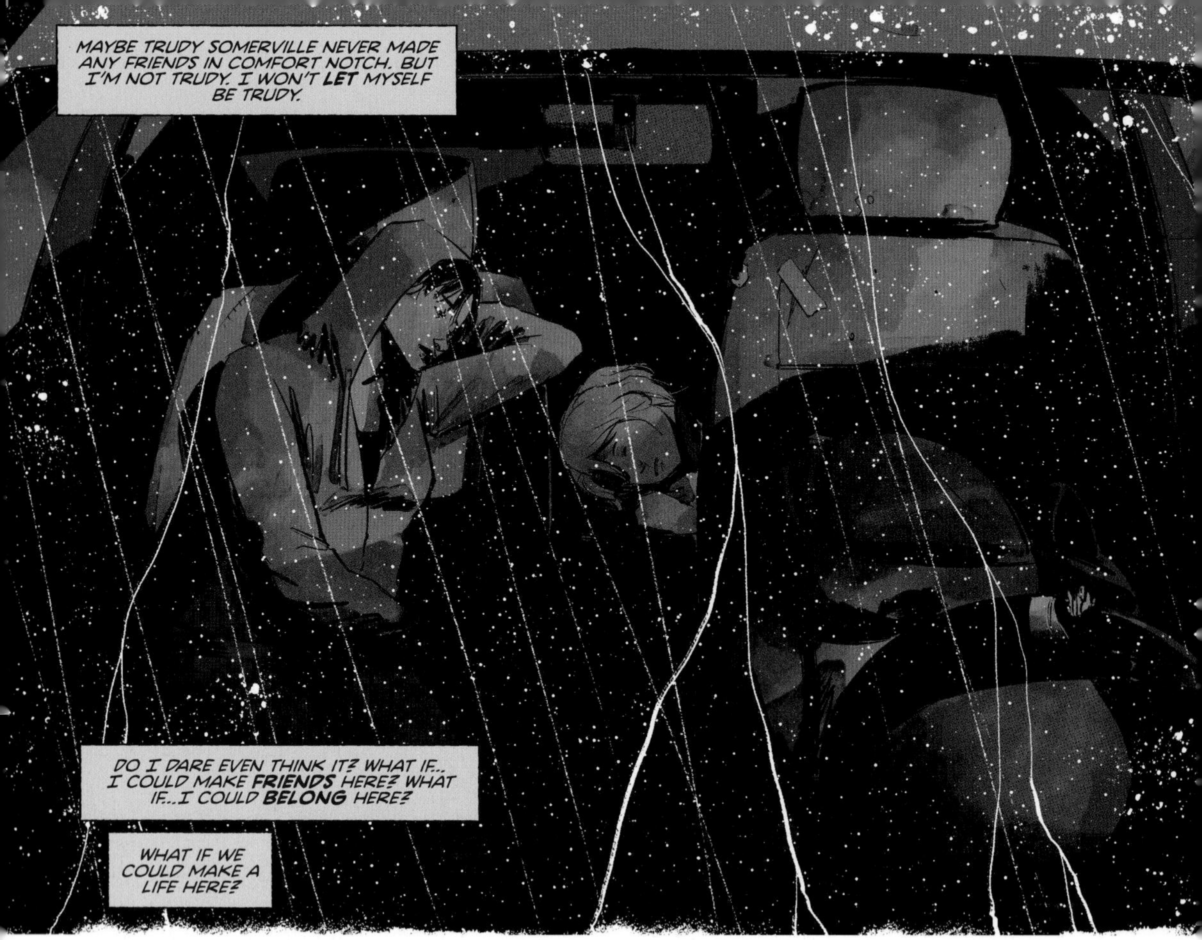
MAYBE TRUDY SOMERVILLE NEVER MADE ANY FRIENDS IN COMFORT NOTCH. BUT I'M NOT TRUDY. I WON'T LET MYSELF BE TRUDY.
DO I DARE EVEN THINK IT? WHAT IF... I COULD MAKE FRIENDS HERE? WHAT IF...I COULD BELONG HERE?
WHAT IF WE COULD MAKE A LIFE HERE?

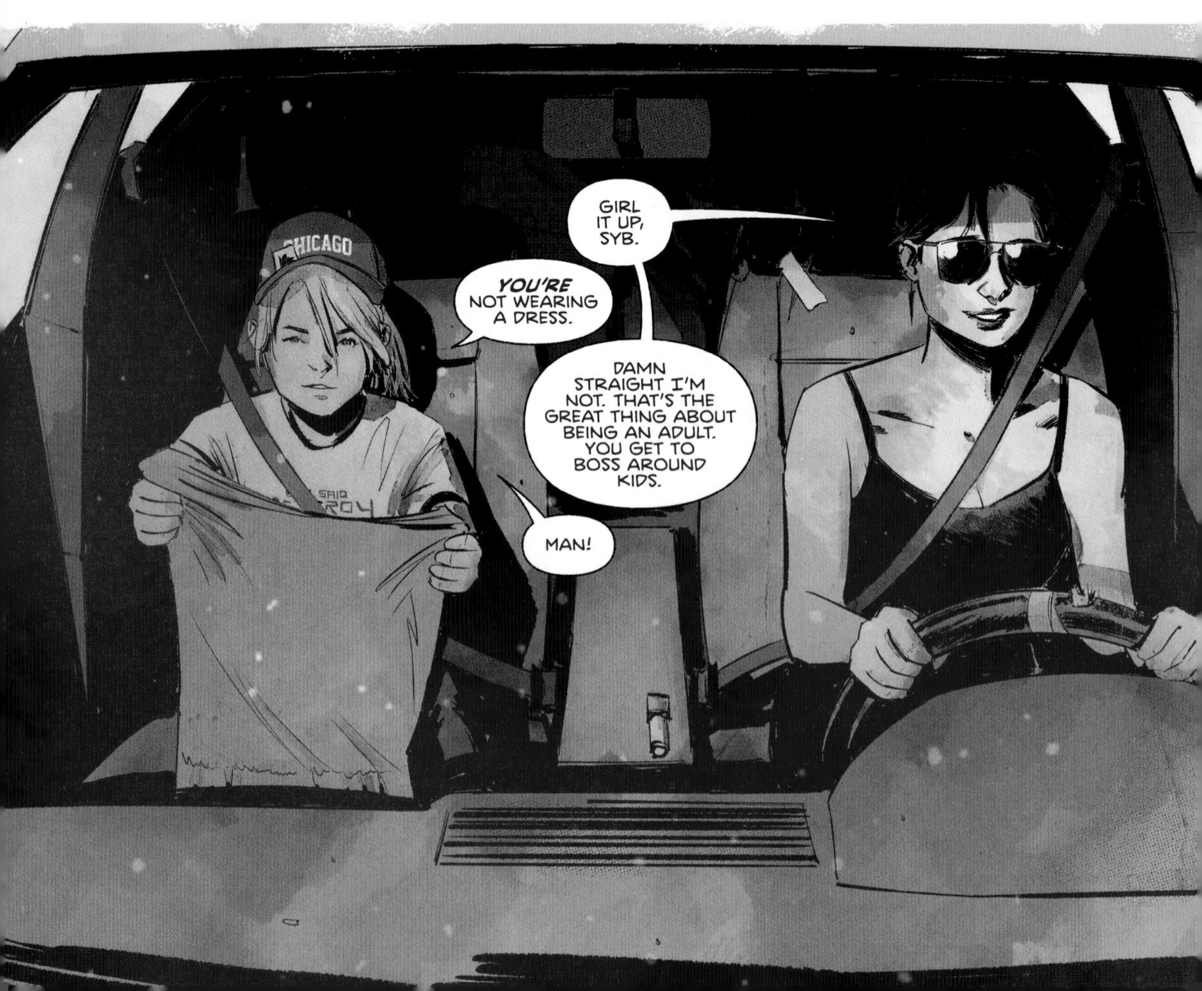
CHICAGO
GIRL IT UP, SYB.
YOU'RE NOT WEARING A DRESS.
DAMN STRAIGHT I'M NOT. THAT'S THE GREAT THING ABOUT BEING AN ADULT. YOU GET TO BOSS AROUND KIDS.
MAN!

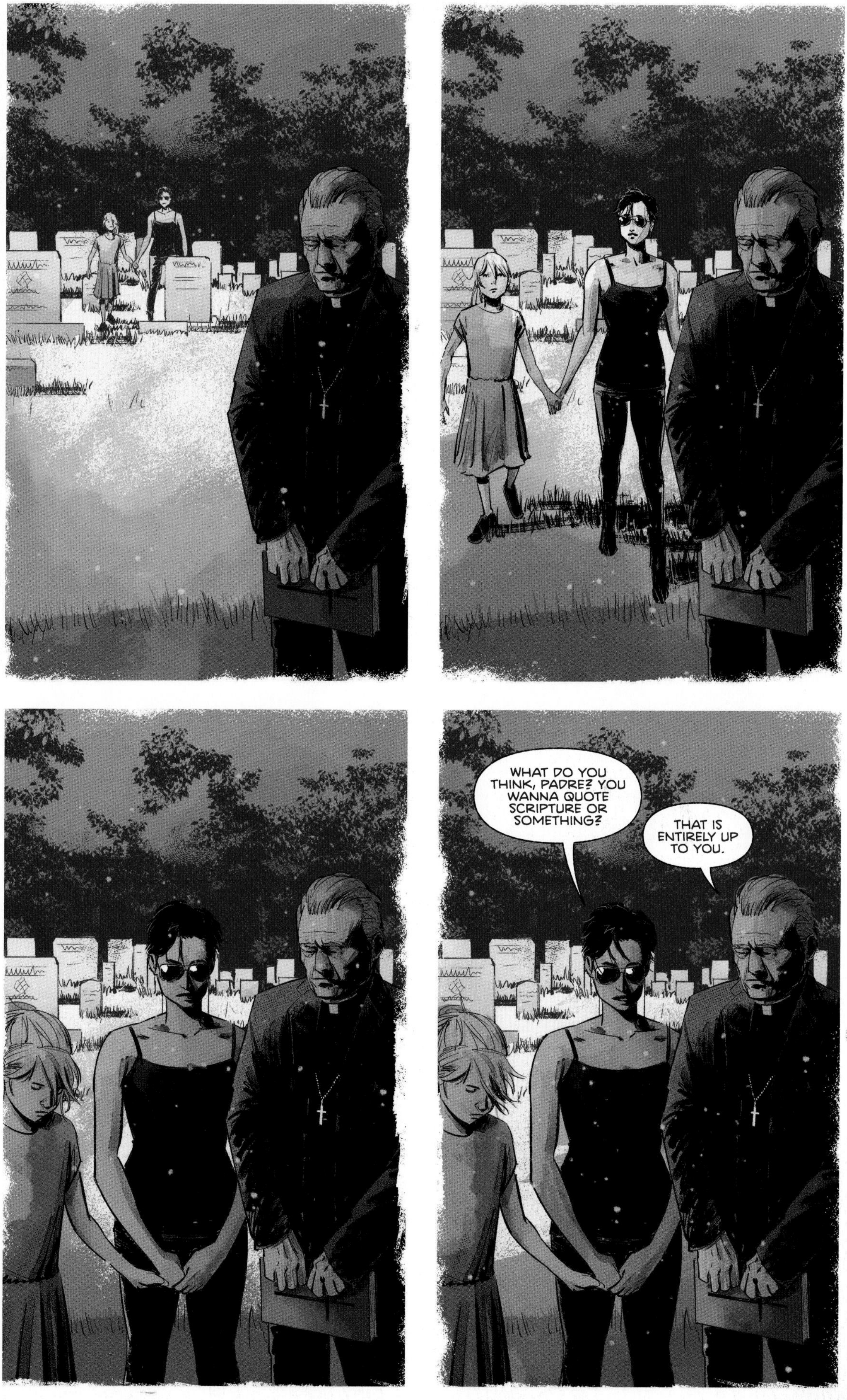
WHAT DO YOU THINK, PADRE? YOU WANNA QUOTE SCRIPTURE OR SOMETHING?
THAT IS ENTIRELY UP TO YOU.

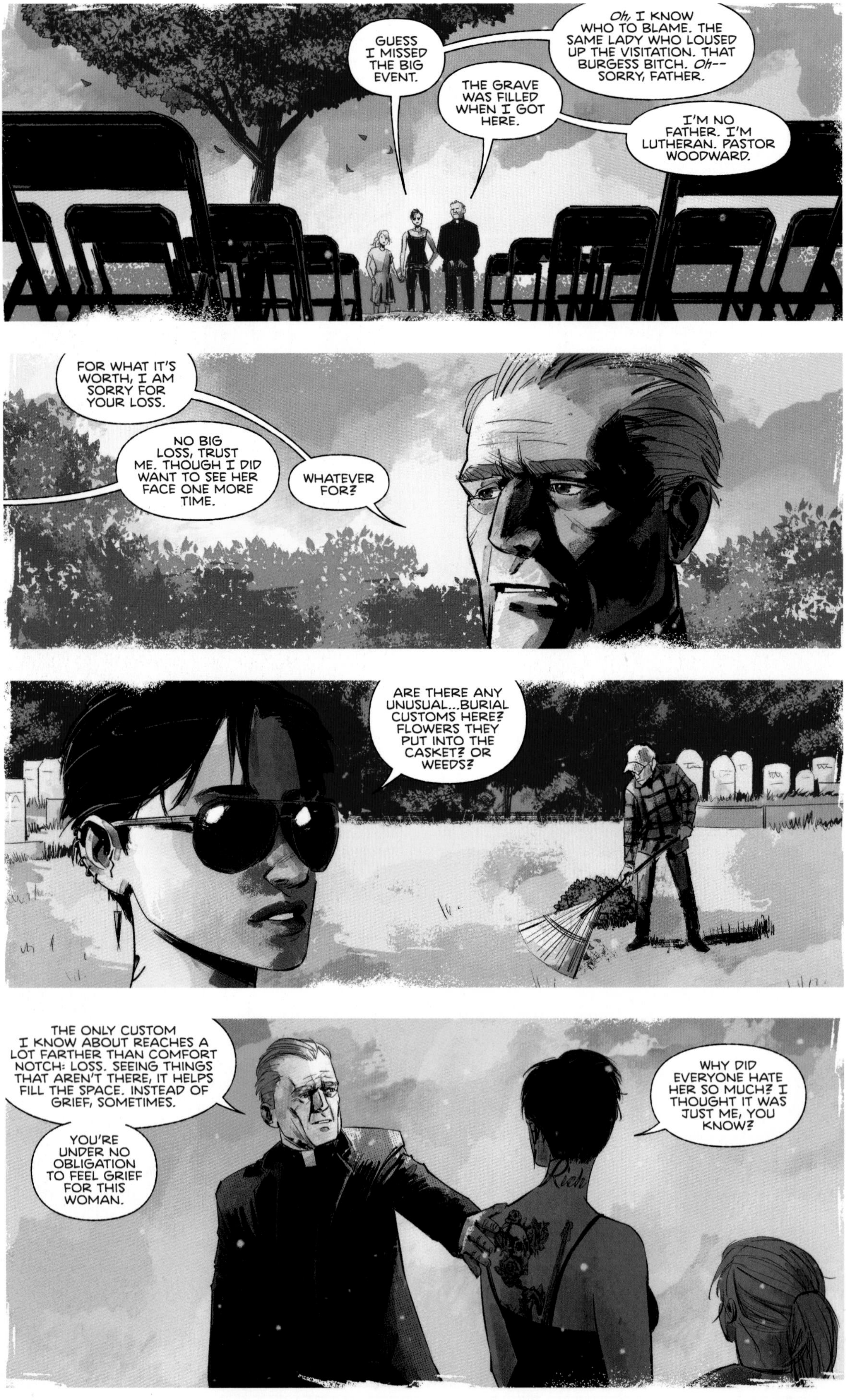
GUESS I MISSED THE BIG EVENT.
Oh, I KNOW WHO TO BLAME. THE SAME LADY WHO LOUSED UP THE VISITATION. THAT BURGESS BITCH. *Oh*-- SORRY, FATHER.
THE GRAVE WAS FILLED WHEN I GOT HERE.
I'M NO FATHER. I'M LUTHERAN. PASTOR WOODWARD.
FOR WHAT IT'S WORTH, I AM SORRY FOR YOUR LOSS.
NO BIG LOSS, TRUST ME. THOUGH I DID WANT TO SEE HER FACE ONE MORE TIME.
WHATEVER FOR?
ARE THERE ANY UNUSUAL...BURIAL CUSTOMS HERE? FLOWERS THEY PUT INTO THE CASKET? OR WEEDS?
THE ONLY CUSTOM I KNOW ABOUT REACHES A LOT FARTHER THAN COMFORT NOTCH: LOSS. SEEING THINGS THAT AREN'T THERE, IT HELPS FILL THE SPACE. INSTEAD OF GRIEF, SOMETIMES.
YOU'RE UNDER NO OBLIGATION TO FEEL GRIEF FOR THIS WOMAN.
WHY DID EVERYONE HATE HER SO MUCH? I THOUGHT IT WAS JUST ME, YOU KNOW?

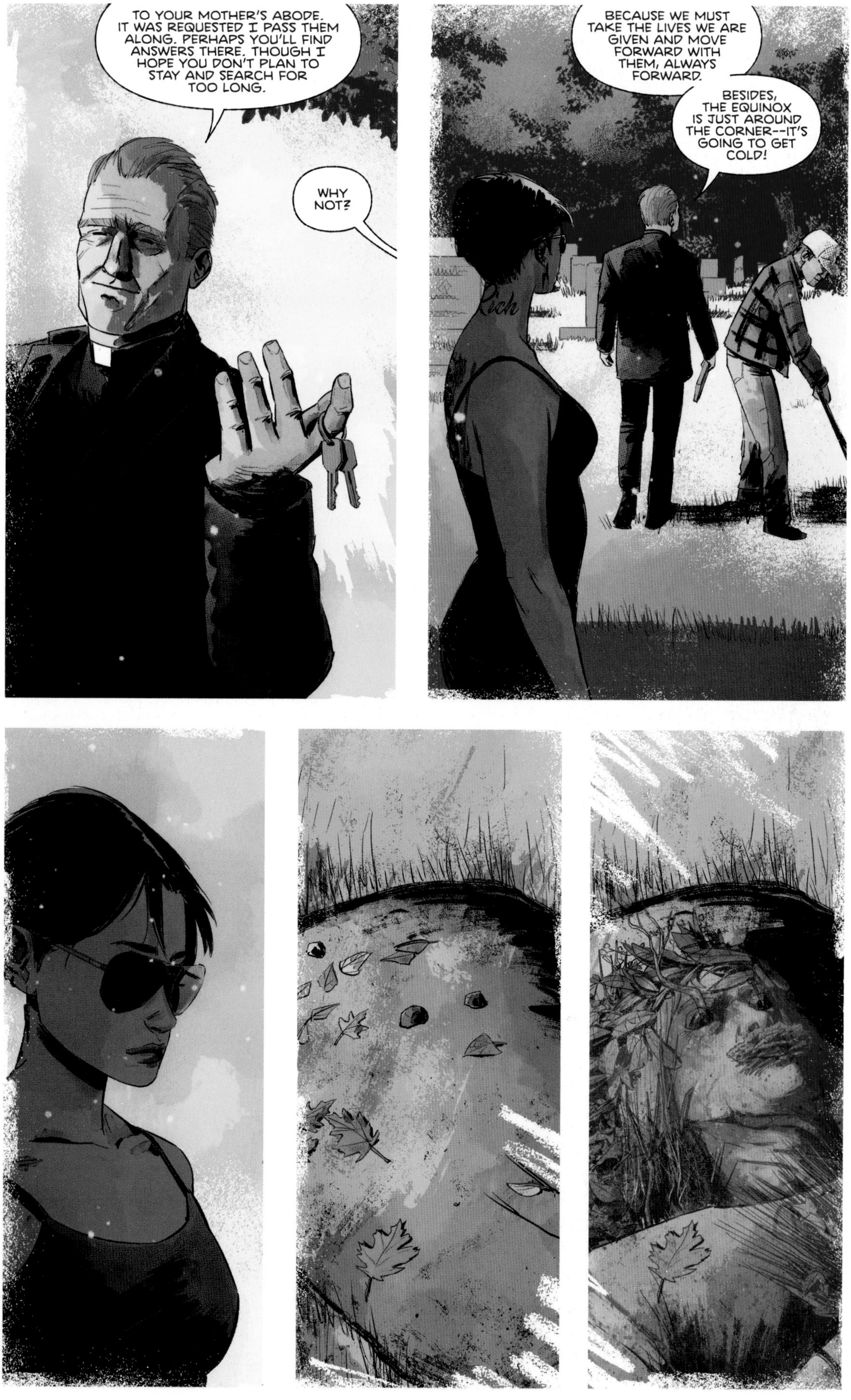
TO YOUR MOTHER'S ABODE. IT WAS REQUESTED I PASS THEM ALONG. PERHAPS YOU'LL FIND ANSWERS THERE. THOUGH I HOPE YOU DON'T PLAN TO STAY AND SEARCH FOR TOO LONG.
WHY NOT?
BECAUSE WE MUST TAKE THE LIVES WE ARE GIVEN AND MOVE FORWARD WITH THEM, ALWAYS FORWARD.
BESIDES, THE EQUINOX IS JUST AROUND THE CORNER--IT'S GOING TO GET COLD!
Rich

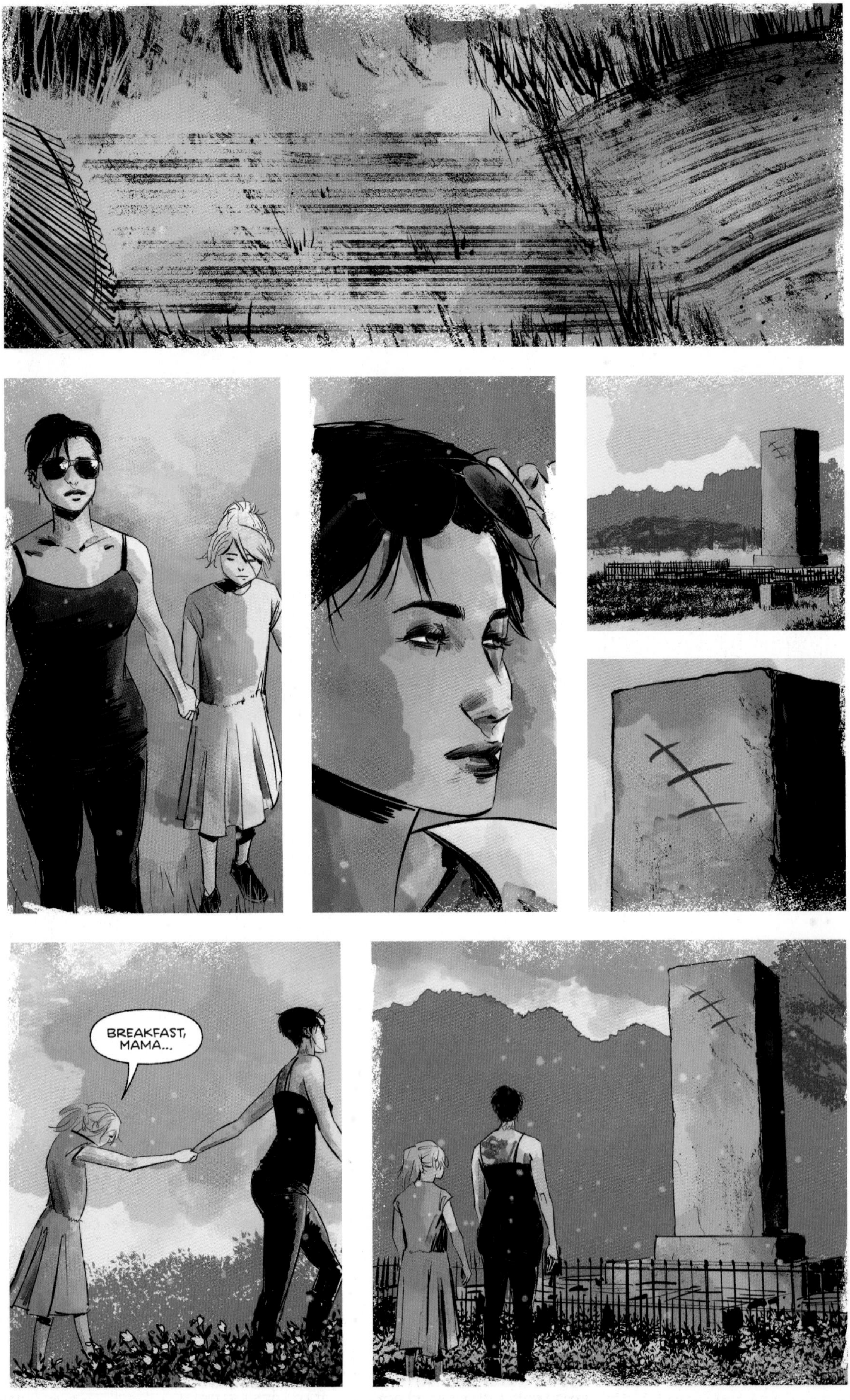
BREAKFAST, MAMA...

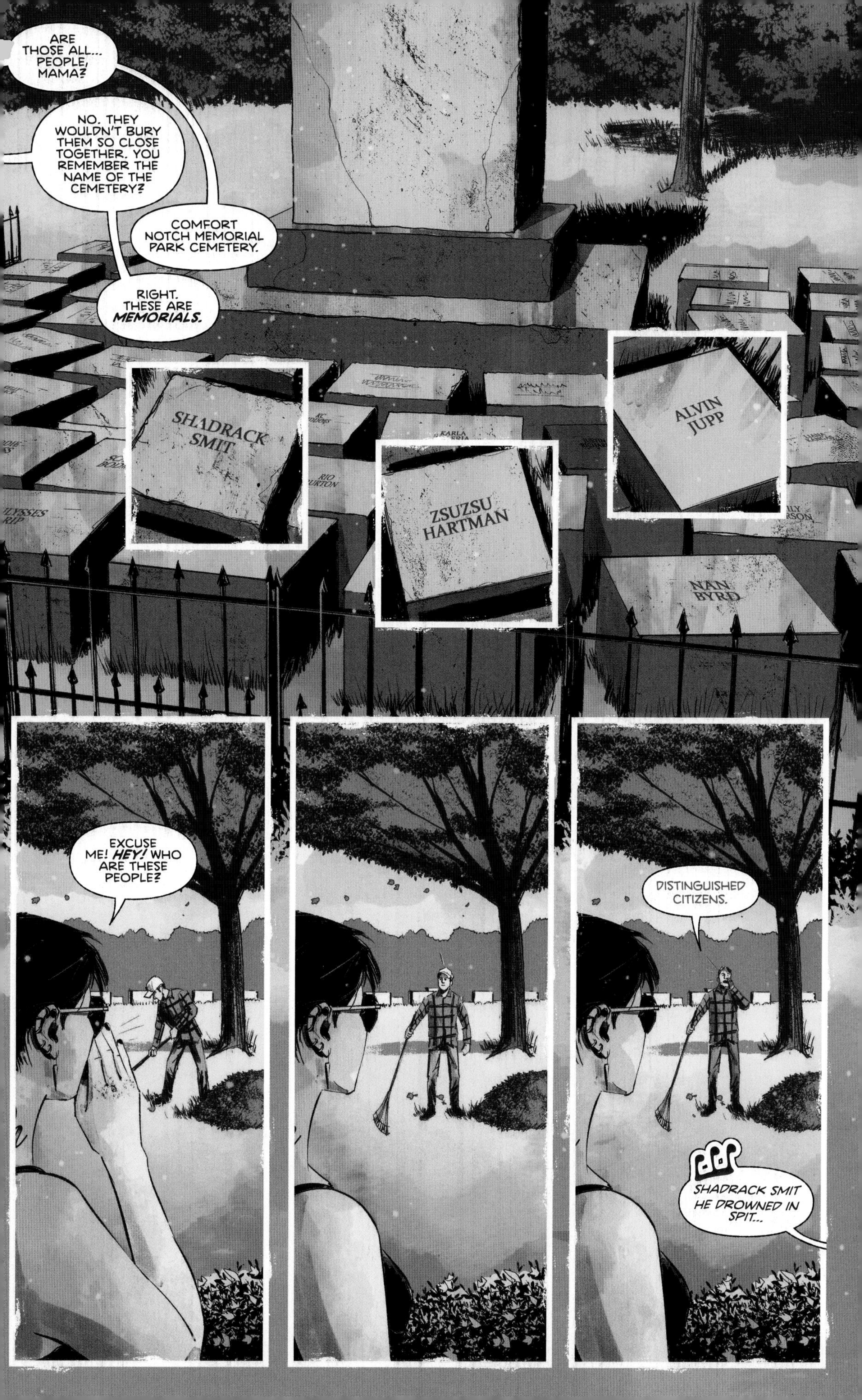
ARE THOSE ALL... PEOPLE, MAMA?
NO. THEY WOULDN'T BURY THEM SO CLOSE TOGETHER. YOU REMEMBER THE NAME OF THE CEMETERY?
COMFORT NOTCH MEMORIAL PARK CEMETERY.
RIGHT. THESE ARE *MEMORIALS.*
SHADRACK SMIT
ZSUZSU HARTMAN
ALVIN JUPP
NAN BYRD
EXCUSE ME! *HEY!* WHO ARE THESE PEOPLE?
DISTINGUISHED CITIZENS.
SHADRACK SMIT HE DROWNED IN SPIT...

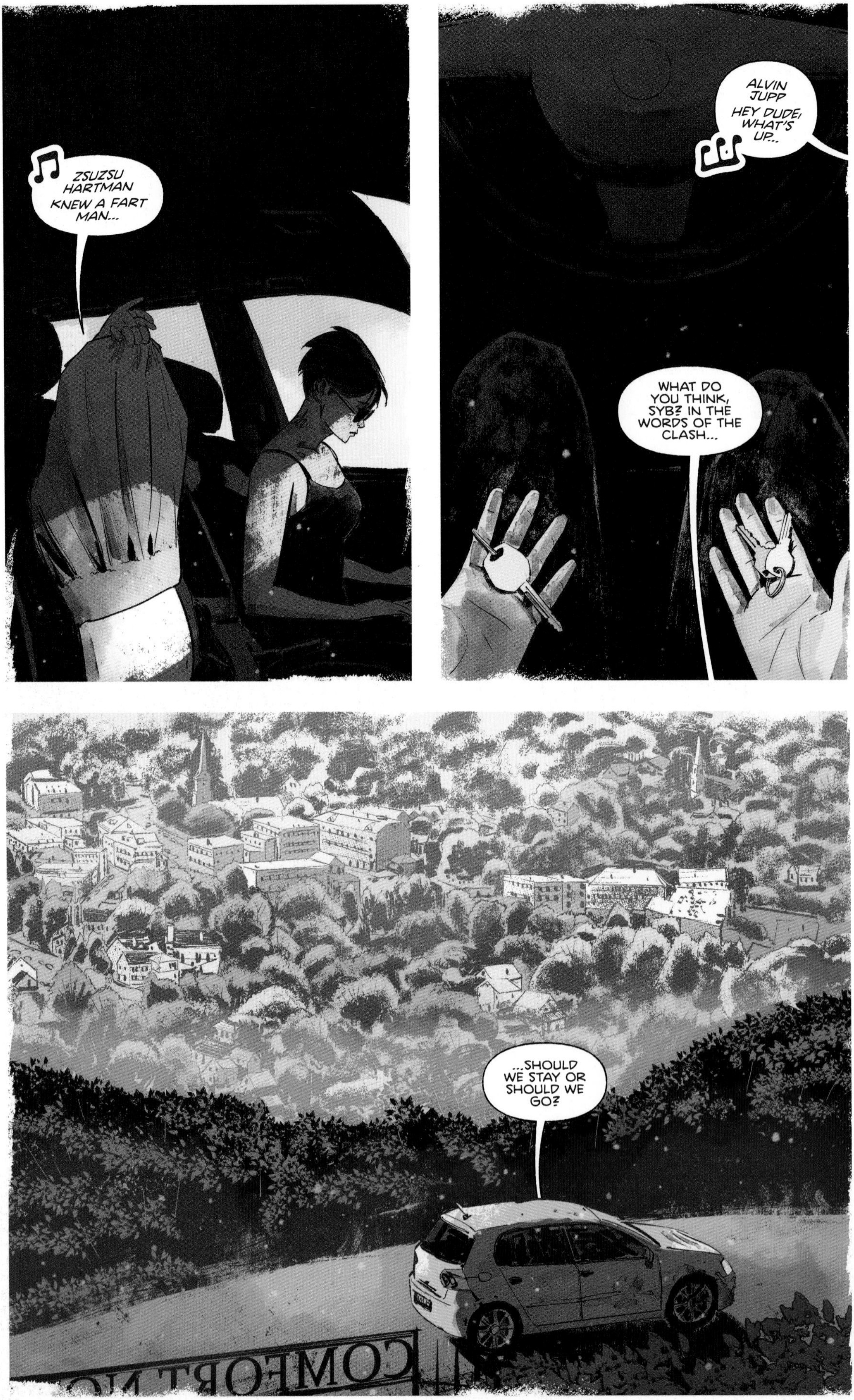
ZSUZSU HARTMAN KNEW A FART MAN...
ALVIN JUPP HEY DUDE, WHAT'S UP...
WHAT DO YOU THINK, SYB? IN THE WORDS OF THE CLASH...
...SHOULD WE STAY OR SHOULD WE GO?

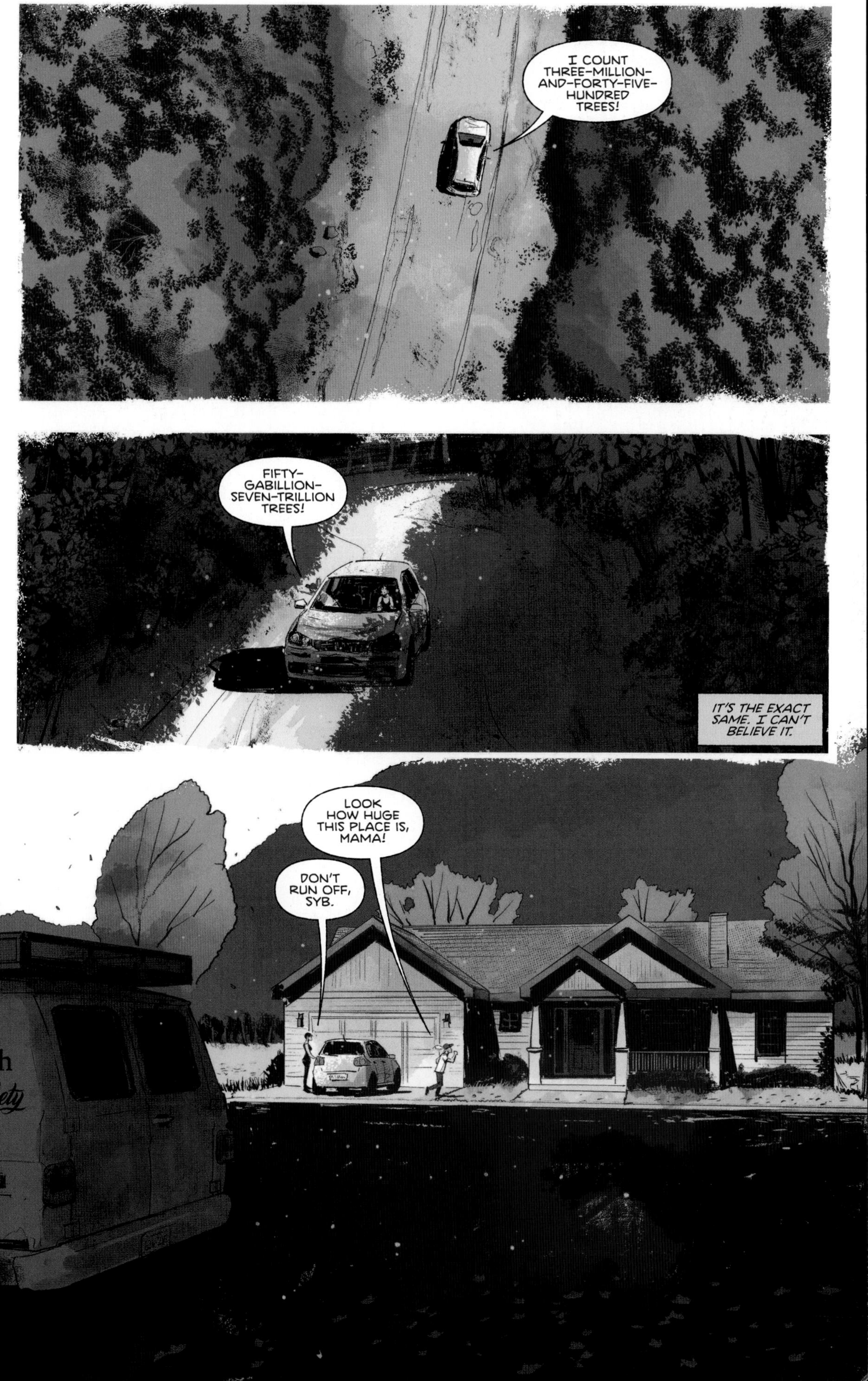
I COUNT THREE-MILLION-AND-FORTY-FIVE-HUNDRED TREES!
FIFTY-GABILLION-SEVEN-TRILLION TREES!
IT'S THE EXACT SAME. I CAN'T BELIEVE IT.
LOOK HOW HUGE THIS PLACE IS, MAMA!
DON'T RUN OFF, SYB.

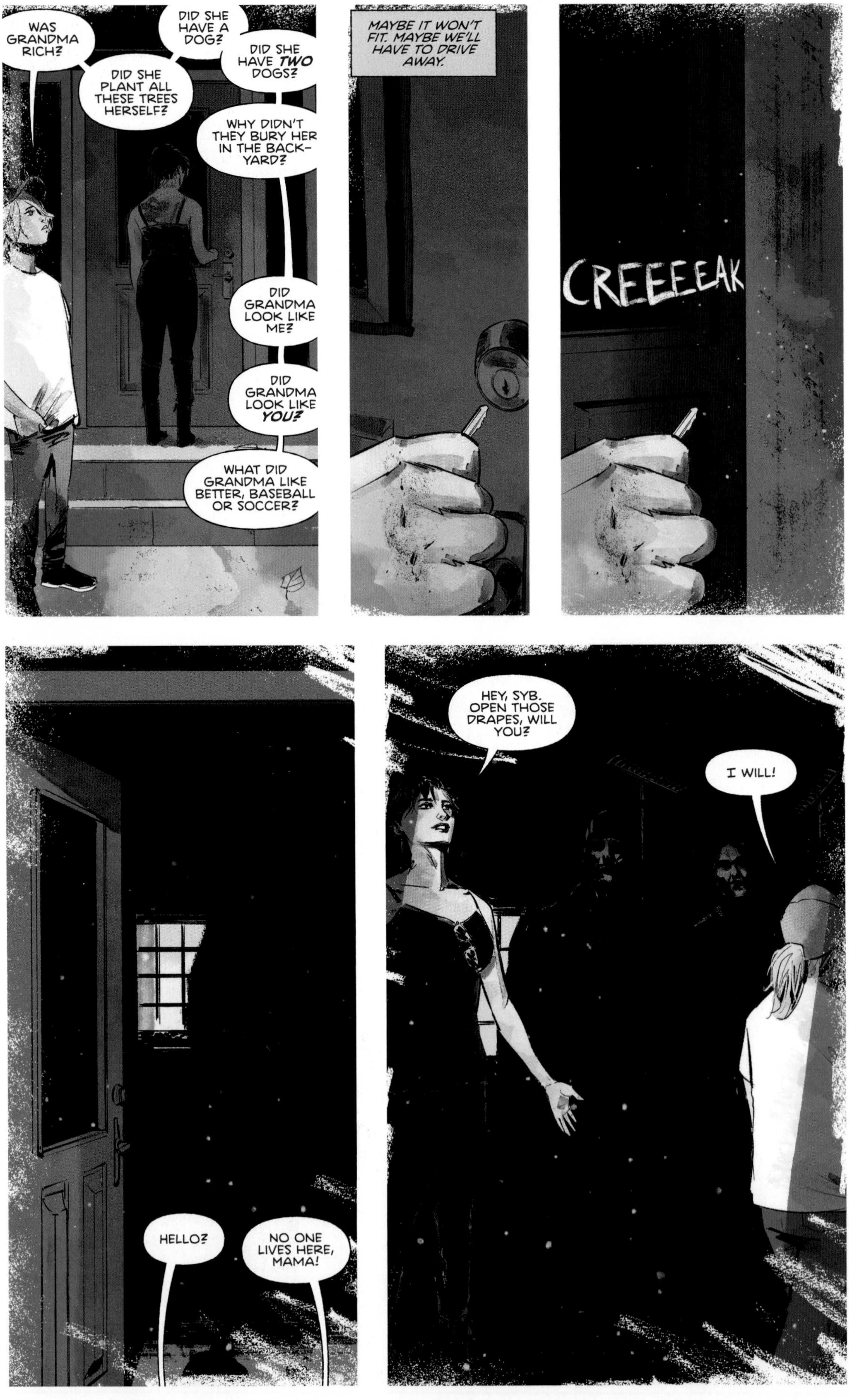
WAS GRANDMA RICH?
DID SHE HAVE A DOG?
DID SHE PLANT ALL THESE TREES HERSELF?
DID SHE HAVE TWO DOGS?
WHY DIDN'T THEY BURY HER IN THE BACK-YARD?
DID GRANDMA LOOK LIKE ME?
DID GRANDMA LOOK LIKE YOU?
WHAT DID GRANDMA LIKE BETTER, BASEBALL OR SOCCER?
MAYBE IT WON'T FIT. MAYBE WE'LL HAVE TO DRIVE AWAY.
CREEEEAK
HELLO?
NO ONE LIVES HERE, MAMA!
HEY, SYB. OPEN THOSE DRAPES, WILL YOU?
I WILL!

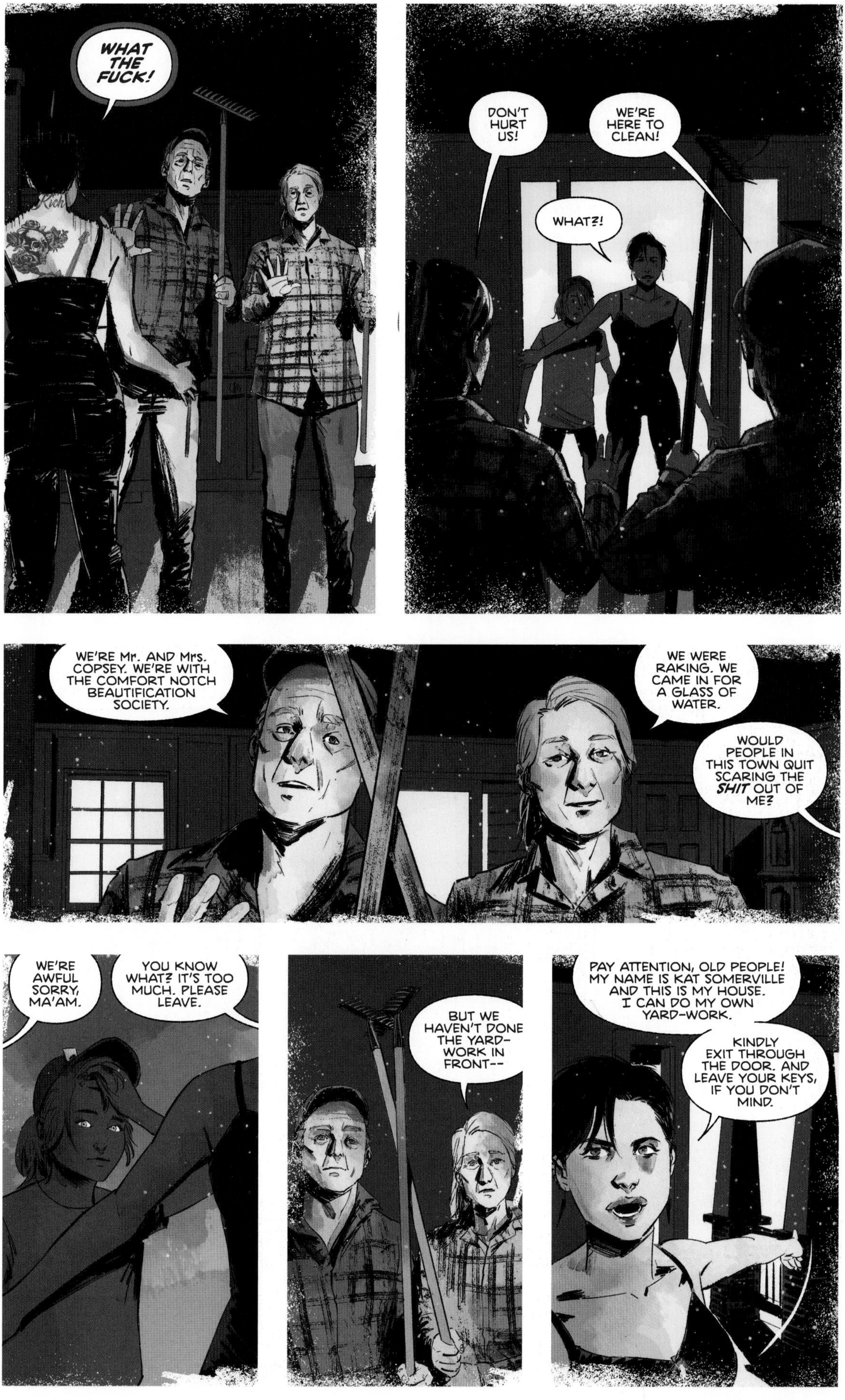
WHAT THE FUCK!
DON'T HURT US!
WE'RE HERE TO CLEAN!
WHAT?!
WE'RE Mr. AND Mrs. COPSEY. WE'RE WITH THE COMFORT NOTCH BEAUTIFICATION SOCIETY.
WE WERE RAKING. WE CAME IN FOR A GLASS OF WATER.
WOULD PEOPLE IN THIS TOWN QUIT SCARING THE SHIT OUT OF ME?
WE'RE AWFUL SORRY, MA'AM.
YOU KNOW WHAT? IT'S TOO MUCH. PLEASE LEAVE.
BUT WE HAVEN'T DONE THE YARD-WORK IN FRONT--
PAY ATTENTION, OLD PEOPLE! MY NAME IS KAT SOMERVILLE AND THIS IS MY HOUSE. I CAN DO MY OWN YARD-WORK.
KINDLY EXIT THROUGH THE DOOR. AND LEAVE YOUR KEYS, IF YOU DON'T MIND.

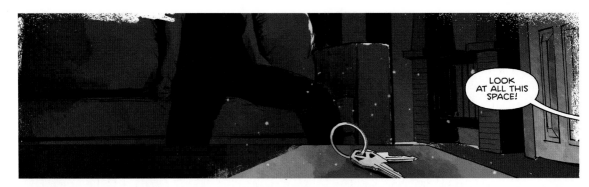

LOOK AT ALL THIS SPACE!

Oh, WOW, CAN THIS BE MY ROOM?

"NO, I WANT THIS ROOM. CAN I HAVE THIS ROOM?"

Uh-oh, THERE'S A BASEMENT. I'M AFRAID OF BASEMENTS.

"THIS PLACE SMELLS BAD, MAMA. IS IT THE SMELL OF GHOSTS?"

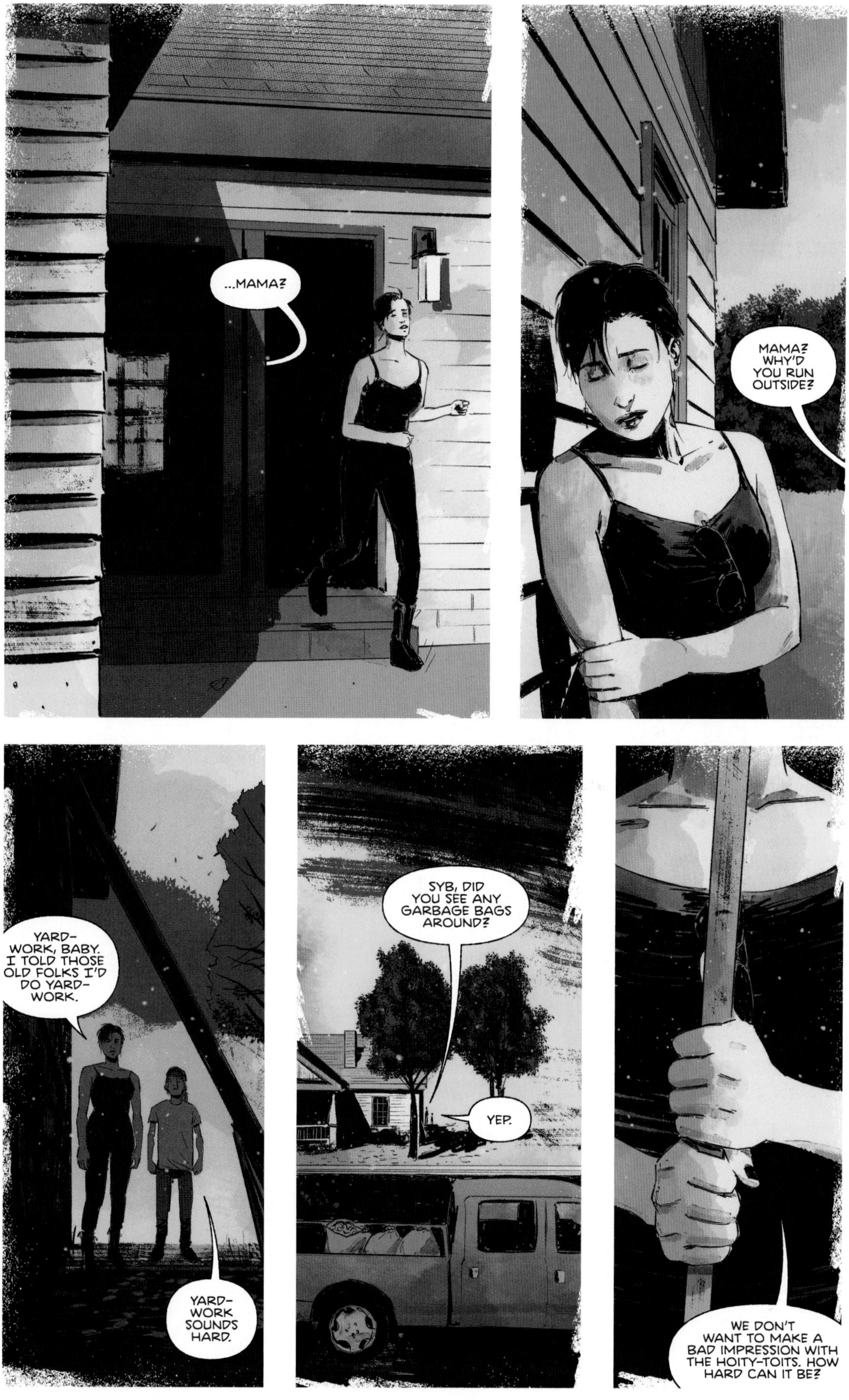
...MAMA?
MAMA? WHY'D YOU RUN OUTSIDE?
YARD-WORK, BABY. I TOLD THOSE OLD FOLKS I'D DO YARD-WORK.
YARD-WORK SOUNDS HARD.
SYB, DID YOU SEE ANY GARBAGE BAGS AROUND?
YEP.
WE DON'T WANT TO MAKE A BAD IMPRESSION WITH THE HOITY-TOITS. HOW HARD CAN IT BE?

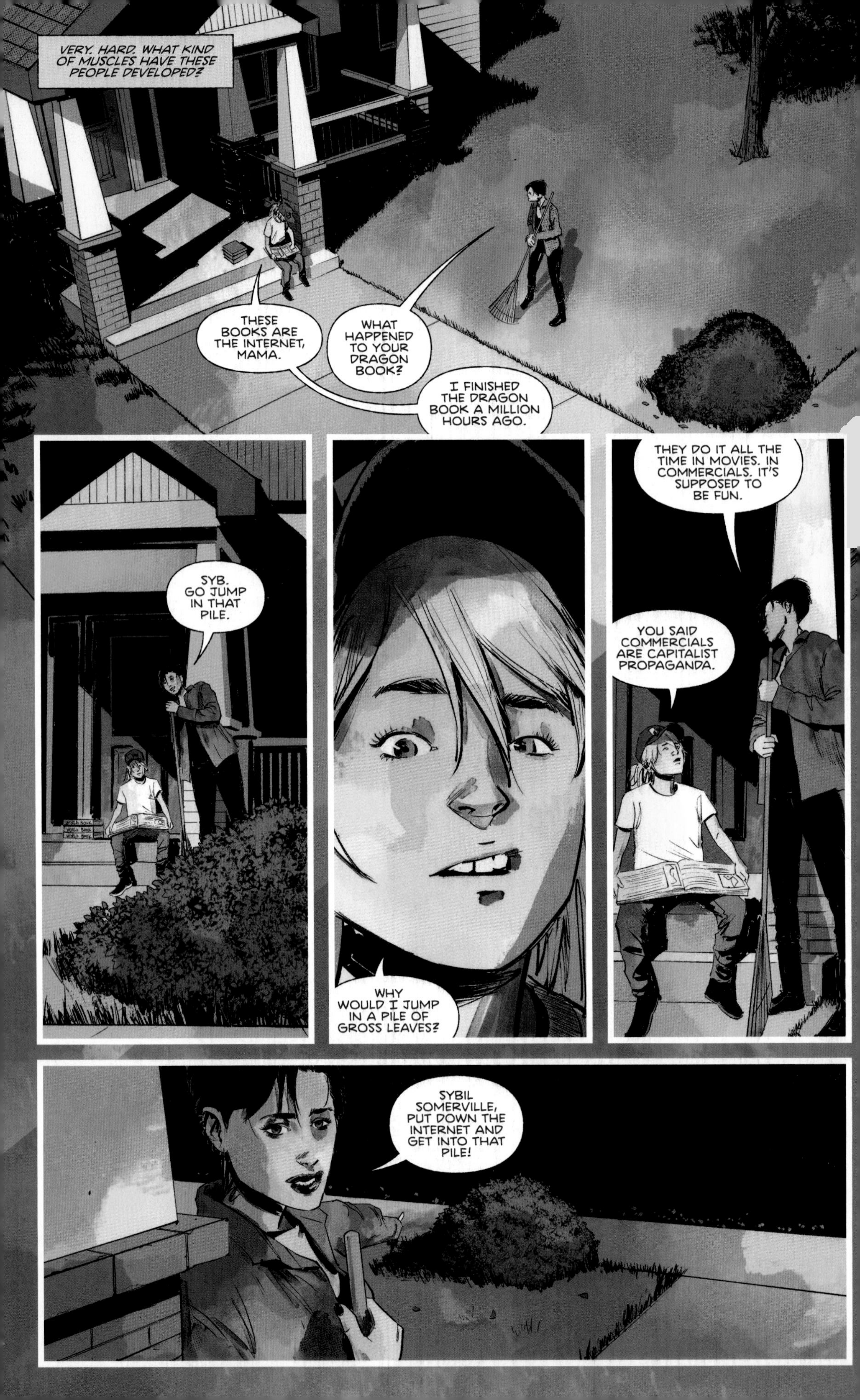
VERY. HARD. WHAT KIND OF MUSCLES HAVE THESE PEOPLE DEVELOPED?
THESE BOOKS ARE THE INTERNET, MAMA.
WHAT HAPPENED TO YOUR DRAGON BOOK?
I FINISHED THE DRAGON BOOK A MILLION HOURS AGO.
SYB. GO JUMP IN THAT PILE.
WHY WOULD I JUMP IN A PILE OF GROSS LEAVES?
THEY DO IT ALL THE TIME IN MOVIES. IN COMMERCIALS. IT'S SUPPOSED TO BE FUN.
YOU SAID COMMERCIALS ARE CAPITALIST PROPAGANDA.
SYBIL SOMERVILLE, PUT DOWN THE INTERNET AND GET INTO THAT PILE!

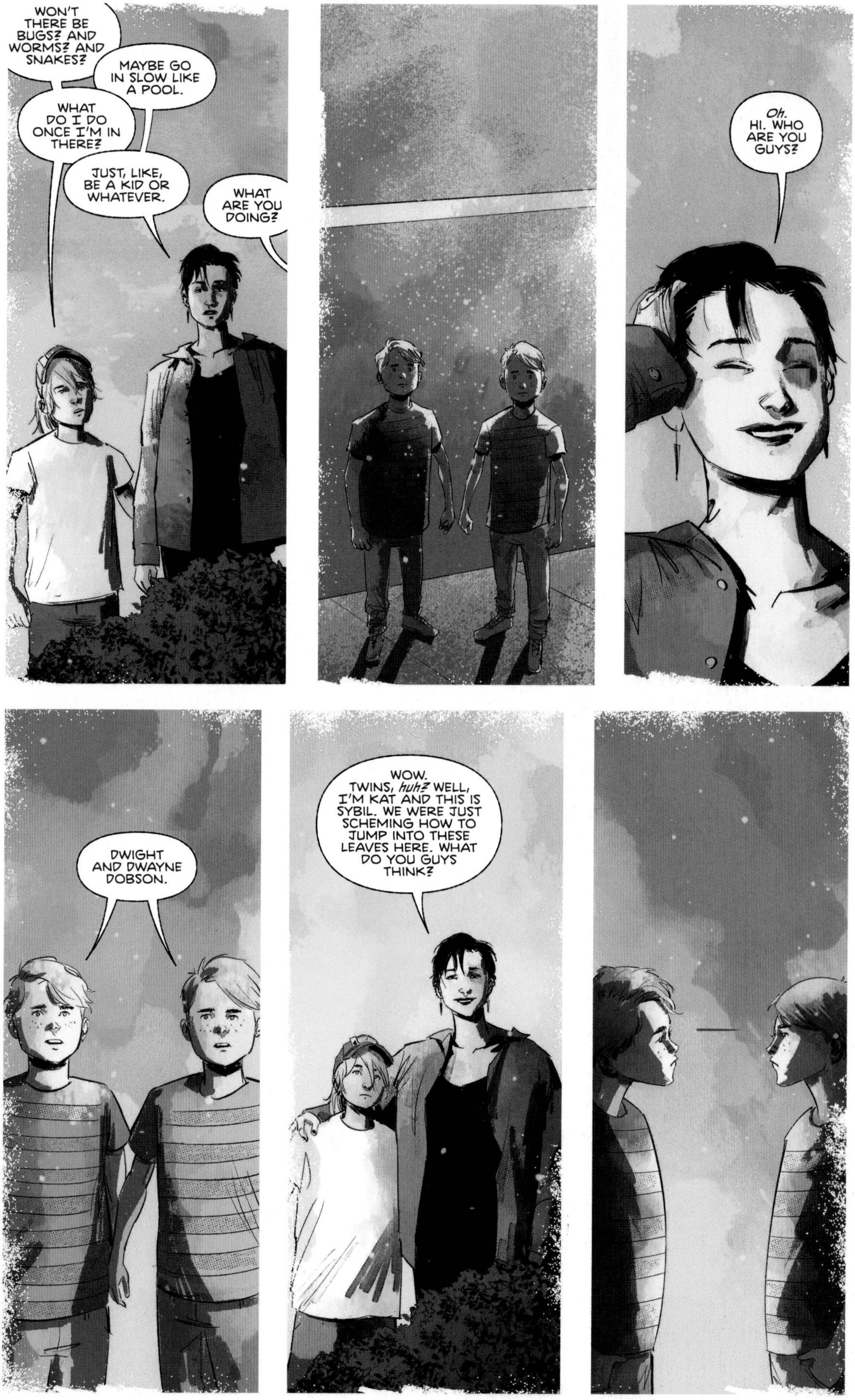
WON'T THERE BE BUGS? AND WORMS? AND SNAKES?
MAYBE GO IN SLOW LIKE A POOL.
WHAT DO I DO ONCE I'M IN THERE?
JUST, LIKE, BE A KID OR WHATEVER.
WHAT ARE YOU DOING?
Oh. HI. WHO ARE YOU GUYS?
DWIGHT AND DWAYNE DOBSON.
WOW. TWINS, huh? WELL, I'M KAT AND THIS IS SYBIL. WE WERE JUST SCHEMING HOW TO JUMP INTO THESE LEAVES HERE. WHAT DO YOU GUYS THINK?

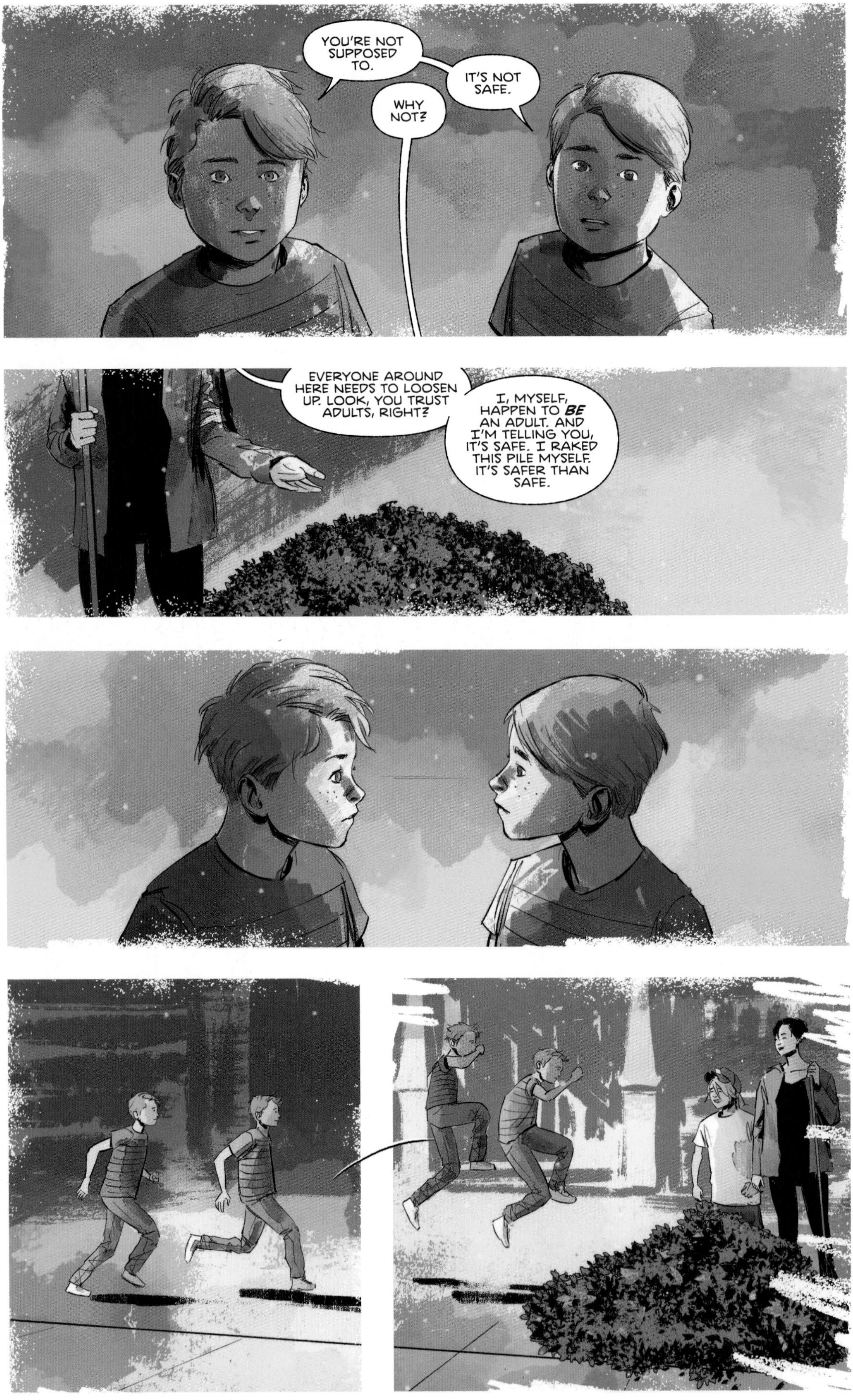
YOU'RE NOT SUPPOSED TO.
WHY NOT?
IT'S NOT SAFE.
EVERYONE AROUND HERE NEEDS TO LOOSEN UP. LOOK, YOU TRUST ADULTS, RIGHT?
I, MYSELF, HAPPEN TO *BE* AN ADULT. AND I'M TELLING YOU, IT'S SAFE. I RAKED THIS PILE MYSELF. IT'S SAFER THAN SAFE.

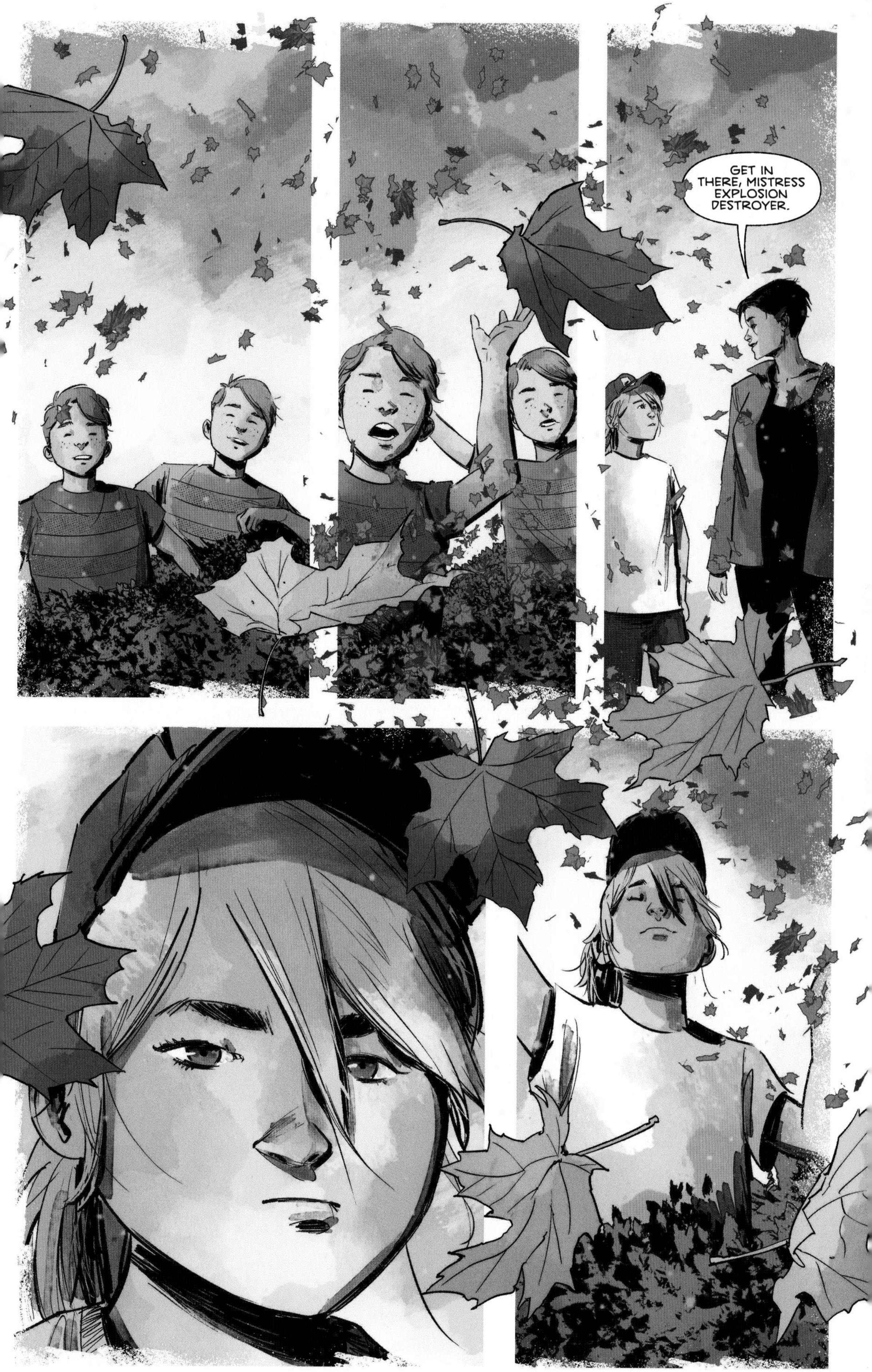
GET IN THERE, MISTRESS EXPLOSION DESTROYER.

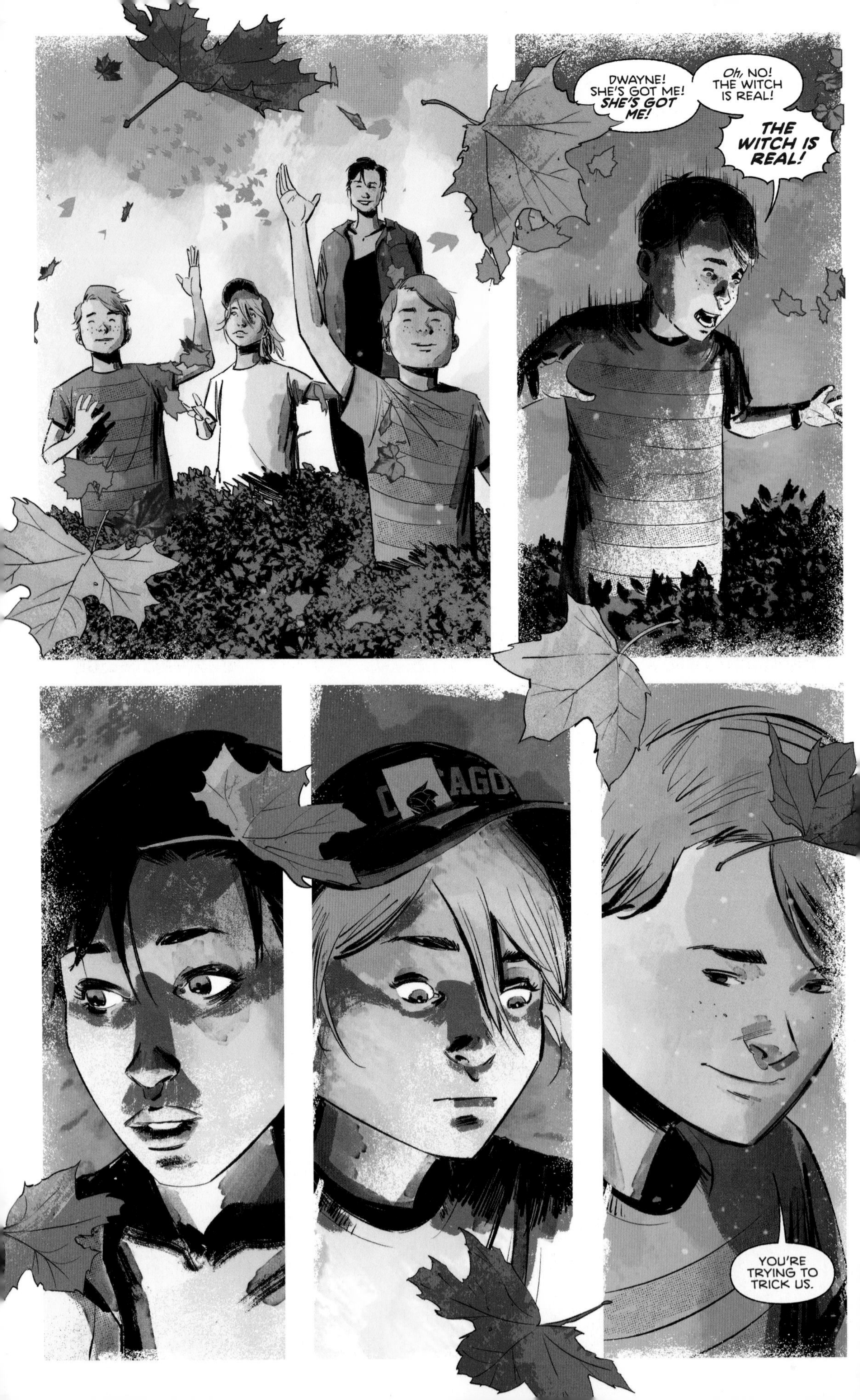
DWAYNE! SHE'S GOT ME! *SHE'S GOT ME!*
Oh, NO! THE WITCH IS REAL!
THE WITCH IS REAL!
AGO
YOU'RE TRYING TO TRICK US.

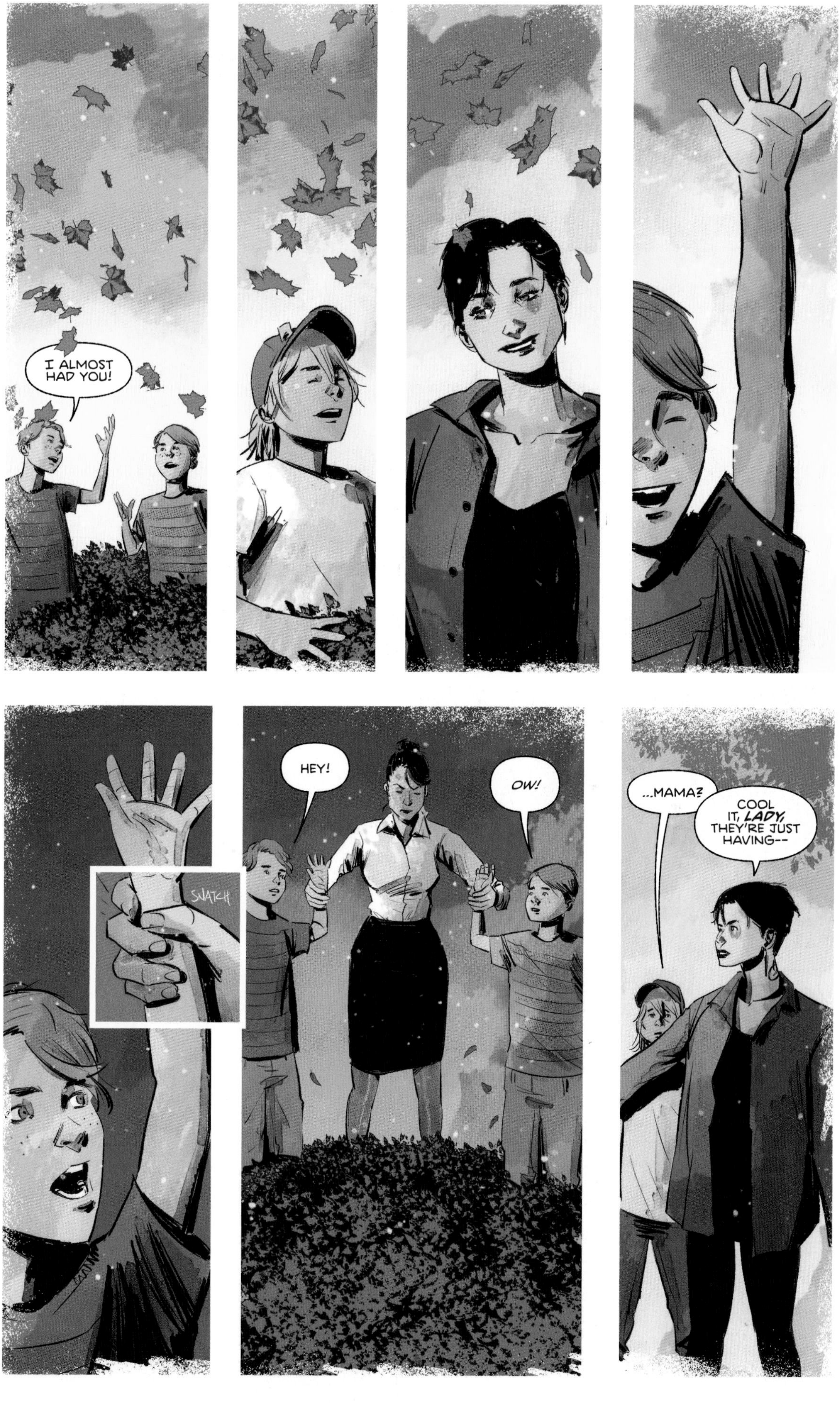
I ALMOST HAD YOU!
SNATCH
HEY!
OW!
...MAMA?
COOL IT, LADY, THEY'RE JUST HAVING--

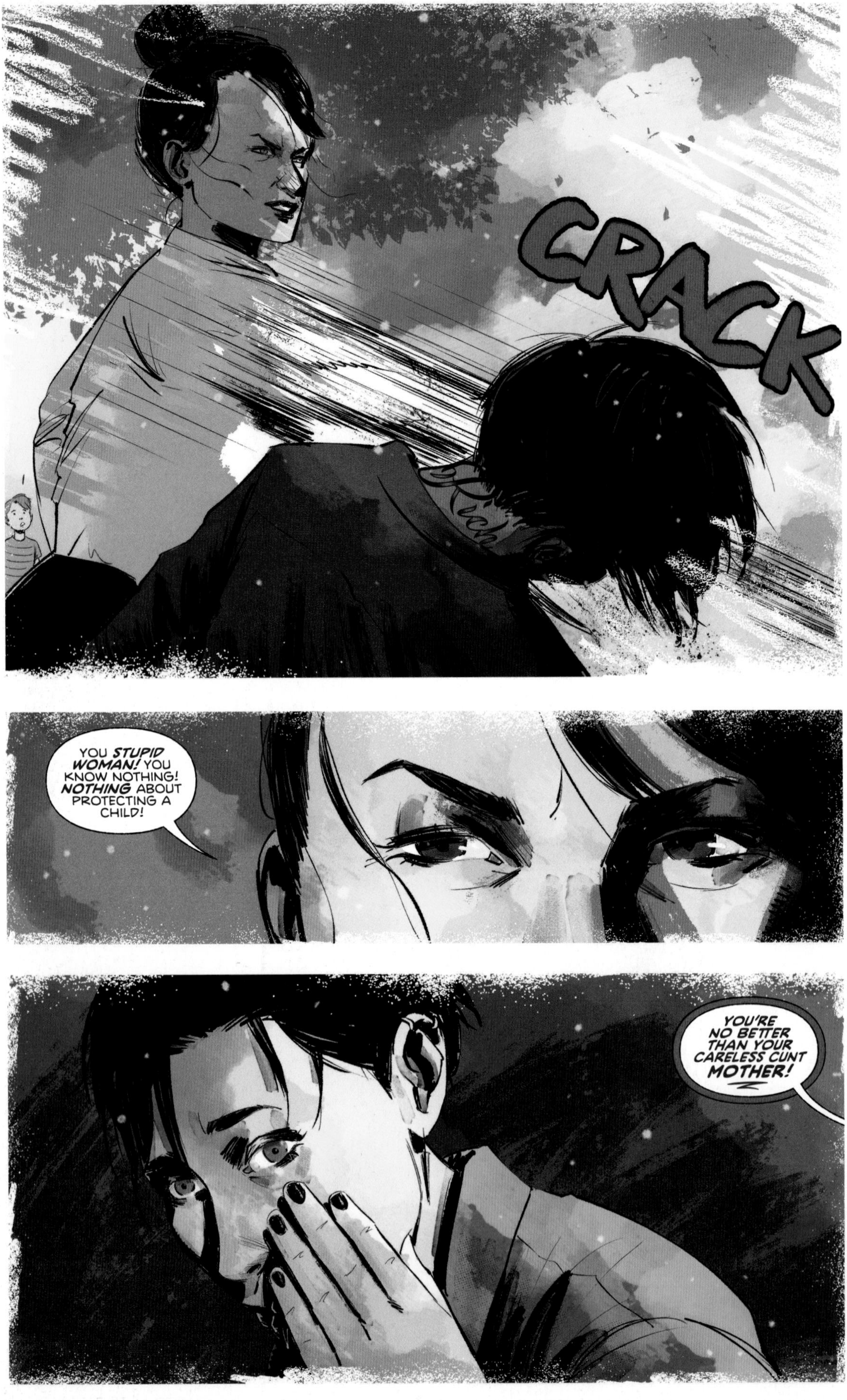
CRACK
YOU STUPID WOMAN! YOU KNOW NOTHING! NOTHING ABOUT PROTECTING A CHILD!
YOU'RE NO BETTER THAN YOUR CARELESS CUNT MOTHER!

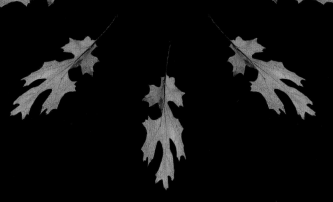

turn stone and tree and leaf and mud.

CHAPTER

THREE

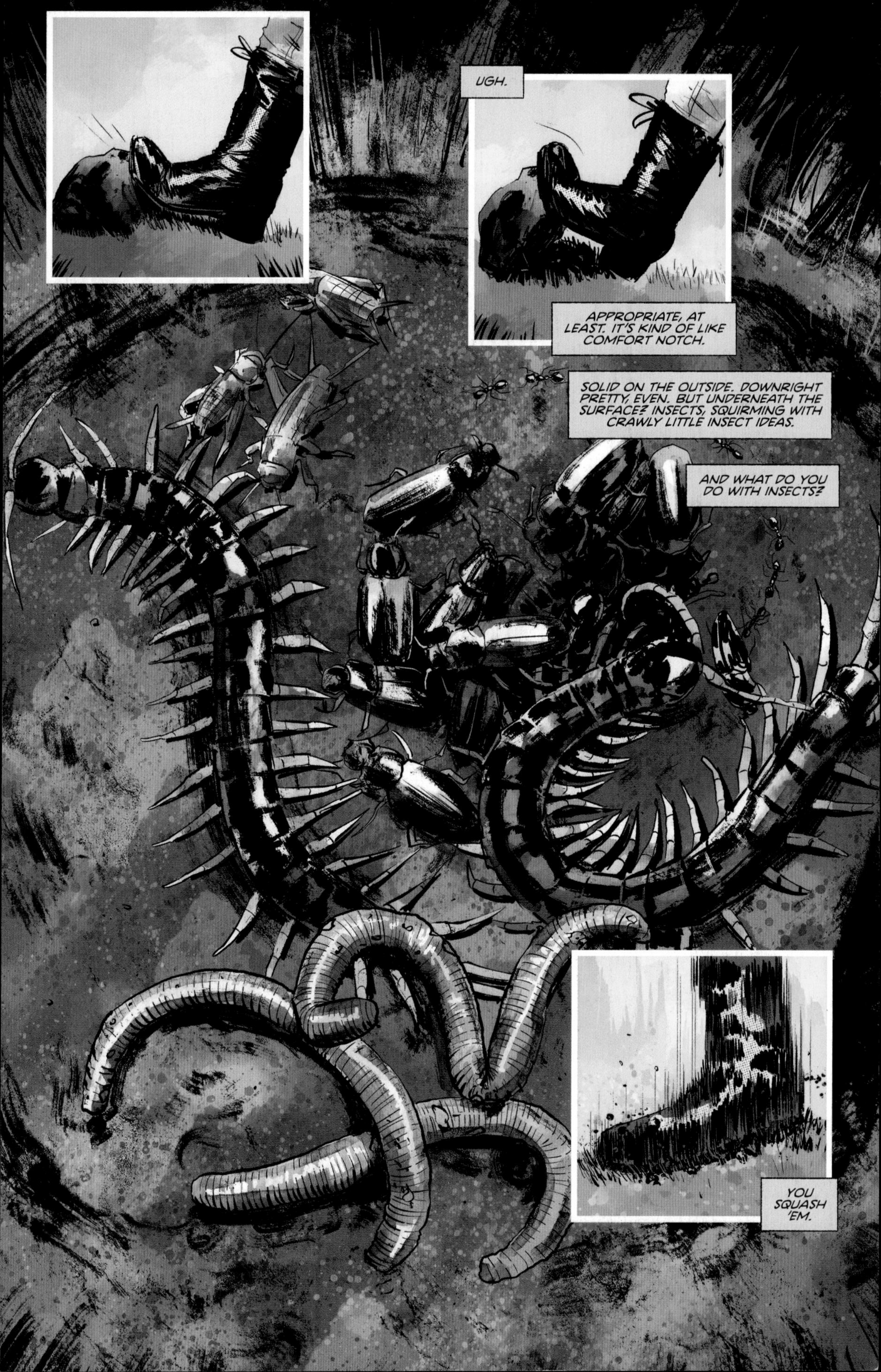
UGH.
APPROPRIATE, AT LEAST. IT'S KIND OF LIKE COMFORT NOTCH.
SOLID ON THE OUTSIDE. DOWNRIGHT PRETTY, EVEN. BUT UNDERNEATH THE SURFACE? INSECTS, SQUIRMING WITH CRAWLY LITTLE INSECT IDEAS.
AND WHAT DO YOU DO WITH INSECTS?
YOU SQUASH 'EM.

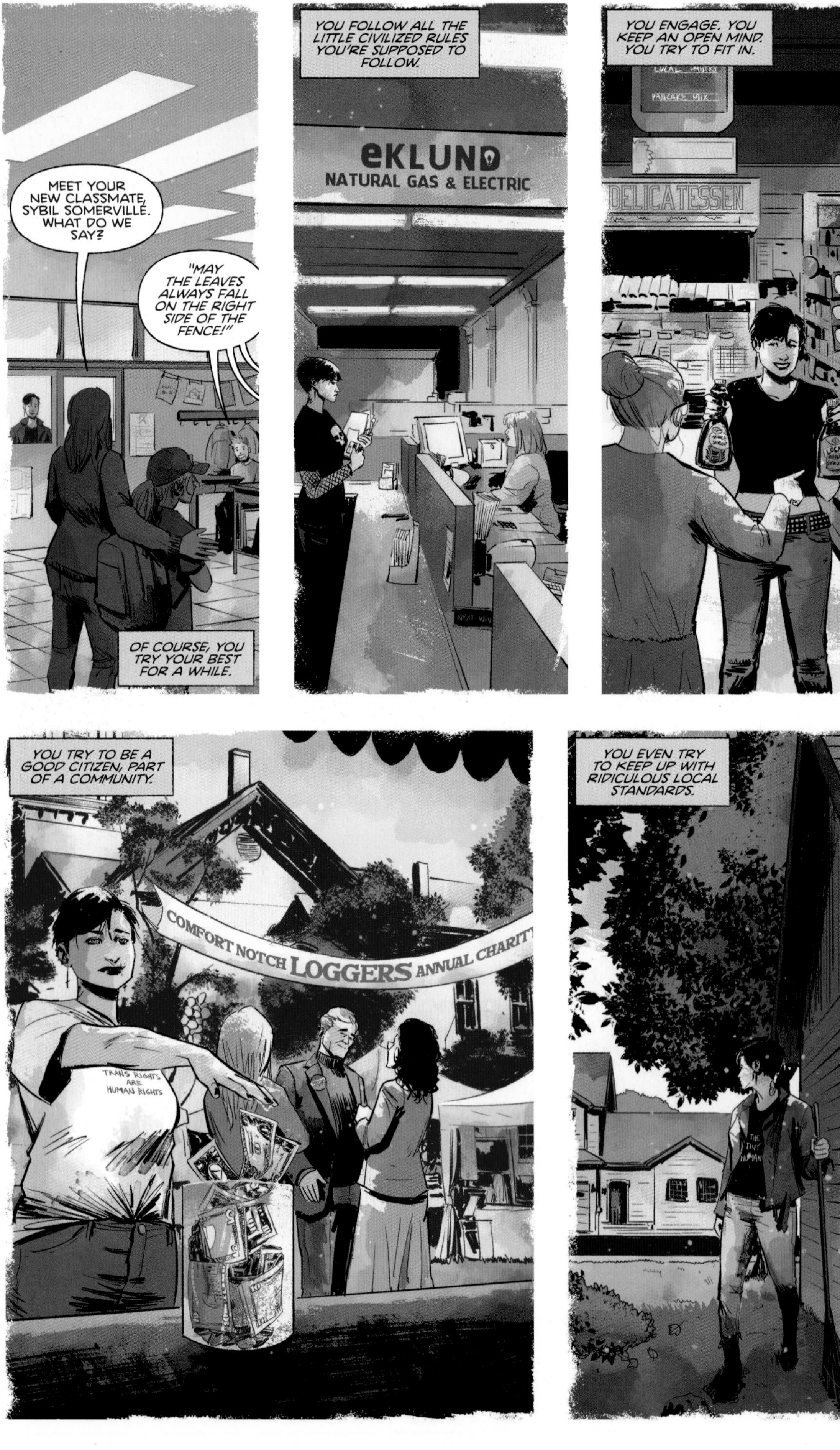
MEET YOUR NEW CLASSMATE, SYBIL SOMERVILLE. WHAT DO WE SAY?
"MAY THE LEAVES ALWAYS FALL ON THE RIGHT SIDE OF THE FENCE!"
OF COURSE, YOU TRY YOUR BEST FOR A WHILE.
YOU FOLLOW ALL THE LITTLE CIVILIZED RULES YOU'RE SUPPOSED TO FOLLOW.
eKLUND
NATURAL GAS & ELECTRIC
YOU ENGAGE. YOU KEEP AN OPEN MIND. YOU TRY TO FIT IN.
PANCAKE MIX
DELICATESSEN
YOU TRY TO BE A GOOD CITIZEN, PART OF A COMMUNITY.
COMFORT NOTCH LOGGERS ANNUAL CHARITY
TRANS RIGHTS ARE HUMAN RIGHTS
YOU EVEN TRY TO KEEP UP WITH RIDICULOUS LOCAL STANDARDS.

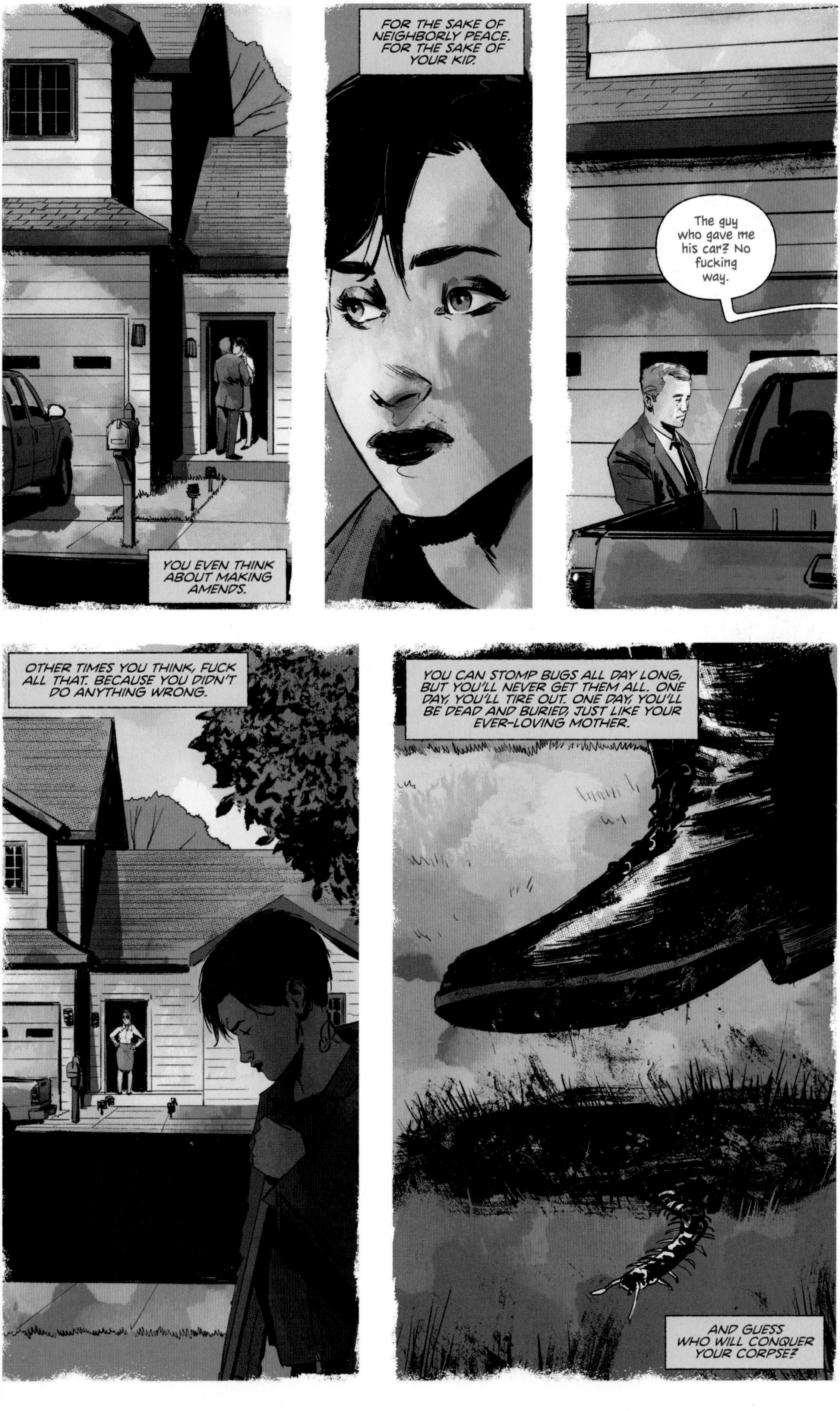
YOU EVEN THINK ABOUT MAKING AMENDS.
FOR THE SAKE OF NEIGHBORLY PEACE. FOR THE SAKE OF YOUR KID.
The guy who gave me his car? No fucking way.
OTHER TIMES YOU THINK, FUCK ALL THAT. BECAUSE YOU DIDN'T DO ANYTHING WRONG.
YOU CAN STOMP BUGS ALL DAY LONG, BUT YOU'LL NEVER GET THEM ALL. ONE DAY, YOU'LL TIRE OUT. ONE DAY, YOU'LL BE DEAD AND BURIED, JUST LIKE YOUR EVER-LOVING MOTHER.
AND GUESS WHO WILL CONQUER YOUR CORPSE?

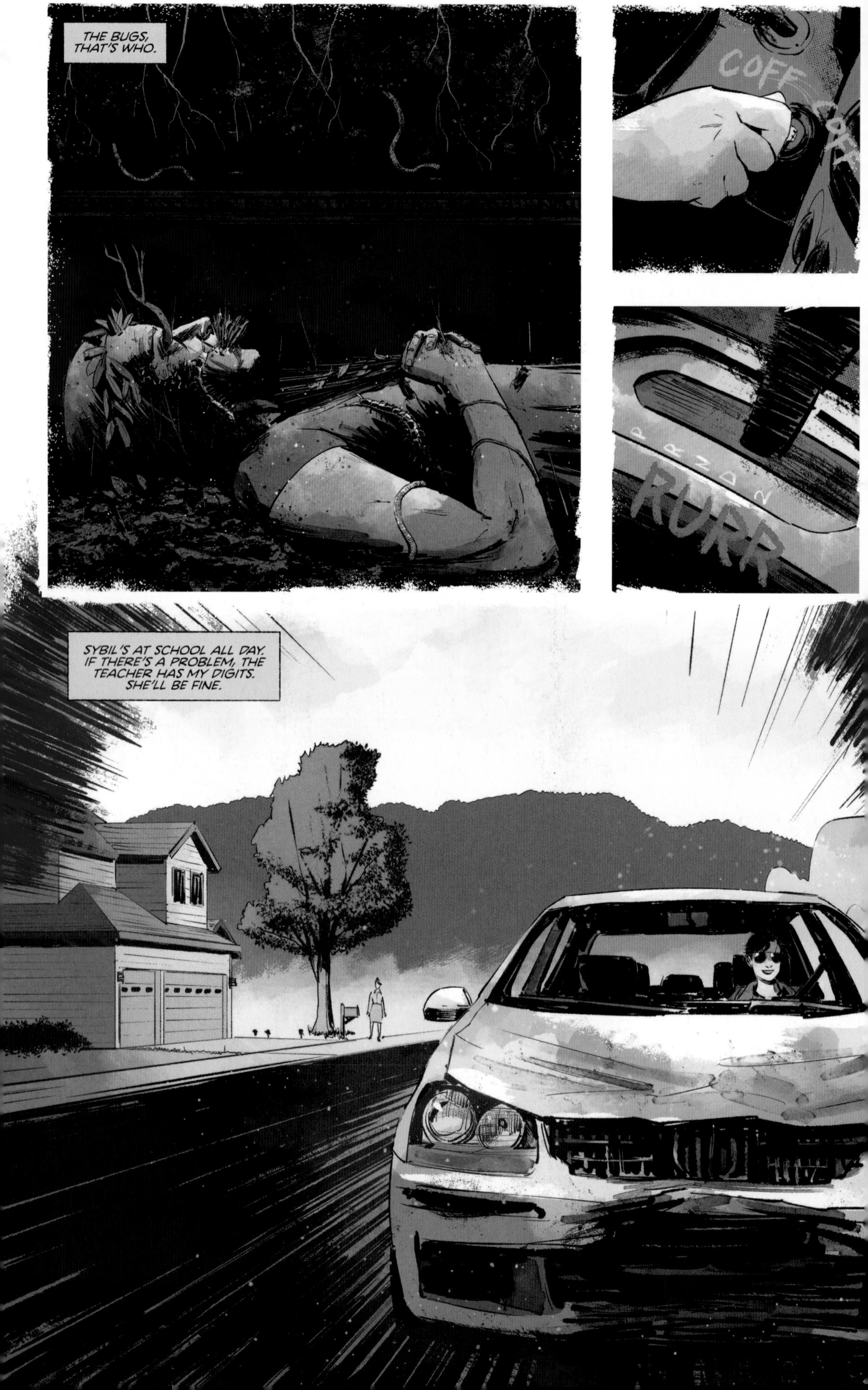
THE BUGS, THAT'S WHO.
COFF COFF
P R D N
RURR
SYBIL'S AT SCHOOL ALL DAY. IF THERE'S A PROBLEM, THE TEACHER HAS MY DIGITS. SHE'LL BE FINE.

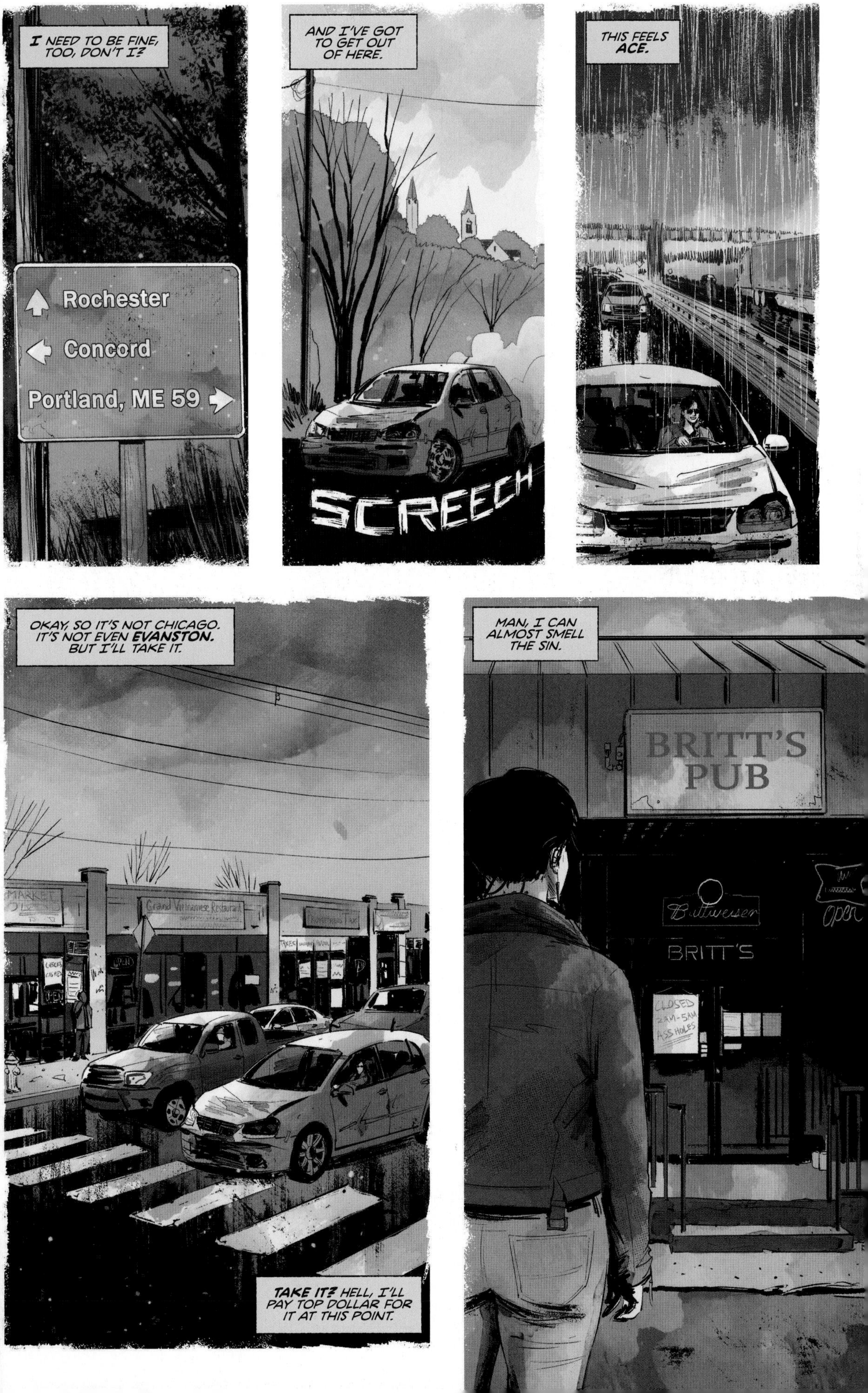
I NEED TO BE FINE, TOO, DON'T I?
Rochester
Concord
Portland, ME 59
AND I'VE GOT TO GET OUT OF HERE.
SCREECH
THIS FEELS ACE.
OKAY, SO IT'S NOT CHICAGO. IT'S NOT EVEN EVANSTON. BUT I'LL TAKE IT.
Grand Vietnamese Restaurant
OPEN
TAKE IT? HELL, I'LL PAY TOP DOLLAR FOR IT AT THIS POINT.
MAN, I CAN ALMOST SMELL THE SIN.
BRITT'S PUB
Budweiser
BRITT'S
Open
CLOSED 2AM-5AM ASSHOLES

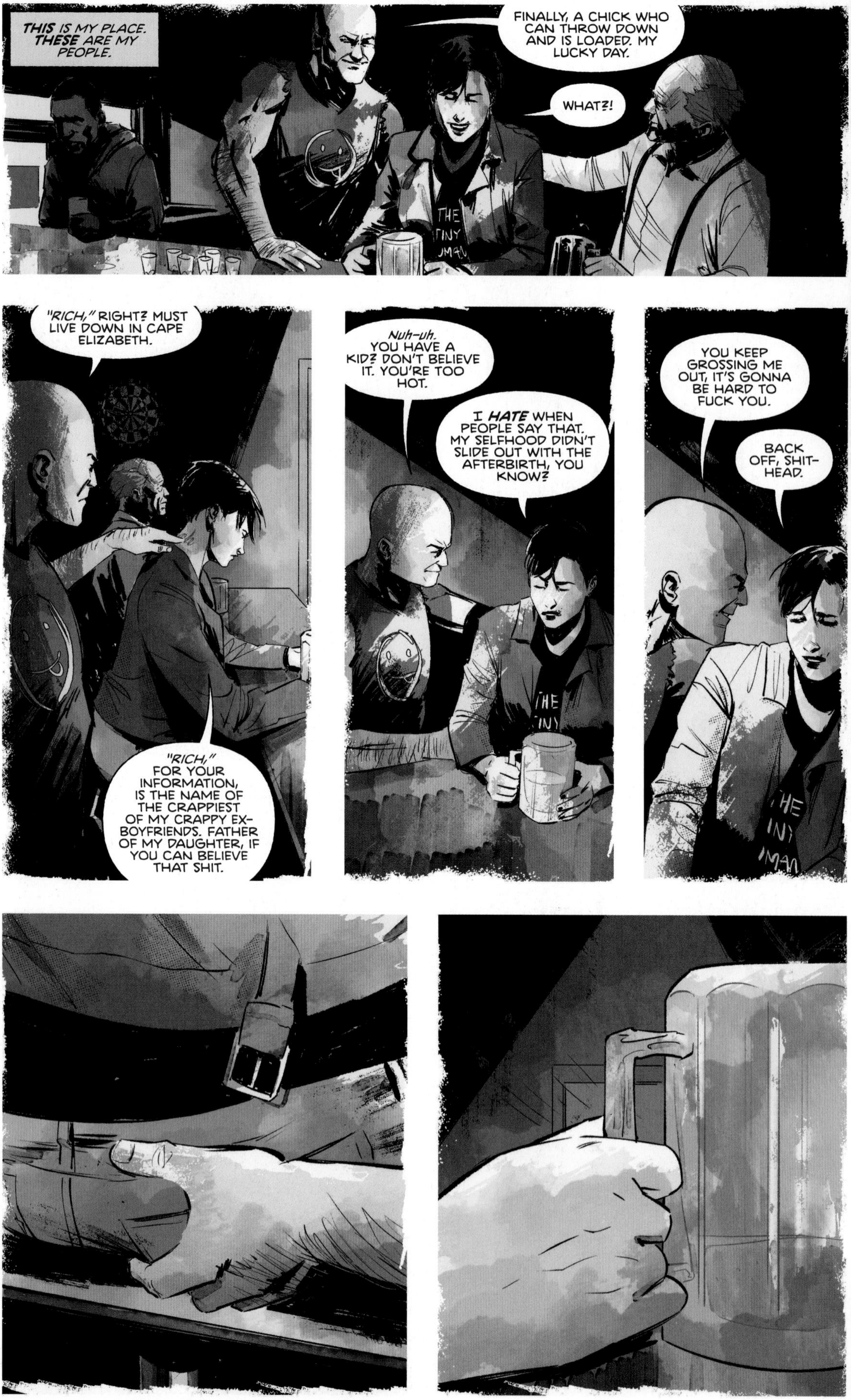
THIS IS MY PLACE. THESE ARE MY PEOPLE.
FINALLY, A CHICK WHO CAN THROW DOWN AND IS LOADED. MY LUCKY DAY.
WHAT?!
"RICH," RIGHT? MUST LIVE DOWN IN CAPE ELIZABETH.
"RICH," FOR YOUR INFORMATION, IS THE NAME OF THE CRAPPIEST OF MY CRAPPY EX-BOYFRIENDS. FATHER OF MY DAUGHTER, IF YOU CAN BELIEVE THAT SHIT.
Nuh-uh. YOU HAVE A KID? DON'T BELIEVE IT. YOU'RE TOO HOT.
I HATE WHEN PEOPLE SAY THAT. MY SELFHOOD DIDN'T SLIDE OUT WITH THE AFTERBIRTH, YOU KNOW?
YOU KEEP GROSSING ME OUT, IT'S GONNA BE HARD TO FUCK YOU.
BACK OFF, SHIT-HEAD.

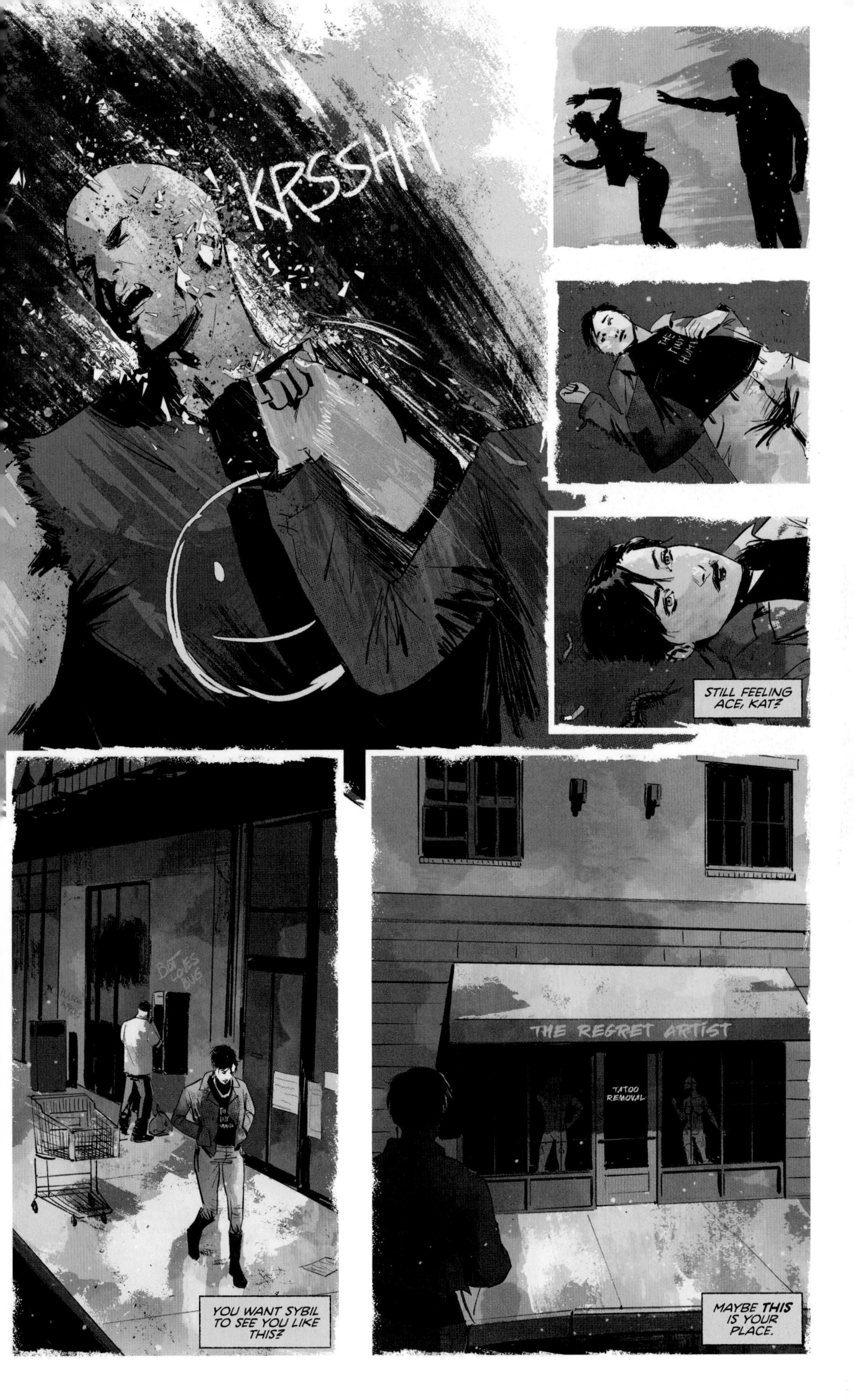
KRSSHH
STILL FEELING ACE, KAT?
YOU WANT SYBIL TO SEE YOU LIKE THIS?
THE REGRET ARTIST
TATOO REMOVAL
MAYBE THIS IS YOUR PLACE.

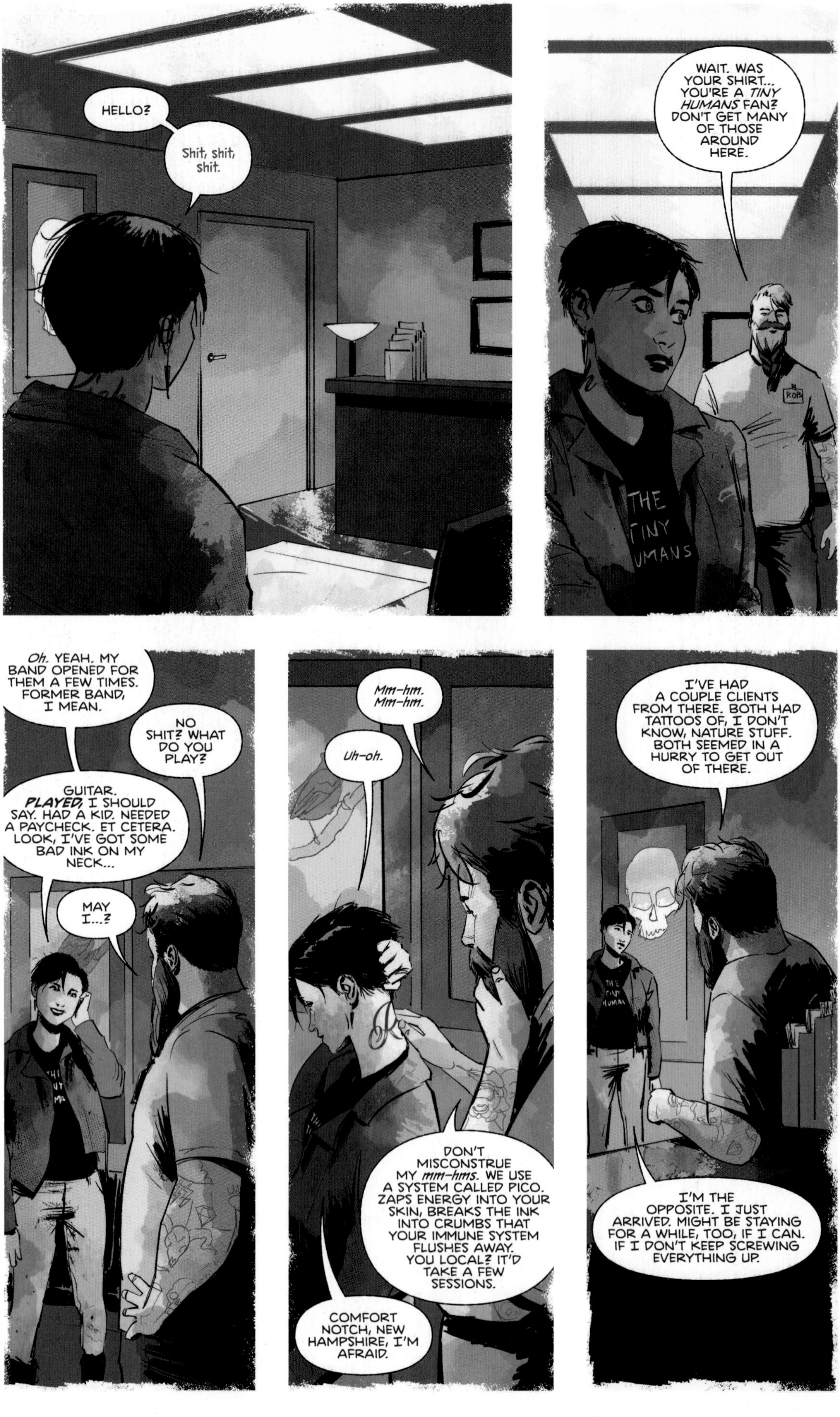
HELLO?
Shit, shit, shit.
WAIT. WAS YOUR SHIRT... YOU'RE A TINY HUMANS FAN? DON'T GET MANY OF THOSE AROUND HERE.
ROB
THE TINY HUMANS
Oh. YEAH. MY BAND OPENED FOR THEM A FEW TIMES. FORMER BAND, I MEAN.
NO SHIT? WHAT DO YOU PLAY?
GUITAR. PLAYED, I SHOULD SAY. HAD A KID. NEEDED A PAYCHECK. ET CETERA. LOOK, I'VE GOT SOME BAD INK ON MY NECK...
MAY I...?
Mm-hm. Mm-hm.
Uh-oh.
DON'T MISCONSTRUE MY mm-hms. WE USE A SYSTEM CALLED PICO. ZAPS ENERGY INTO YOUR SKIN, BREAKS THE INK INTO CRUMBS THAT YOUR IMMUNE SYSTEM FLUSHES AWAY. YOU LOCAL? IT'D TAKE A FEW SESSIONS.
COMFORT NOTCH, NEW HAMPSHIRE, I'M AFRAID.
I'VE HAD A COUPLE CLIENTS FROM THERE. BOTH HAD TATTOOS OF, I DON'T KNOW, NATURE STUFF. BOTH SEEMED IN A HURRY TO GET OUT OF THERE.
I'M THE OPPOSITE. I JUST ARRIVED. MIGHT BE STAYING FOR A WHILE, TOO, IF I CAN. IF I DON'T KEEP SCREWING EVERYTHING UP.

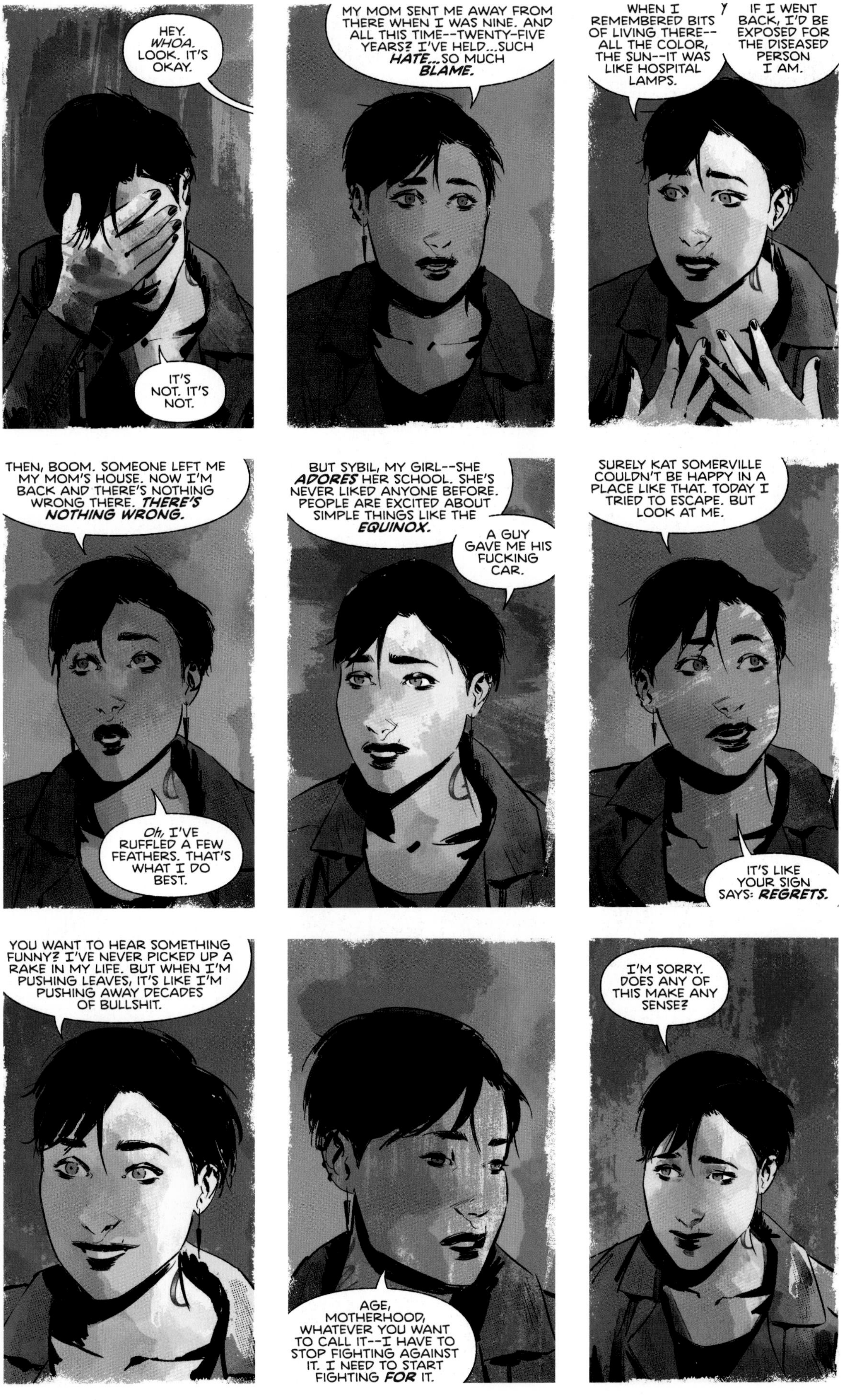
HEY. *WHOA.* LOOK. IT'S OKAY.
IT'S NOT. IT'S NOT.
MY MOM SENT ME AWAY FROM THERE WHEN I WAS NINE. AND ALL THIS TIME--TWENTY-FIVE YEARS? I'VE HELD...SUCH **HATE...** SO MUCH **BLAME.**
WHEN I REMEMBERED BITS OF LIVING THERE--ALL THE COLOR, THE SUN--IT WAS LIKE HOSPITAL LAMPS.
IF I WENT BACK, I'D BE EXPOSED FOR THE DISEASED PERSON I AM.
THEN, BOOM. SOMEONE LEFT ME MY MOM'S HOUSE. NOW I'M BACK AND THERE'S NOTHING WRONG THERE. **THERE'S NOTHING WRONG.**
Oh, I'VE RUFFLED A FEW FEATHERS. THAT'S WHAT I DO BEST.
BUT SYBIL, MY GIRL--SHE **ADORES** HER SCHOOL. SHE'S NEVER LIKED ANYONE BEFORE. PEOPLE ARE EXCITED ABOUT SIMPLE THINGS LIKE THE **EQUINOX.**
A GUY GAVE ME HIS FUCKING CAR.
SURELY KAT SOMERVILLE COULDN'T BE HAPPY IN A PLACE LIKE THAT. TODAY I TRIED TO ESCAPE. BUT LOOK AT ME.
IT'S LIKE YOUR SIGN SAYS: **REGRETS.**
YOU WANT TO HEAR SOMETHING FUNNY? I'VE NEVER PICKED UP A RAKE IN MY LIFE. BUT WHEN I'M PUSHING LEAVES, IT'S LIKE I'M PUSHING AWAY DECADES OF BULLSHIT.
AGE, MOTHERHOOD, WHATEVER YOU WANT TO CALL IT--I HAVE TO STOP FIGHTING AGAINST IT. I NEED TO START FIGHTING **FOR** IT.
I'M SORRY. DOES ANY OF THIS MAKE ANY SENSE?

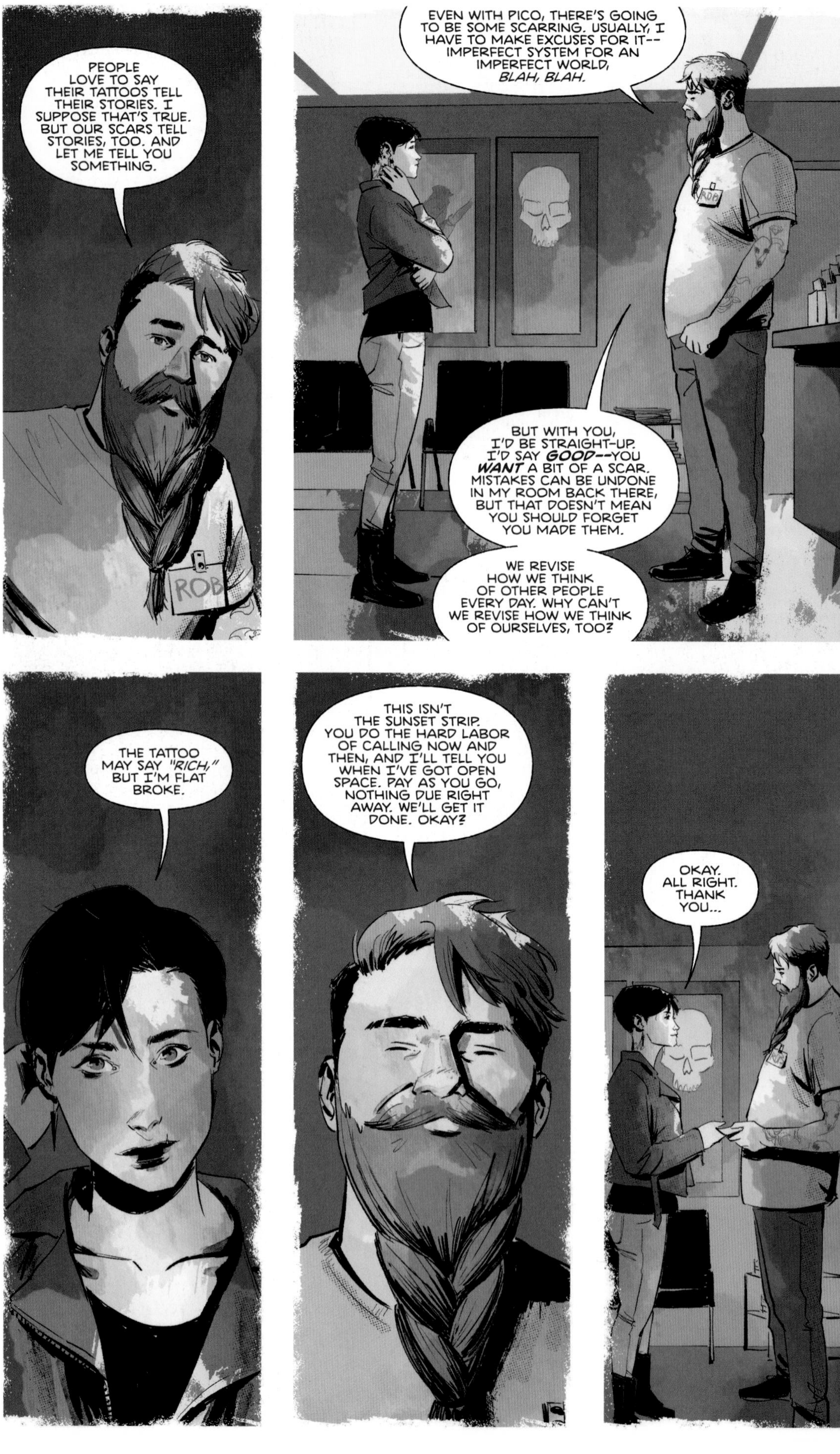
PEOPLE LOVE TO SAY THEIR TATTOOS TELL THEIR STORIES. I SUPPOSE THAT'S TRUE. BUT OUR SCARS TELL STORIES, TOO. AND LET ME TELL YOU SOMETHING.
ROB
EVEN WITH PICO, THERE'S GOING TO BE SOME SCARRING. USUALLY, I HAVE TO MAKE EXCUSES FOR IT--IMPERFECT SYSTEM FOR AN IMPERFECT WORLD, *BLAH, BLAH.*
ROB
BUT WITH YOU, I'D BE STRAIGHT-UP. I'D SAY ***GOOD***--YOU ***WANT*** A BIT OF A SCAR. MISTAKES CAN BE UNDONE IN MY ROOM BACK THERE, BUT THAT DOESN'T MEAN YOU SHOULD FORGET YOU MADE THEM.
WE REVISE HOW WE THINK OF OTHER PEOPLE EVERY DAY. WHY CAN'T WE REVISE HOW WE THINK OF OURSELVES, TOO?
THE TATTOO MAY SAY *"RICH,"* BUT I'M FLAT BROKE.
THIS ISN'T THE SUNSET STRIP. YOU DO THE HARD LABOR OF CALLING NOW AND THEN, AND I'LL TELL YOU WHEN I'VE GOT OPEN SPACE. PAY AS YOU GO, NOTHING DUE RIGHT AWAY. WE'LL GET IT DONE. OKAY?
OKAY. ALL RIGHT. THANK YOU...

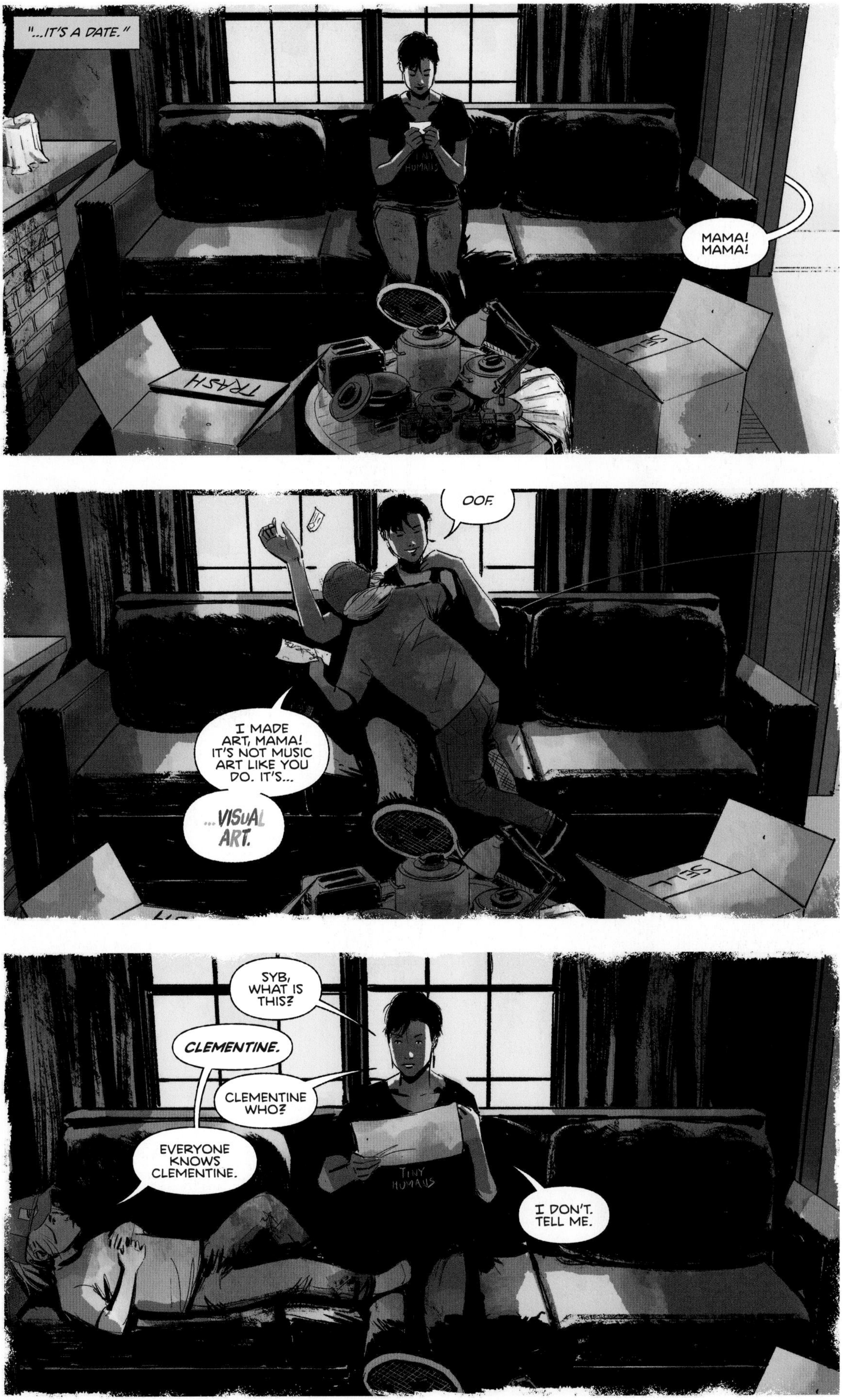
"...IT'S A DATE."
MAMA! MAMA!
TRASH
SELL
OOF.
I MADE ART, MAMA! IT'S NOT MUSIC ART LIKE YOU DO. IT'S...
...VISUAL ART.
SYB, WHAT IS THIS?
CLEMENTINE.
CLEMENTINE WHO?
EVERYONE KNOWS CLEMENTINE.
I DON'T. TELL ME.

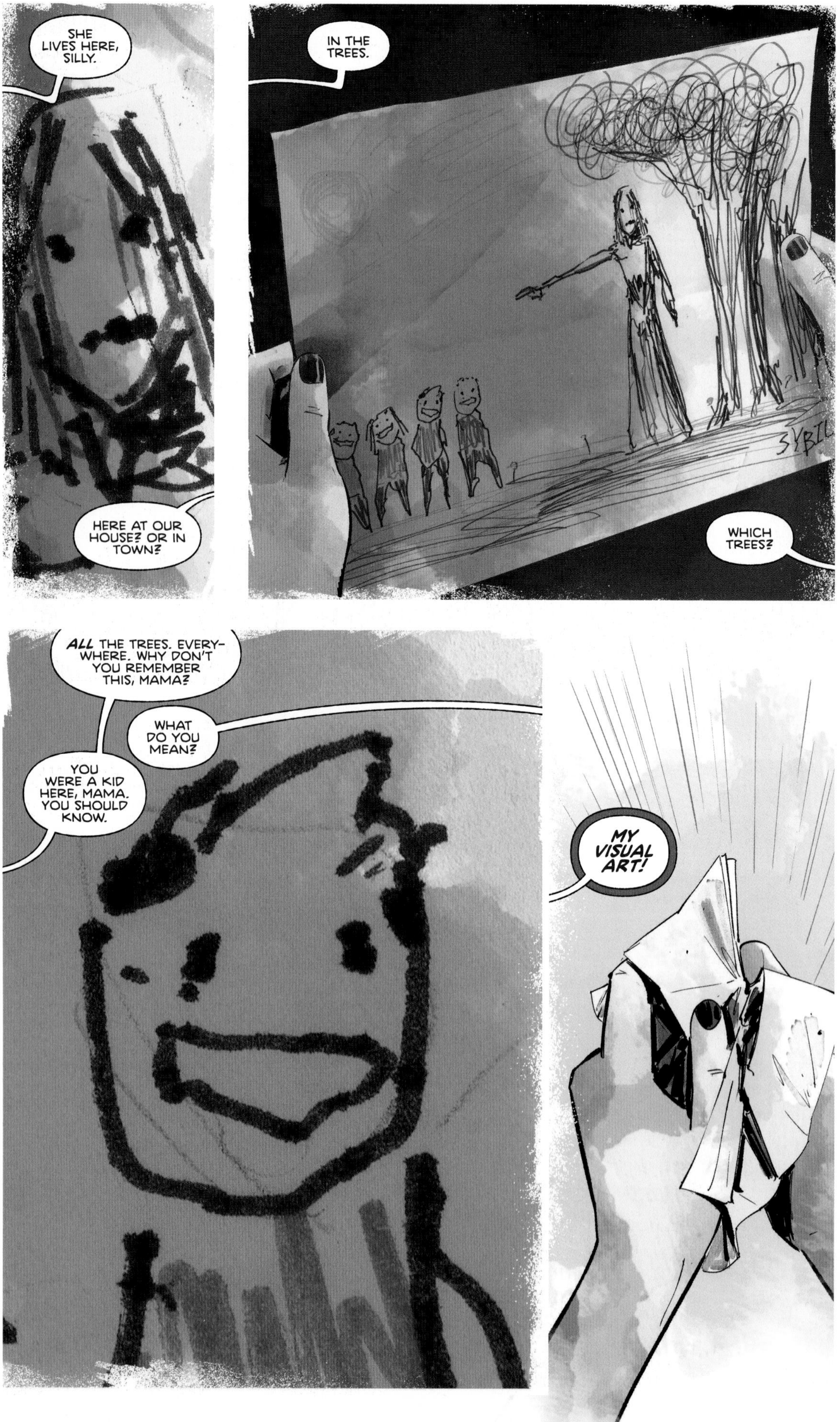
SHE LIVES HERE, SILLY.
HERE AT OUR HOUSE? OR IN TOWN?
IN THE TREES.
SYBIL
WHICH TREES?
ALL THE TREES. EVERYWHERE. WHY DON'T YOU REMEMBER THIS, MAMA?
WHAT DO YOU MEAN?
YOU WERE A KID HERE, MAMA. YOU SHOULD KNOW.
MY VISUAL ART!

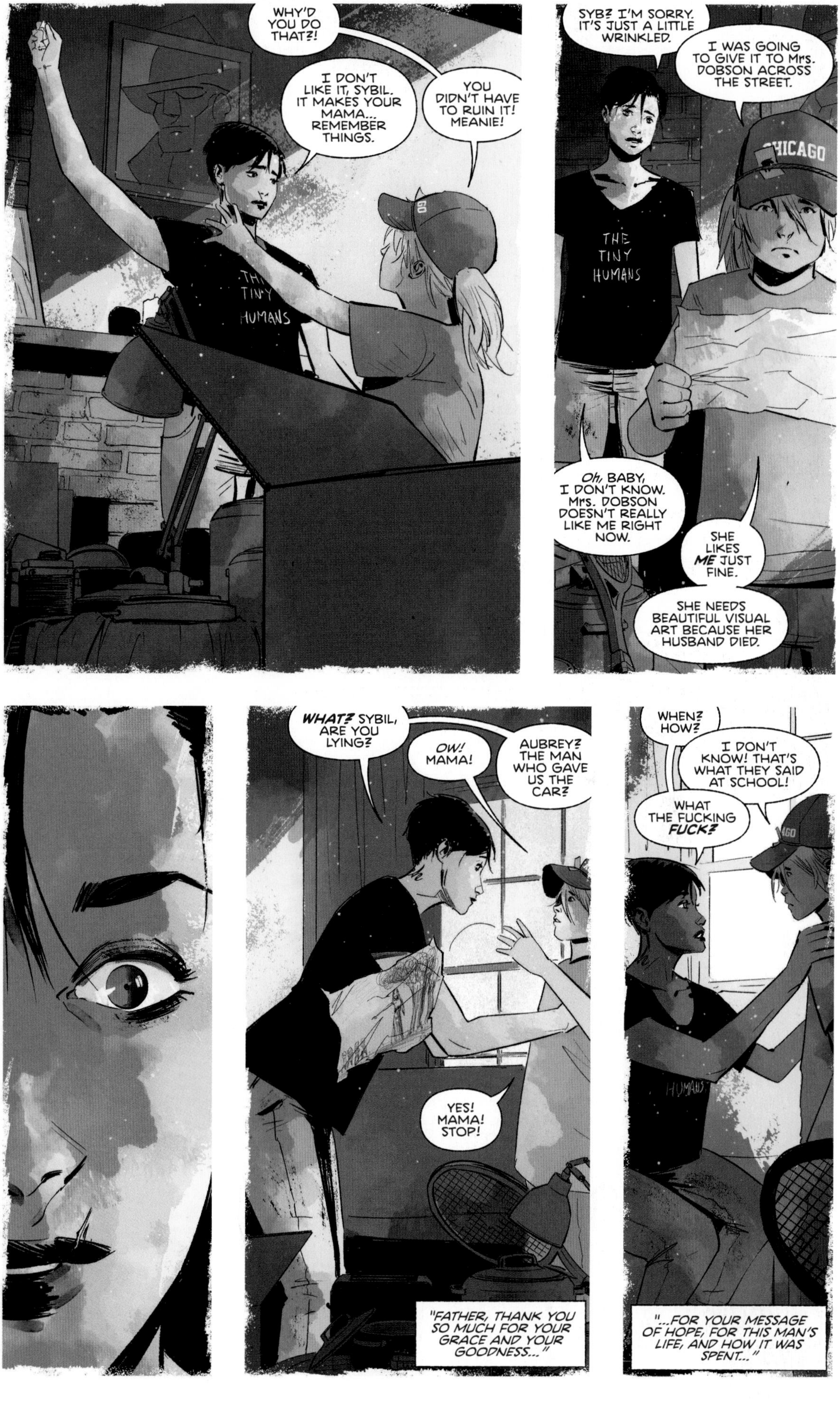
WHY'D YOU DO THAT?!
I DON'T LIKE IT, SYBIL. IT MAKES YOUR MAMA... REMEMBER THINGS.
YOU DIDN'T HAVE TO RUIN IT! MEANIE!
THE TINY HUMANS
SYB? I'M SORRY. IT'S JUST A LITTLE WRINKLED.
I WAS GOING TO GIVE IT TO Mrs. DOBSON ACROSS THE STREET.
CHICAGO
THE TINY HUMANS
Oh, BABY, I DON'T KNOW. Mrs. DOBSON DOESN'T REALLY LIKE ME RIGHT NOW.
SHE LIKES ***ME*** JUST FINE.
SHE NEEDS BEAUTIFUL VISUAL ART BECAUSE HER HUSBAND DIED.
WHAT? SYBIL, ARE YOU LYING?
OW! MAMA!
AUBREY? THE MAN WHO GAVE US THE CAR?
YES! MAMA! STOP!
"FATHER, THANK YOU SO MUCH FOR YOUR GRACE AND YOUR GOODNESS..."
WHEN? HOW?
I DON'T KNOW! THAT'S WHAT THEY SAID AT SCHOOL!
WHAT THE FUCKING ***FUCK?***
HUMANS
"...FOR YOUR MESSAGE OF HOPE, FOR THIS MAN'S LIFE, AND HOW IT WAS SPENT..."

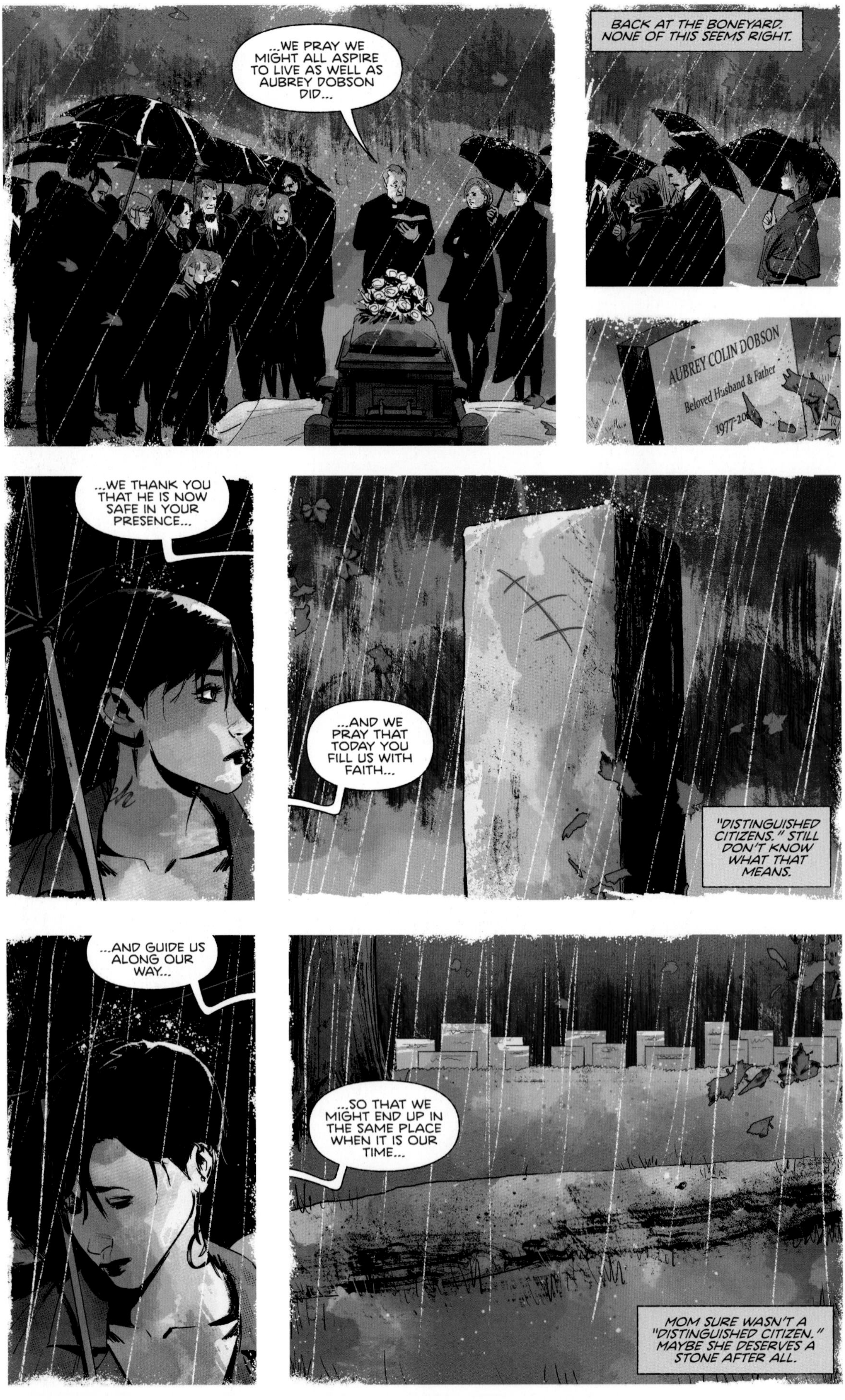
...WE PRAY WE MIGHT ALL ASPIRE TO LIVE AS WELL AS AUBREY DOBSON DID...
BACK AT THE BONEYARD. NONE OF THIS SEEMS RIGHT.
AUBREY COLIN DOBSON
Beloved Husband & Father
...WE THANK YOU THAT HE IS NOW SAFE IN YOUR PRESENCE...
...AND WE PRAY THAT TODAY YOU FILL US WITH FAITH...
"DISTINGUISHED CITIZENS." STILL DON'T KNOW WHAT THAT MEANS.
...AND GUIDE US ALONG OUR WAY...
...SO THAT WE MIGHT END UP IN THE SAME PLACE WHEN IT IS OUR TIME...
MOM SURE WASN'T A "DISTINGUISHED CITIZEN." MAYBE SHE DESERVES A STONE AFTER ALL.

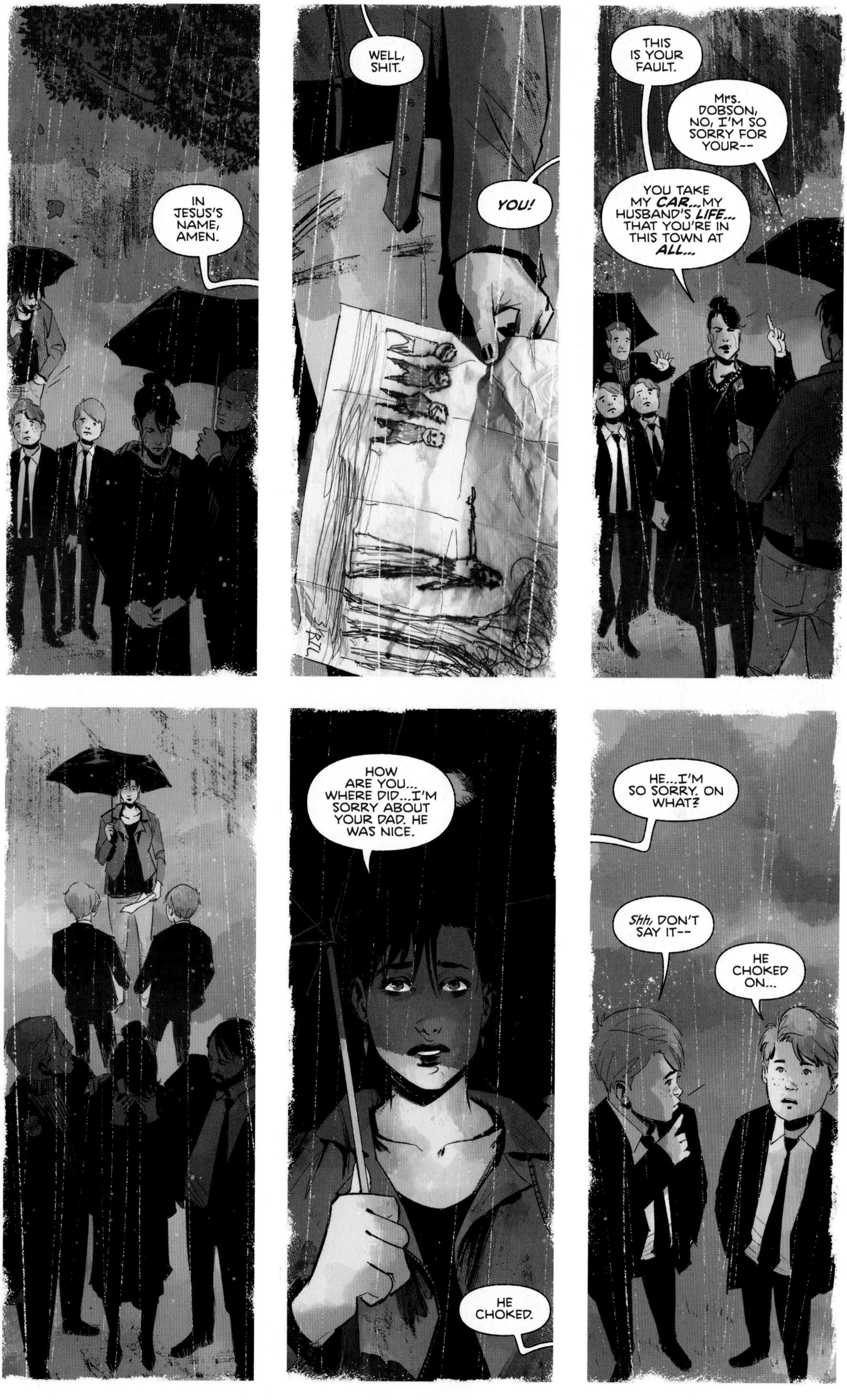
IN JESUS'S NAME, AMEN.
WELL, SHIT.
YOU!
THIS IS YOUR FAULT.
Mrs. DOBSON, NO, I'M SO SORRY FOR YOUR--
YOU TAKE MY CAR...MY HUSBAND'S LIFE... THAT YOU'RE IN THIS TOWN AT ALL...
HOW ARE YOU... WHERE DID...I'M SORRY ABOUT YOUR DAD. HE WAS NICE.
HE CHOKED.
HE...I'M SO SORRY. ON WHAT?
Shh, DON'T SAY IT--
HE CHOKED ON...

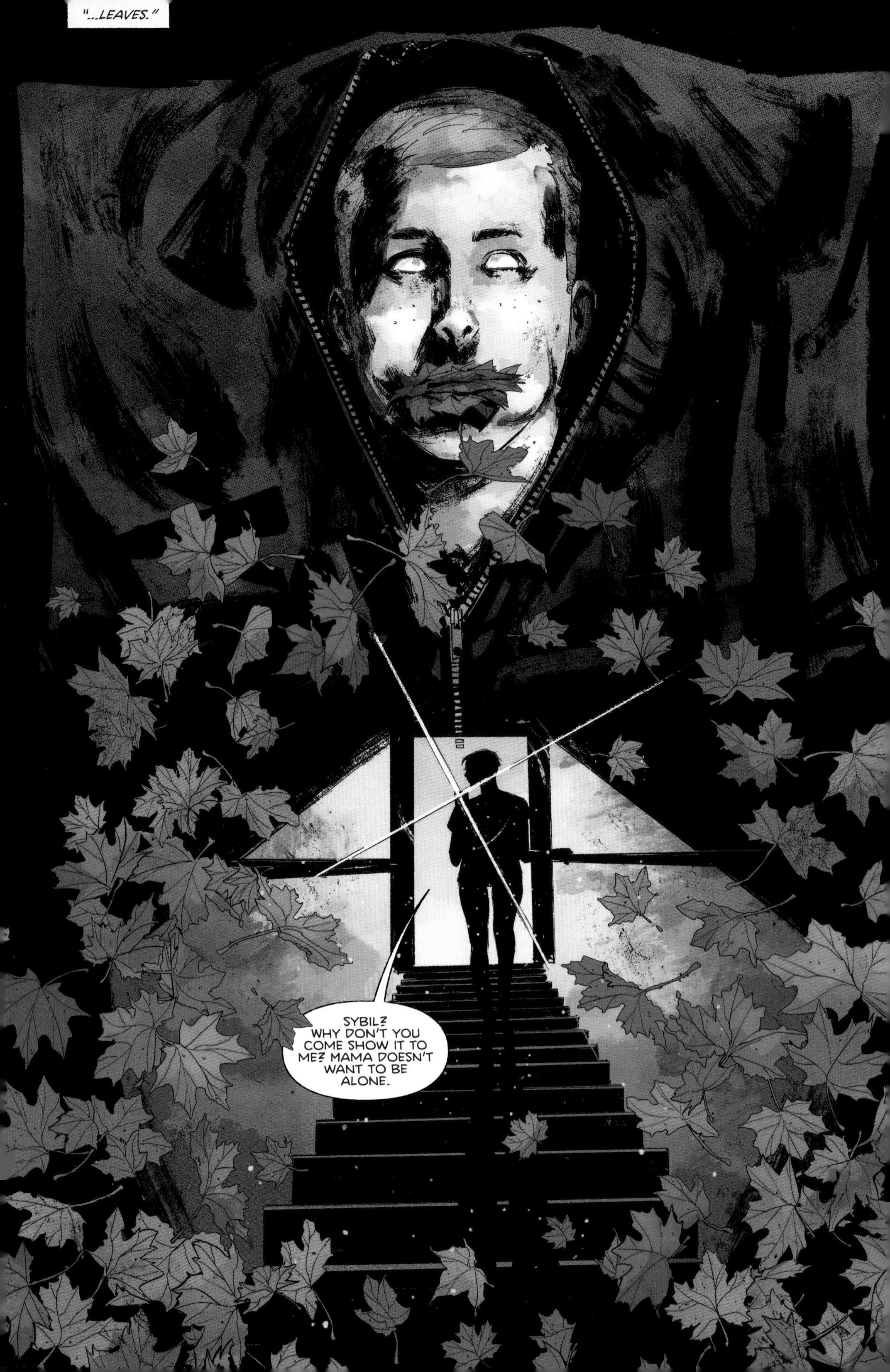
"...LEAVES."
SYBIL? WHY DON'T YOU COME SHOW IT TO ME? MAMA DOESN'T WANT TO BE ALONE.

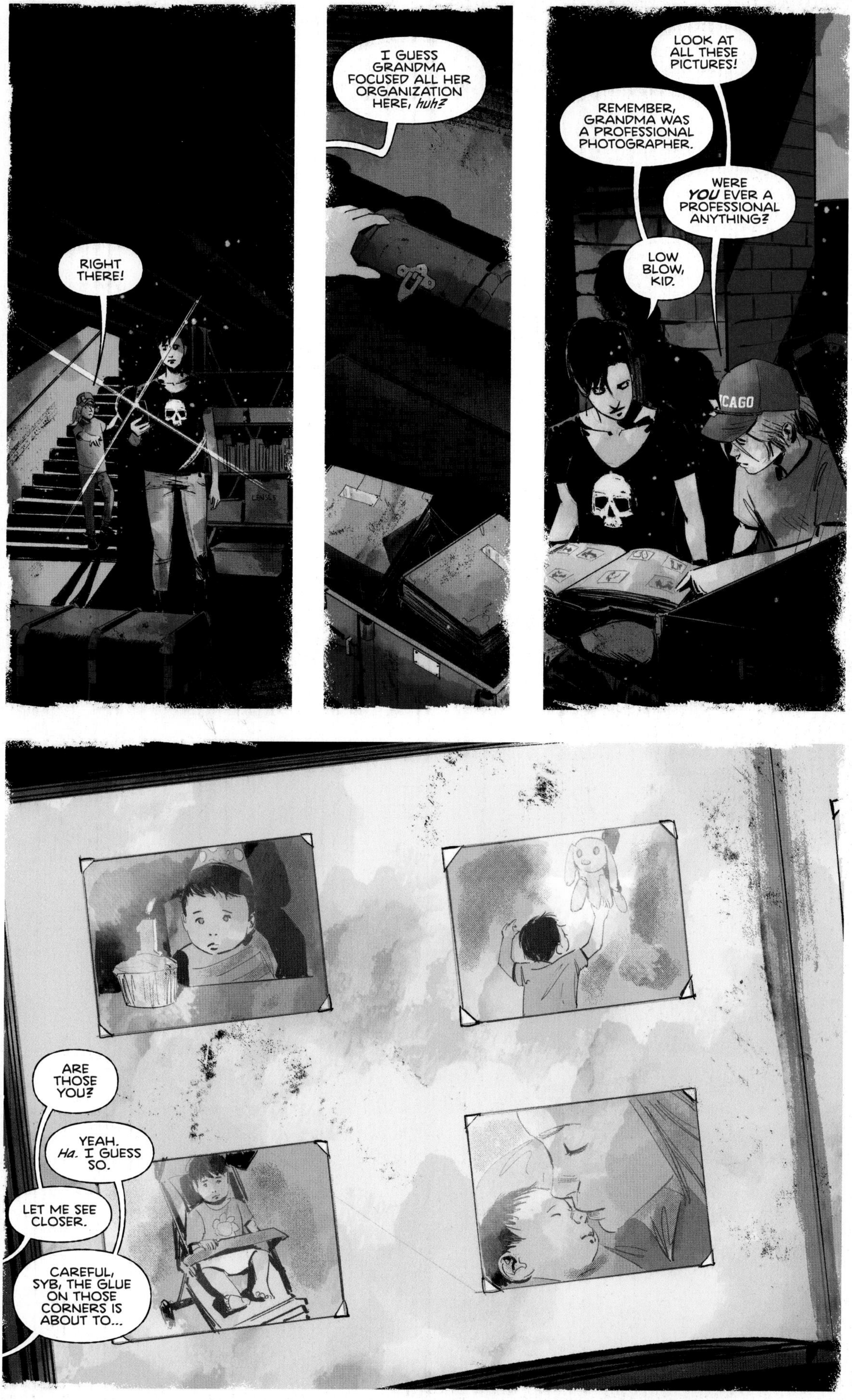
RIGHT THERE!
I GUESS GRANDMA FOCUSED ALL HER ORGANIZATION HERE, *huh?*
LOOK AT ALL THESE PICTURES!
REMEMBER, GRANDMA WAS A PROFESSIONAL PHOTOGRAPHER.
WERE ***YOU*** EVER A PROFESSIONAL ANYTHING?
LOW BLOW, KID.
CAGO
ARE THOSE YOU?
YEAH. *Ha.* I GUESS SO.
LET ME SEE CLOSER.
CAREFUL, SYB, THE GLUE ON THOSE CORNERS IS ABOUT TO...

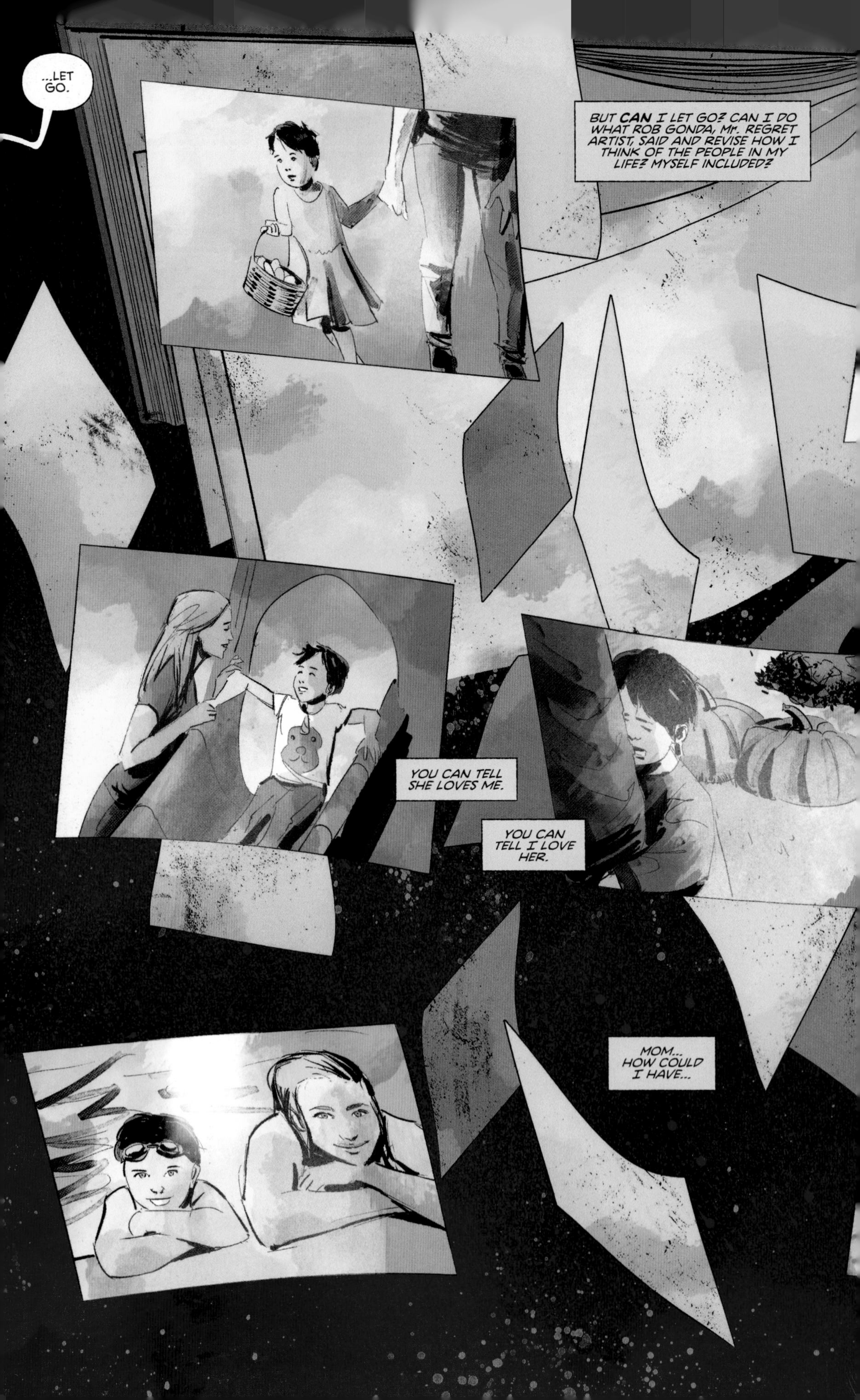
...LET GO.
BUT CAN I LET GO? CAN I DO WHAT ROB GONDA, Mr. REGRET ARTIST, SAID AND REVISE HOW I THINK OF THE PEOPLE IN MY LIFE? MYSELF INCLUDED?
YOU CAN TELL SHE LOVES ME.
YOU CAN TELL I LOVE HER.
MOM... HOW COULD I HAVE...

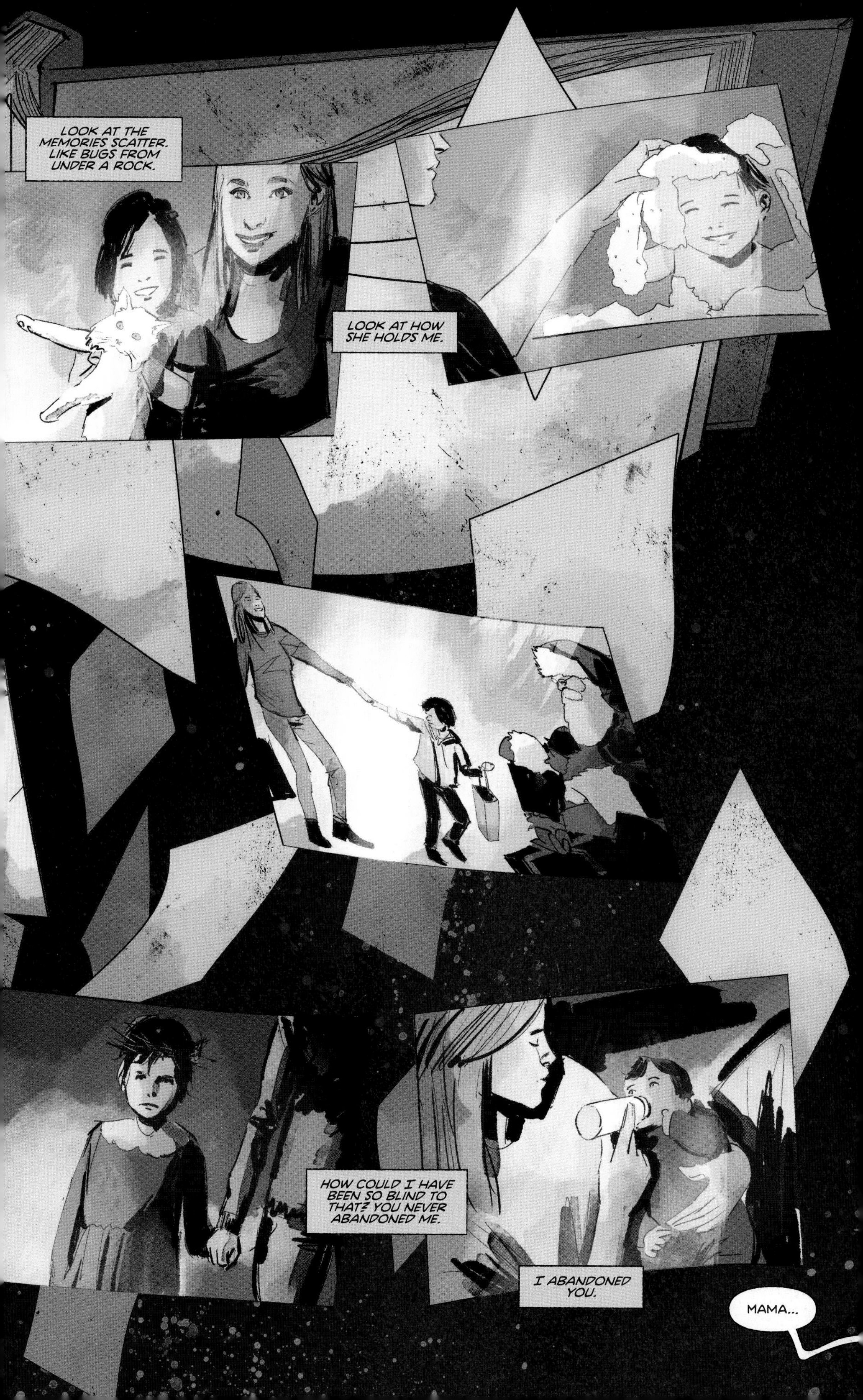
LOOK AT THE MEMORIES SCATTER. LIKE BUGS FROM UNDER A ROCK.
LOOK AT HOW SHE HOLDS ME.
HOW COULD I HAVE BEEN SO BLIND TO THAT? YOU NEVER ABANDONED ME.
I ABANDONED YOU.
MAMA...

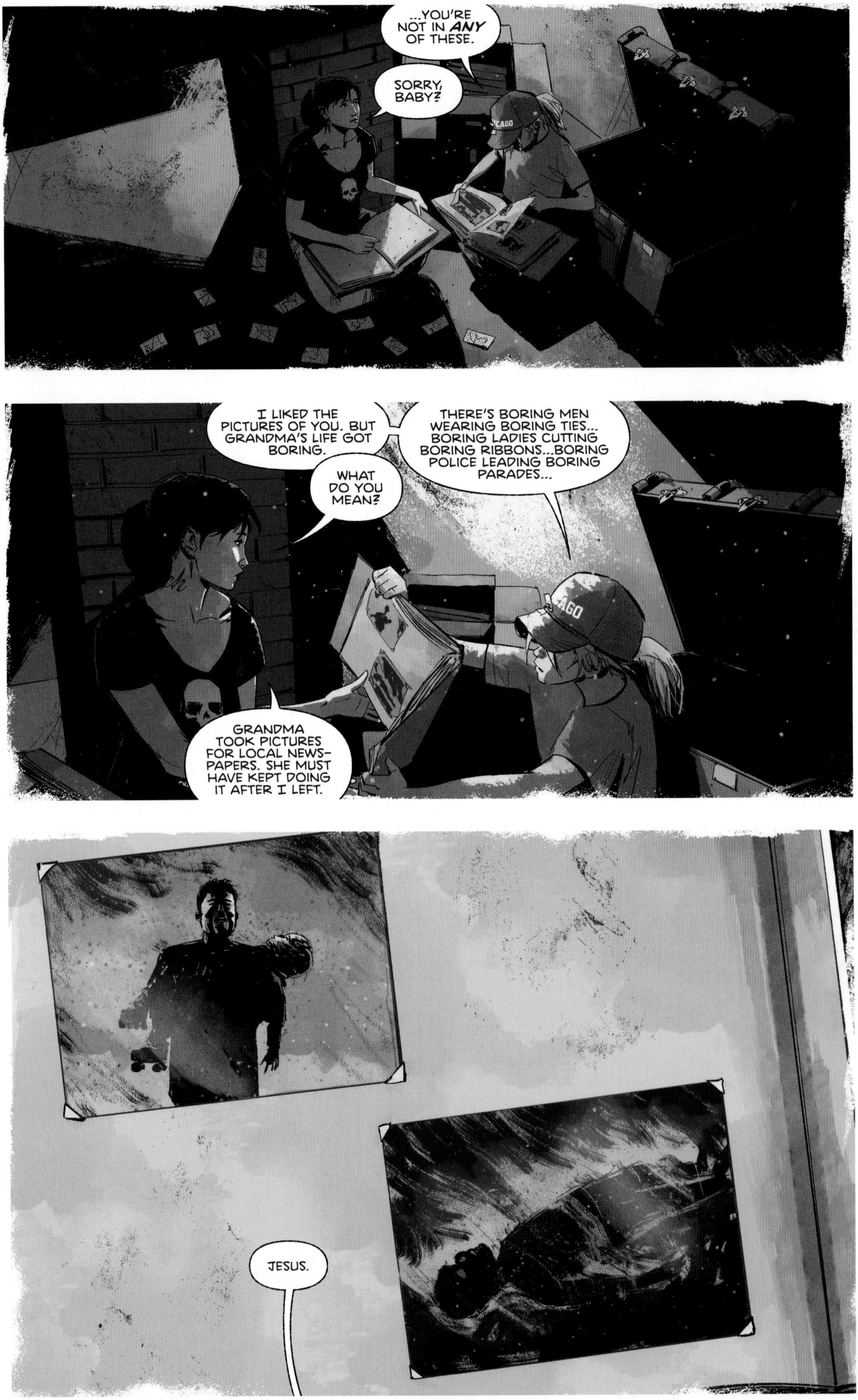

...YOU'RE NOT IN ANY OF THESE.
SORRY, BABY?
I LIKED THE PICTURES OF YOU. BUT GRANDMA'S LIFE GOT BORING.
THERE'S BORING MEN WEARING BORING TIES... BORING LADIES CUTTING BORING RIBBONS...BORING POLICE LEADING BORING PARADES...
WHAT DO YOU MEAN?
GRANDMA TOOK PICTURES FOR LOCAL NEWS-PAPERS. SHE MUST HAVE KEPT DOING IT AFTER I LEFT.
JESUS.

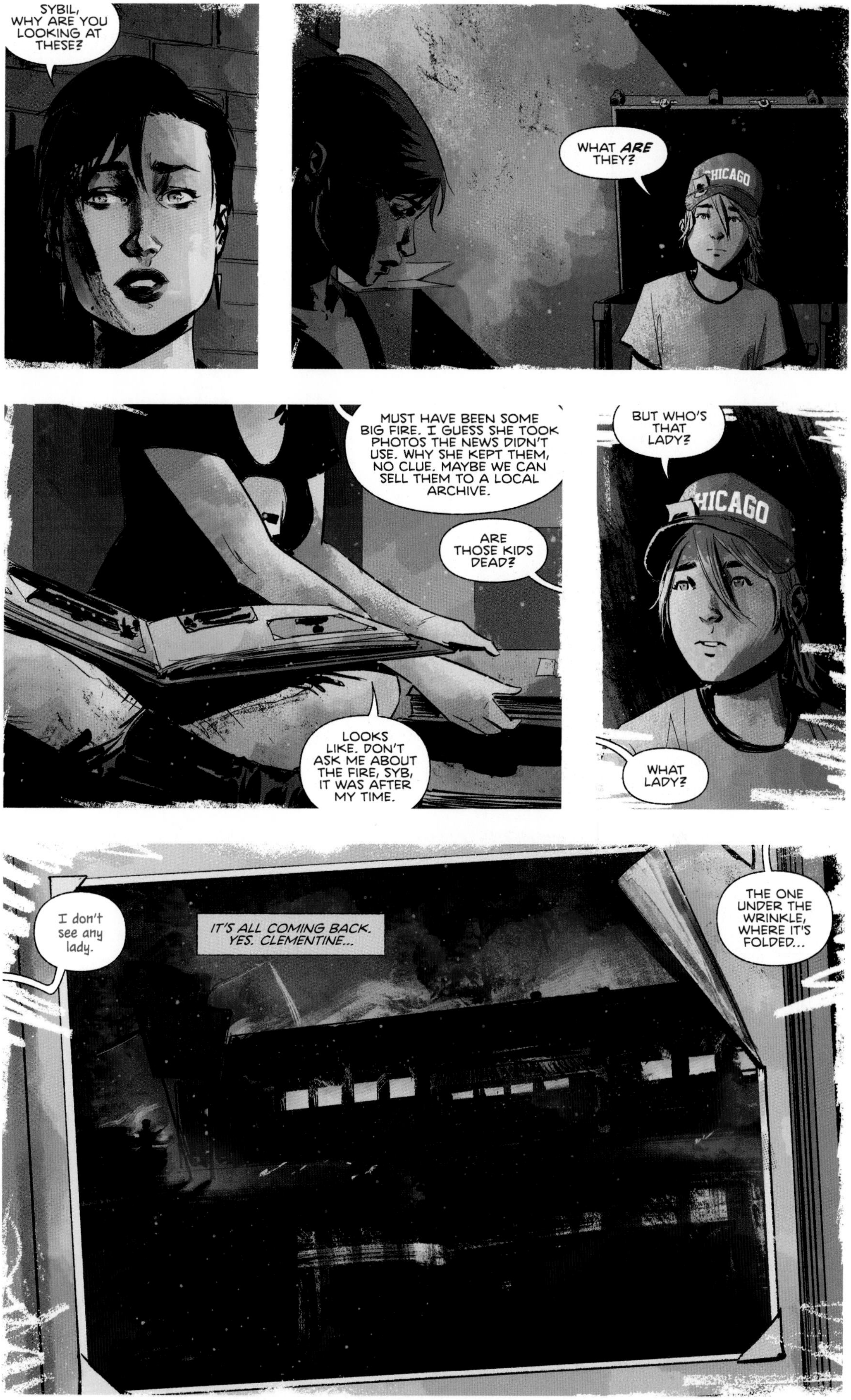
SYBIL, WHY ARE YOU LOOKING AT THESE?
WHAT ARE THEY?
CHICAGO
MUST HAVE BEEN SOME BIG FIRE. I GUESS SHE TOOK PHOTOS THE NEWS DIDN'T USE. WHY SHE KEPT THEM, NO CLUE. MAYBE WE CAN SELL THEM TO A LOCAL ARCHIVE.
ARE THOSE KIDS DEAD?
LOOKS LIKE. DON'T ASK ME ABOUT THE FIRE, SYB, IT WAS AFTER MY TIME.
BUT WHO'S THAT LADY?
CHICAGO
WHAT LADY?
I don't see any lady.
IT'S ALL COMING BACK. YES. CLEMENTINE...
THE ONE UNDER THE WRINKLE, WHERE IT'S FOLDED...

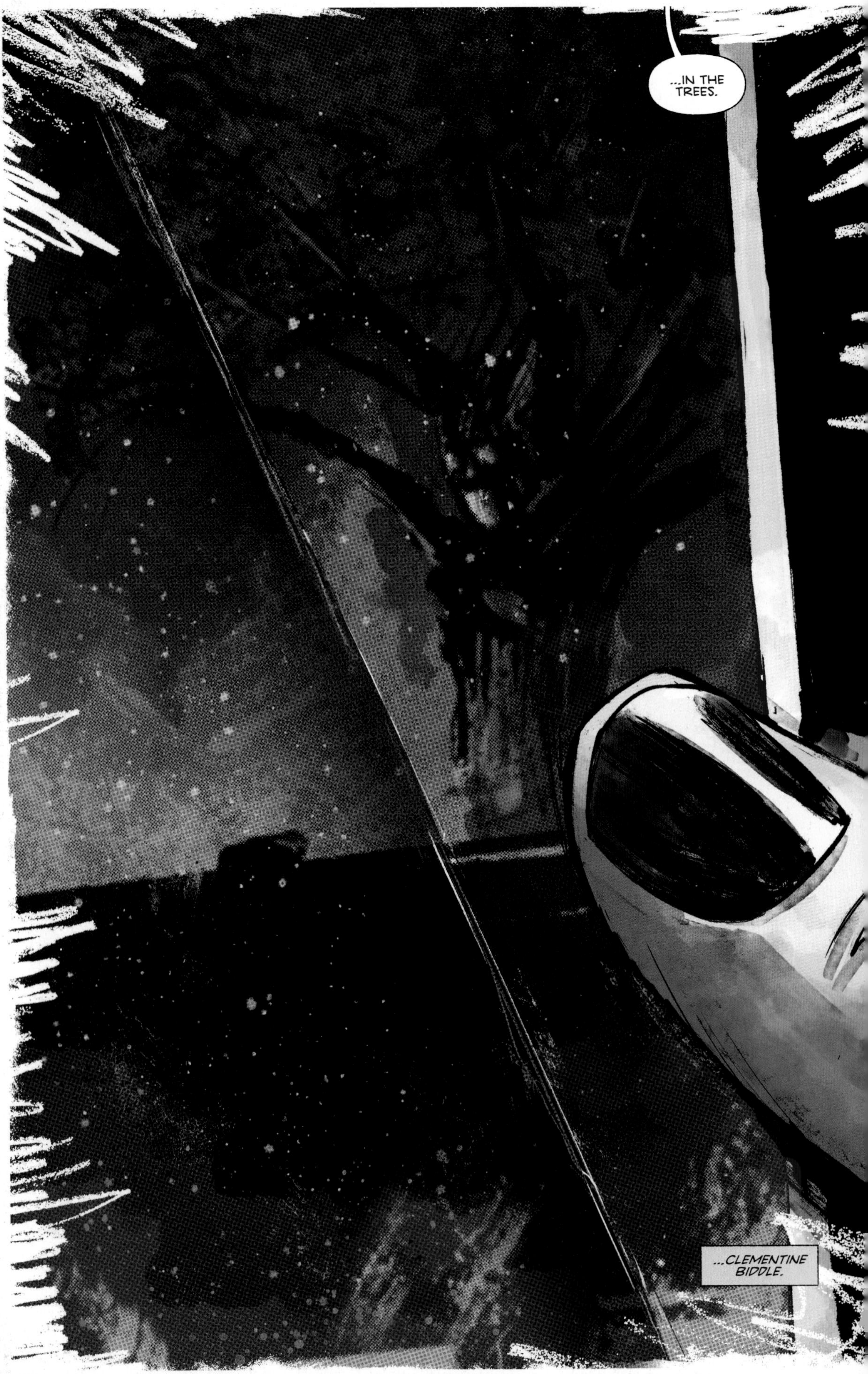
...IN THE TREES.
...CLEMENTINE BIDDLE.

Watch your feet now watch your nose—

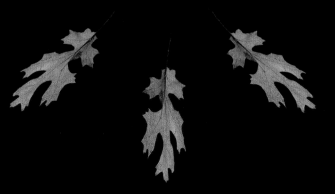

CHAPTER

FOUR

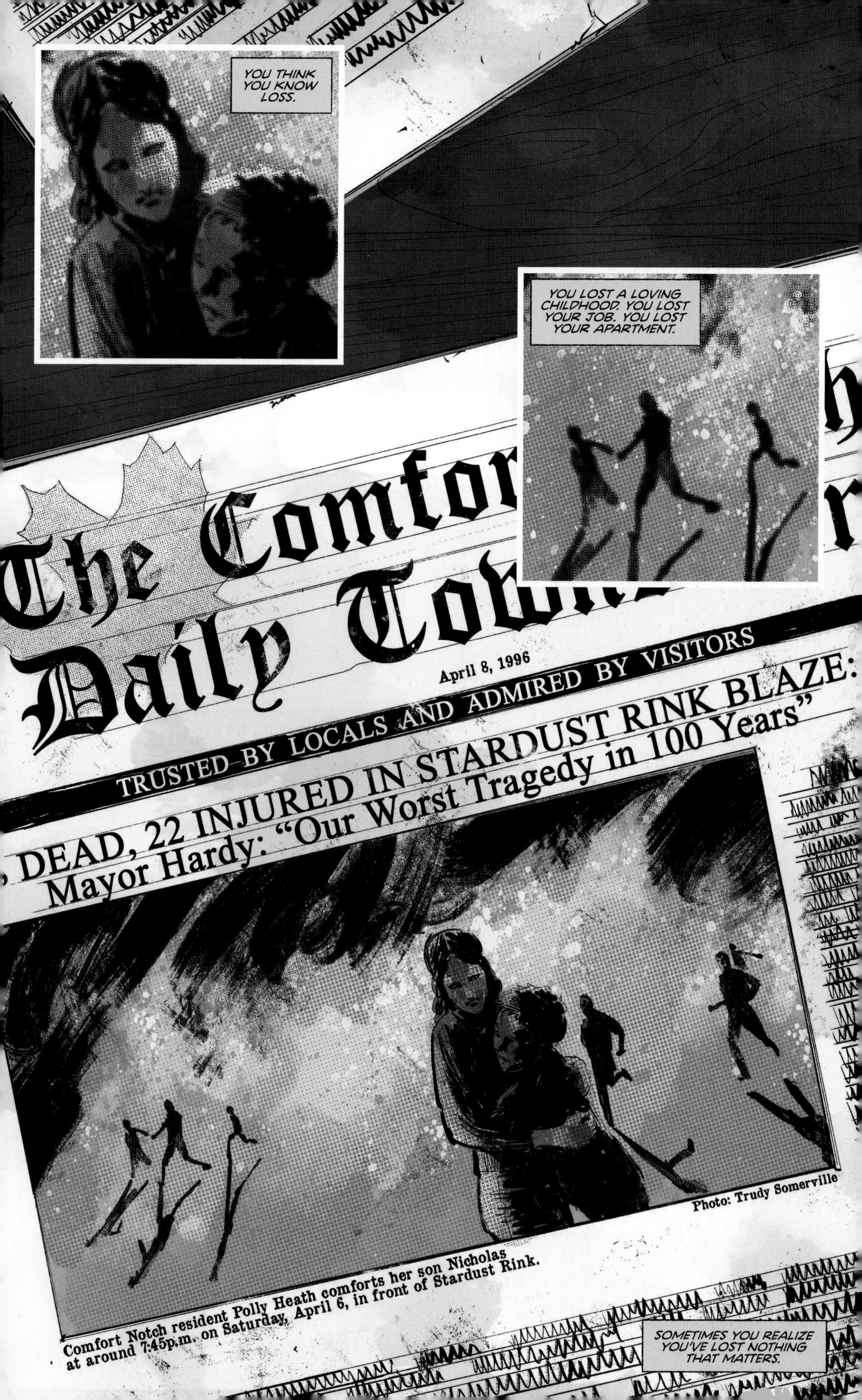
YOU THINK YOU KNOW LOSS.
YOU LOST A LOVING CHILDHOOD. YOU LOST YOUR JOB. YOU LOST YOUR APARTMENT.
The Comfor
Daily Town
April 8, 1996
TRUSTED BY LOCALS AND ADMIRED BY VISITORS
DEAD, 22 INJURED IN STARDUST RINK BLAZE:
Mayor Hardy: "Our Worst Tragedy in 100 Years"
Photo: Trudy Somerville
Comfort Notch resident Polly Heath comforts her son Nicholas at around 7:45p.m. on Saturday, April 6, in front of Stardust Rink.
SOMETIMES YOU REALIZE YOU'VE LOST NOTHING THAT MATTERS.

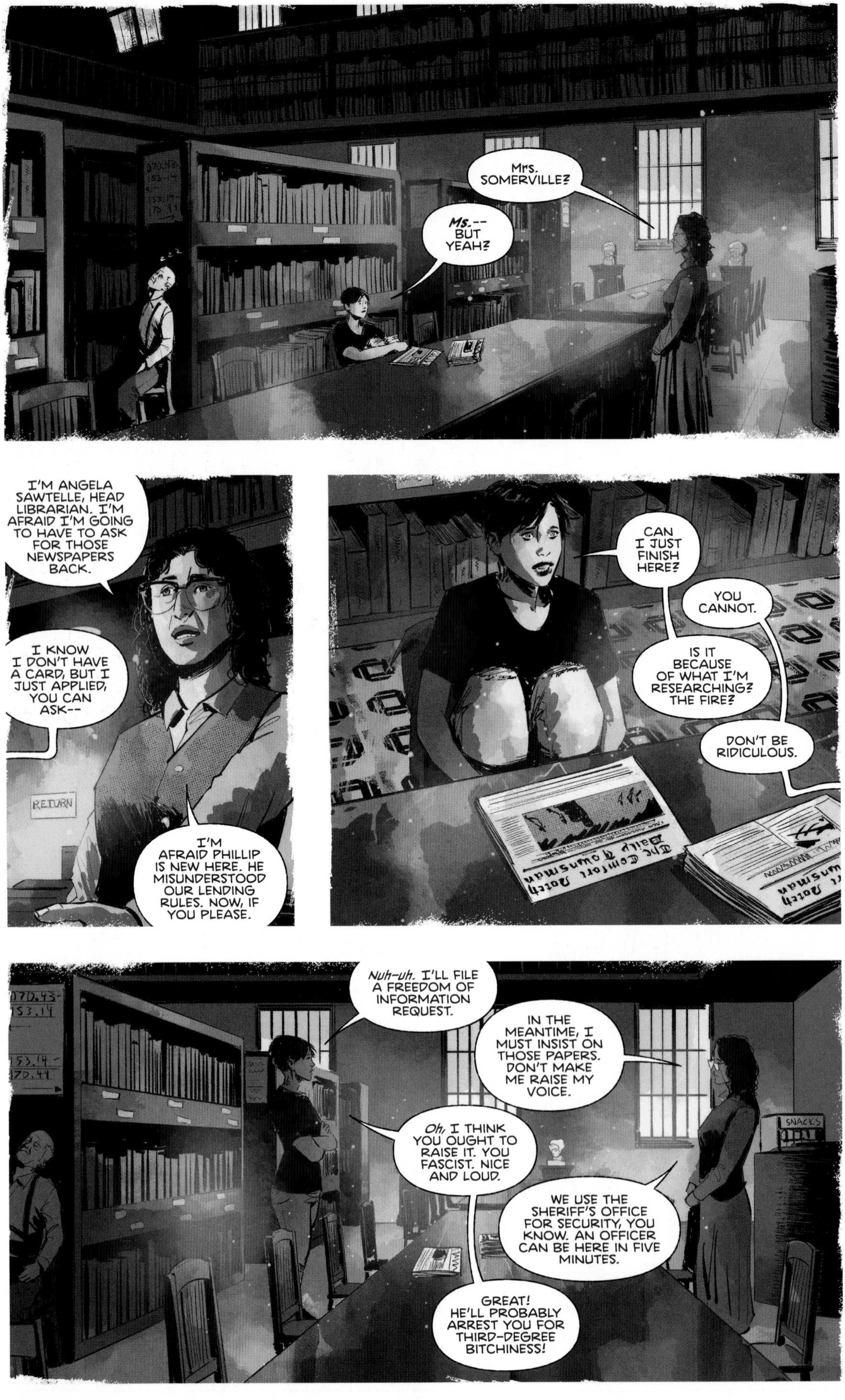
Mrs. SOMERVILLE?
Ms.-- BUT YEAH?
I'M ANGELA SAWTELLE, HEAD LIBRARIAN. I'M AFRAID I'M GOING TO HAVE TO ASK FOR THOSE NEWSPAPERS BACK.
I KNOW I DON'T HAVE A CARD, BUT I JUST APPLIED, YOU CAN ASK--
RETURN
I'M AFRAID PHILLIP IS NEW HERE. HE MISUNDERSTOOD OUR LENDING RULES. NOW, IF YOU PLEASE.
CAN I JUST FINISH HERE?
YOU CANNOT.
IS IT BECAUSE OF WHAT I'M RESEARCHING? THE FIRE?
DON'T BE RIDICULOUS.
Nuh-uh. I'LL FILE A FREEDOM OF INFORMATION REQUEST.
IN THE MEANTIME, I MUST INSIST ON THOSE PAPERS. DON'T MAKE ME RAISE MY VOICE.
Oh, I THINK YOU OUGHT TO RAISE IT. YOU FASCIST. NICE AND LOUD.
SNACKS
WE USE THE SHERIFF'S OFFICE FOR SECURITY, YOU KNOW. AN OFFICER CAN BE HERE IN FIVE MINUTES.
GREAT! HE'LL PROBABLY ARREST YOU FOR THIRD-DEGREE BITCHINESS!

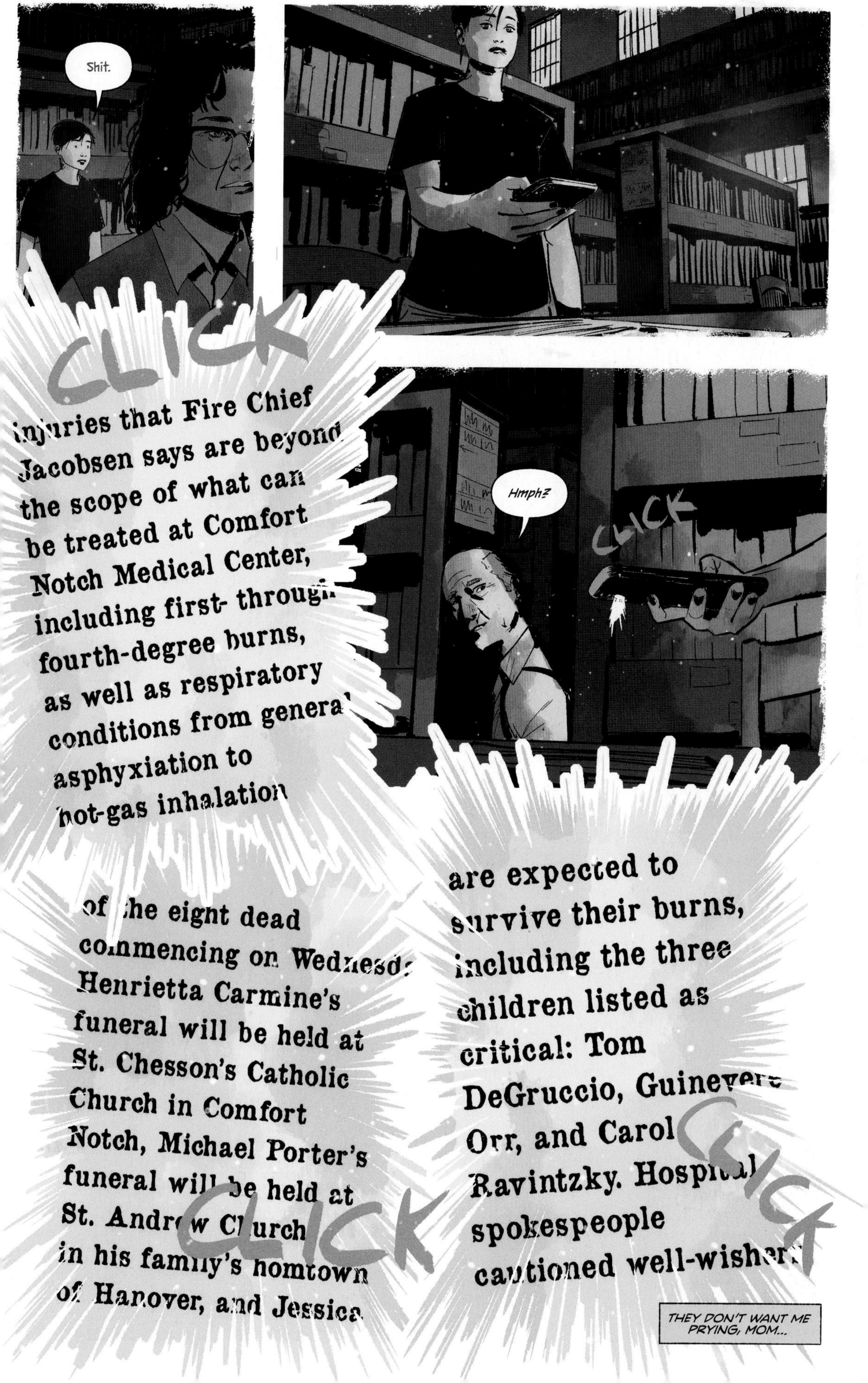

Shit.

Hmph?

CLICK

injuries that Fire Chief Jacobsen says are beyond the scope of what can be treated at Comfort Notch Medical Center, including first- through fourth-degree burns, as well as respiratory conditions from general asphyxiation to hot-gas inhalation

of the eight dead commencing on Wednesd: Henrietta Carmine's funeral will be held at St. Chesson's Catholic Church in Comfort Notch, Michael Porter's funeral will be held at St. Andrew Church in his family's homtown of Hanover, and Jessica

are expected to survive their burns, including the three children listed as critical: Tom DeGruccio, Guinevere Orr, and Carol Ravintzky. Hospital spokespeople cautioned well-wishers

CLICK
CLICK
CLICK

THEY DON'T WANT ME PRYING, MOM...

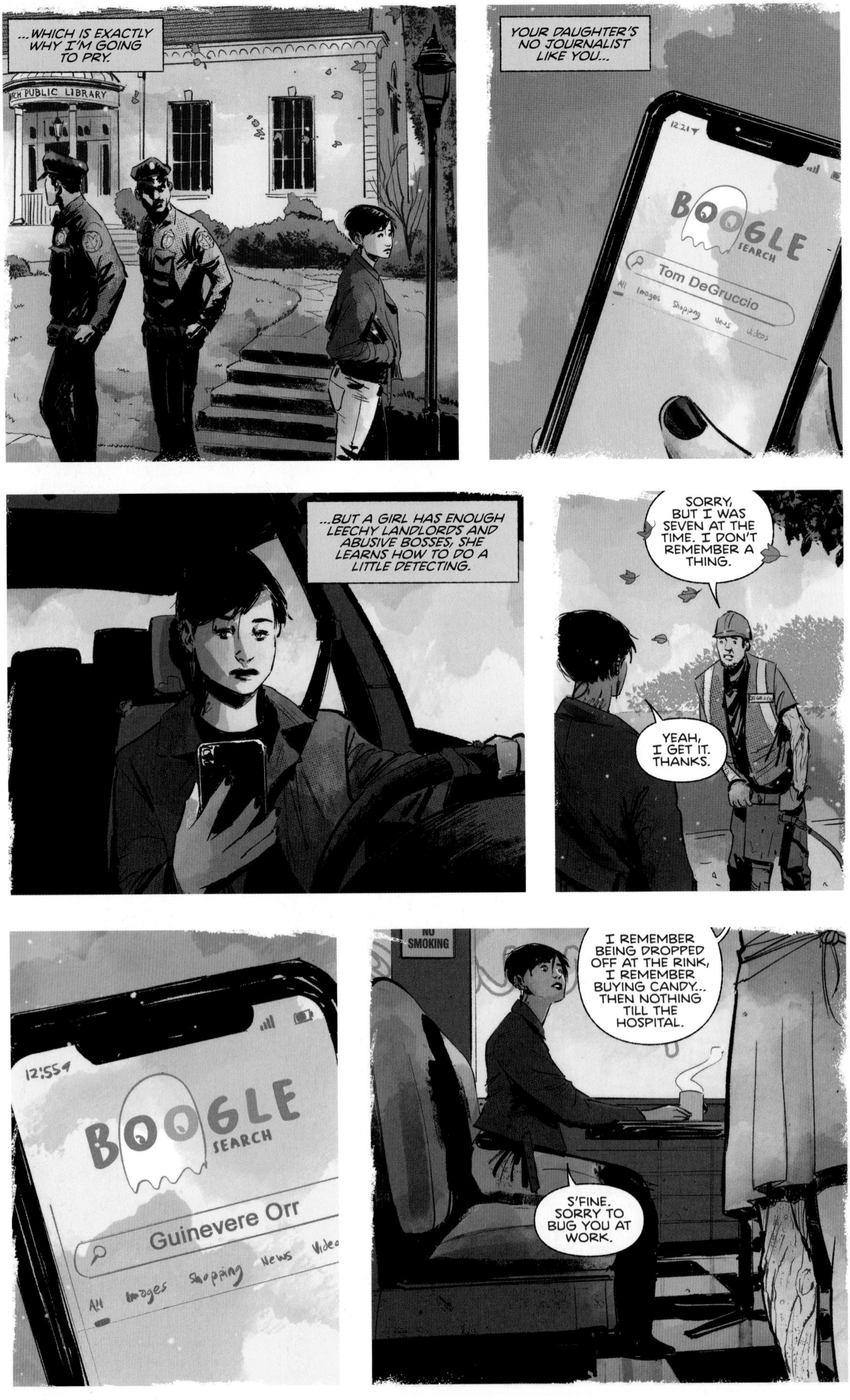
...WHICH IS EXACTLY WHY I'M GOING TO PRY.
PUBLIC LIBRARY
YOUR DAUGHTER'S NO JOURNALIST LIKE YOU...
BOOGLE SEARCH
Tom DeGruccio
All Images Shopping News Videos
...BUT A GIRL HAS ENOUGH LEECHY LANDLORDS AND ABUSIVE BOSSES, SHE LEARNS HOW TO DO A LITTLE DETECTING.
SORRY, BUT I WAS SEVEN AT THE TIME. I DON'T REMEMBER A THING.
YEAH, I GET IT. THANKS.
BOOGLE SEARCH
Guinevere Orr
All Images Shopping News Video
NO SMOKING
I REMEMBER BEING DROPPED OFF AT THE RINK, I REMEMBER BUYING CANDY... THEN NOTHING TILL THE HOSPITAL.
S'FINE. SORRY TO BUG YOU AT WORK.

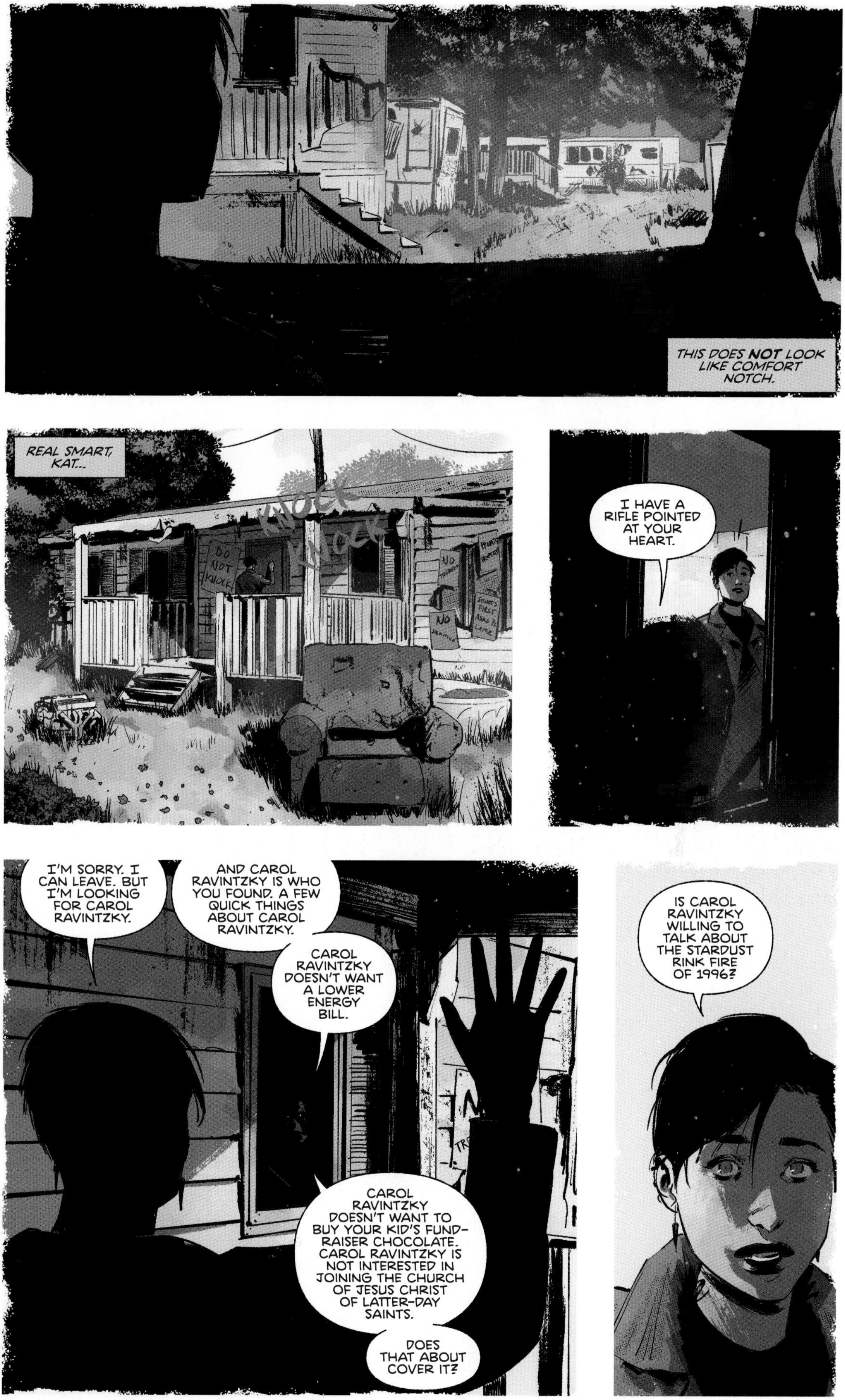
THIS DOES NOT LOOK LIKE COMFORT NOTCH.
REAL SMART, KAT...
KNOCK KNOCK
DO NOT KNOCK
I HAVE A RIFLE POINTED AT YOUR HEART.
I'M SORRY. I CAN LEAVE. BUT I'M LOOKING FOR CAROL RAVINTZKY.
AND CAROL RAVINTZKY IS WHO YOU FOUND. A FEW QUICK THINGS ABOUT CAROL RAVINTZKY.
CAROL RAVINTZKY DOESN'T WANT A LOWER ENERGY BILL.
CAROL RAVINTZKY DOESN'T WANT TO BUY YOUR KID'S FUND-RAISER CHOCOLATE. CAROL RAVINTZKY IS NOT INTERESTED IN JOINING THE CHURCH OF JESUS CHRIST OF LATTER-DAY SAINTS.
DOES THAT ABOUT COVER IT?
IS CAROL RAVINTZKY WILLING TO TALK ABOUT THE STARDUST RINK FIRE OF 1996?

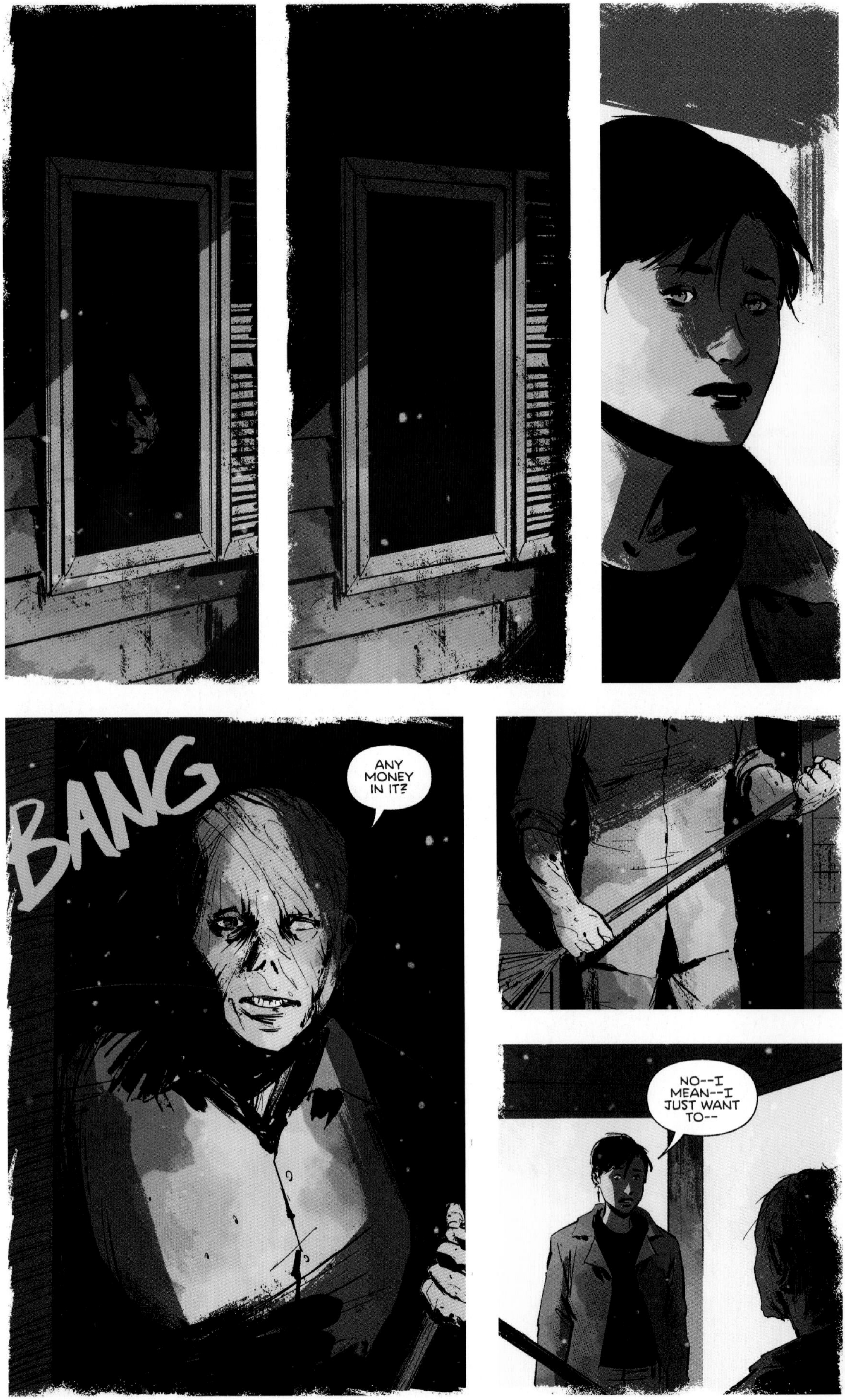
BANG
ANY MONEY IN IT?
NO--I MEAN--I JUST WANT TO--

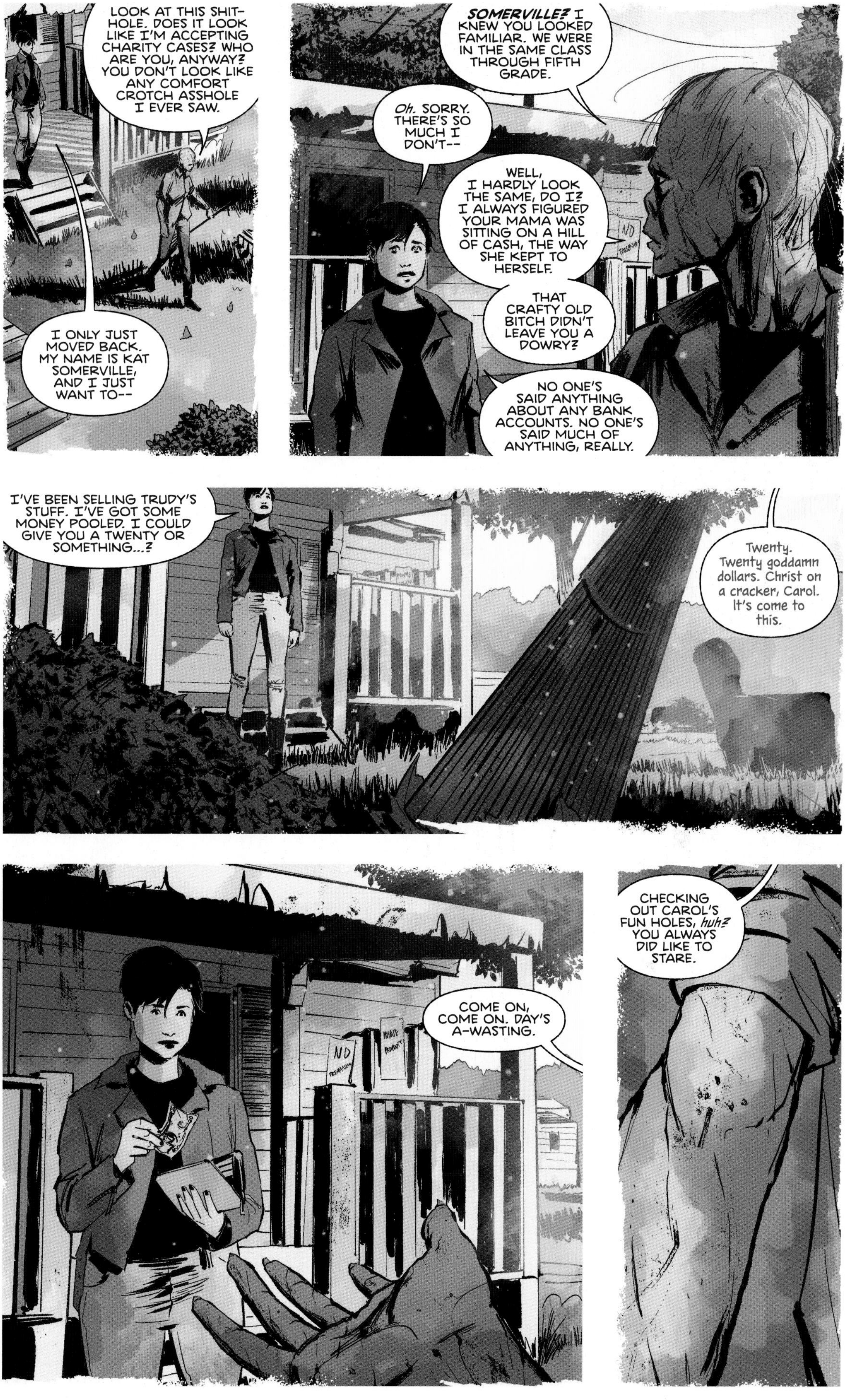
LOOK AT THIS SHIT-HOLE. DOES IT LOOK LIKE I'M ACCEPTING CHARITY CASES? WHO ARE YOU, ANYWAY? YOU DON'T LOOK LIKE ANY COMFORT CROTCH ASSHOLE I EVER SAW.
I ONLY JUST MOVED BACK. MY NAME IS KAT SOMERVILLE, AND I JUST WANT TO--
SOMERVILLE? I KNEW YOU LOOKED FAMILIAR. WE WERE IN THE SAME CLASS THROUGH FIFTH GRADE.
Oh. SORRY. THERE'S SO MUCH I DON'T--
WELL, I HARDLY LOOK THE SAME, DO I? I ALWAYS FIGURED YOUR MAMA WAS SITTING ON A HILL OF CASH, THE WAY SHE KEPT TO HERSELF.
THAT CRAFTY OLD BITCH DIDN'T LEAVE YOU A DOWRY?
NO ONE'S SAID ANYTHING ABOUT ANY BANK ACCOUNTS. NO ONE'S SAID MUCH OF ANYTHING, REALLY.
I'VE BEEN SELLING TRUDY'S STUFF. I'VE GOT SOME MONEY POOLED. I COULD GIVE YOU A TWENTY OR SOMETHING...?
Twenty. Twenty goddamn dollars. Christ on a cracker, Carol. It's come to this.
COME ON, COME ON. DAY'S A-WASTING.
CHECKING OUT CAROL'S FUN HOLES, huh? YOU ALWAYS DID LIKE TO STARE.

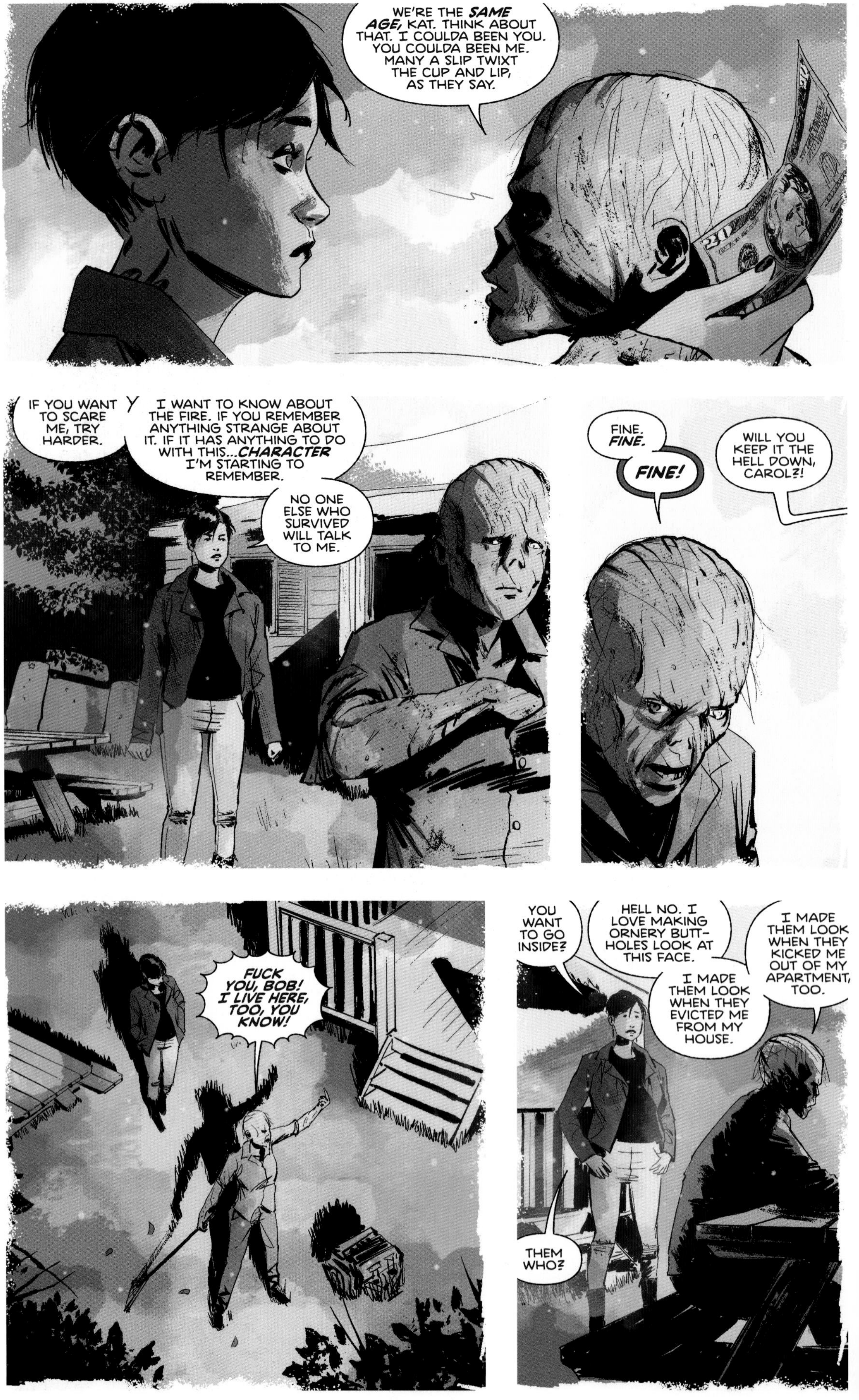

WE'RE THE **SAME AGE,** KAT. THINK ABOUT THAT. I COULDA BEEN YOU. YOU COULDA BEEN ME. MANY A SLIP TWIXT THE CUP AND LIP, AS THEY SAY.
IF YOU WANT TO SCARE ME, TRY HARDER.
I WANT TO KNOW ABOUT THE FIRE. IF YOU REMEMBER ANYTHING STRANGE ABOUT IT. IF IT HAS ANYTHING TO DO WITH THIS...**CHARACTER** I'M STARTING TO REMEMBER.
NO ONE ELSE WHO SURVIVED WILL TALK TO ME.
WILL YOU KEEP IT THE HELL DOWN, CAROL?!
FINE. **FINE.**
FINE!
FUCK YOU, BOB! I LIVE HERE, TOO, YOU KNOW!
YOU WANT TO GO INSIDE?
HELL NO. I LOVE MAKING ORNERY BUTT-HOLES LOOK AT THIS FACE.
I MADE THEM LOOK WHEN THEY EVICTED ME FROM MY HOUSE.
I MADE THEM LOOK WHEN THEY KICKED ME OUT OF MY APARTMENT, TOO.
THEM WHO?

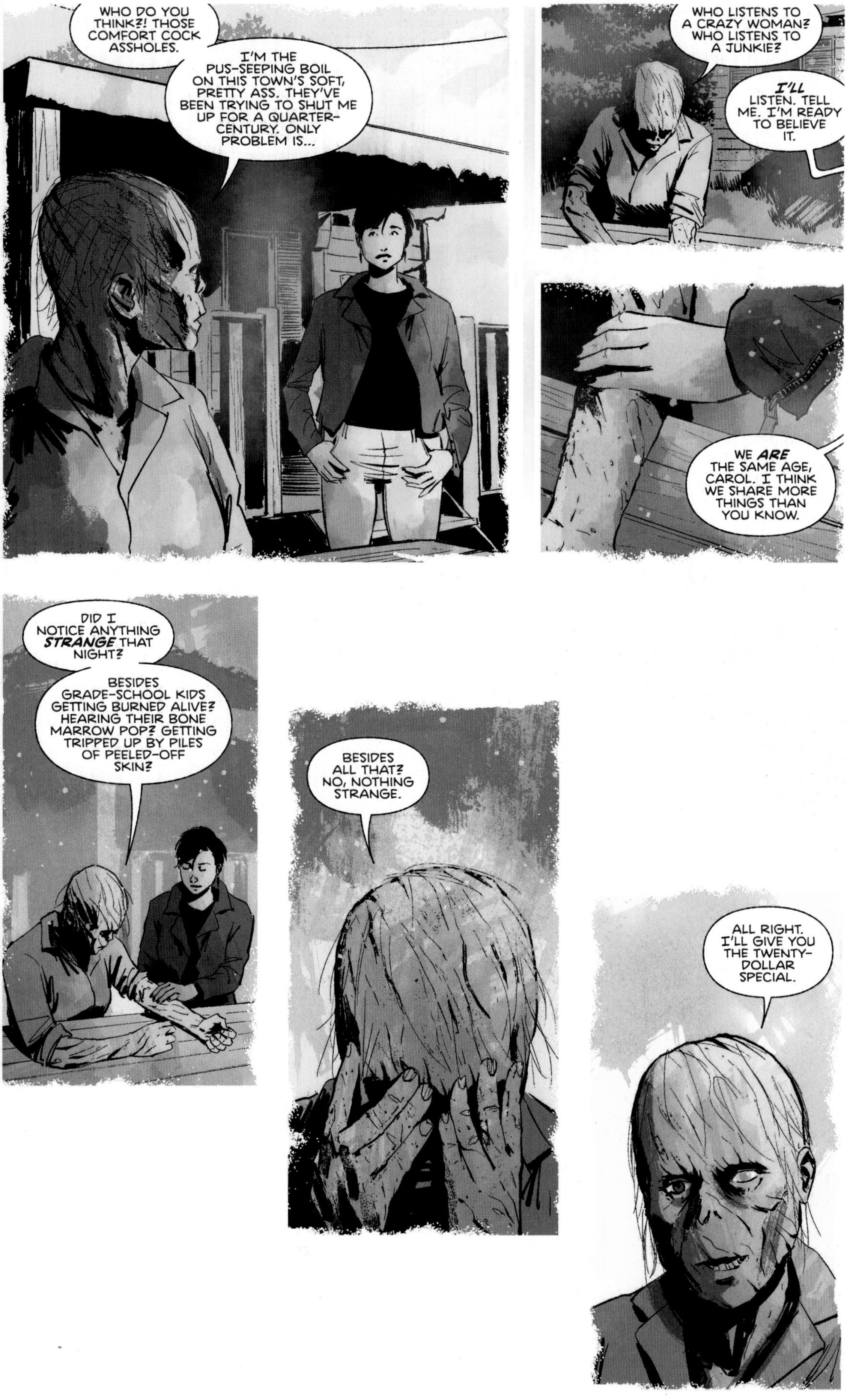
WHO DO YOU THINK?! THOSE COMFORT COCK ASSHOLES.
I'M THE PUS-SEEPING BOIL ON THIS TOWN'S SOFT, PRETTY ASS. THEY'VE BEEN TRYING TO SHUT ME UP FOR A QUARTER-CENTURY. ONLY PROBLEM IS...
WHO LISTENS TO A CRAZY WOMAN? WHO LISTENS TO A JUNKIE?
I'LL LISTEN. TELL ME. I'M READY TO BELIEVE IT.
WE *ARE* THE SAME AGE, CAROL. I THINK WE SHARE MORE THINGS THAN YOU KNOW.
DID I NOTICE ANYTHING *STRANGE* THAT NIGHT?
BESIDES GRADE-SCHOOL KIDS GETTING BURNED ALIVE? HEARING THEIR BONE MARROW POP? GETTING TRIPPED UP BY PILES OF PEELED-OFF SKIN?
BESIDES ALL THAT? NO, NOTHING STRANGE.
ALL RIGHT. I'LL GIVE YOU THE TWENTY-DOLLAR SPECIAL.

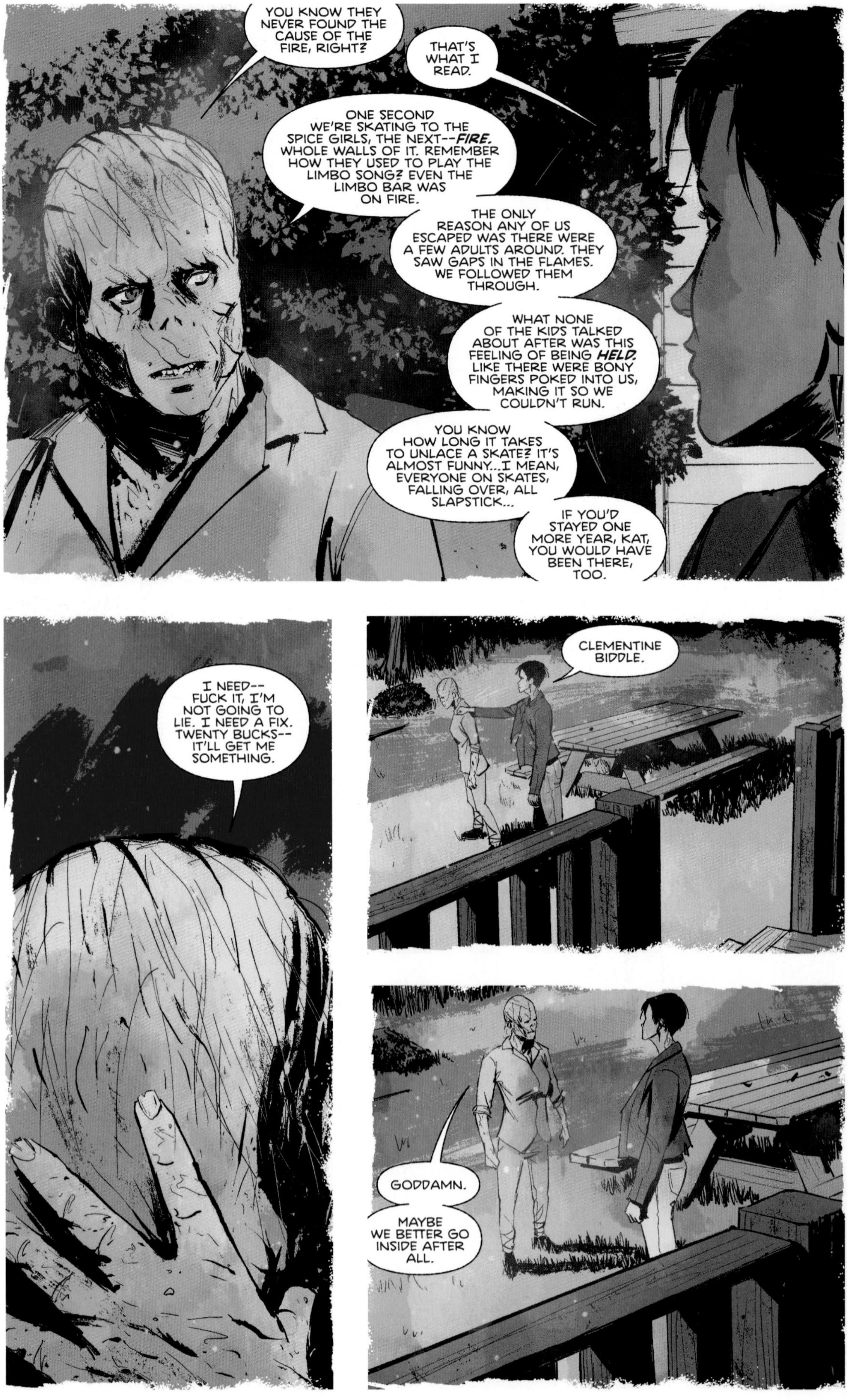
YOU KNOW THEY NEVER FOUND THE CAUSE OF THE FIRE, RIGHT?
THAT'S WHAT I READ.
ONE SECOND WE'RE SKATING TO THE SPICE GIRLS, THE NEXT--*FIRE.* WHOLE WALLS OF IT. REMEMBER HOW THEY USED TO PLAY THE LIMBO SONG? EVEN THE LIMBO BAR WAS ON FIRE.
THE ONLY REASON ANY OF US ESCAPED WAS THERE WERE A FEW ADULTS AROUND. THEY SAW GAPS IN THE FLAMES. WE FOLLOWED THEM THROUGH.
WHAT NONE OF THE KIDS TALKED ABOUT AFTER WAS THIS FEELING OF BEING *HELD.* LIKE THERE WERE BONY FINGERS POKED INTO US, MAKING IT SO WE COULDN'T RUN.
YOU KNOW HOW LONG IT TAKES TO UNLACE A SKATE? IT'S ALMOST FUNNY...I MEAN, EVERYONE ON SKATES, FALLING OVER, ALL SLAPSTICK...
IF YOU'D STAYED ONE MORE YEAR, KAT, YOU WOULD HAVE BEEN THERE, TOO.
I NEED--FUCK IT, I'M NOT GOING TO LIE. I NEED A FIX. TWENTY BUCKS--IT'LL GET ME SOMETHING.
CLEMENTINE BIDDLE.
GODDAMN.
MAYBE WE BETTER GO INSIDE AFTER ALL.

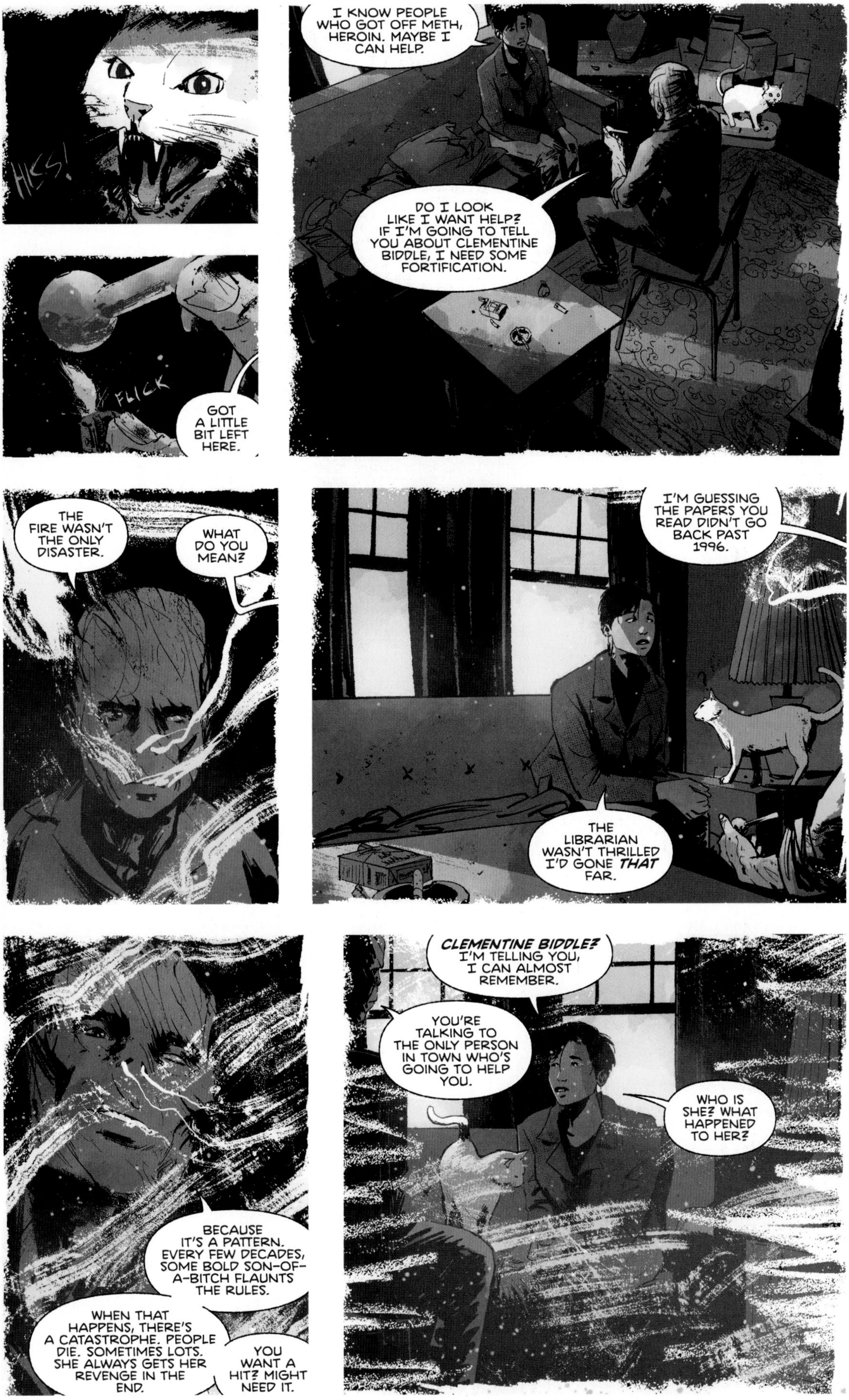
HISS!
I KNOW PEOPLE WHO GOT OFF METH, HEROIN. MAYBE I CAN HELP.
DO I LOOK LIKE I WANT HELP? IF I'M GOING TO TELL YOU ABOUT CLEMENTINE BIDDLE, I NEED SOME FORTIFICATION.
FLICK
GOT A LITTLE BIT LEFT HERE.
THE FIRE WASN'T THE ONLY DISASTER.
WHAT DO YOU MEAN?
I'M GUESSING THE PAPERS YOU READ DIDN'T GO BACK PAST 1996.
THE LIBRARIAN WASN'T THRILLED I'D GONE *THAT* FAR.
BECAUSE IT'S A PATTERN. EVERY FEW DECADES, SOME BOLD SON-OF-A-BITCH FLAUNTS THE RULES.
WHEN THAT HAPPENS, THERE'S A CATASTROPHE. PEOPLE DIE. SOMETIMES LOTS. SHE ALWAYS GETS HER REVENGE IN THE END.
YOU WANT A HIT? MIGHT NEED IT.
CLEMENTINE BIDDLE? I'M TELLING YOU, I CAN ALMOST REMEMBER.
YOU'RE TALKING TO THE ONLY PERSON IN TOWN WHO'S GOING TO HELP YOU.
WHO IS SHE? WHAT HAPPENED TO HER?

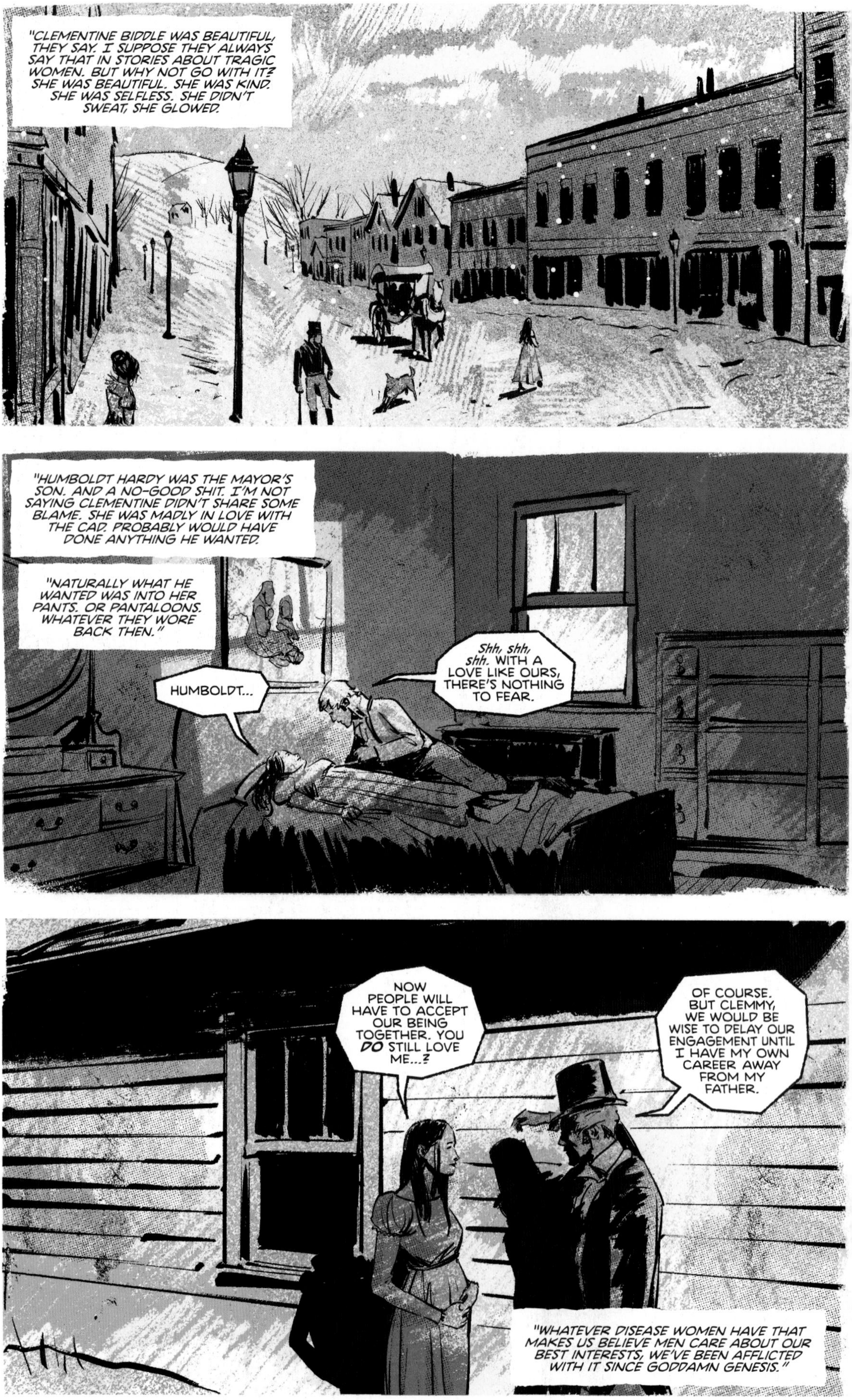
"CLEMENTINE BIDDLE WAS BEAUTIFUL, THEY SAY. I SUPPOSE THEY ALWAYS SAY THAT IN STORIES ABOUT TRAGIC WOMEN. BUT WHY NOT GO WITH IT? SHE WAS BEAUTIFUL. SHE WAS KIND. SHE WAS SELFLESS. SHE DIDN'T SWEAT, SHE GLOWED.
"HUMBOLDT HARDY WAS THE MAYOR'S SON. AND A NO-GOOD SHIT. I'M NOT SAYING CLEMENTINE DIDN'T SHARE SOME BLAME. SHE WAS MADLY IN LOVE WITH THE CAD. PROBABLY WOULD HAVE DONE ANYTHING HE WANTED.
"NATURALLY WHAT HE WANTED WAS INTO HER PANTS. OR PANTALOONS. WHATEVER THEY WORE BACK THEN."
HUMBOLDT...
Shh, shh, shh. WITH A LOVE LIKE OURS, THERE'S NOTHING TO FEAR.
NOW PEOPLE WILL HAVE TO ACCEPT OUR BEING TOGETHER. YOU ***DO*** STILL LOVE ME...?
OF COURSE. BUT CLEMMY, WE WOULD BE WISE TO DELAY OUR ENGAGEMENT UNTIL I HAVE MY OWN CAREER AWAY FROM MY FATHER.
"WHATEVER DISEASE WOMEN HAVE THAT MAKES US BELIEVE MEN CARE ABOUT OUR BEST INTERESTS, WE'VE BEEN AFFLICTED WITH IT SINCE GODDAMN GENESIS."

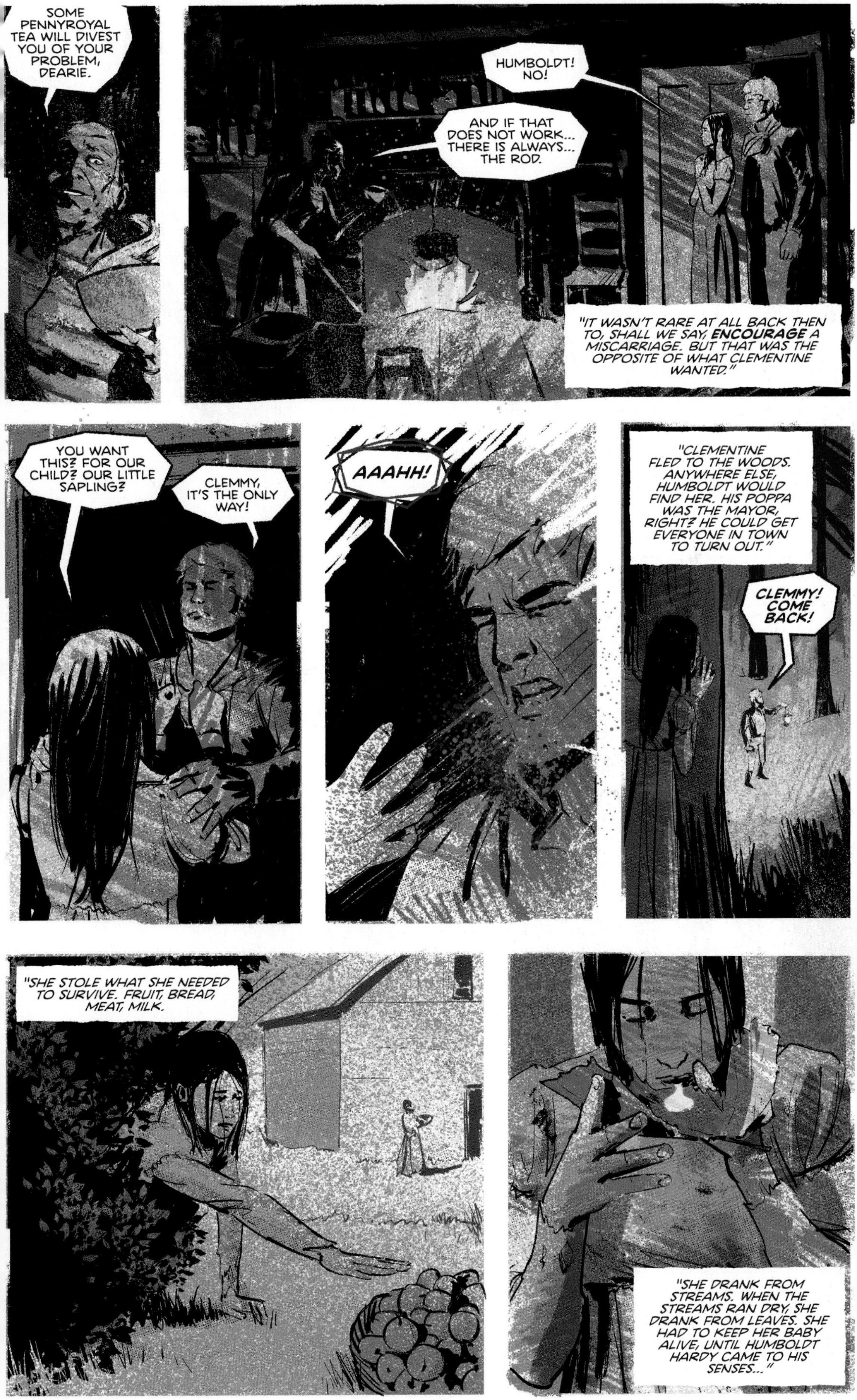
SOME PENNYROYAL TEA WILL DIVEST YOU OF YOUR PROBLEM, DEARIE.
HUMBOLDT! NO!
AND IF THAT DOES NOT WORK... THERE IS ALWAYS... THE ROD.
"IT WASN'T RARE AT ALL BACK THEN TO, SHALL WE SAY, ENCOURAGE A MISCARRIAGE. BUT THAT WAS THE OPPOSITE OF WHAT CLEMENTINE WANTED."
YOU WANT THIS? FOR OUR CHILD? OUR LITTLE SAPLING?
CLEMMY, IT'S THE ONLY WAY!
AAAHH!
"CLEMENTINE FLED TO THE WOODS. ANYWHERE ELSE, HUMBOLDT WOULD FIND HER. HIS POPPA WAS THE MAYOR, RIGHT? HE COULD GET EVERYONE IN TOWN TO TURN OUT."
CLEMMY! COME BACK!
"SHE STOLE WHAT SHE NEEDED TO SURVIVE. FRUIT, BREAD, MEAT, MILK.
"SHE DRANK FROM STREAMS. WHEN THE STREAMS RAN DRY, SHE DRANK FROM LEAVES. SHE HAD TO KEEP HER BABY ALIVE, UNTIL HUMBOLDT HARDY CAME TO HIS SENSES..."

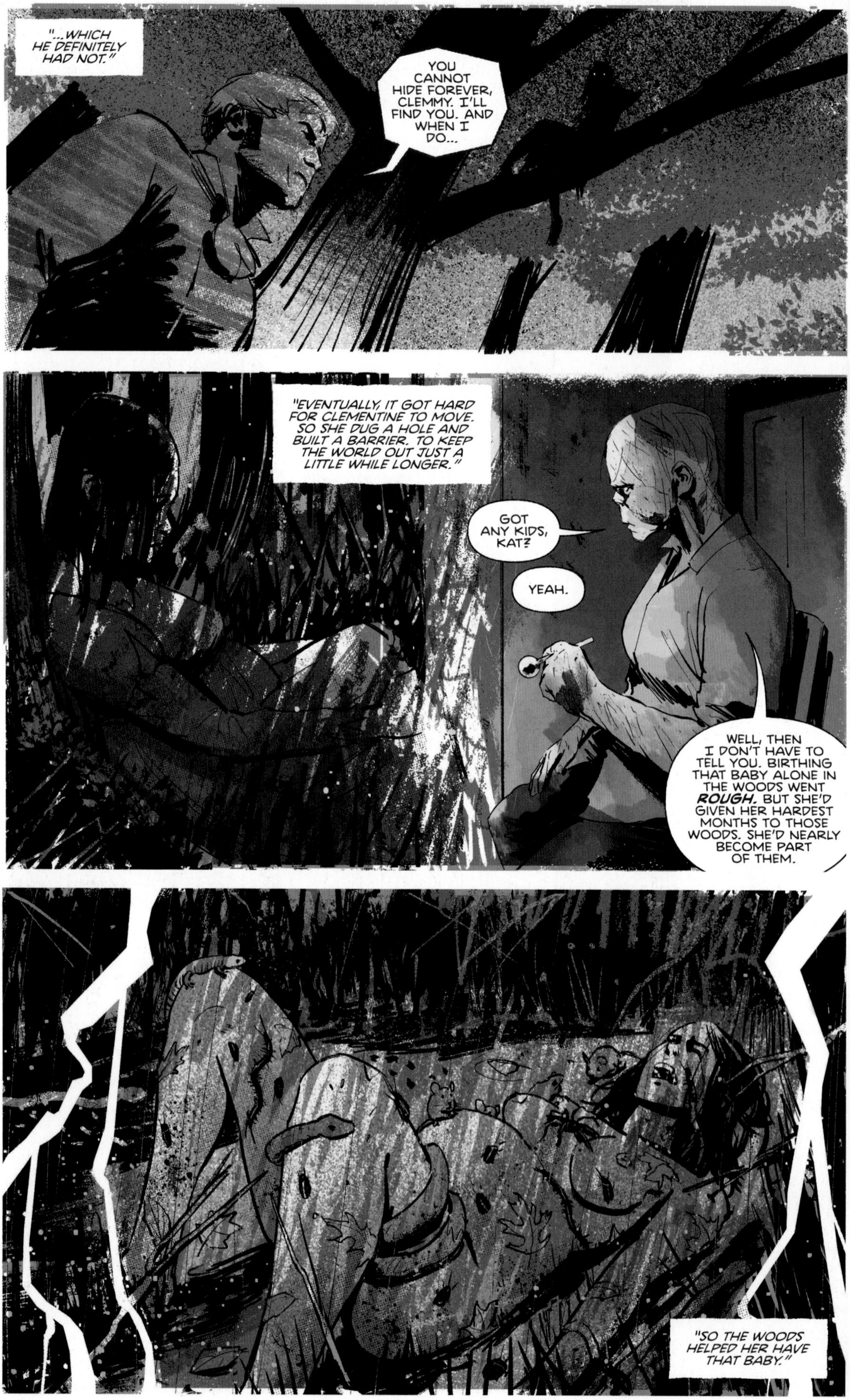
"...WHICH HE DEFINITELY HAD NOT."
YOU CANNOT HIDE FOREVER, CLEMMY. I'LL FIND YOU. AND WHEN I DO...
"EVENTUALLY, IT GOT HARD FOR CLEMENTINE TO MOVE. SO SHE DUG A HOLE AND BUILT A BARRIER. TO KEEP THE WORLD OUT JUST A LITTLE WHILE LONGER."
GOT ANY KIDS, KAT?
YEAH.
WELL, THEN I DON'T HAVE TO TELL YOU. BIRTHING THAT BABY ALONE IN THE WOODS WENT ROUGH. BUT SHE'D GIVEN HER HARDEST MONTHS TO THOSE WOODS. SHE'D NEARLY BECOME PART OF THEM.
"SO THE WOODS HELPED HER HAVE THAT BABY."

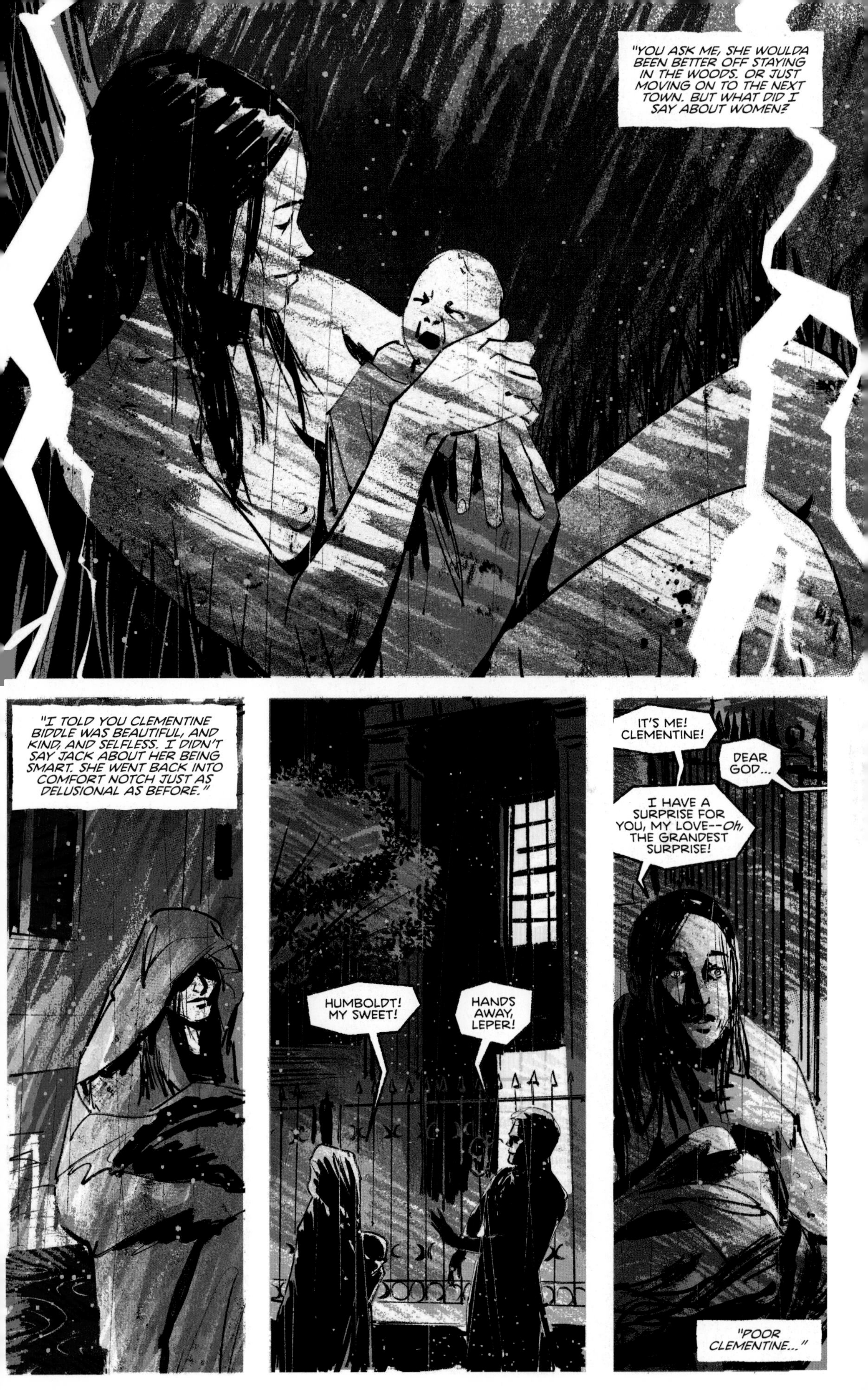
"YOU ASK ME, SHE WOULDA BEEN BETTER OFF STAYING IN THE WOODS. OR JUST MOVING ON TO THE NEXT TOWN. BUT WHAT DID I SAY ABOUT WOMEN?
"I TOLD YOU CLEMENTINE BIDDLE WAS BEAUTIFUL, AND KIND, AND SELFLESS. I DIDN'T SAY JACK ABOUT HER BEING SMART. SHE WENT BACK INTO COMFORT NOTCH JUST AS DELUSIONAL AS BEFORE."
HUMBOLDT! MY SWEET!
HANDS AWAY, LEPER!
IT'S ME! CLEMENTINE!
DEAR GOD...
I HAVE A SURPRISE FOR YOU, MY LOVE--*Oh*, THE GRANDEST SURPRISE!
"POOR CLEMENTINE..."

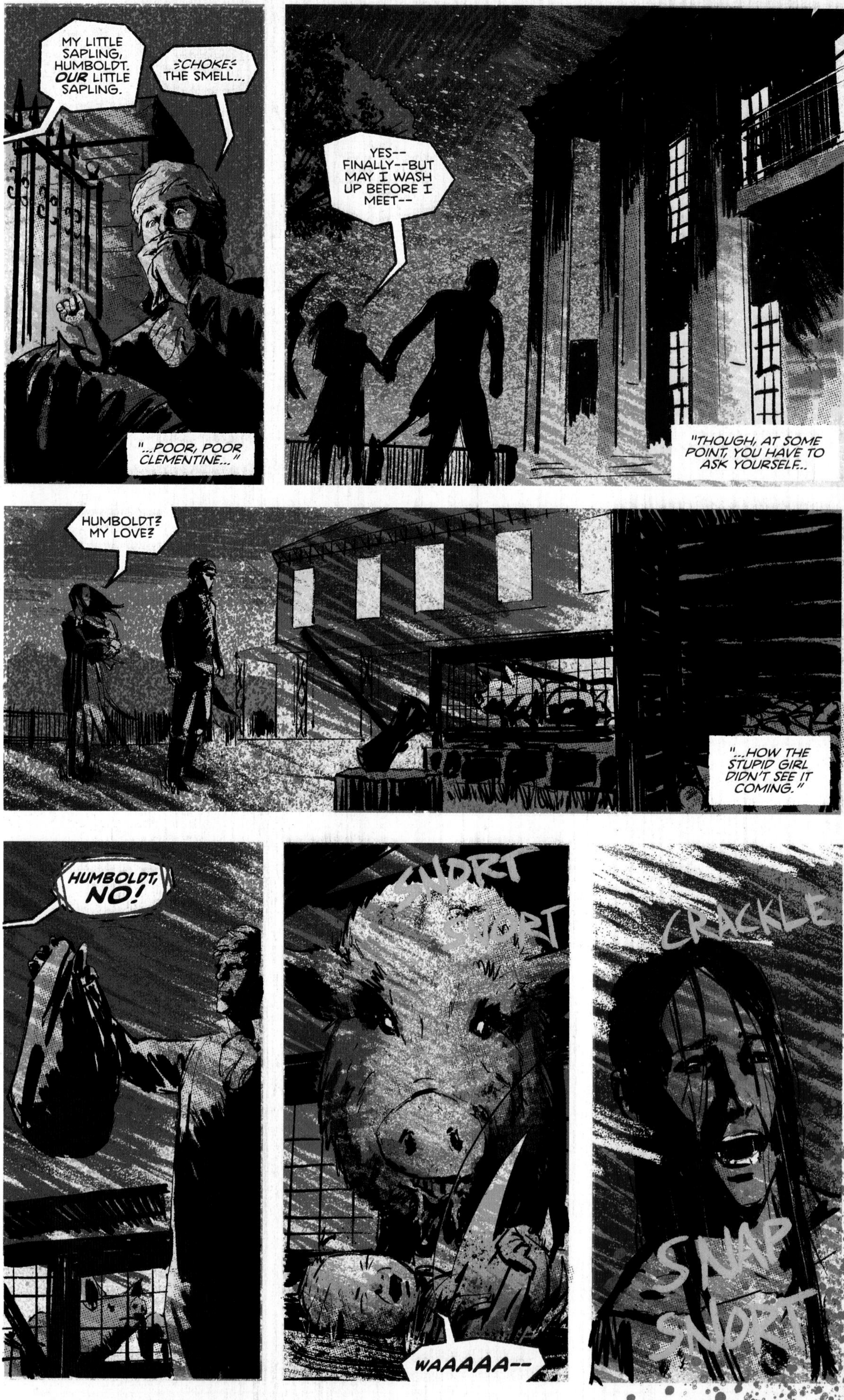
MY LITTLE SAPLING, HUMBOLDT. OUR LITTLE SAPLING.
CHOKE THE SMELL...
"...POOR, POOR CLEMENTINE..."
YES-- FINALLY--BUT MAY I WASH UP BEFORE I MEET--
"THOUGH, AT SOME POINT, YOU HAVE TO ASK YOURSELF...
HUMBOLDT? MY LOVE?
"...HOW THE STUPID GIRL DIDN'T SEE IT COMING."
HUMBOLDT, NO!
SNORT
SNORT
WAAAAA--
CRACKLE
SNAP
SNORT

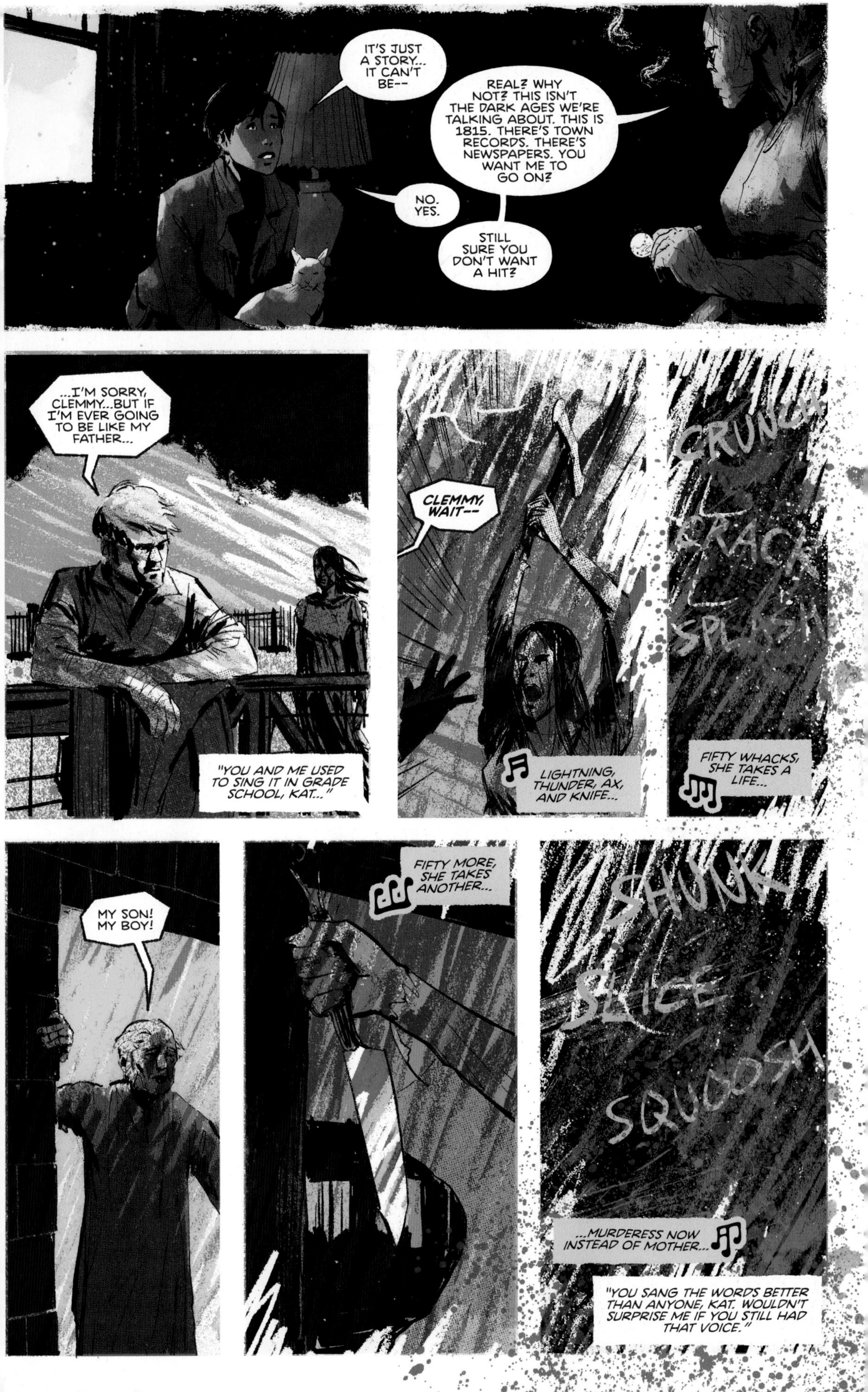
IT'S JUST A STORY... IT CAN'T BE--
REAL? WHY NOT? THIS ISN'T THE DARK AGES WE'RE TALKING ABOUT. THIS IS 1815. THERE'S TOWN RECORDS. THERE'S NEWSPAPERS. YOU WANT ME TO GO ON?
NO. YES.
STILL SURE YOU DON'T WANT A HIT?
...I'M SORRY, CLEMMY...BUT IF I'M EVER GOING TO BE LIKE MY FATHER...
"YOU AND ME USED TO SING IT IN GRADE SCHOOL, KAT..."
CLEMMY, WAIT--
LIGHTNING, THUNDER, AX, AND KNIFE...
CRUNCH
CRACK
SPLASH
FIFTY WHACKS, SHE TAKES A LIFE...
MY SON! MY BOY!
FIFTY MORE, SHE TAKES ANOTHER...
SHUNK
SLICE
SQUOOSH
...MURDERESS NOW INSTEAD OF MOTHER...
"YOU SANG THE WORDS BETTER THAN ANYONE, KAT. WOULDN'T SURPRISE ME IF YOU STILL HAD THAT VOICE."

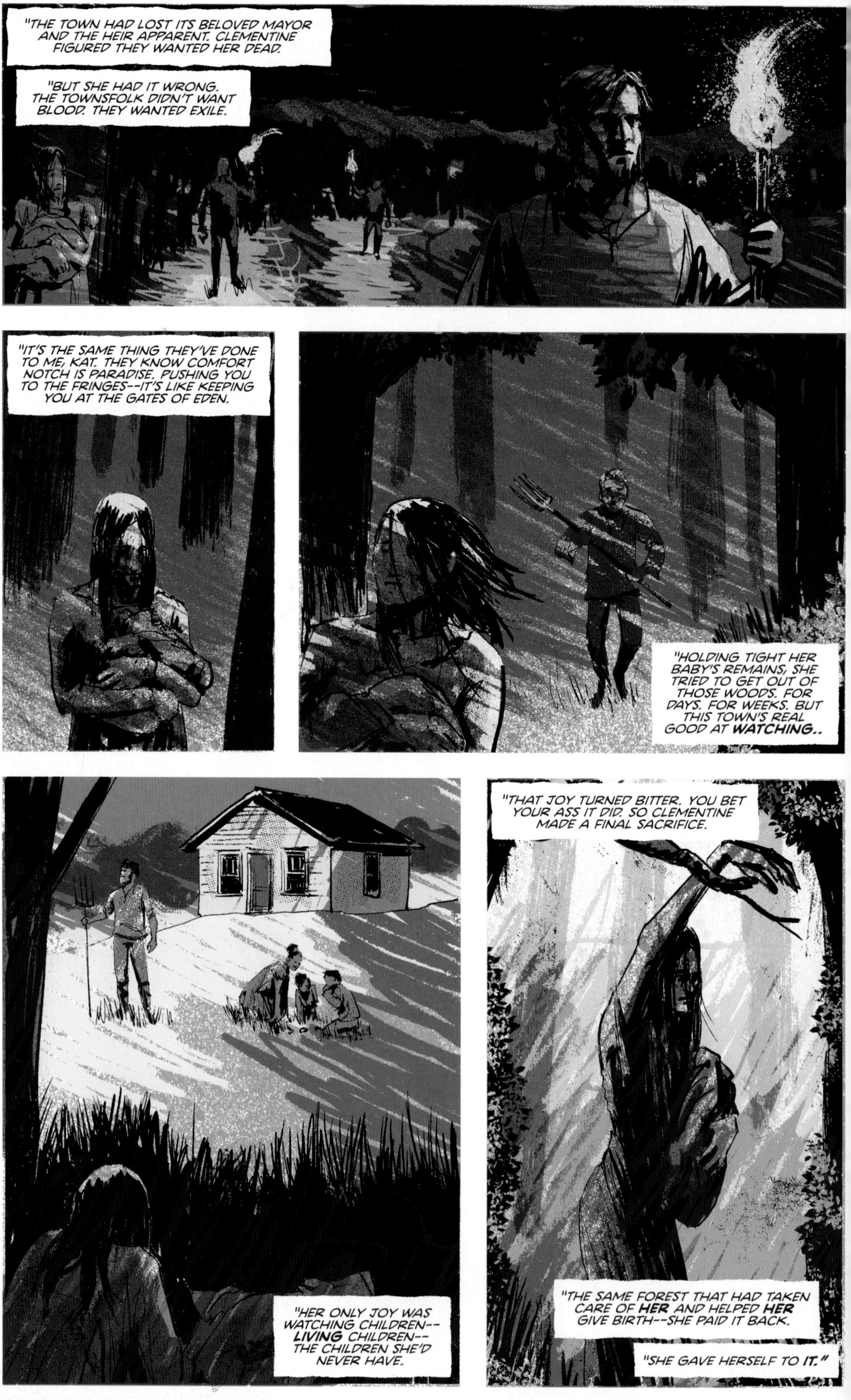
"THE TOWN HAD LOST ITS BELOVED MAYOR AND THE HEIR APPARENT. CLEMENTINE FIGURED THEY WANTED HER DEAD.
"BUT SHE HAD IT WRONG. THE TOWNSFOLK DIDN'T WANT BLOOD. THEY WANTED EXILE.
"IT'S THE SAME THING THEY'VE DONE TO ME, KAT. THEY KNOW COMFORT NOTCH IS PARADISE. PUSHING YOU TO THE FRINGES--IT'S LIKE KEEPING YOU AT THE GATES OF EDEN.
"HOLDING TIGHT HER BABY'S REMAINS, SHE TRIED TO GET OUT OF THOSE WOODS. FOR DAYS. FOR WEEKS. BUT THIS TOWN'S REAL GOOD AT **WATCHING.**.
"HER ONLY JOY WAS WATCHING CHILDREN-- **LIVING** CHILDREN-- THE CHILDREN SHE'D NEVER HAVE.
"THAT JOY TURNED BITTER. YOU BET YOUR ASS IT DID. SO CLEMENTINE MADE A FINAL SACRIFICE.
"THE SAME FOREST THAT HAD TAKEN CARE OF **HER** AND HELPED **HER** GIVE BIRTH--SHE PAID IT BACK.
"SHE GAVE HERSELF TO **IT.**"

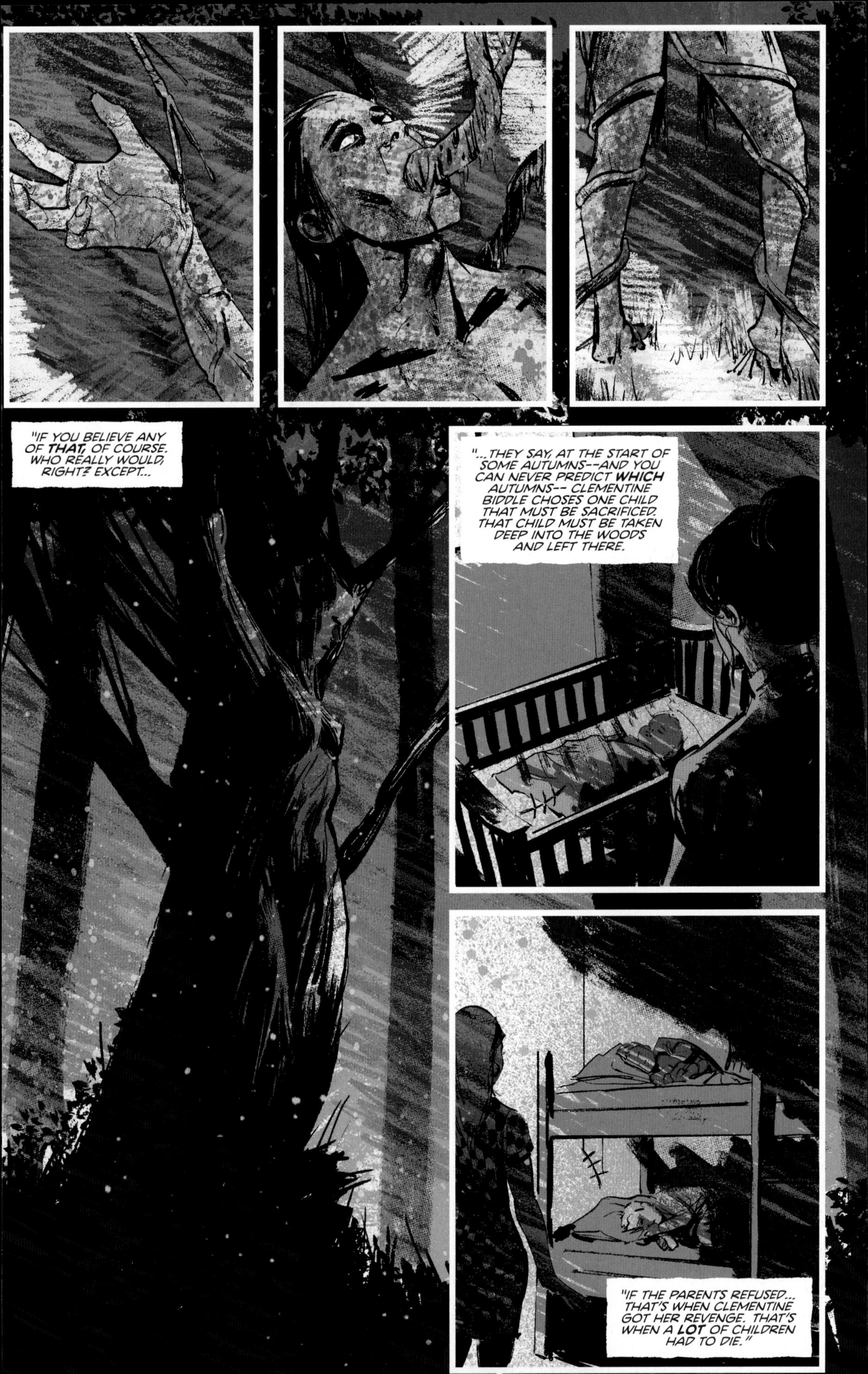
"IF YOU BELIEVE ANY OF THAT, OF COURSE. WHO REALLY WOULD, RIGHT? EXCEPT...
"...THEY SAY, AT THE START OF SOME AUTUMNS--AND YOU CAN NEVER PREDICT WHICH AUTUMNS-- CLEMENTINE BIDDLE CHOSES ONE CHILD THAT MUST BE SACRIFICED. THAT CHILD MUST BE TAKEN DEEP INTO THE WOODS AND LEFT THERE.
"IF THE PARENTS REFUSED... THAT'S WHEN CLEMENTINE GOT HER REVENGE. THAT'S WHEN A LOT OF CHILDREN HAD TO DIE."

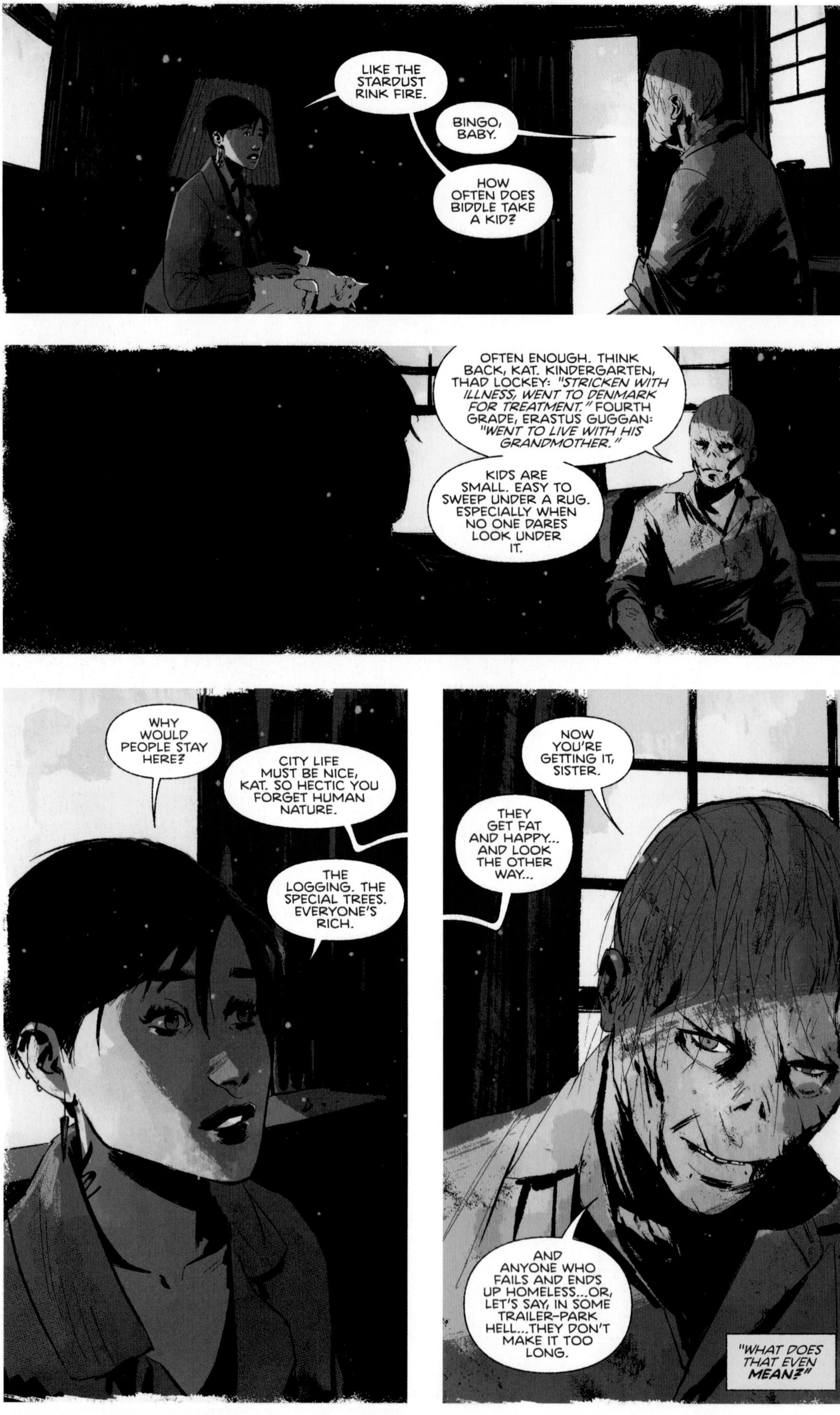
LIKE THE STARDUST RINK FIRE.
BINGO, BABY.
HOW OFTEN DOES BIDDLE TAKE A KID?
OFTEN ENOUGH. THINK BACK, KAT. KINDERGARTEN, THAD LOCKEY: *"STRICKEN WITH ILLNESS, WENT TO DENMARK FOR TREATMENT."* FOURTH GRADE, ERASTUS GUGGAN: *"WENT TO LIVE WITH HIS GRANDMOTHER."*
KIDS ARE SMALL. EASY TO SWEEP UNDER A RUG. ESPECIALLY WHEN NO ONE DARES LOOK UNDER IT.
WHY WOULD PEOPLE STAY HERE?
CITY LIFE MUST BE NICE, KAT. SO HECTIC YOU FORGET HUMAN NATURE.
THE LOGGING. THE SPECIAL TREES. EVERYONE'S RICH.
NOW YOU'RE GETTING IT, SISTER.
THEY GET FAT AND HAPPY... AND LOOK THE OTHER WAY...
AND ANYONE WHO FAILS AND ENDS UP HOMELESS...OR, LET'S SAY, IN SOME TRAILER-PARK HELL...THEY DON'T MAKE IT TOO LONG.
*"WHAT DOES THAT EVEN **MEAN?**"*

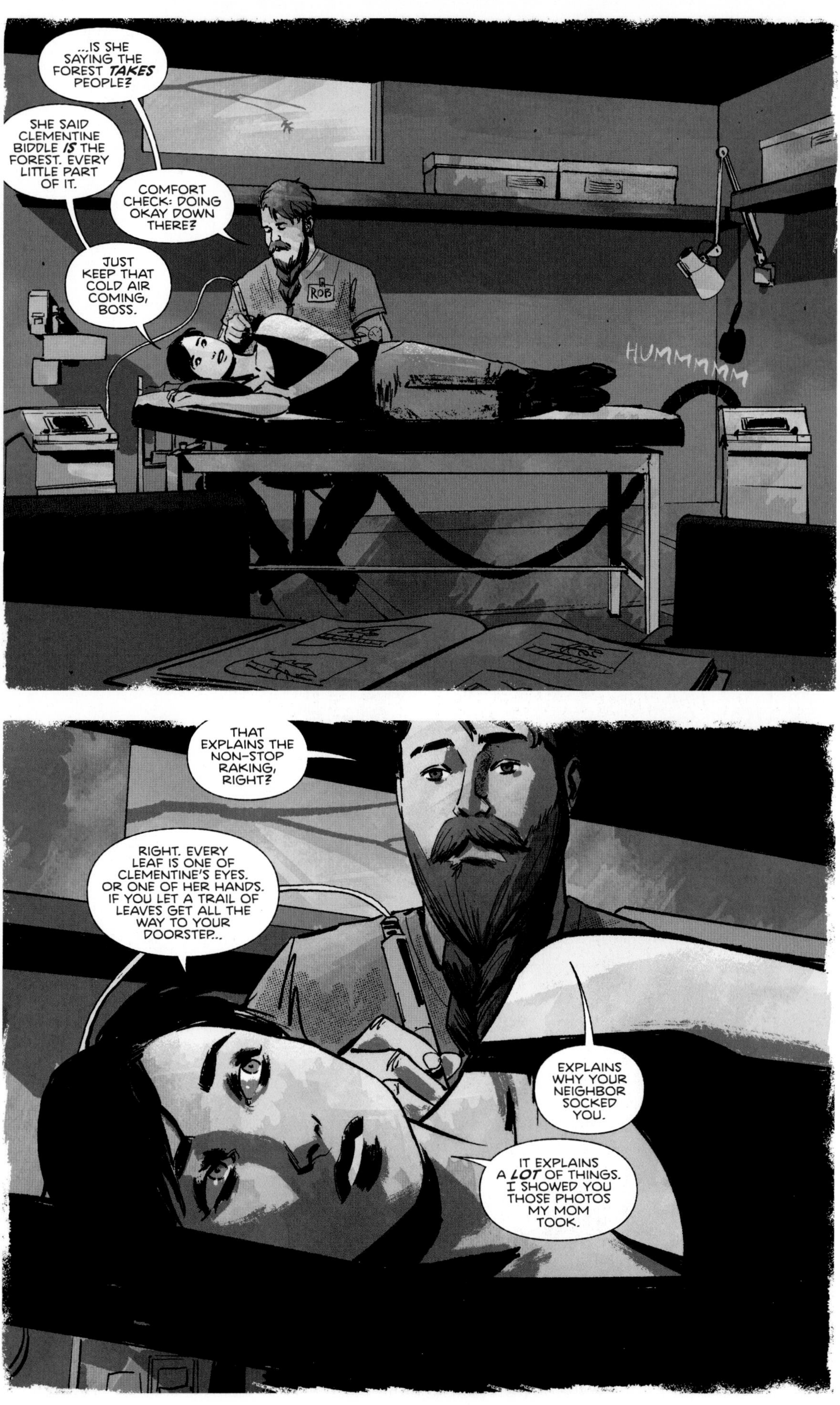
...IS SHE SAYING THE FOREST *TAKES* PEOPLE?
SHE SAID CLEMENTINE BIDDLE *IS* THE FOREST. EVERY LITTLE PART OF IT.
COMFORT CHECK: DOING OKAY DOWN THERE?
ROB
JUST KEEP THAT COLD AIR COMING, BOSS.
HUMMMMM
THAT EXPLAINS THE NON-STOP RAKING, RIGHT?
RIGHT. EVERY LEAF IS ONE OF CLEMENTINE'S EYES. OR ONE OF HER HANDS. IF YOU LET A TRAIL OF LEAVES GET ALL THE WAY TO YOUR DOORSTEP...
EXPLAINS WHY YOUR NEIGHBOR SOCKED YOU.
IT EXPLAINS A *LOT* OF THINGS. I SHOWED YOU THOSE PHOTOS MY MOM TOOK.

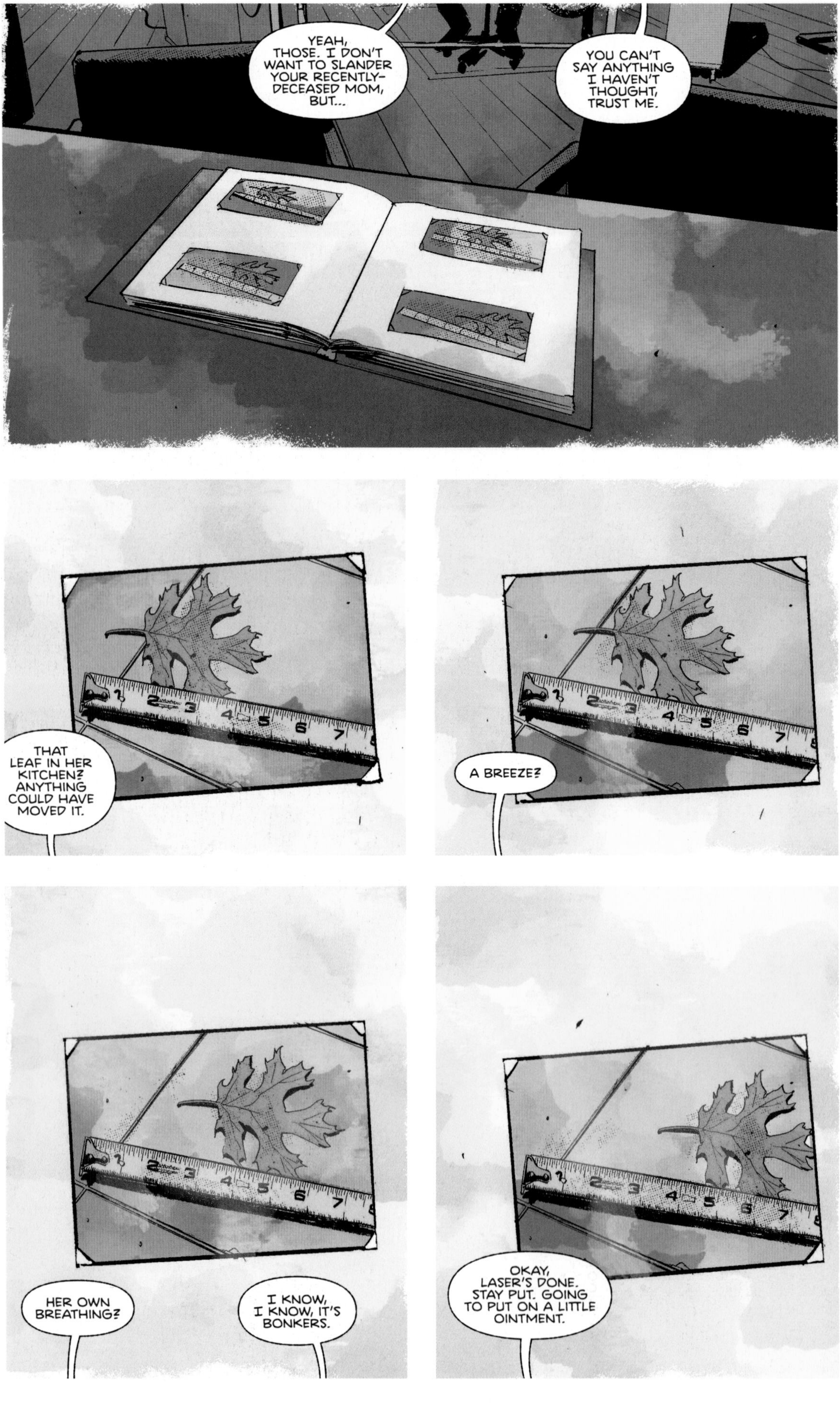
YEAH, THOSE. I DON'T WANT TO SLANDER YOUR RECENTLY-DECEASED MOM, BUT...
YOU CAN'T SAY ANYTHING I HAVEN'T THOUGHT, TRUST ME.
THAT LEAF IN HER KITCHEN? ANYTHING COULD HAVE MOVED IT.
A BREEZE?
HER OWN BREATHING?
I KNOW, I KNOW, IT'S BONKERS.
OKAY, LASER'S DONE. STAY PUT. GOING TO PUT ON A LITTLE OINTMENT.

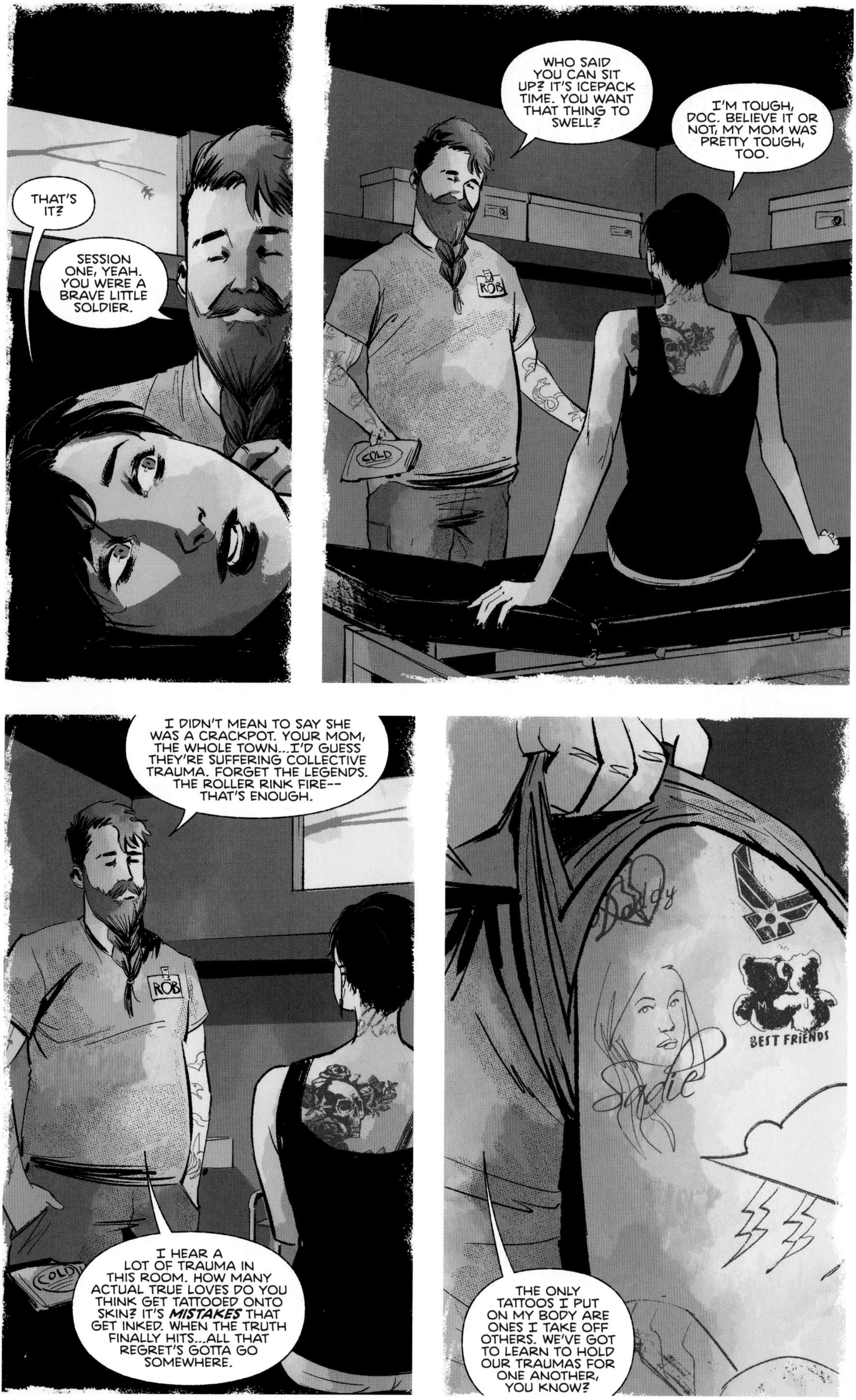
THAT'S IT?
SESSION ONE, YEAH. YOU WERE A BRAVE LITTLE SOLDIER.
WHO SAID YOU CAN SIT UP? IT'S ICEPACK TIME. YOU WANT THAT THING TO SWELL?
ROB
COLD
I'M TOUGH, DOC. BELIEVE IT OR NOT, MY MOM WAS PRETTY TOUGH, TOO.
I DIDN'T MEAN TO SAY SHE WAS A CRACKPOT. YOUR MOM, THE WHOLE TOWN...I'D GUESS THEY'RE SUFFERING COLLECTIVE TRAUMA. FORGET THE LEGENDS. THE ROLLER RINK FIRE-- THAT'S ENOUGH.
ROB
I HEAR A LOT OF TRAUMA IN THIS ROOM. HOW MANY ACTUAL TRUE LOVES DO YOU THINK GET TATTOOED ONTO SKIN? IT'S MISTAKES THAT GET INKED. WHEN THE TRUTH FINALLY HITS...ALL THAT REGRET'S GOTTA GO SOMEWHERE.
BEST FRIENDS
Sadie
THE ONLY TATTOOS I PUT ON MY BODY ARE ONES I TAKE OFF OTHERS. WE'VE GOT TO LEARN TO HOLD OUR TRAUMAS FOR ONE ANOTHER, YOU KNOW?

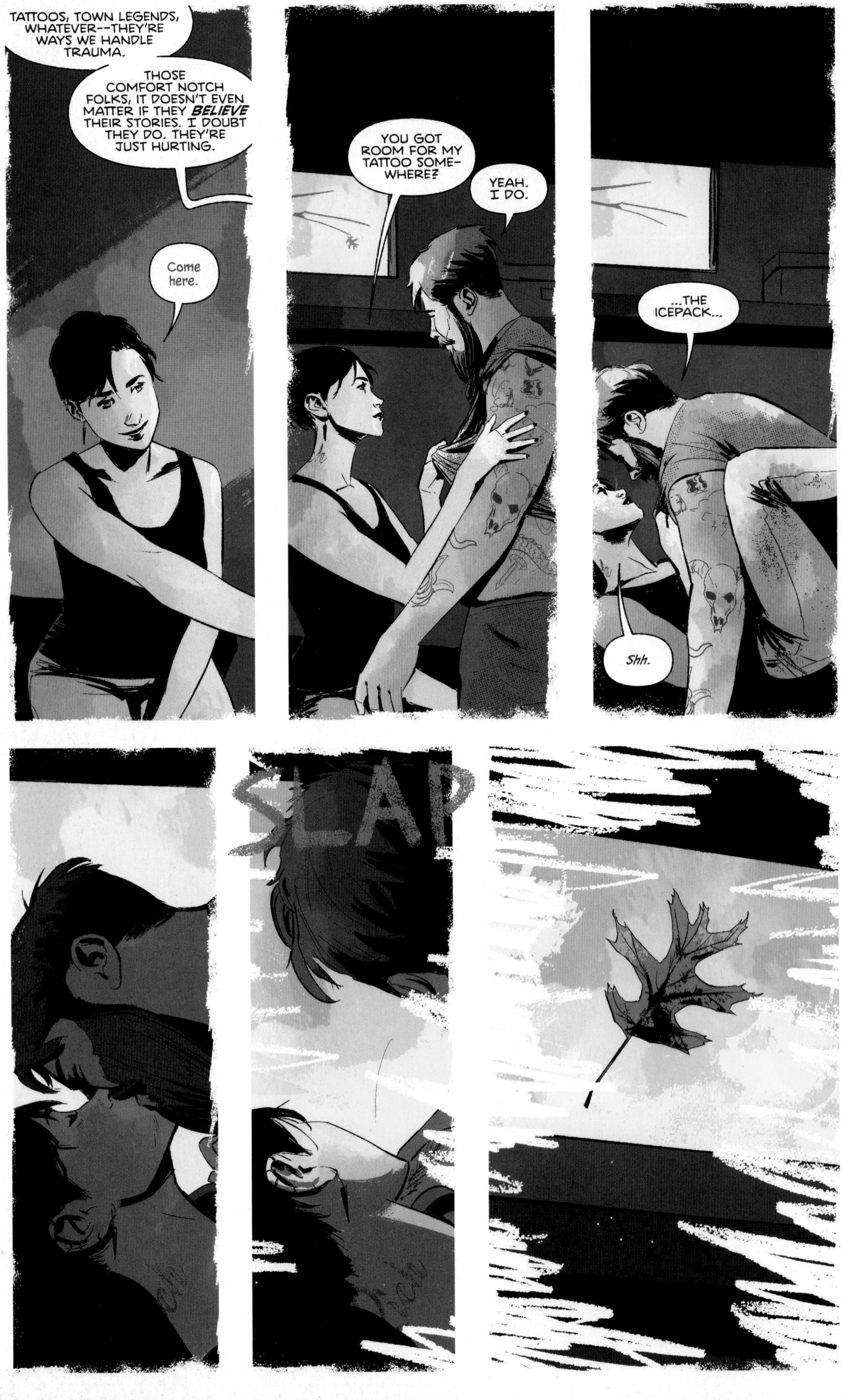

TATTOOS, TOWN LEGENDS, WHATEVER--THEY'RE WAYS WE HANDLE TRAUMA.
THOSE COMFORT NOTCH FOLKS, IT DOESN'T EVEN MATTER IF THEY *BELIEVE* THEIR STORIES. I DOUBT THEY DO. THEY'RE JUST HURTING.
Come here.
YOU GOT ROOM FOR MY TATTOO SOME-WHERE?
YEAH. I DO.
...THE ICEPACK...
Shh.
SLAP

Biddle, Biddle,

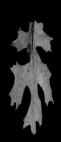

CHAPTER

FIVE

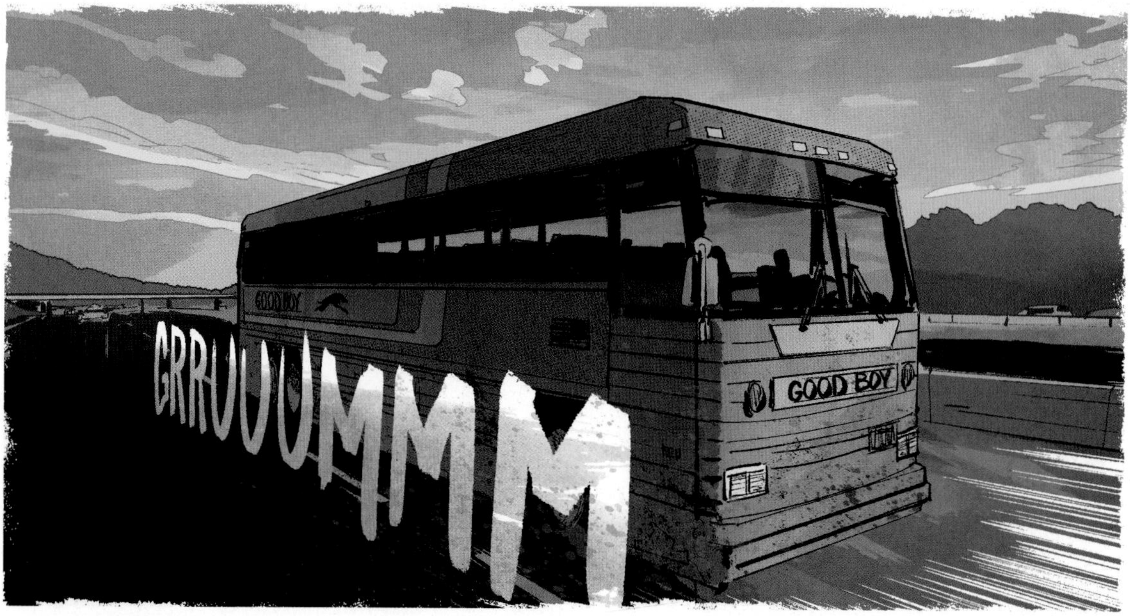
GRRUUUMMMM
GOOD BOY
GOOD BOY

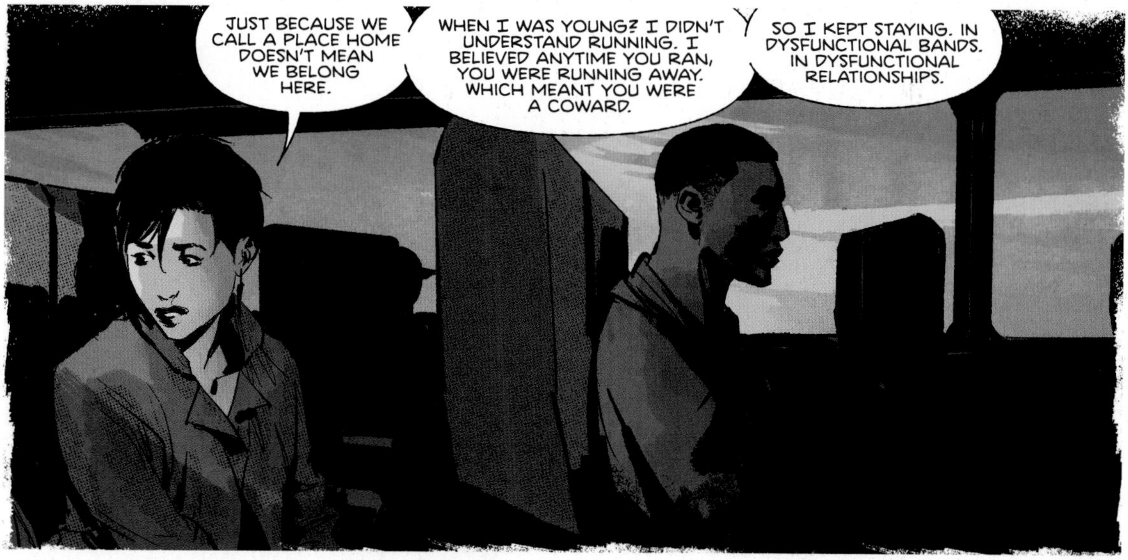
JUST BECAUSE WE CALL A PLACE HOME DOESN'T MEAN WE BELONG HERE.
WHEN I WAS YOUNG? I DIDN'T UNDERSTAND RUNNING. I BELIEVED ANYTIME YOU RAN, YOU WERE RUNNING AWAY. WHICH MEANT YOU WERE A COWARD.
SO I KEPT STAYING. IN DYSFUNCTIONAL BANDS. IN DYSFUNCTIONAL RELATIONSHIPS.

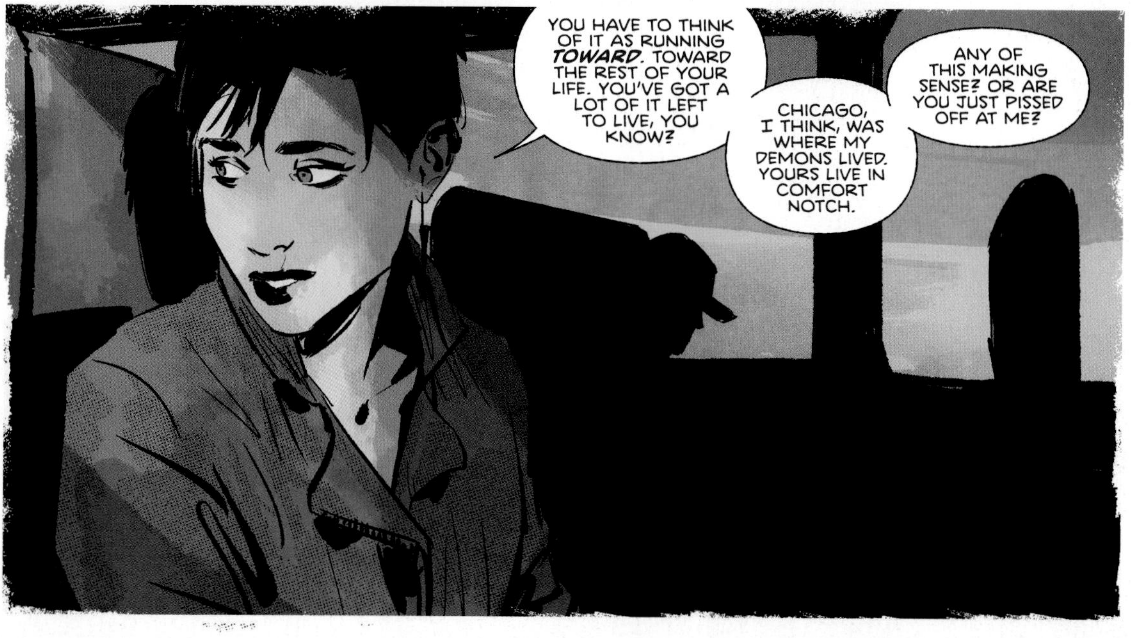
YOU HAVE TO THINK OF IT AS RUNNING *TOWARD*. TOWARD THE REST OF YOUR LIFE. YOU'VE GOT A LOT OF IT LEFT TO LIVE, YOU KNOW?
CHICAGO, I THINK, WAS WHERE MY DEMONS LIVED. YOURS LIVE IN COMFORT NOTCH.
ANY OF THIS MAKING SENSE? OR ARE YOU JUST PISSED OFF AT ME?

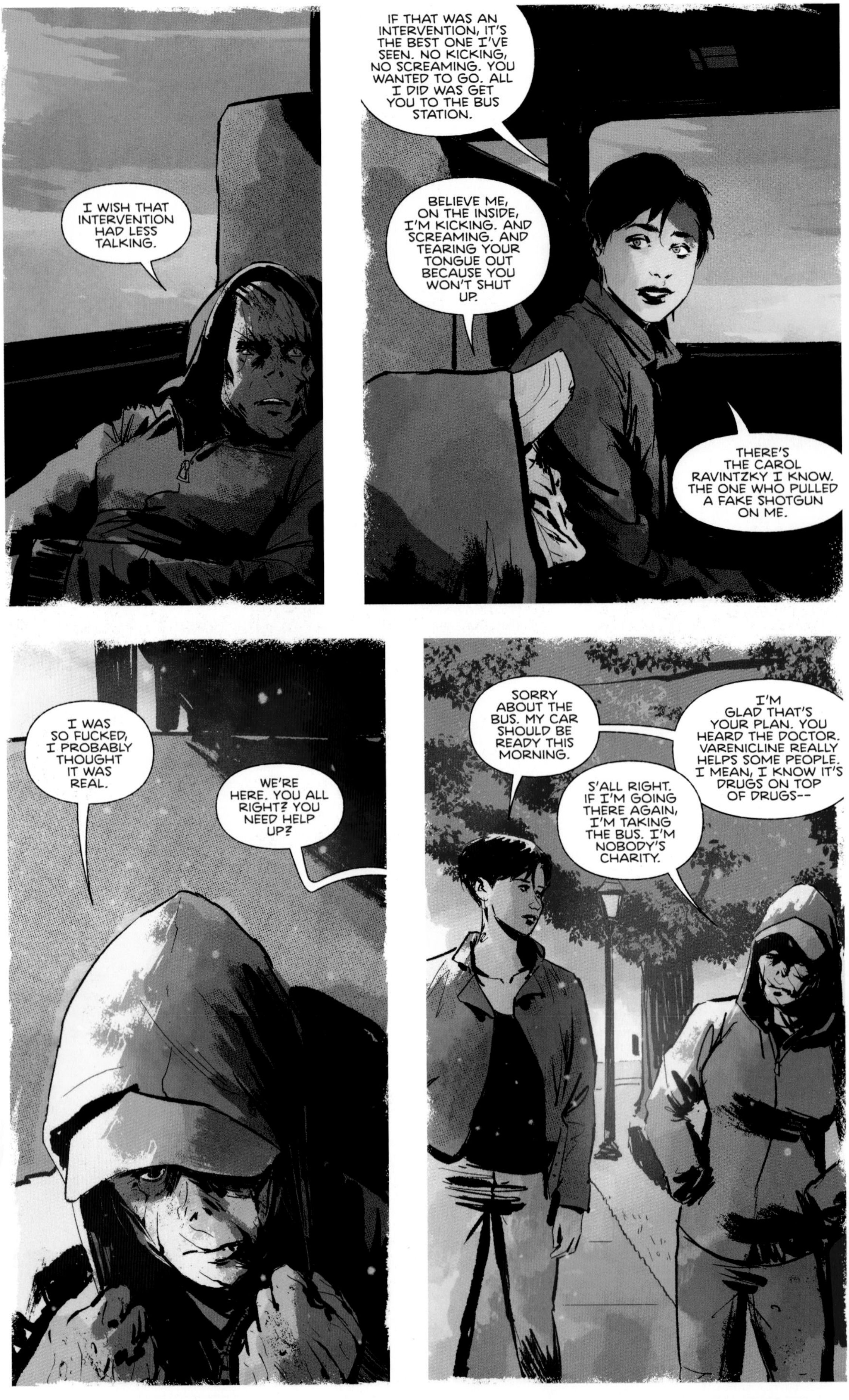
IF THAT WAS AN INTERVENTION, IT'S THE BEST ONE I'VE SEEN. NO KICKING, NO SCREAMING. YOU WANTED TO GO. ALL I DID WAS GET YOU TO THE BUS STATION.
I WISH THAT INTERVENTION HAD LESS TALKING.
BELIEVE ME, ON THE INSIDE, I'M KICKING. AND SCREAMING. AND TEARING YOUR TONGUE OUT BECAUSE YOU WON'T SHUT UP.
THERE'S THE CAROL RAVINTZKY I KNOW. THE ONE WHO PULLED A FAKE SHOTGUN ON ME.
I WAS SO FUCKED, I PROBABLY THOUGHT IT WAS REAL.
WE'RE HERE. YOU ALL RIGHT? YOU NEED HELP UP?
SORRY ABOUT THE BUS. MY CAR SHOULD BE READY THIS MORNING.
S'ALL RIGHT. IF I'M GOING THERE AGAIN, I'M TAKING THE BUS. I'M NOBODY'S CHARITY.
I'M GLAD THAT'S YOUR PLAN. YOU HEARD THE DOCTOR. VARENICLINE REALLY HELPS SOME PEOPLE. I MEAN, I KNOW IT'S DRUGS ON TOP OF DRUGS--

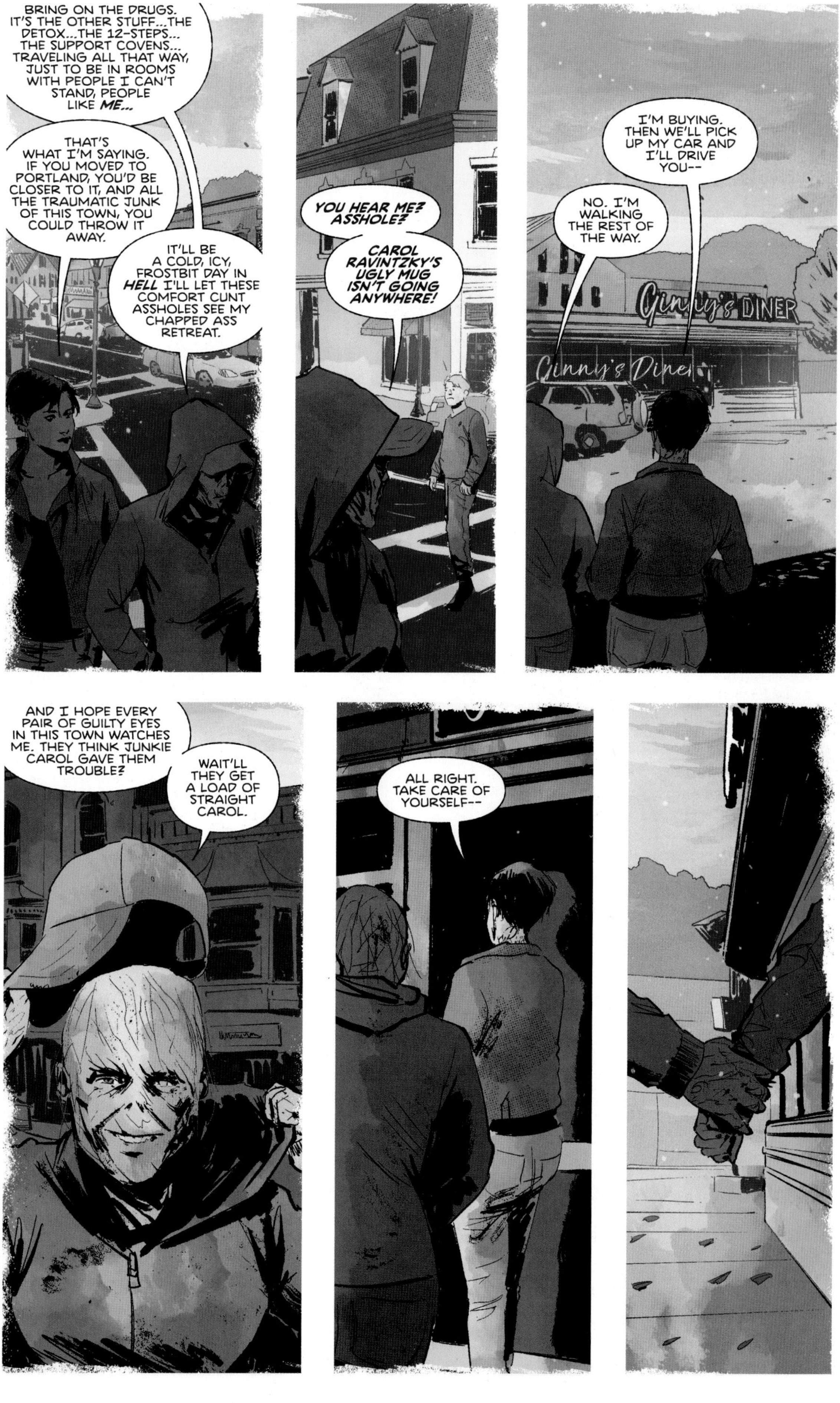
BRING ON THE DRUGS. IT'S THE OTHER STUFF...THE DETOX...THE 12-STEPS... THE SUPPORT COVENS... TRAVELING ALL THAT WAY, JUST TO BE IN ROOMS WITH PEOPLE I CAN'T STAND, PEOPLE LIKE ME...
THAT'S WHAT I'M SAYING. IF YOU MOVED TO PORTLAND, YOU'D BE CLOSER TO IT, AND ALL THE TRAUMATIC JUNK OF THIS TOWN, YOU COULD THROW IT AWAY.
IT'LL BE A COLD, ICY, FROSTBIT DAY IN HELL I'LL LET THESE COMFORT CUNT ASSHOLES SEE MY CHAPPED ASS RETREAT.
YOU HEAR ME? ASSHOLE?
CAROL RAVINTZKY'S UGLY MUG ISN'T GOING ANYWHERE!
I'M BUYING. THEN WE'LL PICK UP MY CAR AND I'LL DRIVE YOU--
NO. I'M WALKING THE REST OF THE WAY.
Ginny's DINER
Ginny's Diner
AND I HOPE EVERY PAIR OF GUILTY EYES IN THIS TOWN WATCHES ME. THEY THINK JUNKIE CAROL GAVE THEM TROUBLE?
WAIT'LL THEY GET A LOAD OF STRAIGHT CAROL.
ALL RIGHT. TAKE CARE OF YOURSELF--

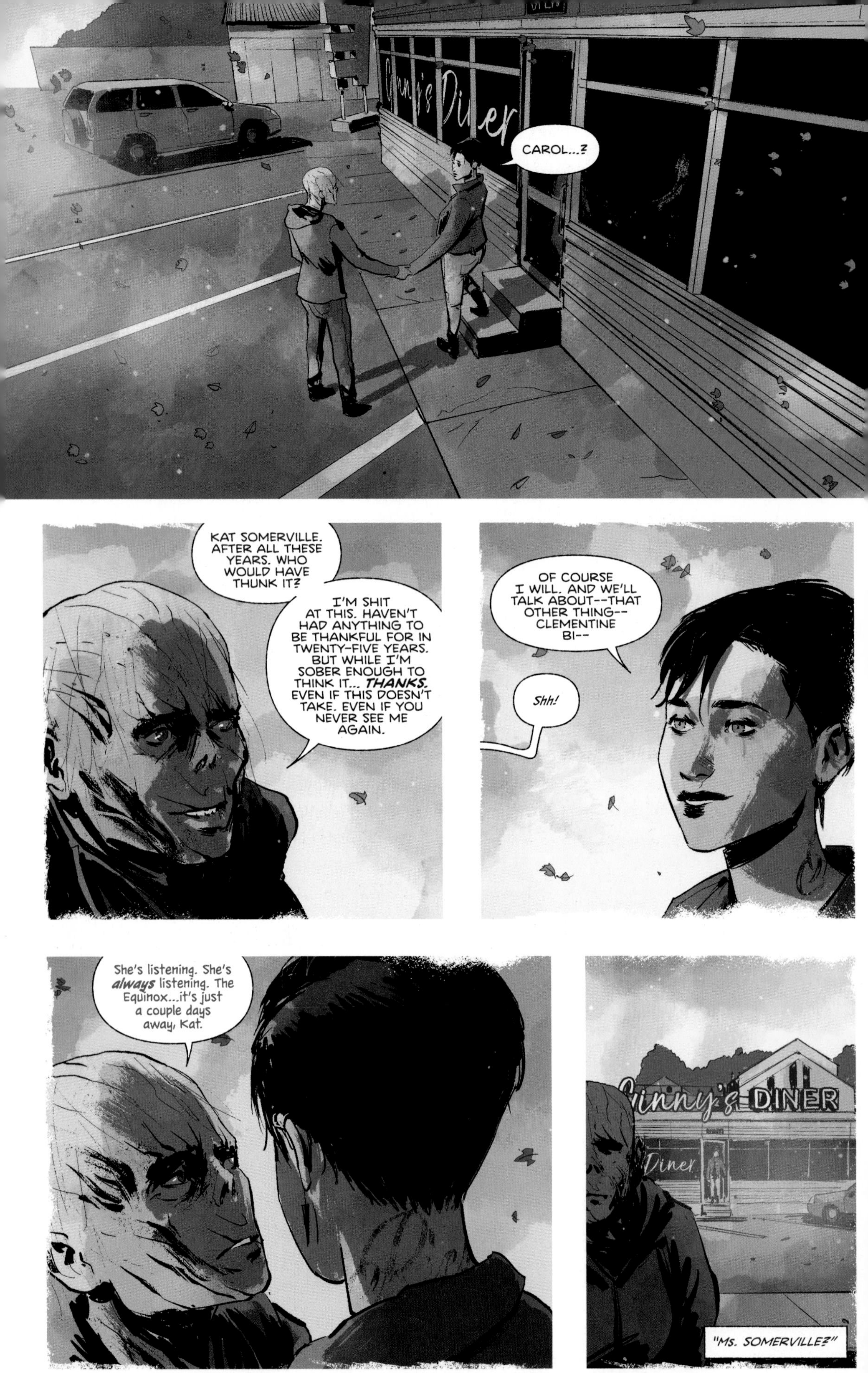
CAROL...?
KAT SOMERVILLE. AFTER ALL THESE YEARS. WHO WOULD HAVE THUNK IT?
I'M SHIT AT THIS. HAVEN'T HAD ANYTHING TO BE THANKFUL FOR IN TWENTY-FIVE YEARS. BUT WHILE I'M SOBER ENOUGH TO THINK IT... *THANKS.* EVEN IF THIS DOESN'T TAKE. EVEN IF YOU NEVER SEE ME AGAIN.
OF COURSE I WILL. AND WE'LL TALK ABOUT--THAT OTHER THING--CLEMENTINE BI--
Shh!
She's listening. She's *always* listening. The Equinox...it's just a couple days away, Kat.
"Ms. SOMERVILLE?"

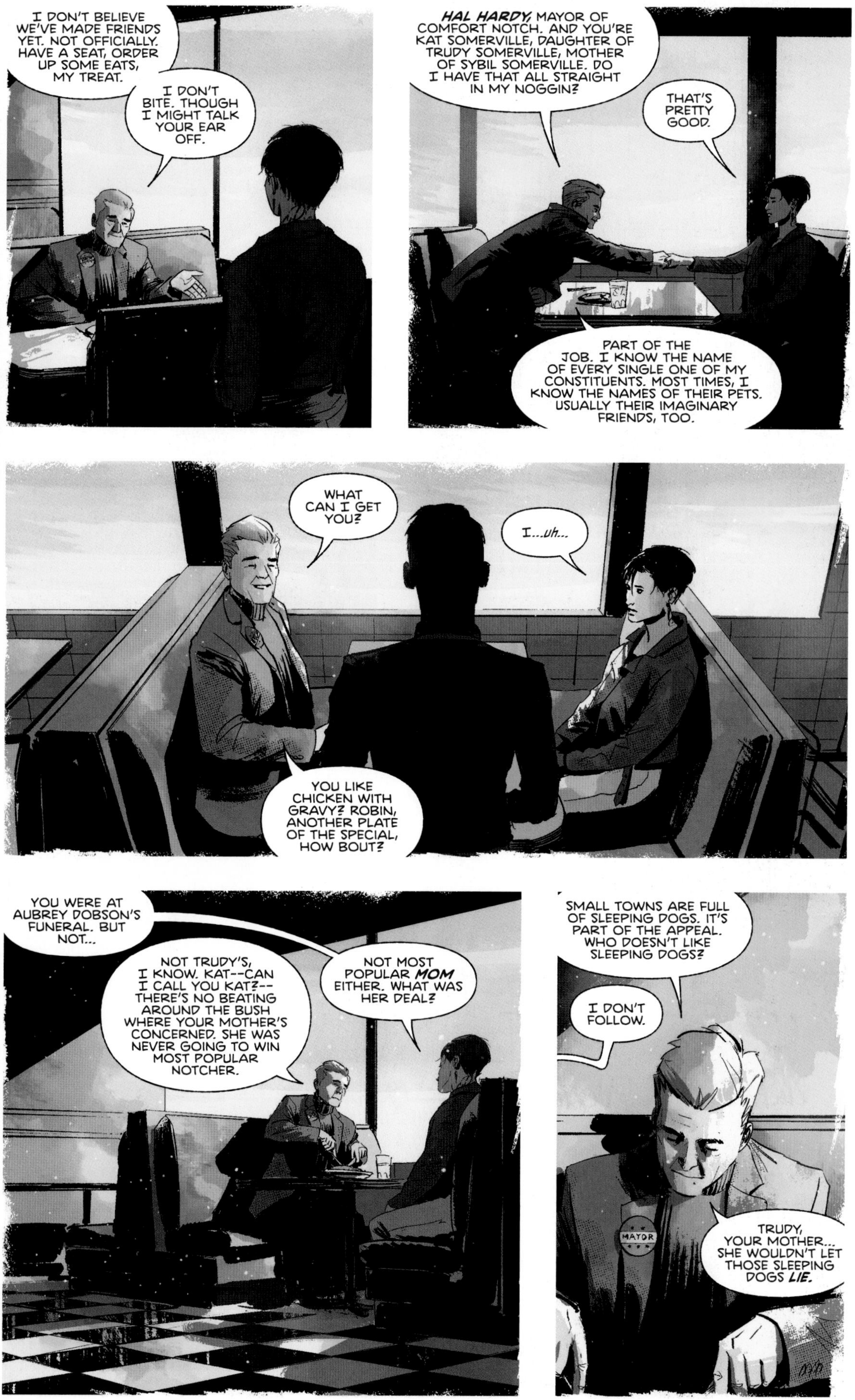
I DON'T BELIEVE WE'VE MADE FRIENDS YET. NOT OFFICIALLY. HAVE A SEAT, ORDER UP SOME EATS, MY TREAT.
I DON'T BITE. THOUGH I MIGHT TALK YOUR EAR OFF.
HAL HARDY, MAYOR OF COMFORT NOTCH. AND YOU'RE KAT SOMERVILLE, DAUGHTER OF TRUDY SOMERVILLE, MOTHER OF SYBIL SOMERVILLE. DO I HAVE THAT ALL STRAIGHT IN MY NOGGIN?
THAT'S PRETTY GOOD.
PART OF THE JOB. I KNOW THE NAME OF EVERY SINGLE ONE OF MY CONSTITUENTS. MOST TIMES, I KNOW THE NAMES OF THEIR PETS. USUALLY THEIR IMAGINARY FRIENDS, TOO.
WHAT CAN I GET YOU?
I... *uh...*
YOU LIKE CHICKEN WITH GRAVY? ROBIN, ANOTHER PLATE OF THE SPECIAL, HOW BOUT?
YOU WERE AT AUBREY DOBSON'S FUNERAL. BUT NOT...
NOT TRUDY'S, I KNOW. KAT--CAN I CALL YOU KAT?--THERE'S NO BEATING AROUND THE BUSH WHERE YOUR MOTHER'S CONCERNED. SHE WAS NEVER GOING TO WIN MOST POPULAR NOTCHER.
NOT MOST POPULAR **MOM** EITHER. WHAT WAS HER DEAL?
SMALL TOWNS ARE FULL OF SLEEPING DOGS. IT'S PART OF THE APPEAL. WHO DOESN'T LIKE SLEEPING DOGS?
I DON'T FOLLOW.
MAYOR
TRUDY, YOUR MOTHER... SHE WOULDN'T LET THOSE SLEEPING DOGS **LIE.**

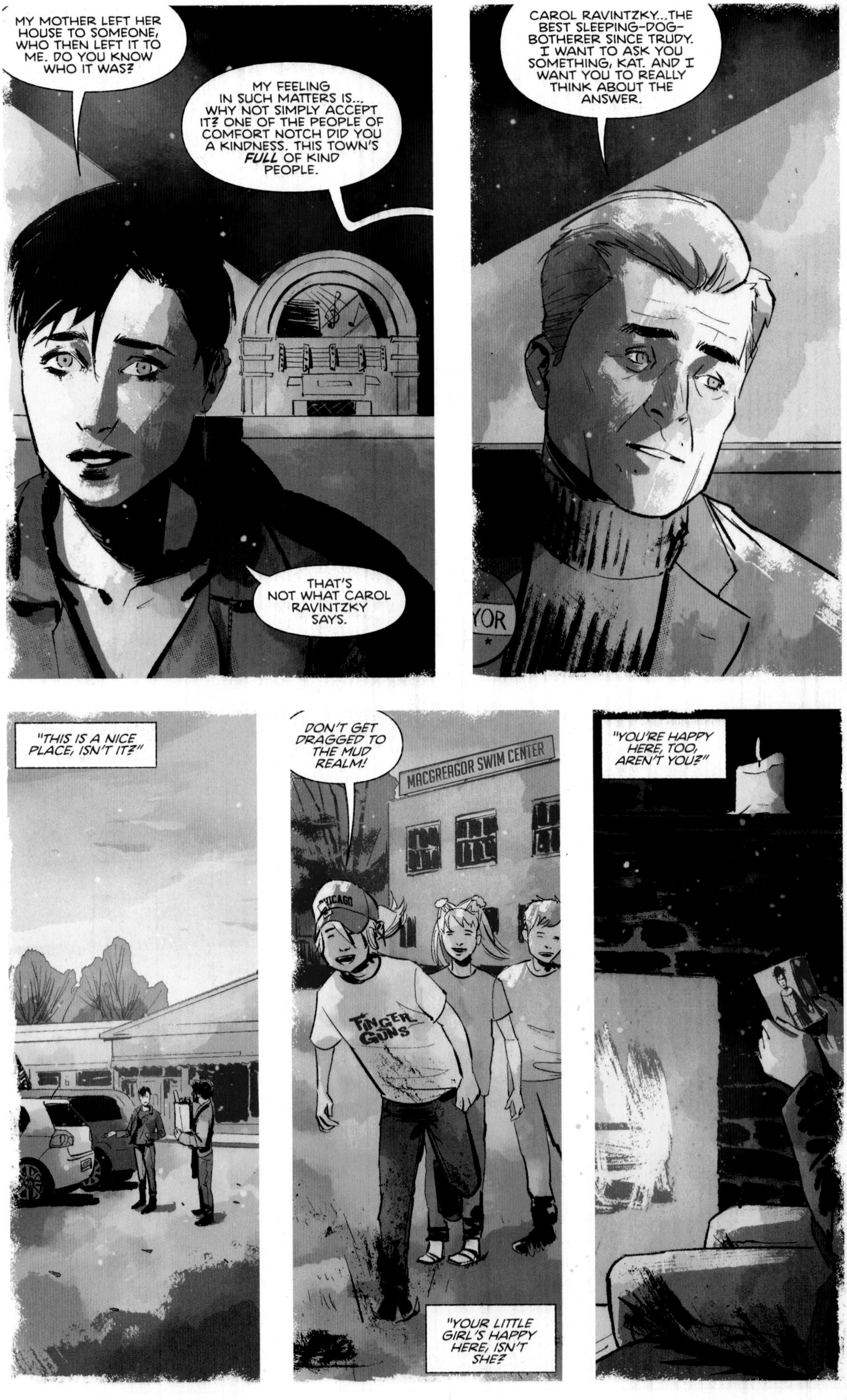
MY MOTHER LEFT HER HOUSE TO SOMEONE, WHO THEN LEFT IT TO ME. DO YOU KNOW WHO IT WAS?
MY FEELING IN SUCH MATTERS IS... WHY NOT SIMPLY ACCEPT IT? ONE OF THE PEOPLE OF COMFORT NOTCH DID YOU A KINDNESS. THIS TOWN'S FULL OF KIND PEOPLE.
THAT'S NOT WHAT CAROL RAVINTZKY SAYS.
CAROL RAVINTZKY...THE BEST SLEEPING-DOG-BOTHERER SINCE TRUDY. I WANT TO ASK YOU SOMETHING, KAT. AND I WANT YOU TO REALLY THINK ABOUT THE ANSWER.
YOR
"THIS IS A NICE PLACE, ISN'T IT?"
DON'T GET DRAGGED TO THE MUD REALM!
MACGREAGOR SWIM CENTER
CHICAGO
FINGER GUNS
"YOUR LITTLE GIRL'S HAPPY HERE, ISN'T SHE?
"YOU'RE HAPPY HERE, TOO, AREN'T YOU?"

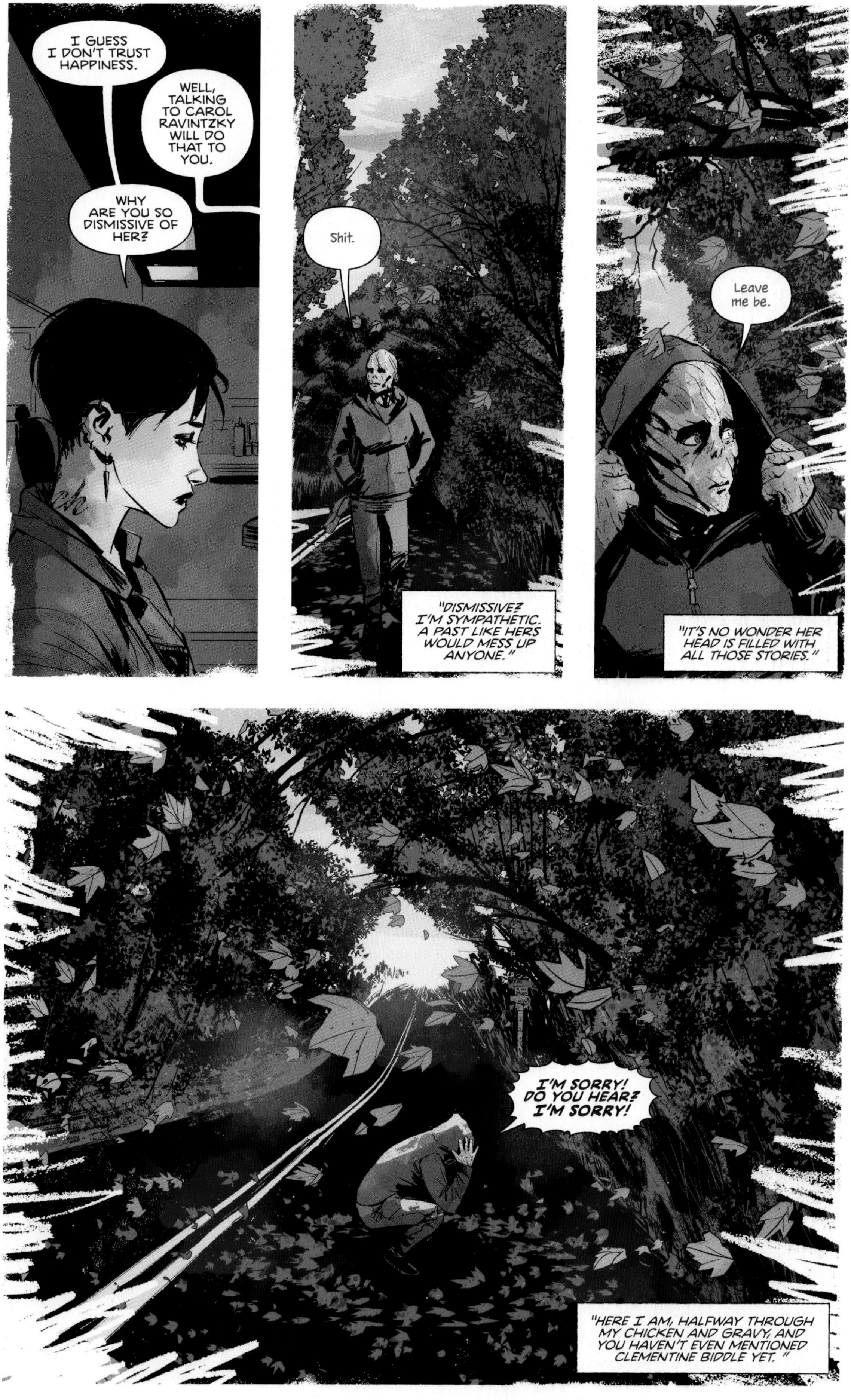

I GUESS I DON'T TRUST HAPPINESS.
WELL, TALKING TO CAROL RAVINTZKY WILL DO THAT TO YOU.
WHY ARE YOU SO DISMISSIVE OF HER?
Shit.
"DISMISSIVE? I'M SYMPATHETIC. A PAST LIKE HERS WOULD MESS UP ANYONE."
Leave me be.
"IT'S NO WONDER HER HEAD IS FILLED WITH ALL THOSE STORIES."
I'M SORRY! DO YOU HEAR? I'M SORRY!
"HERE I AM, HALFWAY THROUGH MY CHICKEN AND GRAVY, AND YOU HAVEN'T EVEN MENTIONED CLEMENTINE BIDDLE YET."

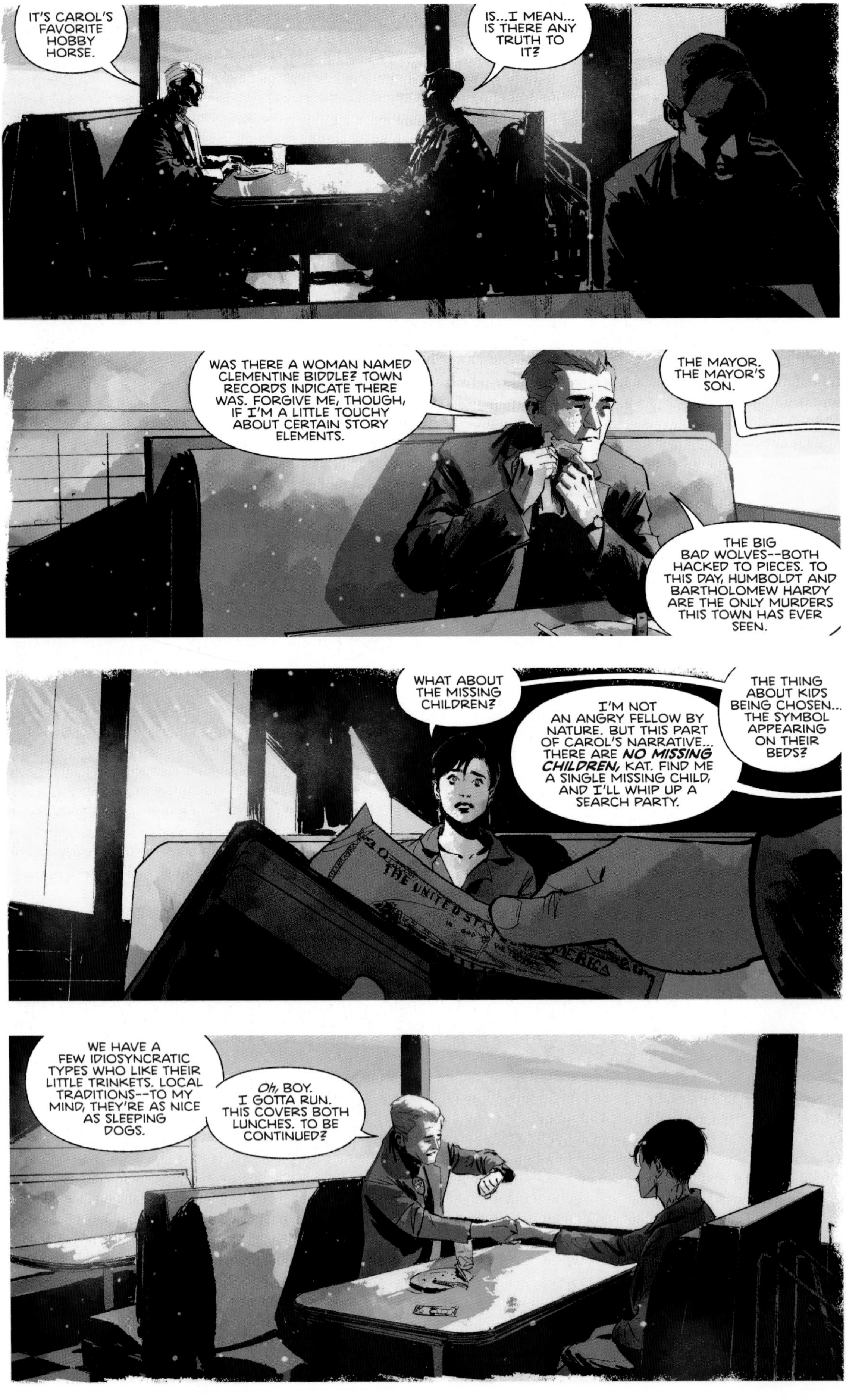
IT'S CAROL'S FAVORITE HOBBY HORSE.
IS...I MEAN... IS THERE ANY TRUTH TO IT?
WAS THERE A WOMAN NAMED CLEMENTINE BIDDLE? TOWN RECORDS INDICATE THERE WAS. FORGIVE ME, THOUGH, IF I'M A LITTLE TOUCHY ABOUT CERTAIN STORY ELEMENTS.
THE MAYOR. THE MAYOR'S SON.
THE BIG BAD WOLVES--BOTH HACKED TO PIECES. TO THIS DAY, HUMBOLDT AND BARTHOLOMEW HARDY ARE THE ONLY MURDERS THIS TOWN HAS EVER SEEN.
WHAT ABOUT THE MISSING CHILDREN?
THE THING ABOUT KIDS BEING CHOSEN... THE SYMBOL APPEARING ON THEIR BEDS?
I'M NOT AN ANGRY FELLOW BY NATURE. BUT THIS PART OF CAROL'S NARRATIVE... THERE ARE NO MISSING CHILDREN, KAT. FIND ME A SINGLE MISSING CHILD, AND I'LL WHIP UP A SEARCH PARTY.
WE HAVE A FEW IDIOSYNCRATIC TYPES WHO LIKE THEIR LITTLE TRINKETS. LOCAL TRADITIONS--TO MY MIND, THEY'RE AS NICE AS SLEEPING DOGS.
Oh, BOY. I GOTTA RUN. THIS COVERS BOTH LUNCHES. TO BE CONTINUED?

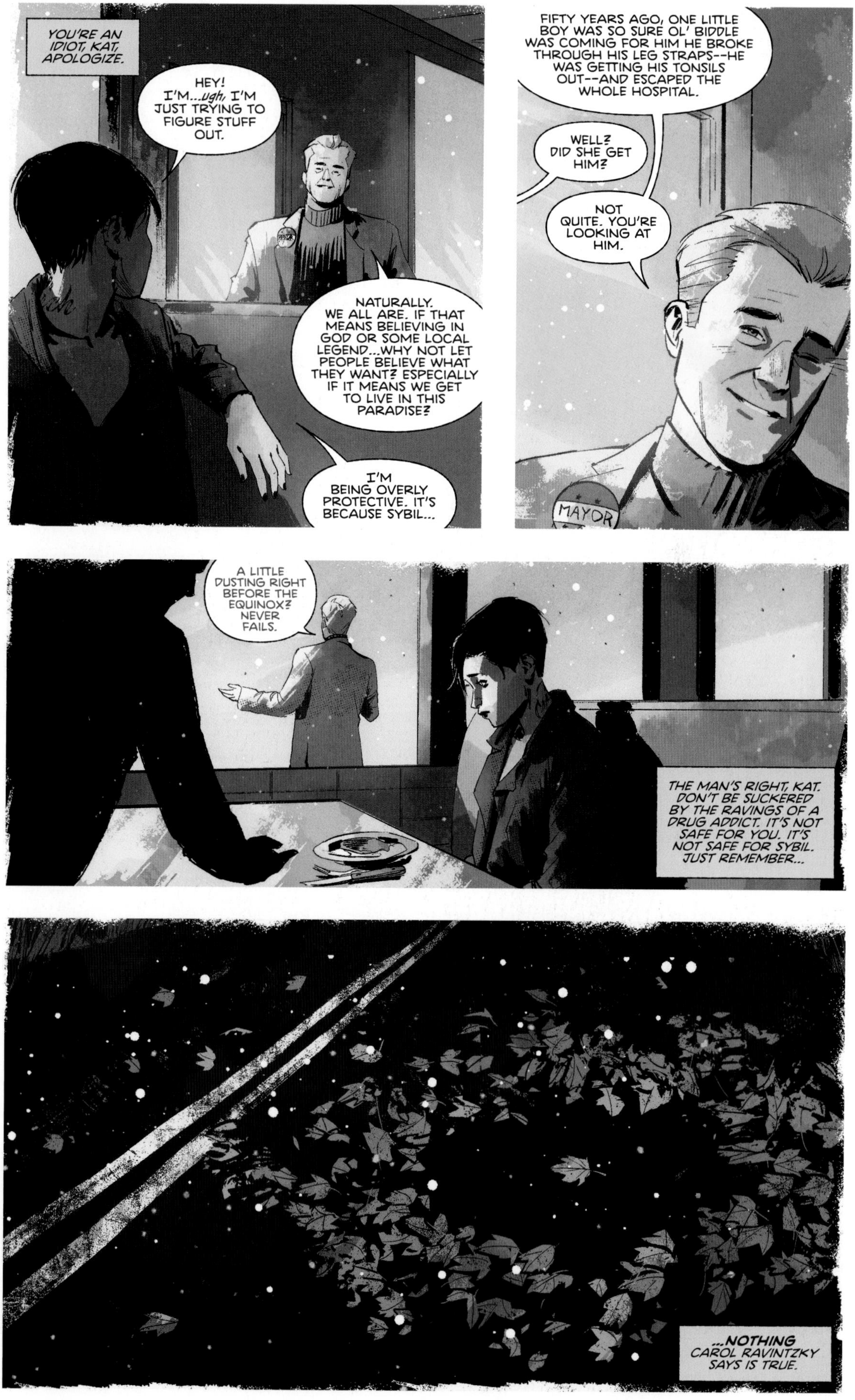
YOU'RE AN IDIOT, KAT, APOLOGIZE.
HEY! I'M...ugh, I'M JUST TRYING TO FIGURE STUFF OUT.
NATURALLY. WE ALL ARE. IF THAT MEANS BELIEVING IN GOD OR SOME LOCAL LEGEND...WHY NOT LET PEOPLE BELIEVE WHAT THEY WANT? ESPECIALLY IF IT MEANS WE GET TO LIVE IN THIS PARADISE?
I'M BEING OVERLY PROTECTIVE. IT'S BECAUSE SYBIL...
FIFTY YEARS AGO, ONE LITTLE BOY WAS SO SURE OL' BIDDLE WAS COMING FOR HIM HE BROKE THROUGH HIS LEG STRAPS--HE WAS GETTING HIS TONSILS OUT--AND ESCAPED THE WHOLE HOSPITAL.
WELL? DID SHE GET HIM?
NOT QUITE. YOU'RE LOOKING AT HIM.
MAYOR
A LITTLE DUSTING RIGHT BEFORE THE EQUINOX? NEVER FAILS.
THE MAN'S RIGHT, KAT. DON'T BE SUCKERED BY THE RAVINGS OF A DRUG ADDICT. IT'S NOT SAFE FOR YOU. IT'S NOT SAFE FOR SYBIL. JUST REMEMBER...
...NOTHING CAROL RAVINTZKY SAYS IS TRUE.

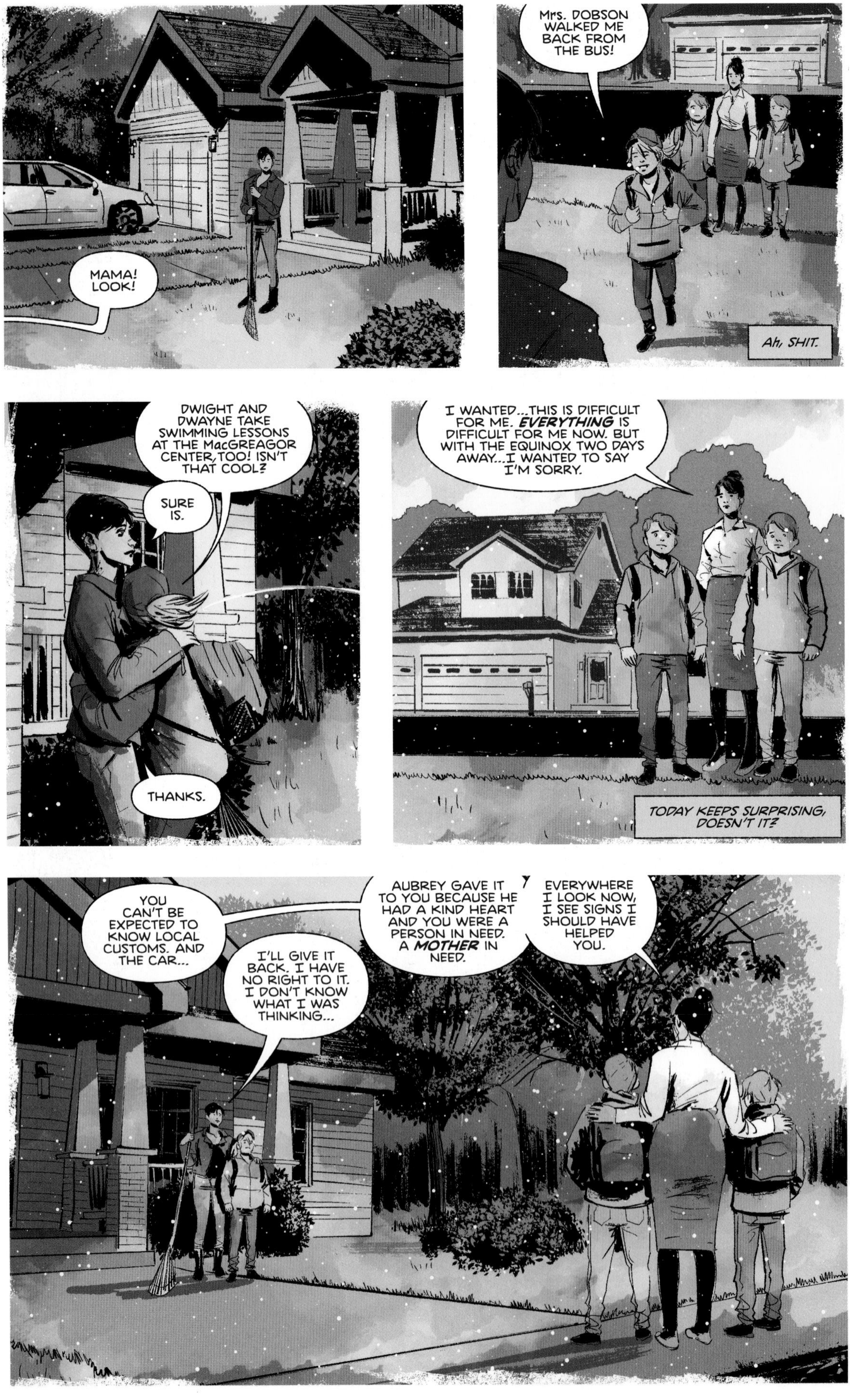
MAMA! LOOK!
Mrs. DOBSON WALKED ME BACK FROM THE BUS!
Ah, SHIT.
DWIGHT AND DWAYNE TAKE SWIMMING LESSONS AT THE MacGREAGOR CENTER, TOO! ISN'T THAT COOL?
SURE IS.
THANKS.
I WANTED...THIS IS DIFFICULT FOR ME. EVERYTHING IS DIFFICULT FOR ME NOW. BUT WITH THE EQUINOX TWO DAYS AWAY...I WANTED TO SAY I'M SORRY.
TODAY KEEPS SURPRISING, DOESN'T IT?
YOU CAN'T BE EXPECTED TO KNOW LOCAL CUSTOMS. AND THE CAR...
I'LL GIVE IT BACK. I HAVE NO RIGHT TO IT. I DON'T KNOW WHAT I WAS THINKING...
AUBREY GAVE IT TO YOU BECAUSE HE HAD A KIND HEART AND YOU WERE A PERSON IN NEED. A MOTHER IN NEED.
EVERYWHERE I LOOK NOW, I SEE SIGNS I SHOULD HAVE HELPED YOU.

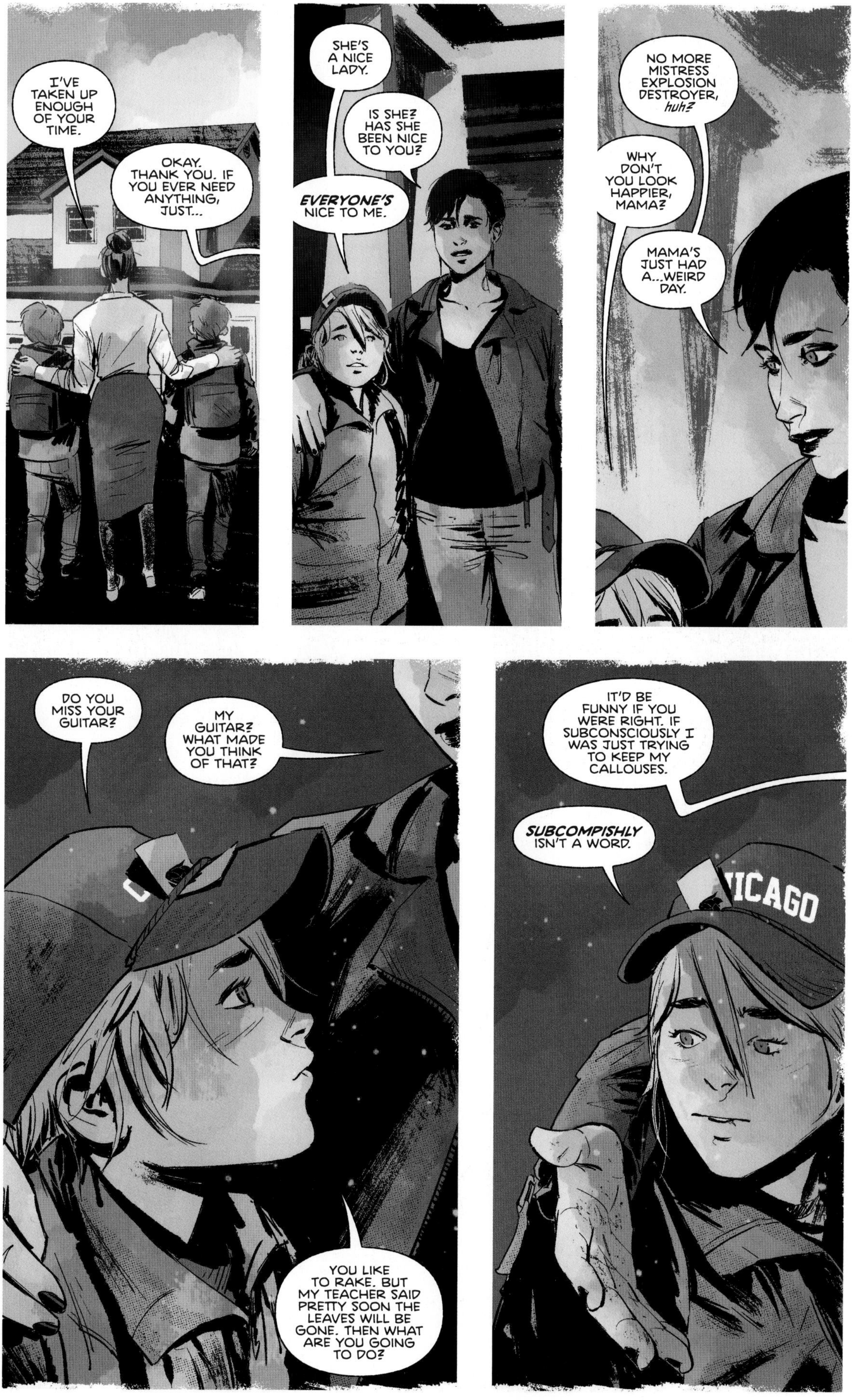
I'VE TAKEN UP ENOUGH OF YOUR TIME.
OKAY. THANK YOU. IF YOU EVER NEED ANYTHING, JUST...
SHE'S A NICE LADY.
IS SHE? HAS SHE BEEN NICE TO YOU?
EVERYONE'S NICE TO ME.
NO MORE MISTRESS EXPLOSION DESTROYER, huh?
WHY DON'T YOU LOOK HAPPIER, MAMA?
MAMA'S JUST HAD A...WEIRD DAY.
DO YOU MISS YOUR GUITAR?
MY GUITAR? WHAT MADE YOU THINK OF THAT?
YOU LIKE TO RAKE. BUT MY TEACHER SAID PRETTY SOON THE LEAVES WILL BE GONE. THEN WHAT ARE YOU GOING TO DO?
IT'D BE FUNNY IF YOU WERE RIGHT. IF SUBCONSCIOUSLY I WAS JUST TRYING TO KEEP MY CALLOUSES.
SUBCOMPISHLY ISN'T A WORD.
ICAGO

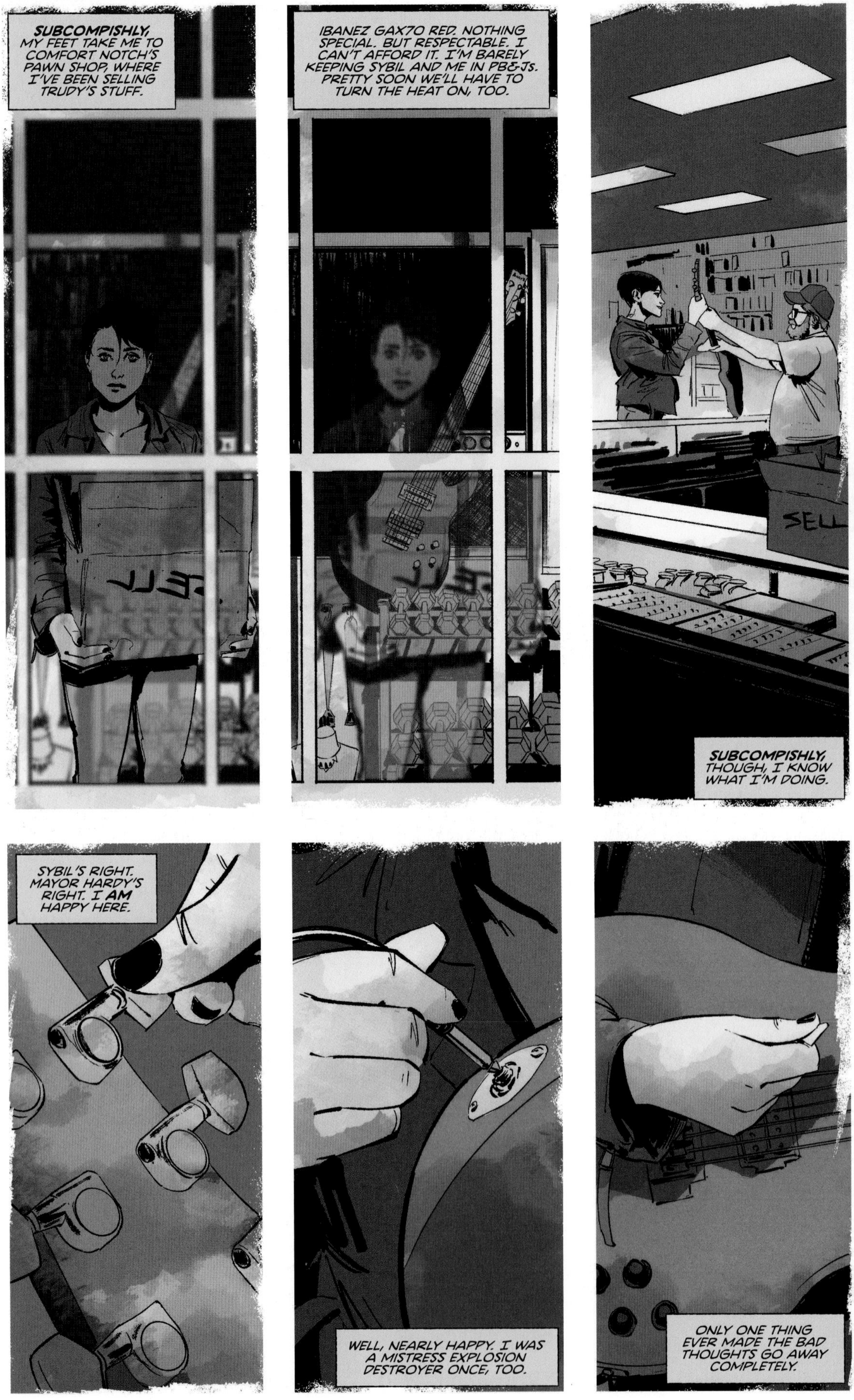
SUBCOMPISHLY, MY FEET TAKE ME TO COMFORT NOTCH'S PAWN SHOP, WHERE I'VE BEEN SELLING TRUDY'S STUFF.
IBANEZ GAX70 RED. NOTHING SPECIAL. BUT RESPECTABLE. I CAN'T AFFORD IT. I'M BARELY KEEPING SYBIL AND ME IN PB&Js. PRETTY SOON WE'LL HAVE TO TURN THE HEAT ON, TOO.
SUBCOMPISHLY, THOUGH, I KNOW WHAT I'M DOING.
SYBIL'S RIGHT. MAYOR HARDY'S RIGHT. I AM HAPPY HERE.
WELL, NEARLY HAPPY. I WAS A MISTRESS EXPLOSION DESTROYER ONCE, TOO.
ONLY ONE THING EVER MADE THE BAD THOUGHTS GO AWAY COMPLETELY.

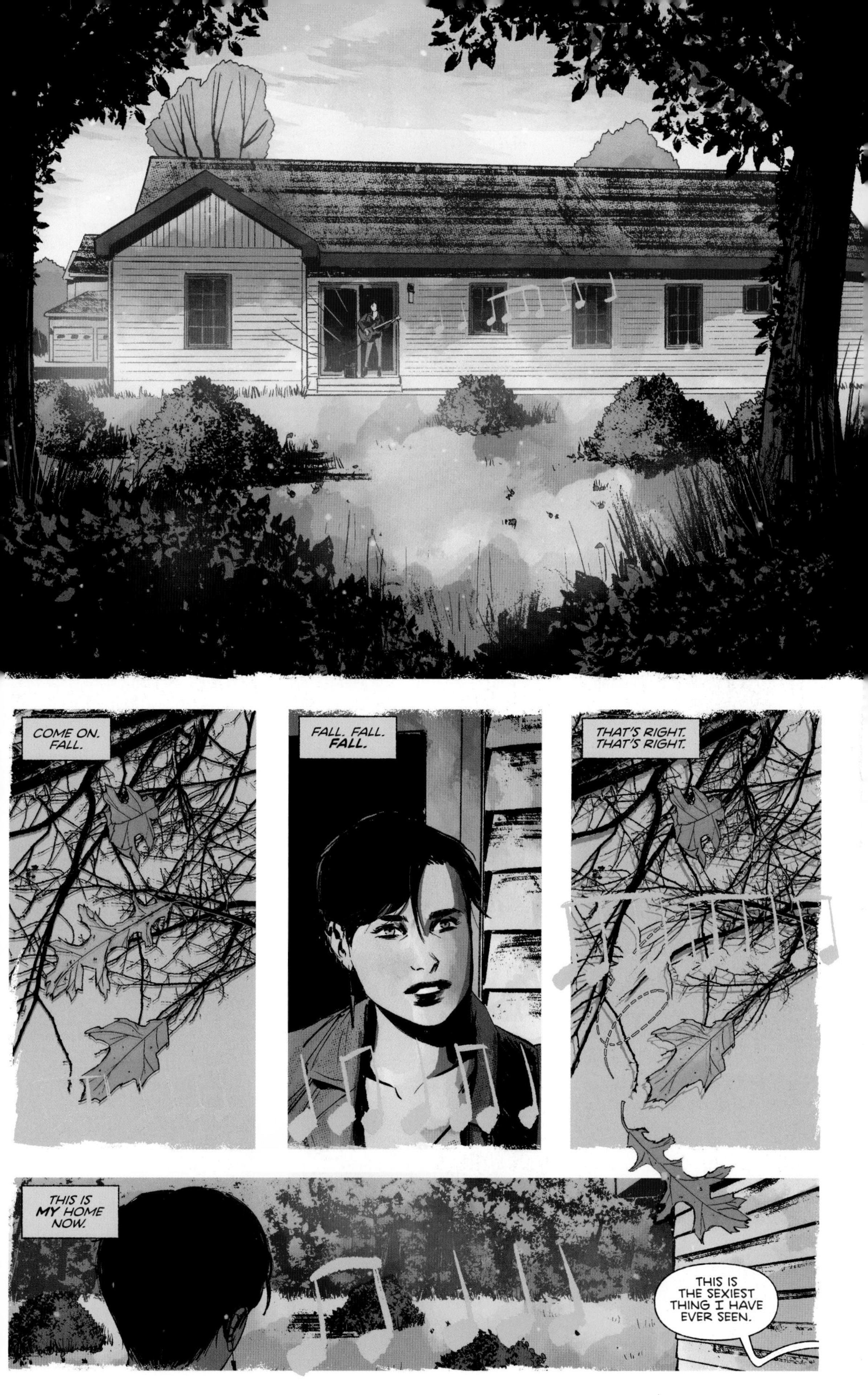
COME ON. FALL.
FALL. FALL. **FALL.**
THAT'S RIGHT. THAT'S RIGHT.
THIS IS **MY** HOME NOW.
THIS IS THE SEXIEST THING I HAVE EVER SEEN.

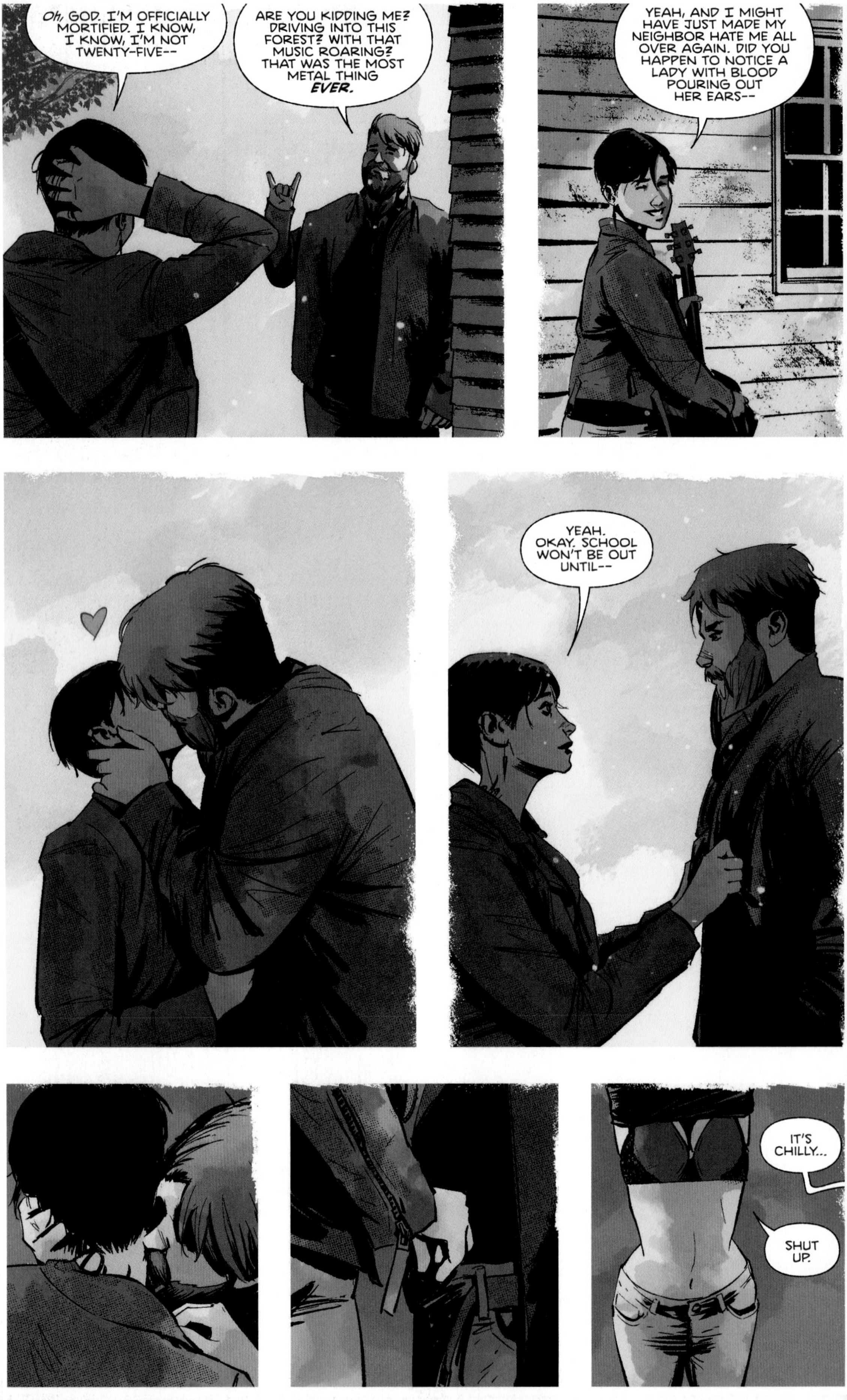
Oh, GOD. I'M OFFICIALLY MORTIFIED. I KNOW, I KNOW, I'M NOT TWENTY-FIVE--
ARE YOU KIDDING ME? DRIVING INTO THIS FOREST? WITH THAT MUSIC ROARING? THAT WAS THE MOST METAL THING ***EVER.***
YEAH, AND I MIGHT HAVE JUST MADE MY NEIGHBOR HATE ME ALL OVER AGAIN. DID YOU HAPPEN TO NOTICE A LADY WITH BLOOD POURING OUT HER EARS--
YEAH. OKAY. SCHOOL WON'T BE OUT UNTIL--
IT'S CHILLY...
SHUT UP.

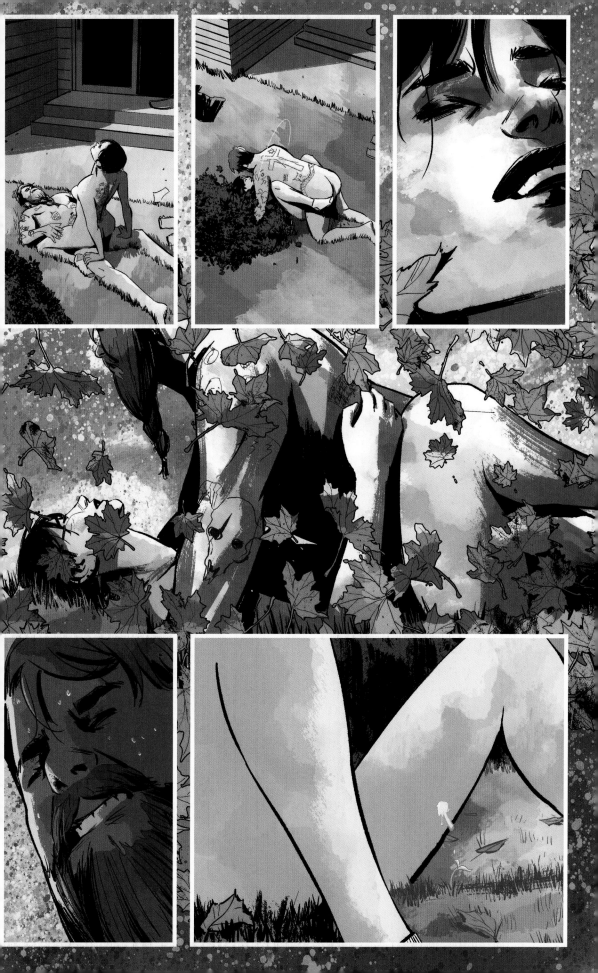

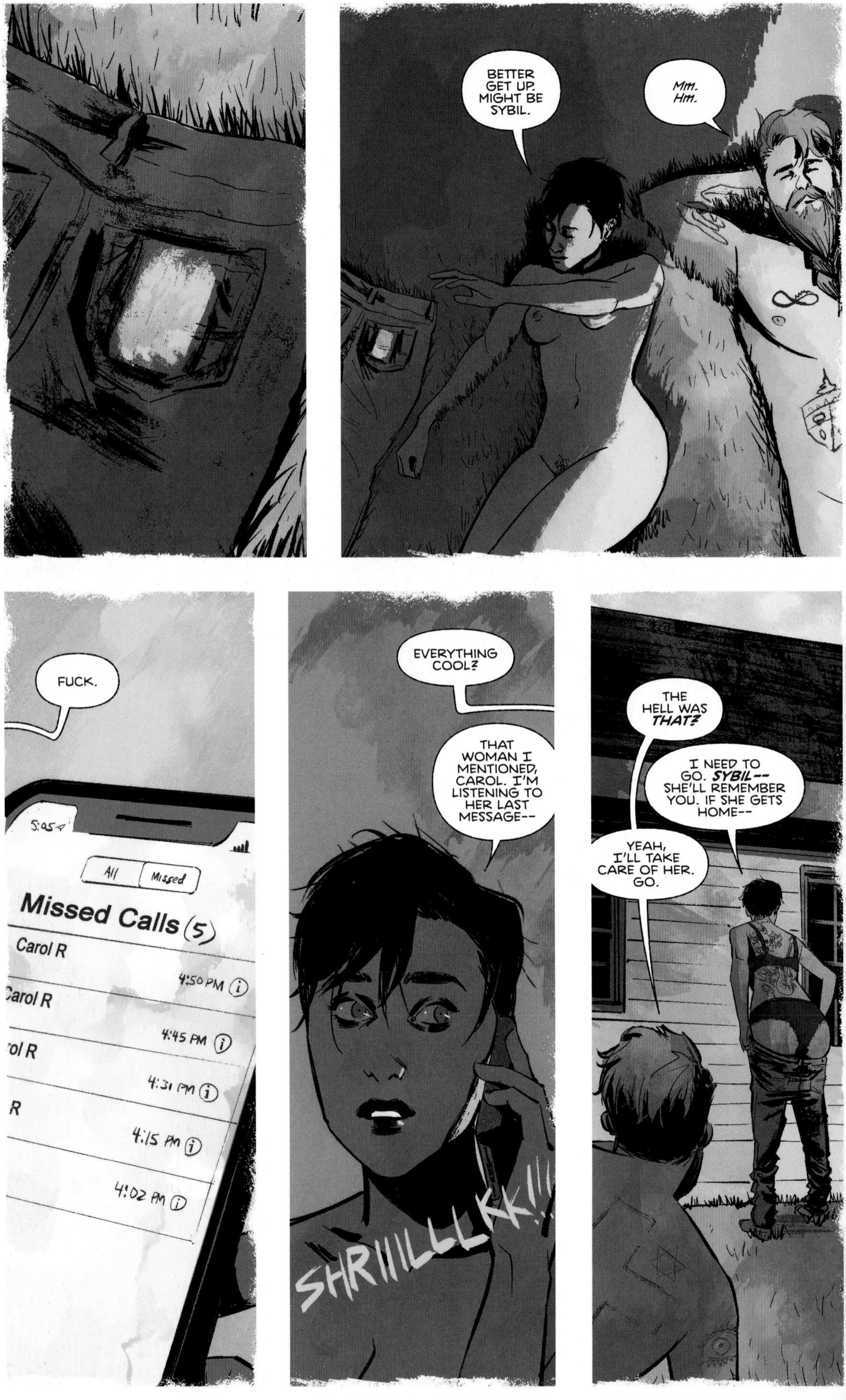
BETTER GET UP. MIGHT BE SYBIL.
Mm. Hm.
FUCK.
5:05
All
Missed
Missed Calls (5)
Carol R
4:50 PM
Carol R
4:45 PM
rol R
4:31 PM
R
4:15 PM
4:02 PM
EVERYTHING COOL?
THAT WOMAN I MENTIONED, CAROL. I'M LISTENING TO HER LAST MESSAGE--
SHRIIILLLKK!!!
THE HELL WAS THAT?
I NEED TO GO. SYBIL-- SHE'LL REMEMBER YOU. IF SHE GETS HOME--
YEAH, I'LL TAKE CARE OF HER. GO.

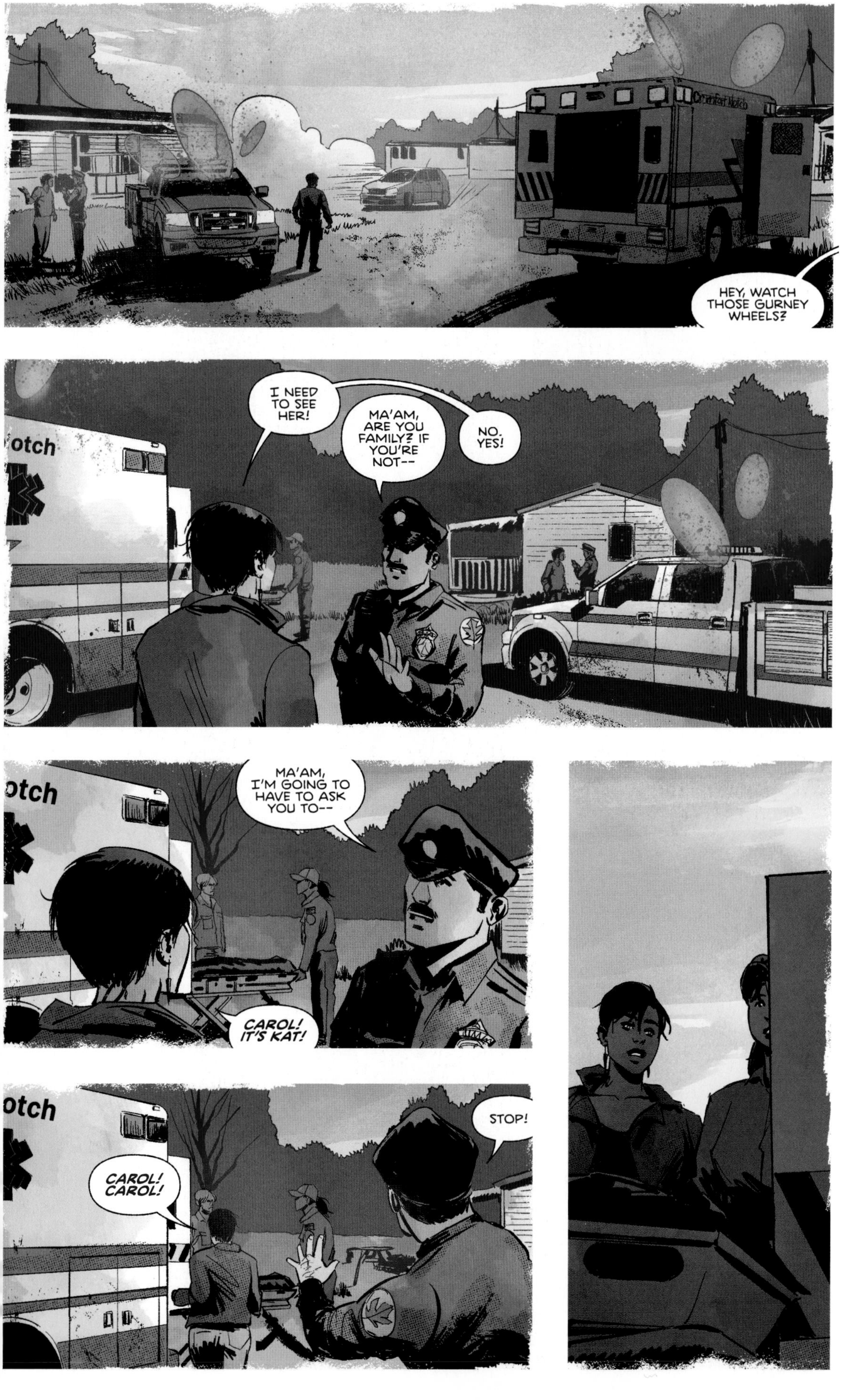
HEY, WATCH THOSE GURNEY WHEELS?
I NEED TO SEE HER!
MA'AM, ARE YOU FAMILY? IF YOU'RE NOT--
NO. YES!
MA'AM, I'M GOING TO HAVE TO ASK YOU TO--
CAROL! IT'S KAT!
STOP!
CAROL! CAROL!

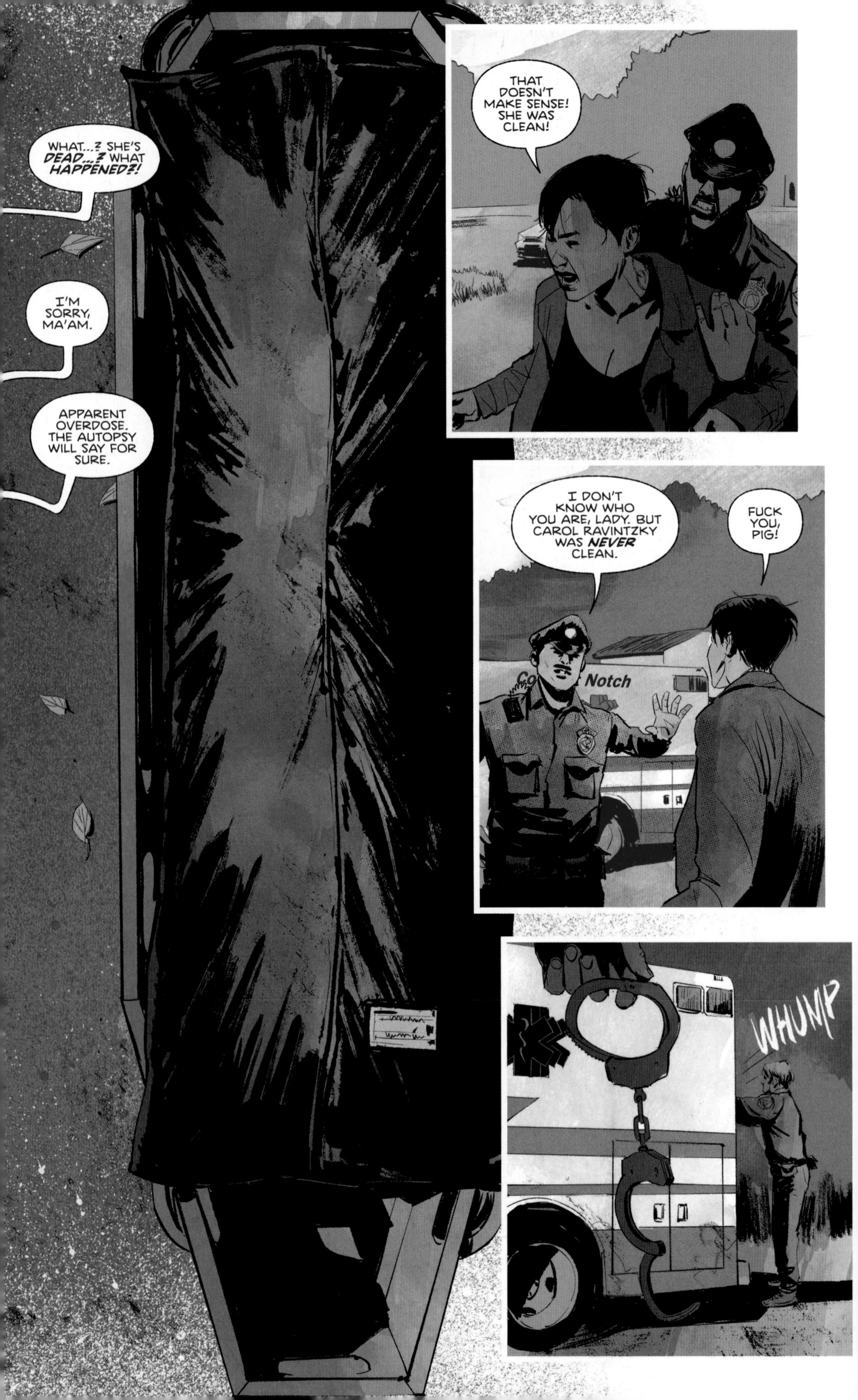
WHAT...? SHE'S DEAD...? WHAT HAPPENED?!
I'M SORRY, MA'AM.
APPARENT OVERDOSE. THE AUTOPSY WILL SAY FOR SURE.
THAT DOESN'T MAKE SENSE! SHE WAS CLEAN!
I DON'T KNOW WHO YOU ARE, LADY. BUT CAROL RAVINTZKY WAS NEVER CLEAN.
FUCK YOU, PIG!
WHUMP

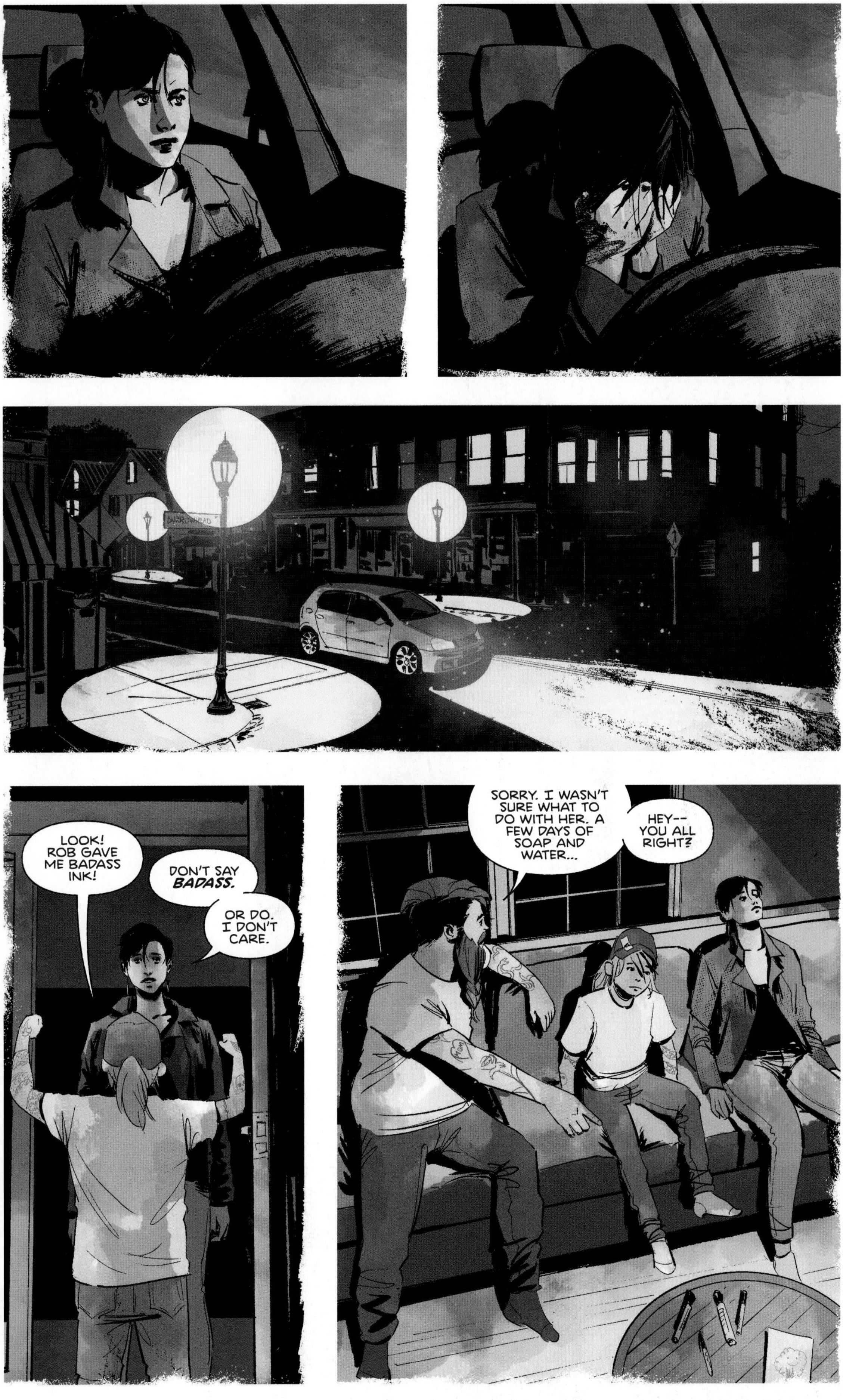
LOOK! ROB GAVE ME BADASS INK!
DON'T SAY ***BADASS.***
OR DO. I DON'T CARE.
SORRY. I WASN'T SURE WHAT TO DO WITH HER. A FEW DAYS OF SOAP AND WATER...
HEY-- YOU ALL RIGHT?

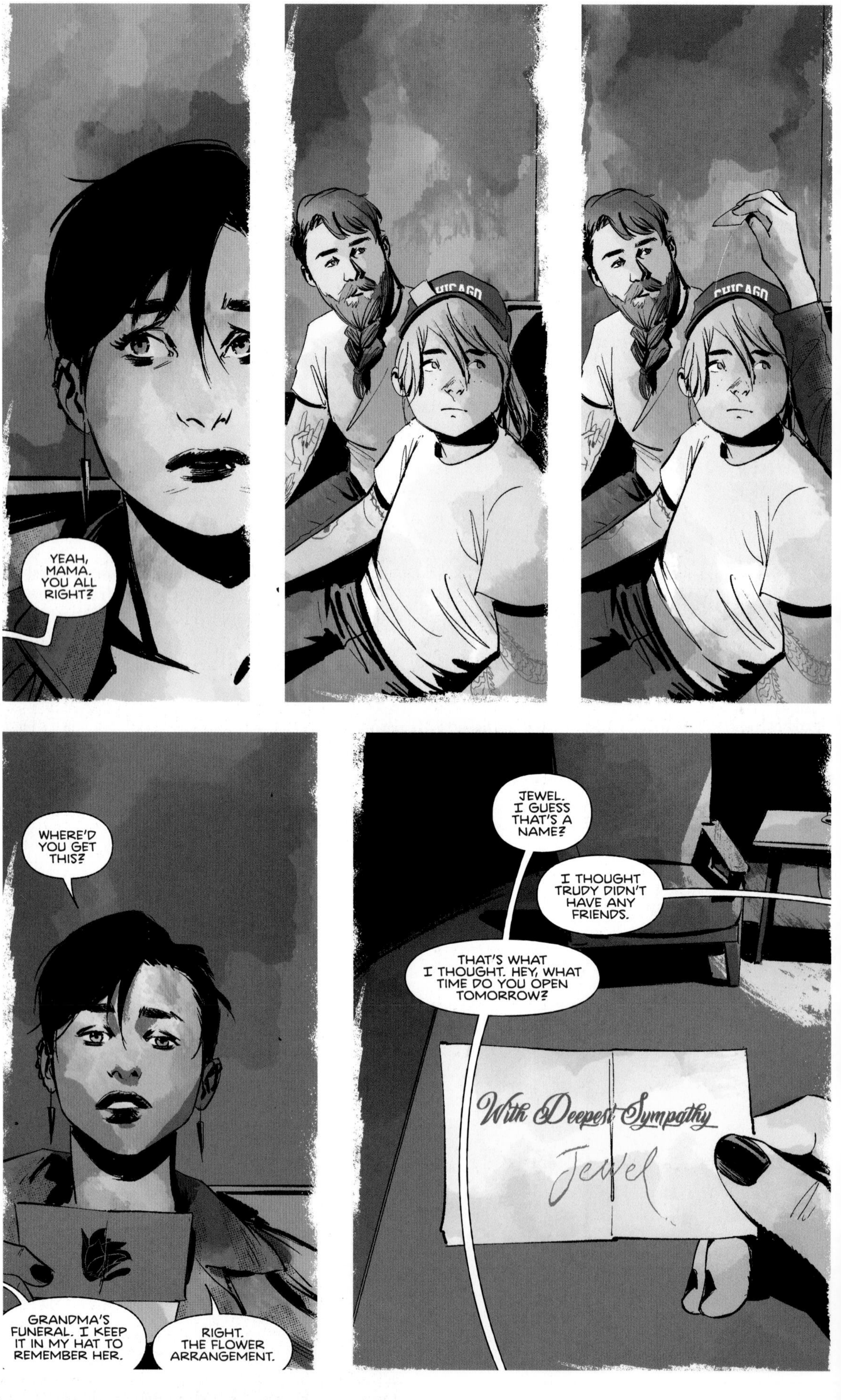
YEAH, MAMA. YOU ALL RIGHT?
CHICAGO
CHICAGO
WHERE'D YOU GET THIS?
GRANDMA'S FUNERAL. I KEEP IT IN MY HAT TO REMEMBER HER.
RIGHT. THE FLOWER ARRANGEMENT.
JEWEL. I GUESS THAT'S A NAME?
I THOUGHT TRUDY DIDN'T HAVE ANY FRIENDS.
THAT'S WHAT I THOUGHT. HEY, WHAT TIME DO YOU OPEN TOMORROW?
With Deepest Sympathy
Jewel

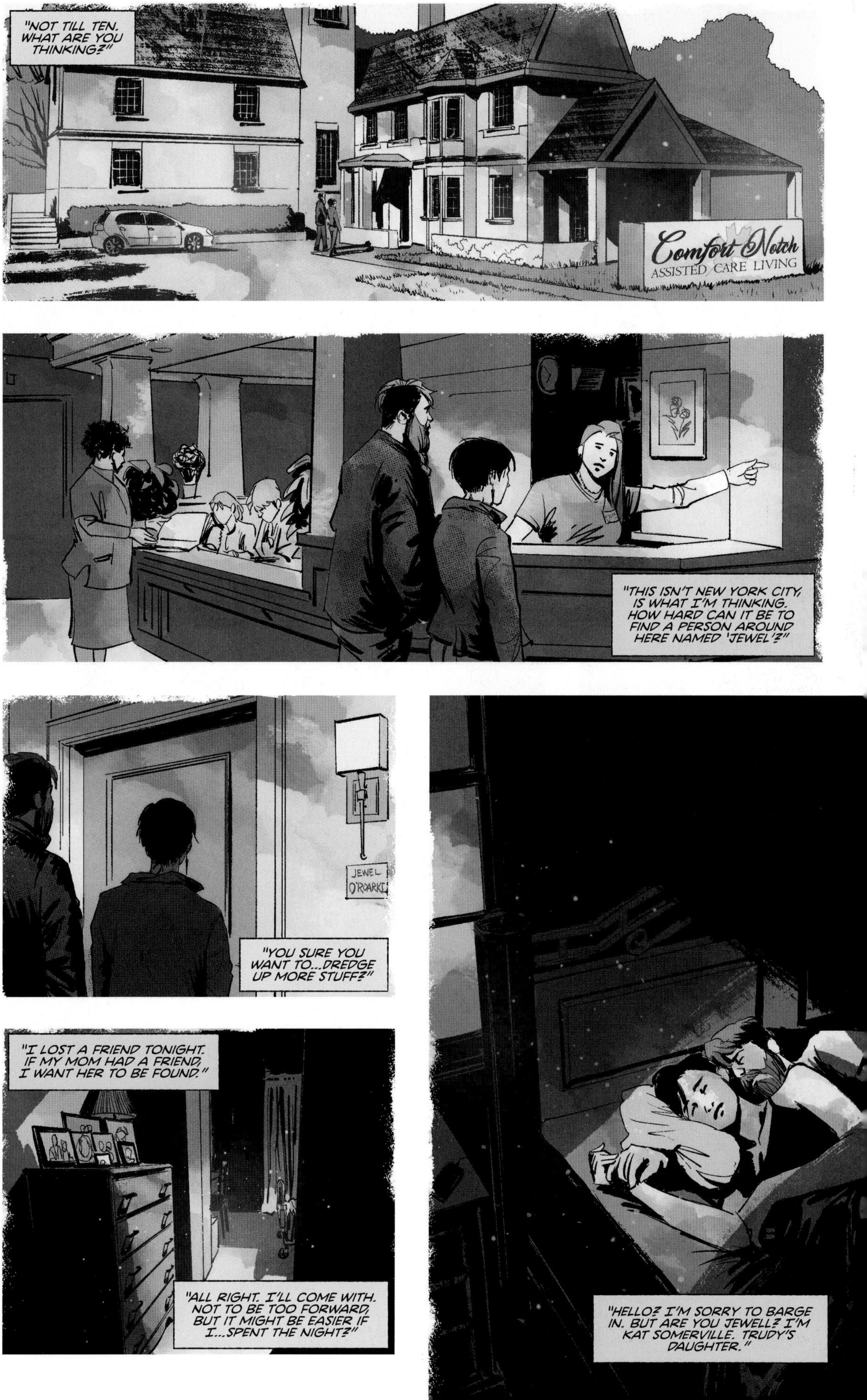
"NOT TILL TEN. WHAT ARE YOU THINKING?"
Comfort Notch
ASSISTED CARE LIVING
"THIS ISN'T NEW YORK CITY, IS WHAT I'M THINKING. HOW HARD CAN IT BE TO FIND A PERSON AROUND HERE NAMED 'JEWEL'?"
JEWEL O'ROARKE
"YOU SURE YOU WANT TO...DREDGE UP MORE STUFF?"
"I LOST A FRIEND TONIGHT. IF MY MOM HAD A FRIEND, I WANT HER TO BE FOUND."
"ALL RIGHT. I'LL COME WITH. NOT TO BE TOO FORWARD, BUT IT MIGHT BE EASIER IF I...SPENT THE NIGHT?"
"HELLO? I'M SORRY TO BARGE IN. BUT ARE YOU JEWELL? I'M KAT SOMERVILLE. TRUDY'S DAUGHTER."

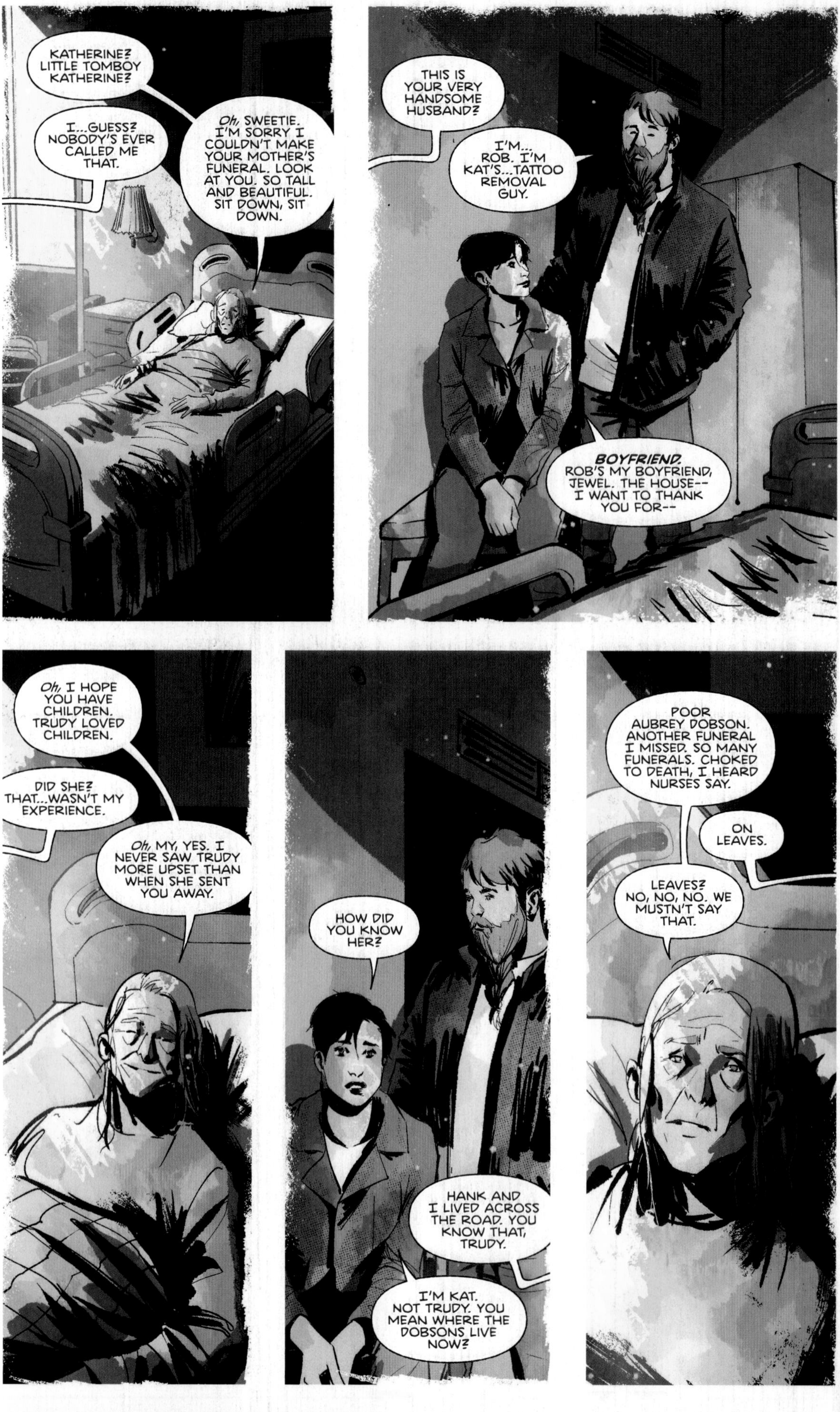
KATHERINE? LITTLE TOMBOY KATHERINE?
I...GUESS? NOBODY'S EVER CALLED ME THAT.
Oh, SWEETIE. I'M SORRY I COULDN'T MAKE YOUR MOTHER'S FUNERAL. LOOK AT YOU. SO TALL AND BEAUTIFUL. SIT DOWN, SIT DOWN.
THIS IS YOUR VERY HANDSOME HUSBAND?
I'M... ROB. I'M KAT'S...TATTOO REMOVAL GUY.
BOYFRIEND. ROB'S MY BOYFRIEND, JEWEL. THE HOUSE-- I WANT TO THANK YOU FOR--
Oh, I HOPE YOU HAVE CHILDREN. TRUDY LOVED CHILDREN.
DID SHE? THAT...WASN'T MY EXPERIENCE.
Oh, MY, YES. I NEVER SAW TRUDY MORE UPSET THAN WHEN SHE SENT YOU AWAY.
HOW DID YOU KNOW HER?
HANK AND I LIVED ACROSS THE ROAD. YOU KNOW THAT, TRUDY.
I'M KAT. NOT TRUDY. YOU MEAN WHERE THE DOBSONS LIVE NOW?
POOR AUBREY DOBSON. ANOTHER FUNERAL I MISSED. SO MANY FUNERALS. CHOKED TO DEATH, I HEARD NURSES SAY.
ON LEAVES.
LEAVES? NO, NO, NO. WE MUSTN'T SAY THAT.

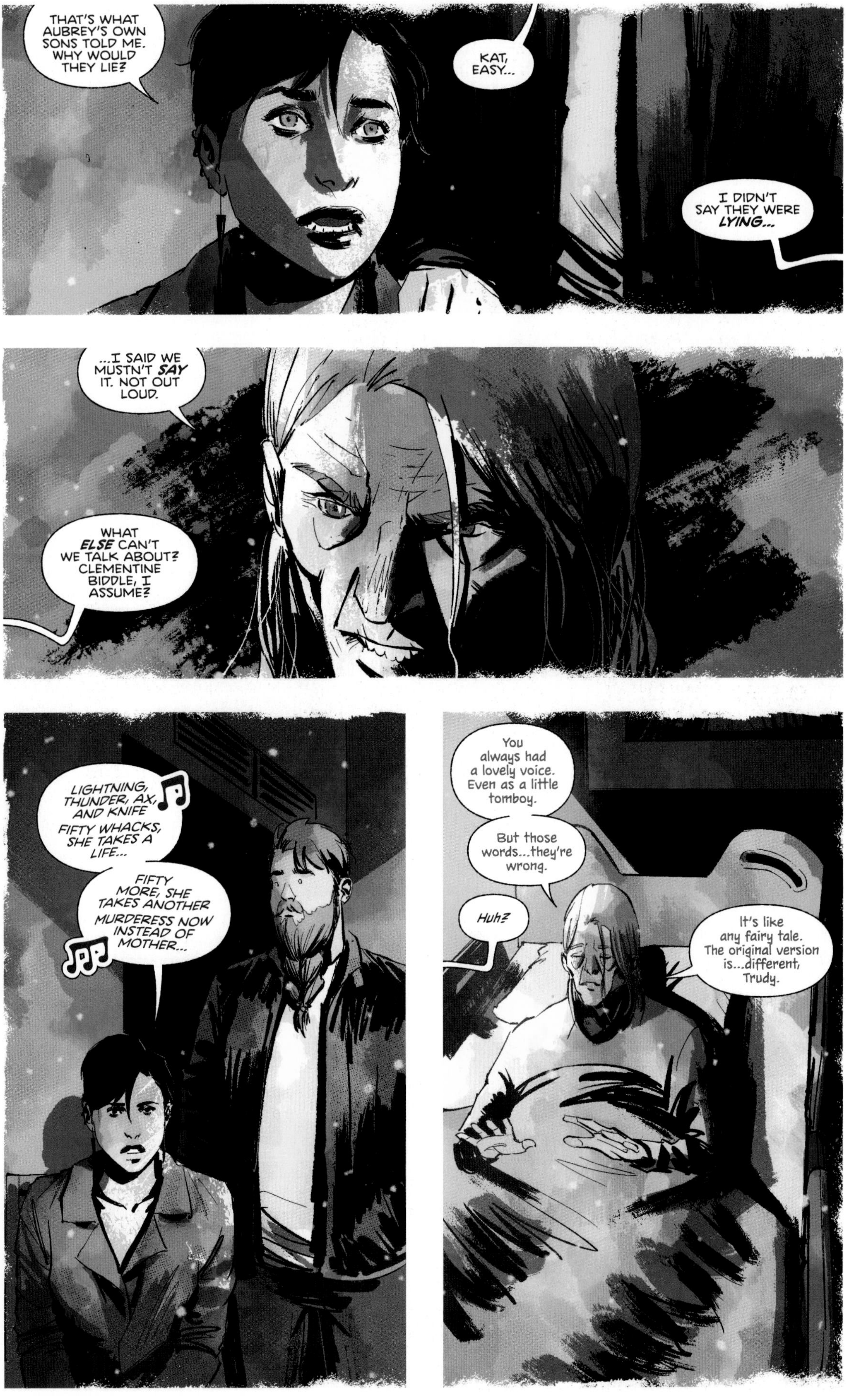
THAT'S WHAT AUBREY'S OWN SONS TOLD ME. WHY WOULD THEY LIE?
KAT, EASY...
I DIDN'T SAY THEY WERE LYING...
...I SAID WE MUSTN'T SAY IT. NOT OUT LOUD.
WHAT ELSE CAN'T WE TALK ABOUT? CLEMENTINE BIDDLE, I ASSUME?
LIGHTNING, THUNDER, AX, AND KNIFE
FIFTY WHACKS, SHE TAKES A LIFE...
FIFTY MORE, SHE TAKES ANOTHER
MURDERESS NOW INSTEAD OF MOTHER...
You always had a lovely voice. Even as a little tomboy.
But those words...they're wrong.
Huh?
It's like any fairy tale. The original version is...different, Trudy.

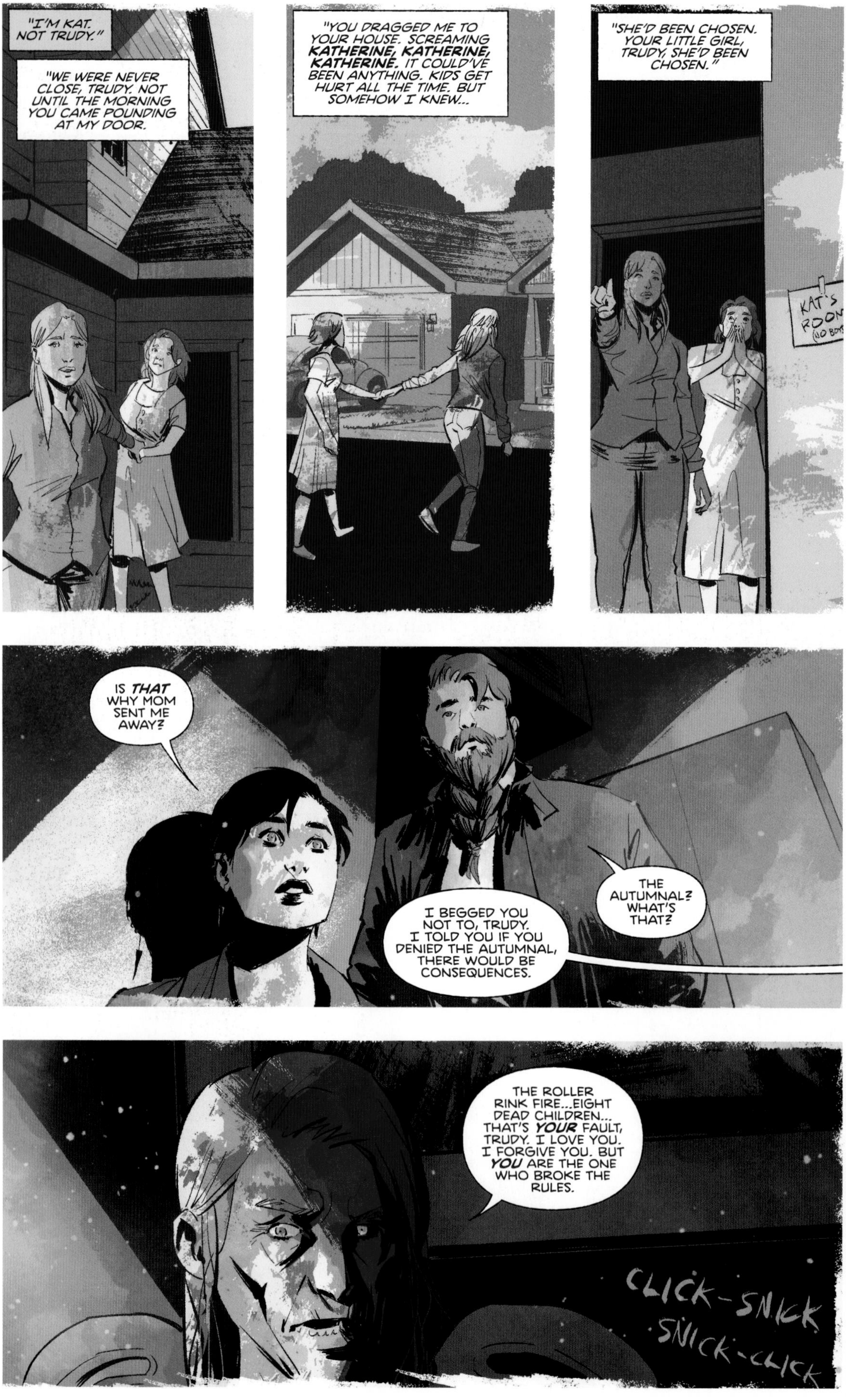
"I'M KAT. NOT TRUDY."
"WE WERE NEVER CLOSE, TRUDY. NOT UNTIL THE MORNING YOU CAME POUNDING AT MY DOOR.
"YOU DRAGGED ME TO YOUR HOUSE. SCREAMING ***KATHERINE, KATHERINE, KATHERINE.*** IT COULD'VE BEEN ANYTHING. KIDS GET HURT ALL THE TIME. BUT SOMEHOW I KNEW...
"SHE'D BEEN CHOSEN. YOUR LITTLE GIRL, TRUDY, SHE'D BEEN CHOSEN."
KAT'S
IS ***THAT*** WHY MOM SENT ME AWAY?
I BEGGED YOU NOT TO, TRUDY. I TOLD YOU IF YOU DENIED THE AUTUMNAL, THERE WOULD BE CONSEQUENCES.
THE AUTUMNAL? WHAT'S THAT?
THE ROLLER RINK FIRE...EIGHT DEAD CHILDREN... THAT'S ***YOUR*** FAULT, TRUDY. I LOVE YOU. I FORGIVE YOU. BUT ***YOU*** ARE THE ONE WHO BROKE THE RULES.
CLICK-SNICK SNICK-CLICK

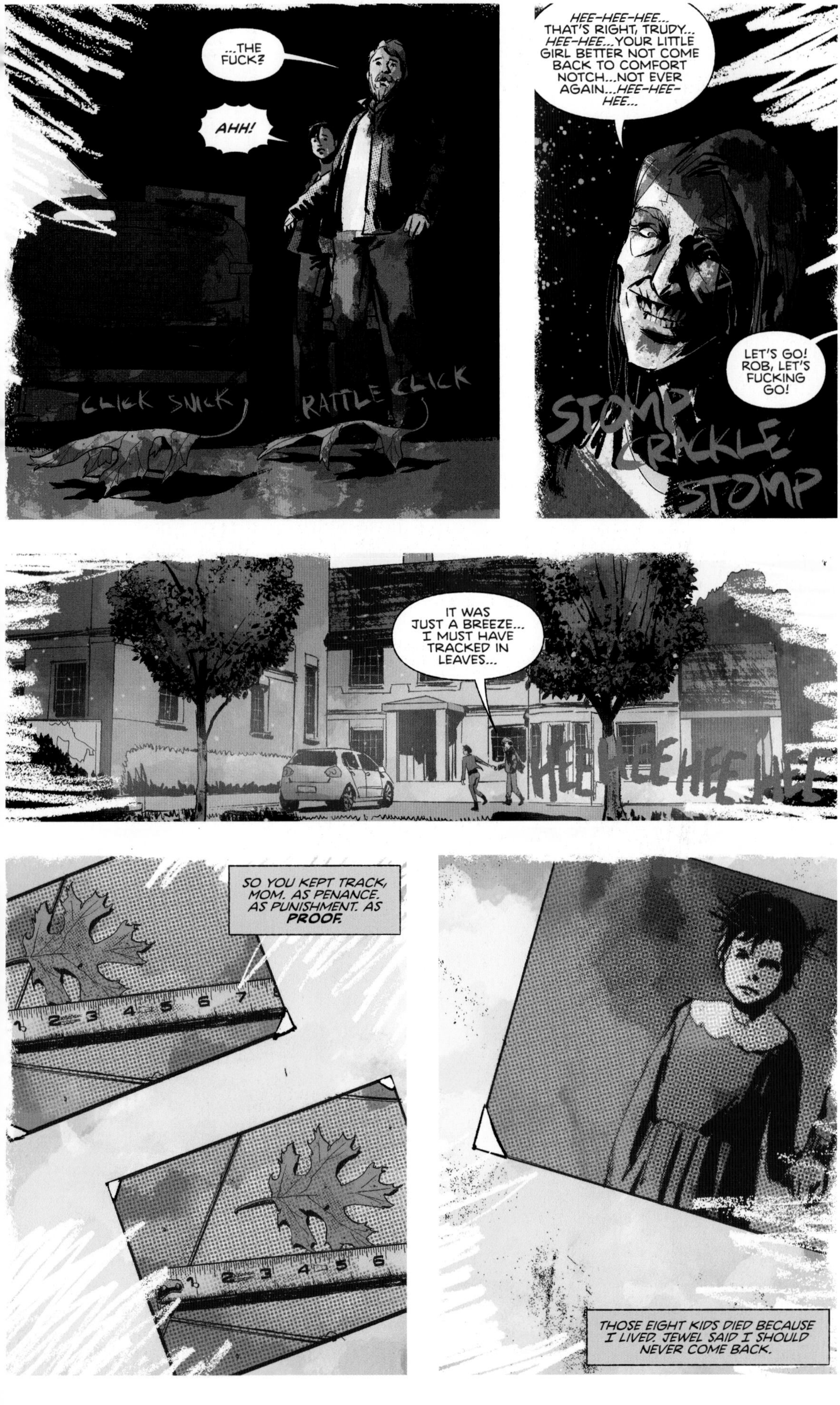
...THE FUCK?
AHH!
CLICK SNICK
RATTLE CLICK
HEE-HEE-HEE... THAT'S RIGHT, TRUDY... HEE-HEE... YOUR LITTLE GIRL BETTER NOT COME BACK TO COMFORT NOTCH...NOT EVER AGAIN...HEE-HEE-HEE...
LET'S GO! ROB, LET'S FUCKING GO!
STOMP
CRACKLE
STOMP
IT WAS JUST A BREEZE... I MUST HAVE TRACKED IN LEAVES...
HEE HEE HEE HEE
SO YOU KEPT TRACK, MOM. AS PENANCE. AS PUNISHMENT. AS PROOF.
THOSE EIGHT KIDS DIED BECAUSE I LIVED. JEWEL SAID I SHOULD NEVER COME BACK.

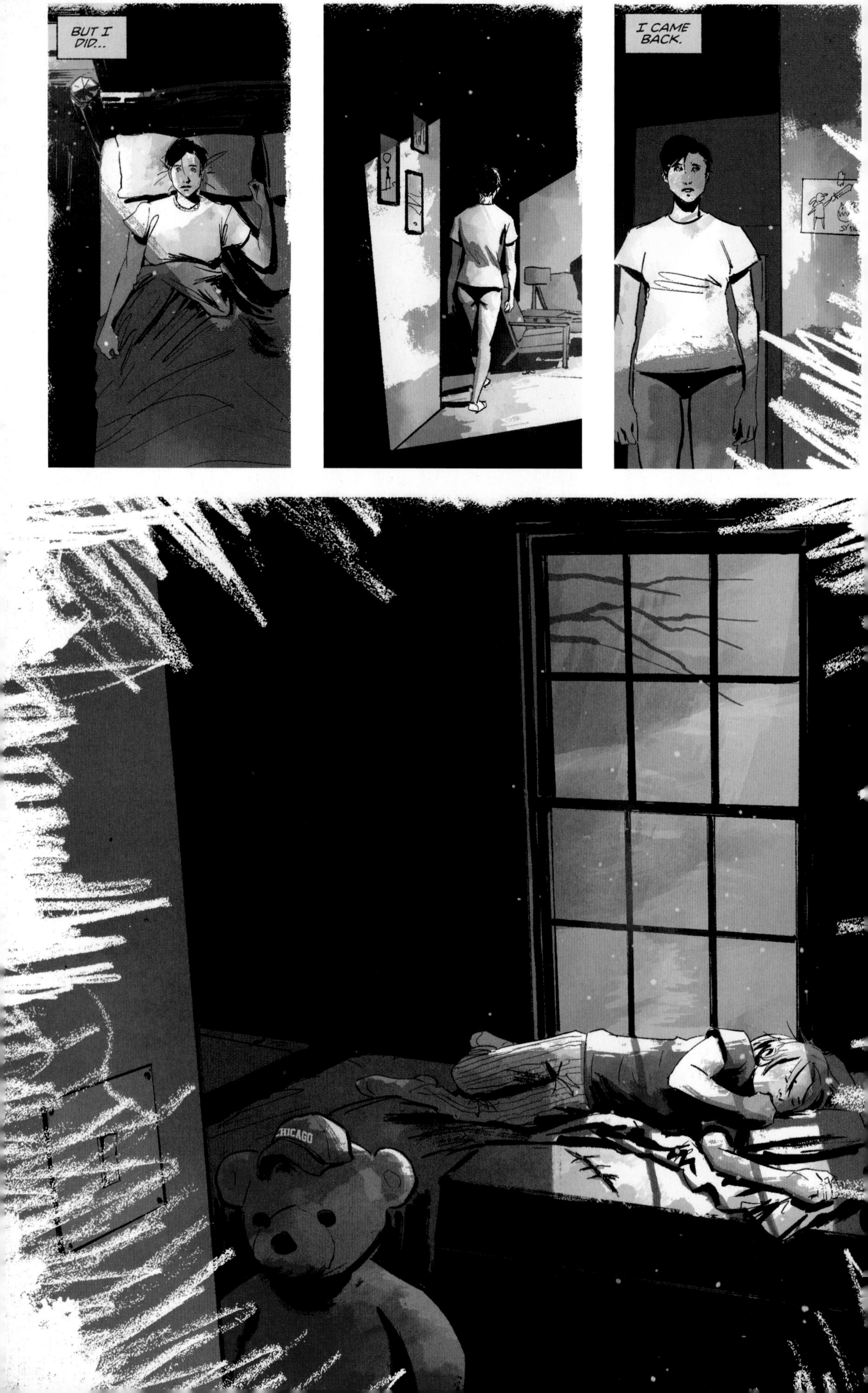
BUT I DID...
I CAME BACK.
CHICAGO

there

CHAPTER
SIX

YOU KNOW MY FRIEND MARTHA WHO WORKS AT WENDY'S? WELL, HER BROTHER, BARRY, IS MARRIED TO LUCY ABRAMS.
WHO'S COUSINS WITH JACKSON ABRAMS, THE MAIL CARRIER?
EXACTLY. AND *JACKSON* DELIVERS MAIL TO *BURGESS FUNERAL HOME.* APPARENTLY HE GOT A GLIMPSE OF CAROL RAVINTZKY'S BODY.
CRUEL GOSSIPS. THEY FOLLOW YOU YOUR WHOLE LIFE.
LIKE ANYONE'S GOING TO CAROL RAVINTZKY'S FUNERAL. THAT'S ABSURD.
WHAT MARTHA SAID BARRY SAID *JACKSON* SAID IS THAT-- GET READY FOR THIS-- ONE OF THE HOLES ON CAROL'S ARMS? YOU KNOW, THE DRUG-NEEDLE HOLES? THERE WAS A *LEAF* POKING FROM IT.
COLD MOUNTAIN
GOOD OMENS
NEIL GAIMAN
*NO MORE MISTRESS EXPLOSION DESTROYER-- NOT FOR SYBIL, AND NOT FOR ME. IN A QUIET TOWN, YOU LEARN TO **KEEP** QUIET. TO LISTEN. TO LET **THEM** EXPOSE **THEMSELVES.***
RIGHT BEFORE JACKSON LEFT, HE SAW BETTY BURGESS PULL THAT LEAF. YOU KNOW, TO GET IT OUT. BUT WHEN SHE PULLED...
WHAT?!
STAY CALM, KAT. STAY CALM.

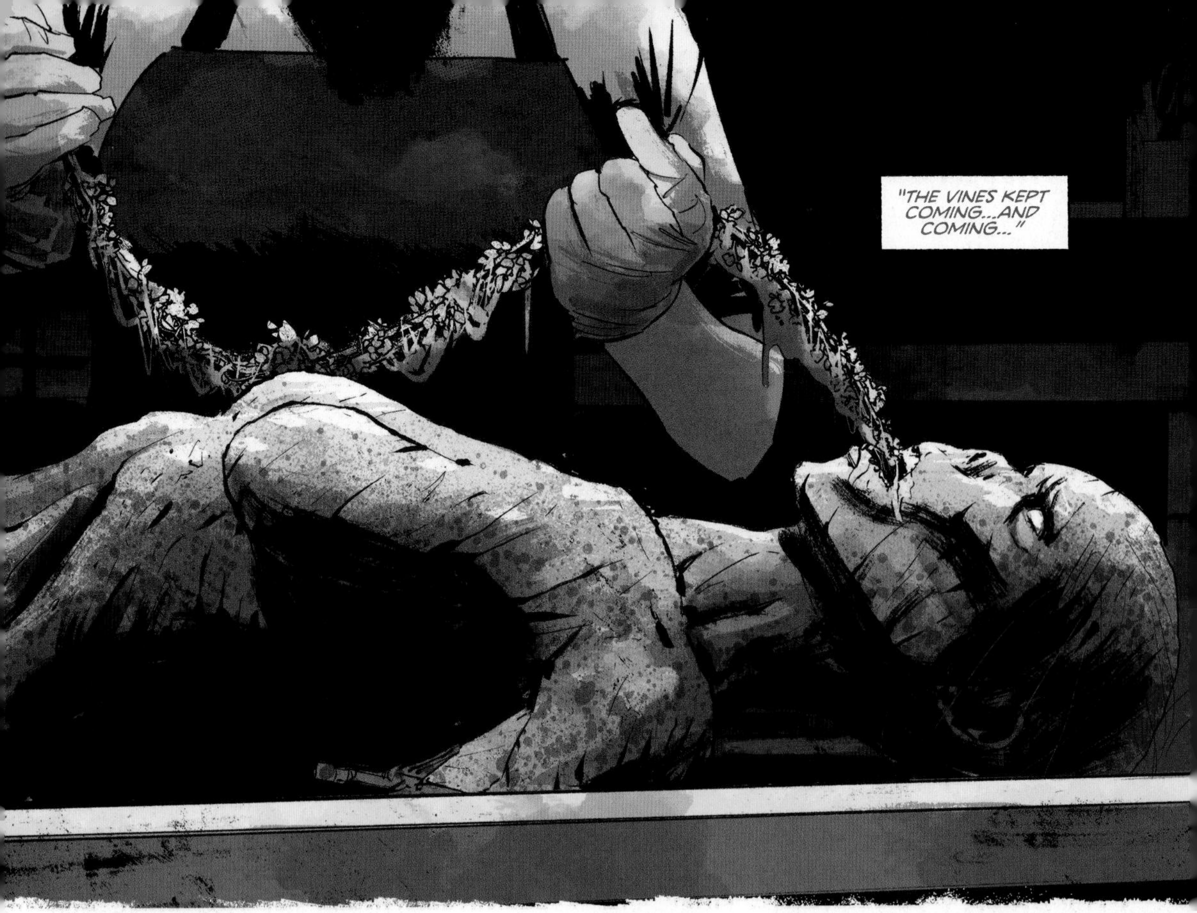
"THE VINES KEPT COMING...AND COMING..."

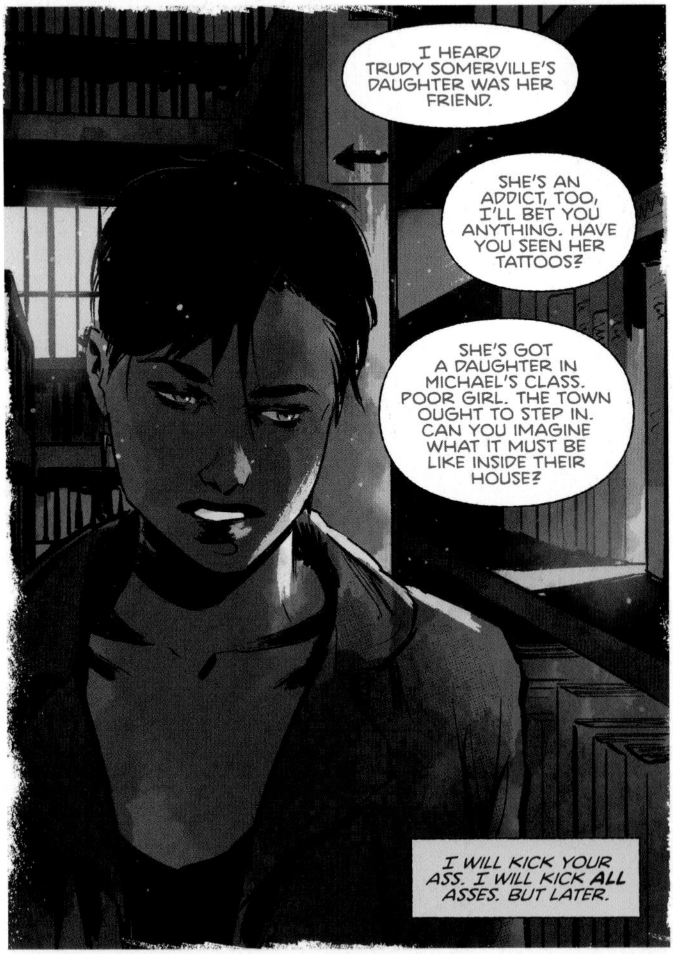
I HEARD TRUDY SOMERVILLE'S DAUGHTER WAS HER FRIEND.
SHE'S AN ADDICT, TOO, I'LL BET YOU ANYTHING. HAVE YOU SEEN HER TATTOOS?
SHE'S GOT A DAUGHTER IN MICHAEL'S CLASS. POOR GIRL. THE TOWN OUGHT TO STEP IN. CAN YOU IMAGINE WHAT IT MUST BE LIKE INSIDE THEIR HOUSE?
I WILL KICK YOUR ASS. I WILL KICK ALL ASSES. BUT LATER.

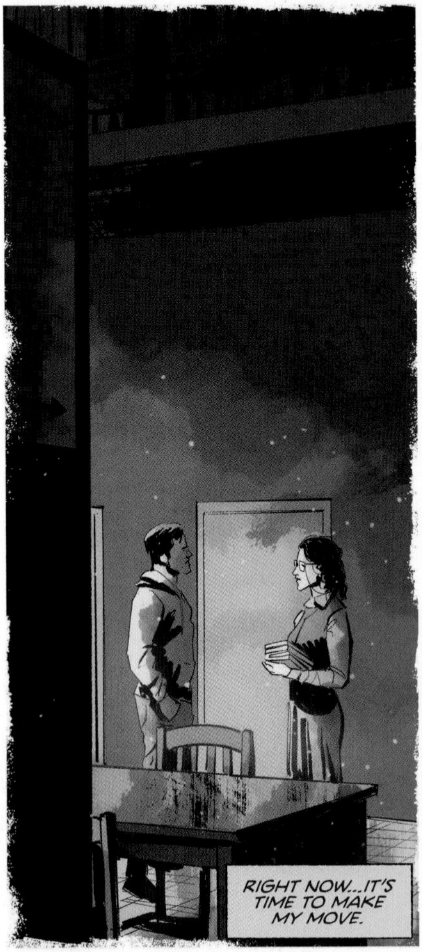
RIGHT NOW...IT'S TIME TO MAKE MY MOVE.

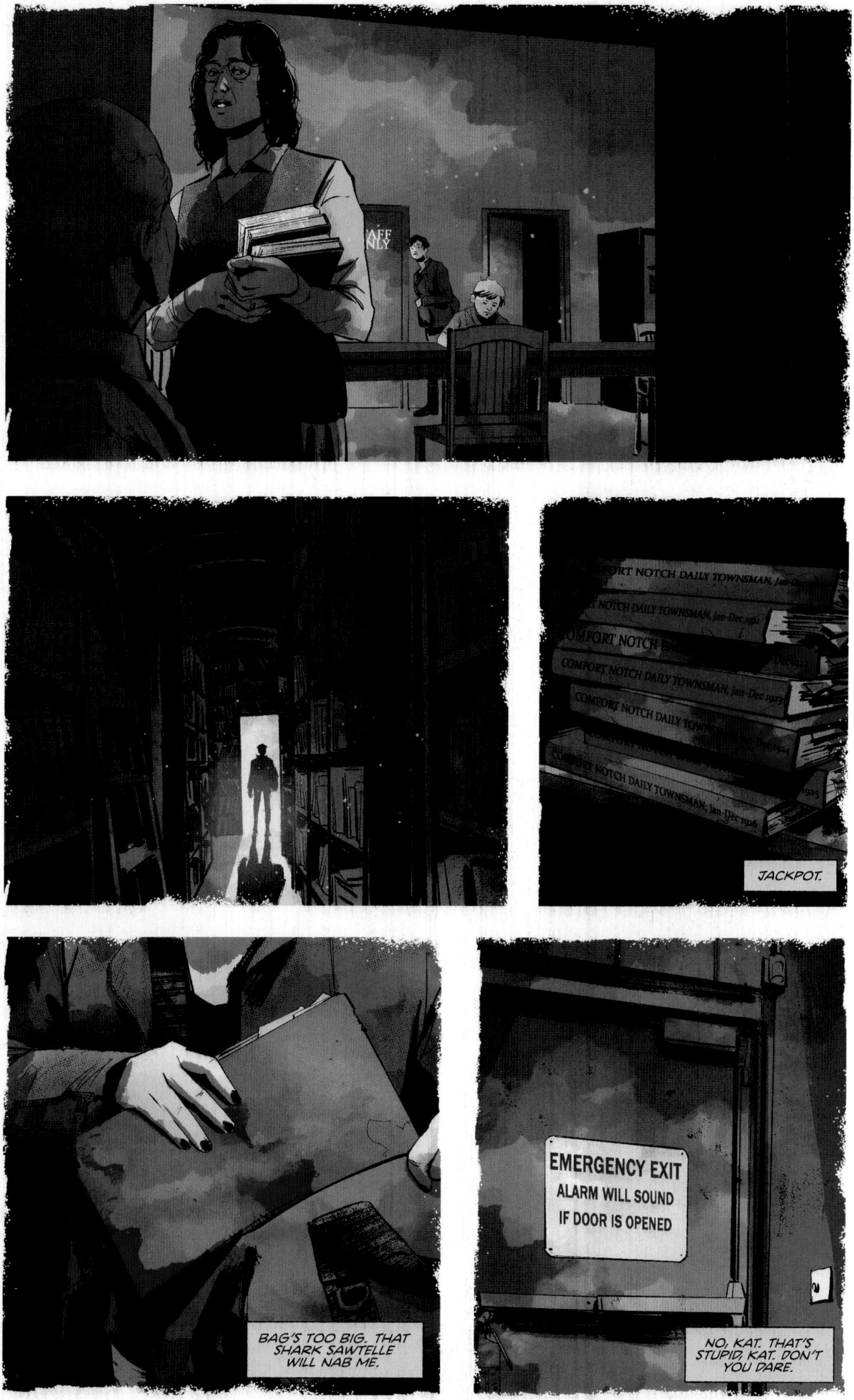
JACKPOT.
BAG'S TOO BIG. THAT SHARK SAWTELLE WILL NAB ME.
EMERGENCY EXIT
ALARM WILL SOUND
IF DOOR IS OPENED
NO, KAT. THAT'S STUPID, KAT. DON'T YOU DARE.

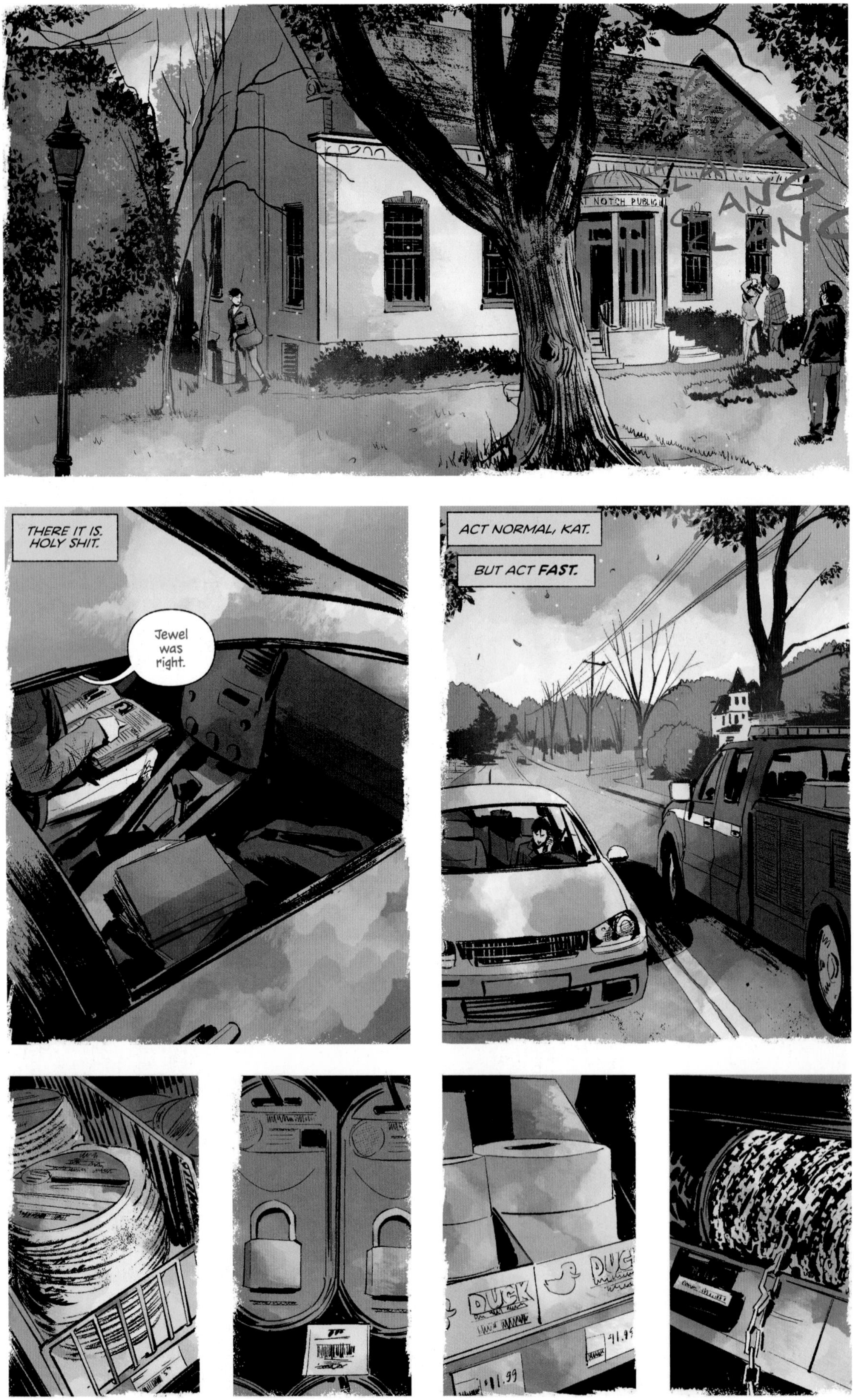
THERE IT IS. HOLY SHIT.
Jewel was right.
ACT NORMAL, KAT.
BUT ACT **FAST.**
DUCK

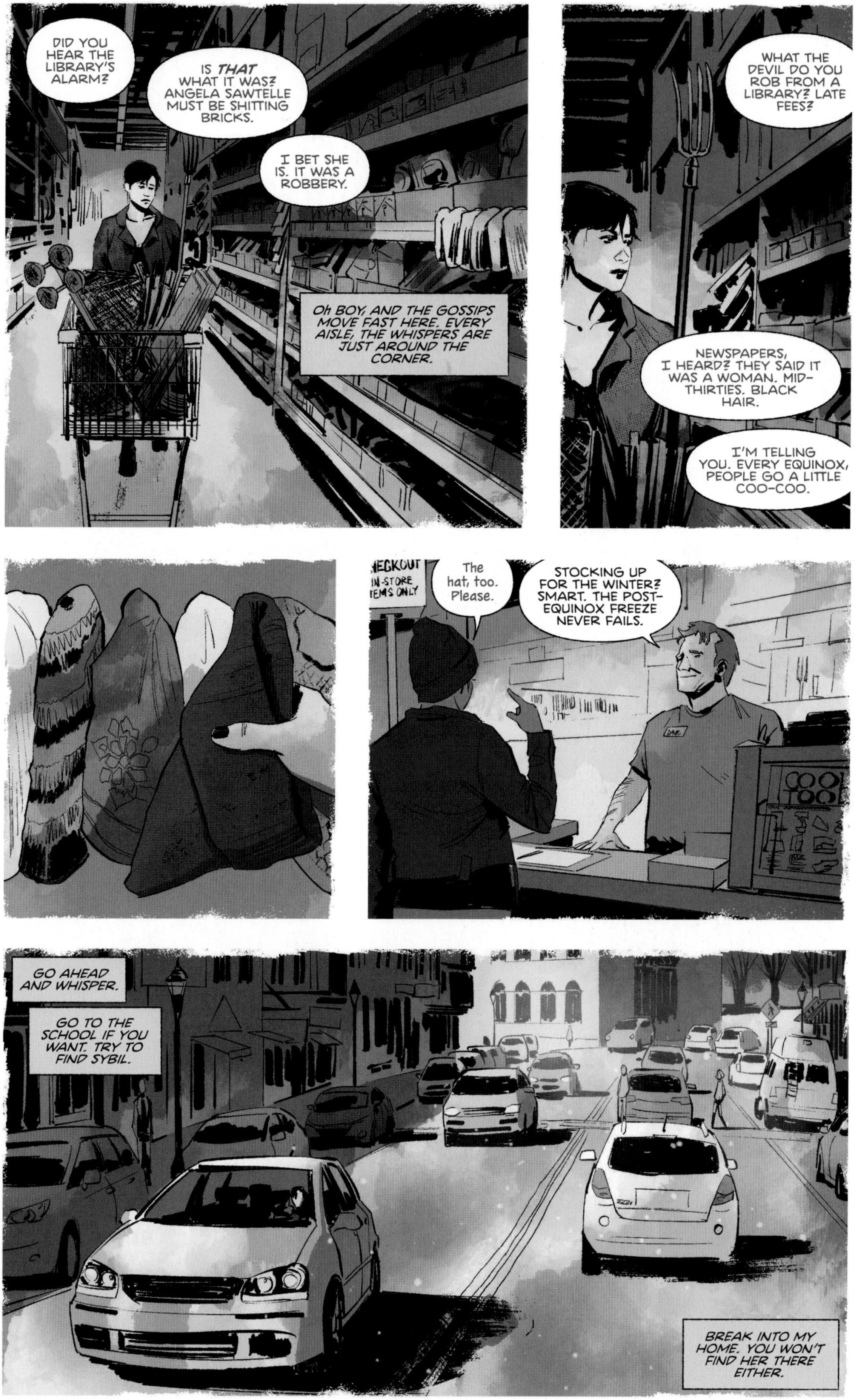
DID YOU HEAR THE LIBRARY'S ALARM?
IS *THAT* WHAT IT WAS? ANGELA SAWTELLE MUST BE SHITTING BRICKS.
I BET SHE IS. IT WAS A ROBBERY.
Oh BOY, AND THE GOSSIPS MOVE FAST HERE. EVERY AISLE, THE WHISPERS ARE JUST AROUND THE CORNER.
WHAT THE DEVIL DO YOU ROB FROM A LIBRARY? LATE FEES?
NEWSPAPERS, I HEARD? THEY SAID IT WAS A WOMAN. MID-THIRTIES. BLACK HAIR.
I'M TELLING YOU. EVERY EQUINOX, PEOPLE GO A LITTLE COO-COO.
ECKOUT
IN-STORE
TEMS ONLY
The hat, too. Please.
STOCKING UP FOR THE WINTER? SMART. THE POST-EQUINOX FREEZE NEVER FAILS.
DAVE
GO AHEAD AND WHISPER.
GO TO THE SCHOOL IF YOU WANT. TRY TO FIND SYBIL.
BREAK INTO MY HOME. YOU WON'T FIND HER THERE EITHER.

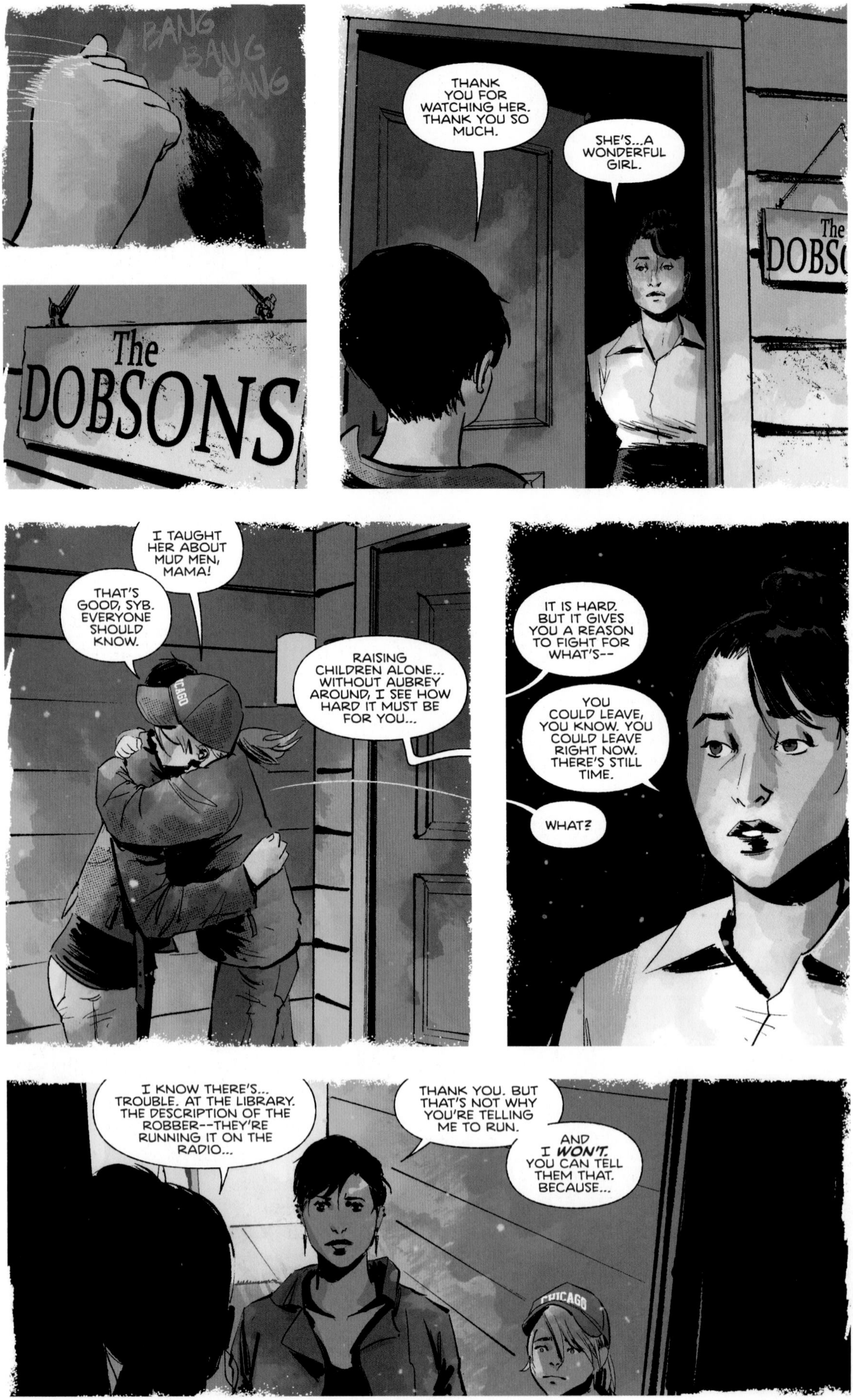
BANG BANG BANG
The DOBSONS
THANK YOU FOR WATCHING HER. THANK YOU SO MUCH.
SHE'S...A WONDERFUL GIRL.
The DOBSONS
I TAUGHT HER ABOUT MUD MEN, MAMA!
THAT'S GOOD, SYB. EVERYONE SHOULD KNOW.
CHICAGO
RAISING CHILDREN ALONE... WITHOUT AUBREY AROUND, I SEE HOW HARD IT MUST BE FOR YOU...
IT IS HARD. BUT IT GIVES YOU A REASON TO FIGHT FOR WHAT'S--
YOU COULD LEAVE, YOU KNOW. YOU COULD LEAVE RIGHT NOW. THERE'S STILL TIME.
WHAT?
I KNOW THERE'S... TROUBLE. AT THE LIBRARY. THE DESCRIPTION OF THE ROBBER--THEY'RE RUNNING IT ON THE RADIO...
THANK YOU. BUT THAT'S NOT WHY YOU'RE TELLING ME TO RUN.
AND I *WON'T.* YOU CAN TELL THEM THAT. BECAUSE...
CHICAGO

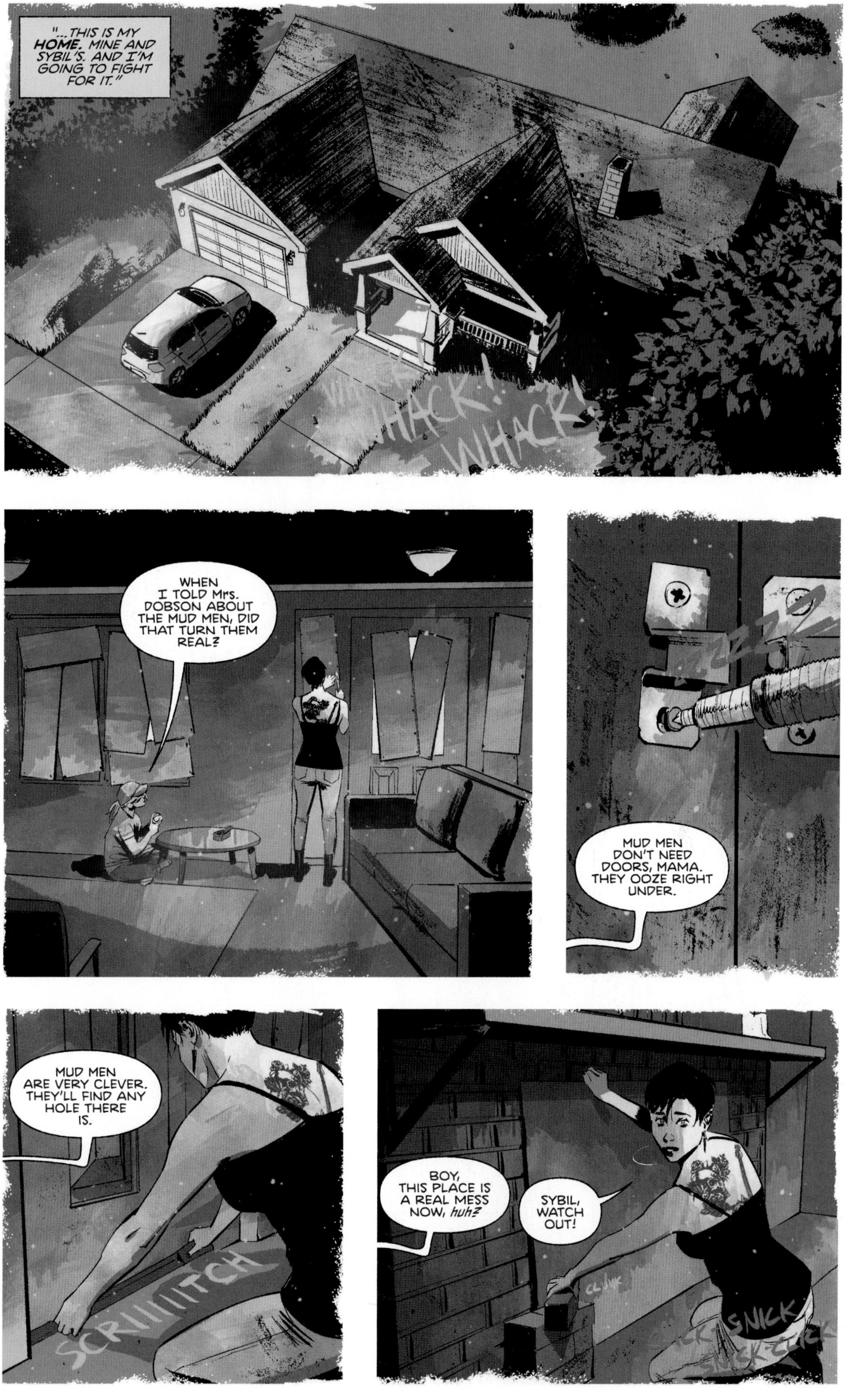
"...THIS IS MY HOME. MINE AND SYBIL'S. AND I'M GOING TO FIGHT FOR IT."
WHACK!
WHACK!
WHEN I TOLD Mrs. DOBSON ABOUT THE MUD MEN, DID THAT TURN THEM REAL?
MUD MEN DON'T NEED DOORS, MAMA. THEY OOZE RIGHT UNDER.
MUD MEN ARE VERY CLEVER. THEY'LL FIND ANY HOLE THERE IS.
SCRIIIITCH
BOY, THIS PLACE IS A REAL MESS NOW, huh?
SYBIL, WATCH OUT!
CLUNK
SNICK

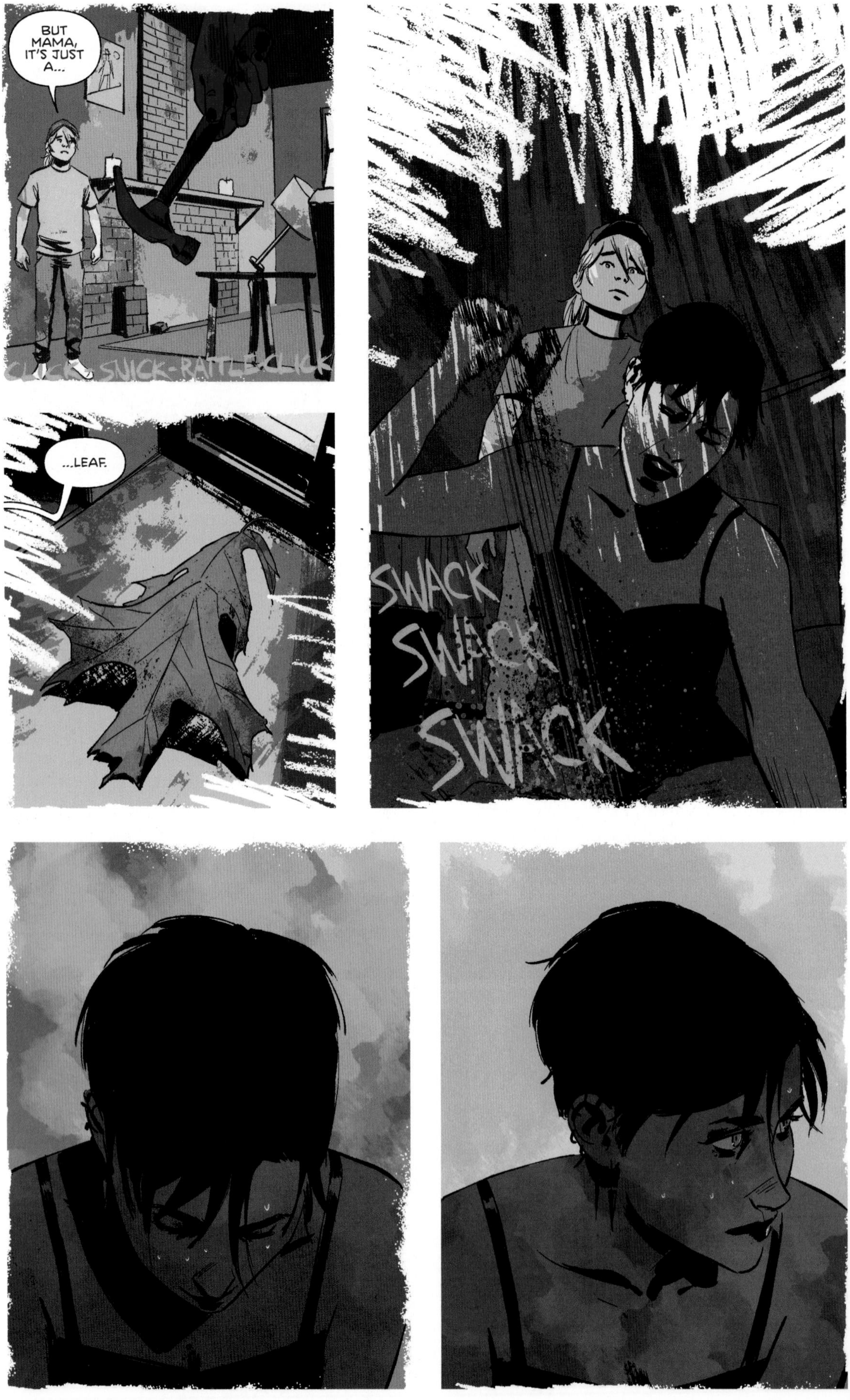
BUT MAMA, IT'S JUST A...
CLICK SNICK-RATTLE-CLICK
...LEAF.
SWACK
SWACK
SWACK

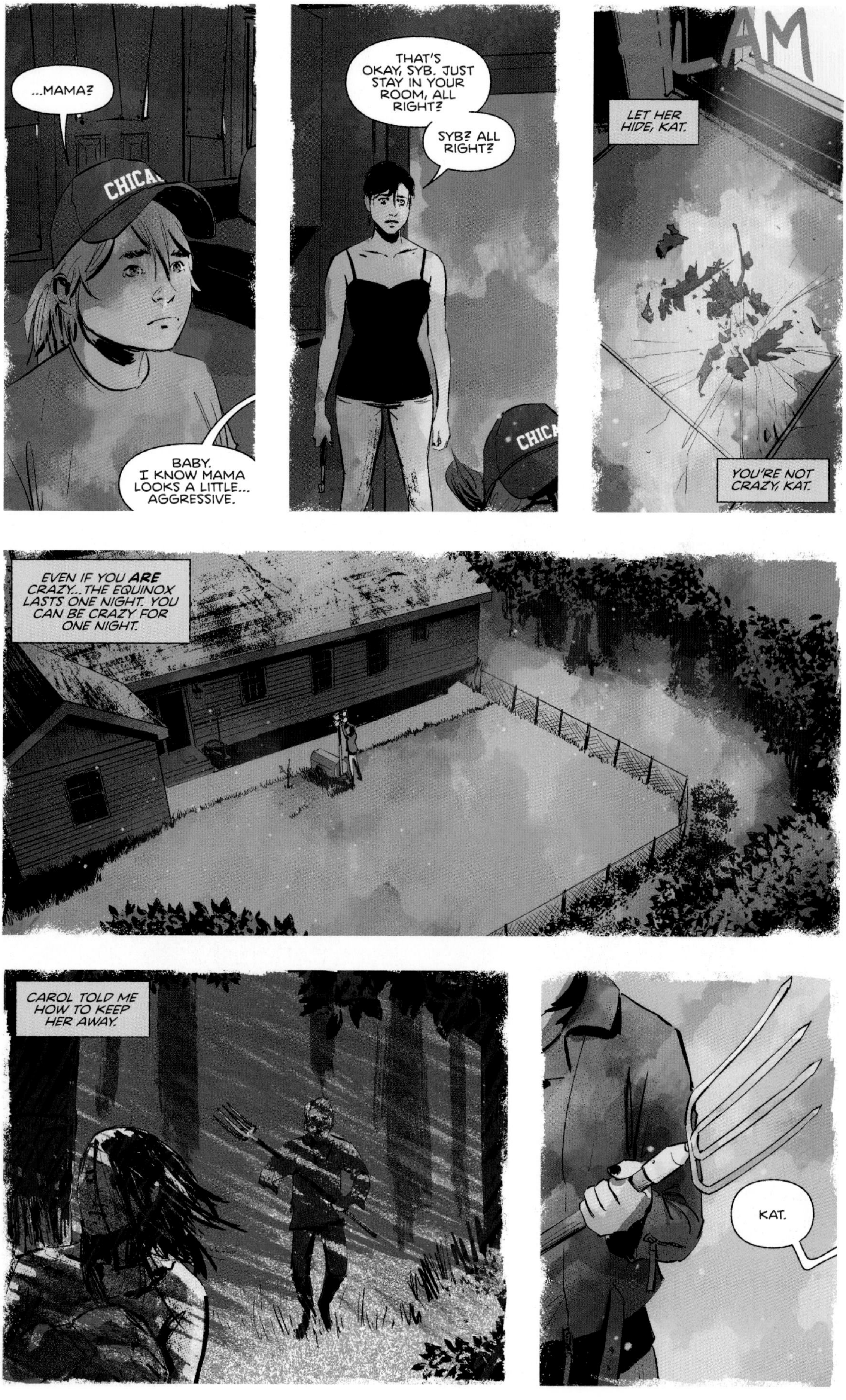
...MAMA?
BABY. I KNOW MAMA LOOKS A LITTLE... AGGRESSIVE.
THAT'S OKAY, SYB. JUST STAY IN YOUR ROOM, ALL RIGHT?
SYB? ALL RIGHT?
SLAM
LET HER HIDE, KAT.
YOU'RE NOT CRAZY, KAT.
EVEN IF YOU **ARE** CRAZY... THE EQUINOX LASTS ONE NIGHT. YOU CAN BE CRAZY FOR ONE NIGHT.
CAROL TOLD ME HOW TO KEEP HER AWAY.
KAT.

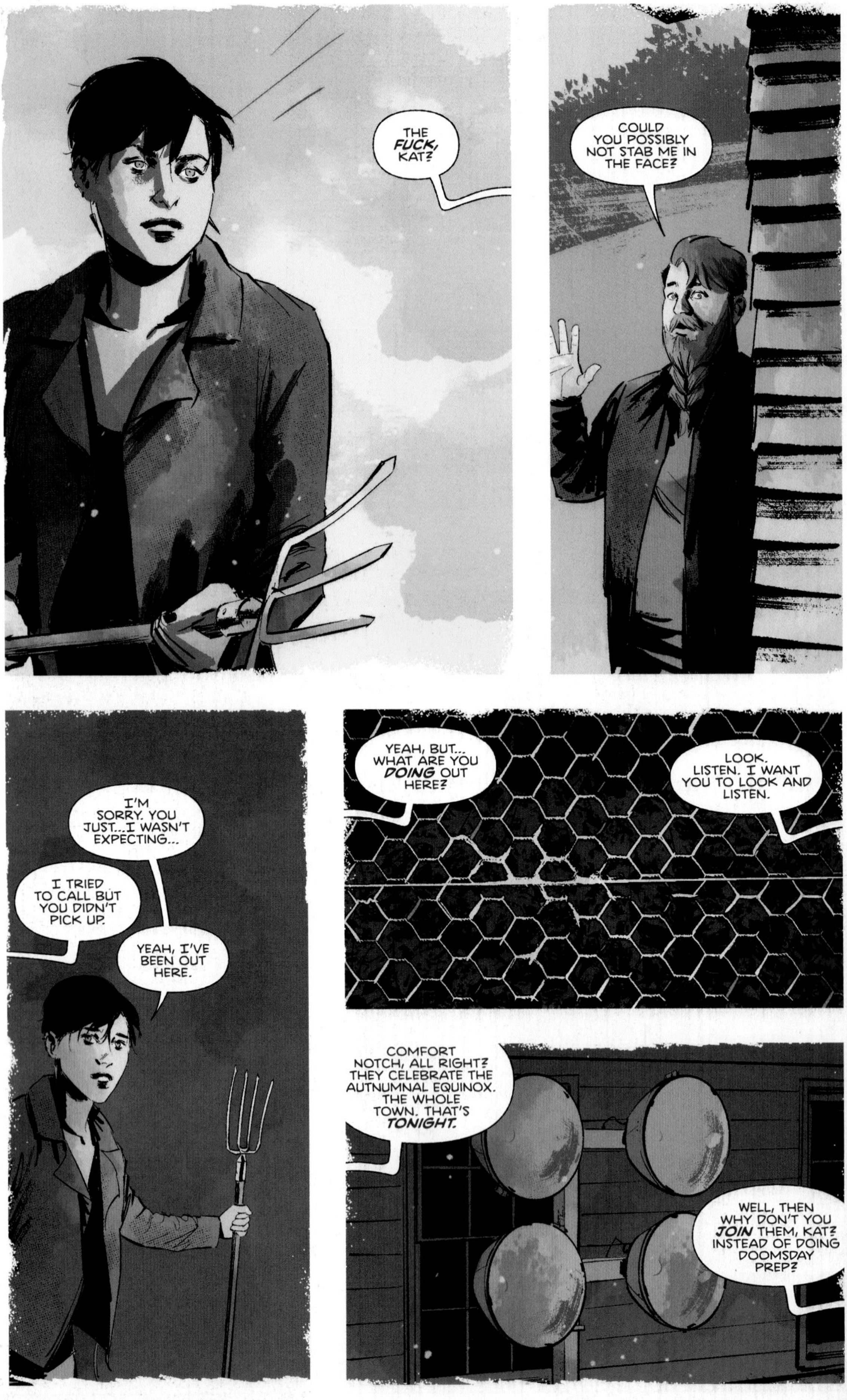
THE *FUCK*, KAT?
COULD YOU POSSIBLY NOT STAB ME IN THE FACE?
I'M SORRY. YOU JUST...I WASN'T EXPECTING...
I TRIED TO CALL BUT YOU DIDN'T PICK UP.
YEAH, I'VE BEEN OUT HERE.
YEAH, BUT... WHAT ARE YOU *DOING* OUT HERE?
LOOK. LISTEN. I WANT YOU TO LOOK AND LISTEN.
COMFORT NOTCH, ALL RIGHT? THEY CELEBRATE THE AUTNUMNAL EQUINOX. THE WHOLE TOWN. THAT'S *TONIGHT.*
WELL, THEN WHY DON'T YOU *JOIN* THEM, KAT? INSTEAD OF DOING DOOMSDAY PREP?

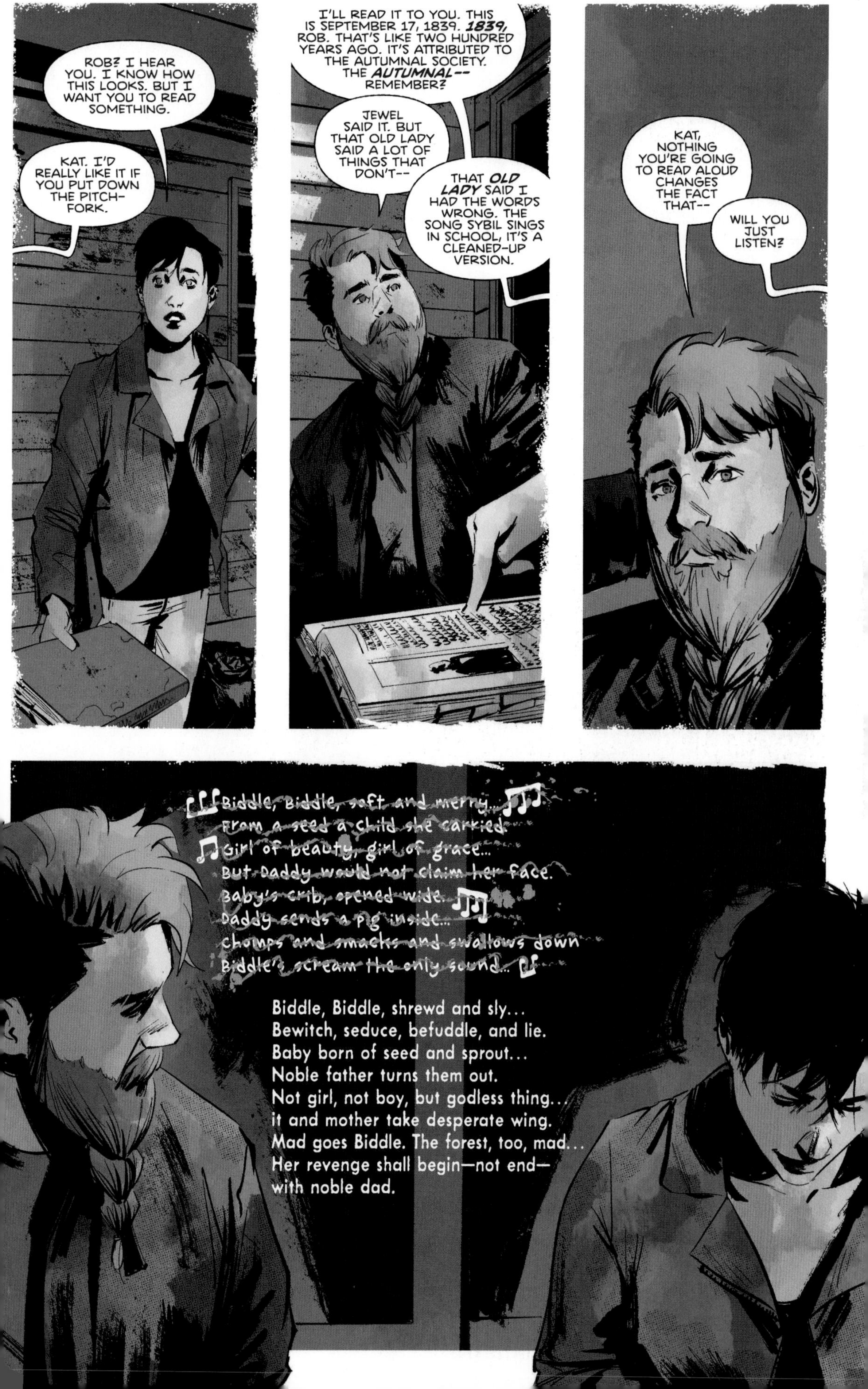
ROB? I HEAR YOU. I KNOW HOW THIS LOOKS. BUT I WANT YOU TO READ SOMETHING.
KAT. I'D REALLY LIKE IT IF YOU PUT DOWN THE PITCH-FORK.
I'LL READ IT TO YOU. THIS IS SEPTEMBER 17, 1839. *1839,* ROB. THAT'S LIKE TWO HUNDRED YEARS AGO. IT'S ATTRIBUTED TO THE AUTUMNAL SOCIETY. THE *AUTUMNAL--* REMEMBER?
JEWEL SAID IT. BUT THAT OLD LADY SAID A LOT OF THINGS THAT DON'T--
THAT *OLD LADY* SAID I HAD THE WORDS WRONG. THE SONG SYBIL SINGS IN SCHOOL, IT'S A CLEANED-UP VERSION.
KAT, NOTHING YOU'RE GOING TO READ ALOUD CHANGES THE FACT THAT--
WILL YOU JUST LISTEN?
Biddle, Biddle, soft and merry...
From a seed a child she carried.
Girl of beauty, girl of grace...
But Daddy would not claim her face.
Baby's crib, opened wide.
Daddy sends a pig inside...
Chomps and smacks and swallows down
Biddle's scream the only sound...
Biddle, Biddle, shrewd and sly...
Bewitch, seduce, befuddle, and lie.
Baby born of seed and sprout...
Noble father turns them out.
Not girl, not boy, but godless thing...
it and mother take desperate wing.
Mad goes Biddle. The forest, too, mad...
Her revenge shall begin—not end—
with noble dad.

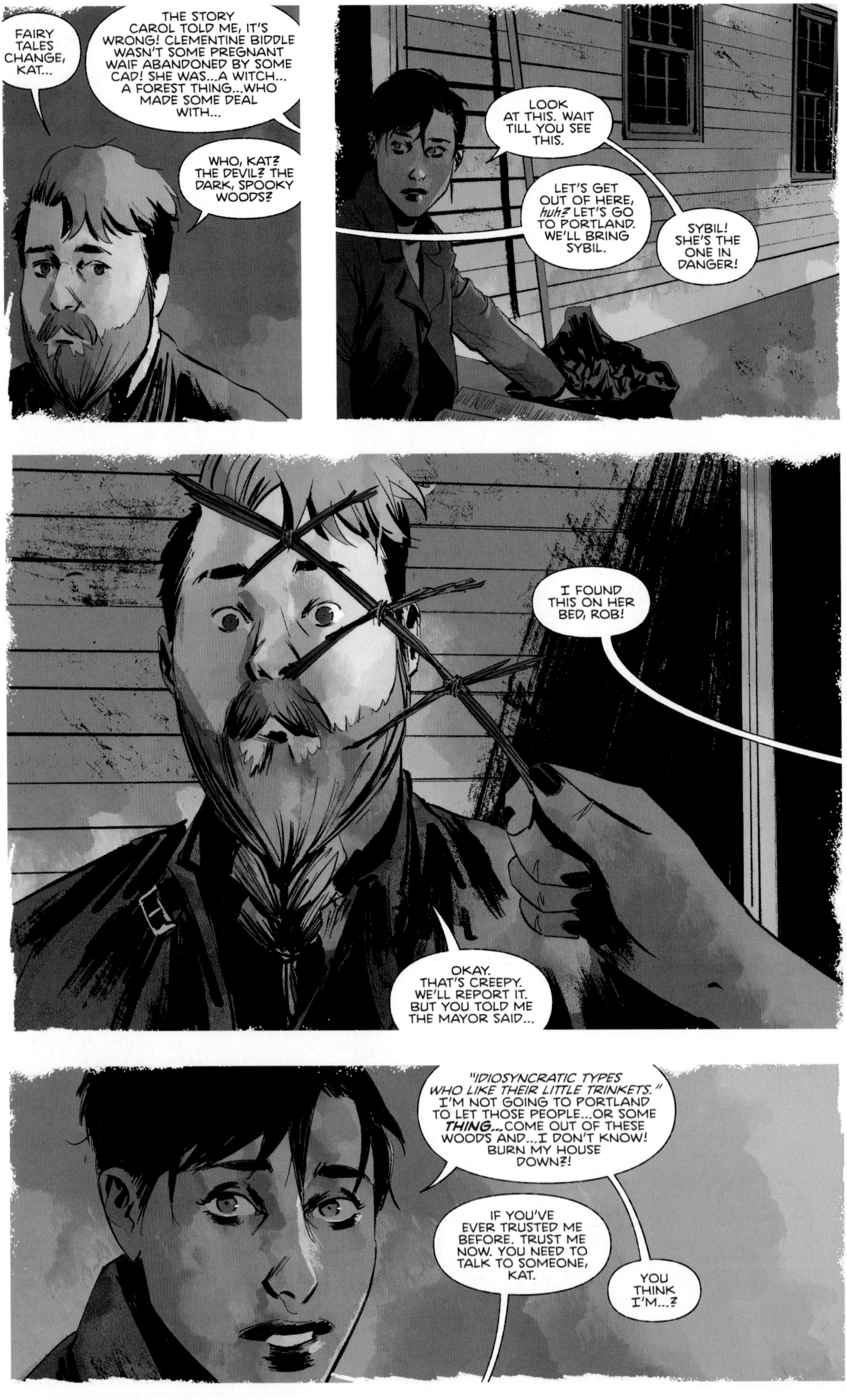
FAIRY TALES CHANGE, KAT...
THE STORY CAROL TOLD ME, IT'S WRONG! CLEMENTINE BIDDLE WASN'T SOME PREGNANT WAIF ABANDONED BY SOME CAD! SHE WAS...A WITCH... A FOREST THING...WHO MADE SOME DEAL WITH...
WHO, KAT? THE DEVIL? THE DARK, SPOOKY WOODS?
LOOK AT THIS. WAIT TILL YOU SEE THIS.
LET'S GET OUT OF HERE, *HUH?* LET'S GO TO PORTLAND. WE'LL BRING SYBIL.
SYBIL! SHE'S THE ONE IN DANGER!
I FOUND THIS ON HER BED, ROB!
OKAY. THAT'S CREEPY. WE'LL REPORT IT. BUT YOU TOLD ME THE MAYOR SAID...
"IDIOSYNCRATIC TYPES WHO LIKE THEIR LITTLE TRINKETS." I'M NOT GOING TO PORTLAND TO LET THOSE PEOPLE...OR SOME ***THING...*** COME OUT OF THESE WOODS AND...I DON'T KNOW! BURN MY HOUSE DOWN?!
IF YOU'VE EVER TRUSTED ME BEFORE. TRUST ME NOW. YOU NEED TO TALK TO SOMEONE, KAT.
YOU THINK I'M...?

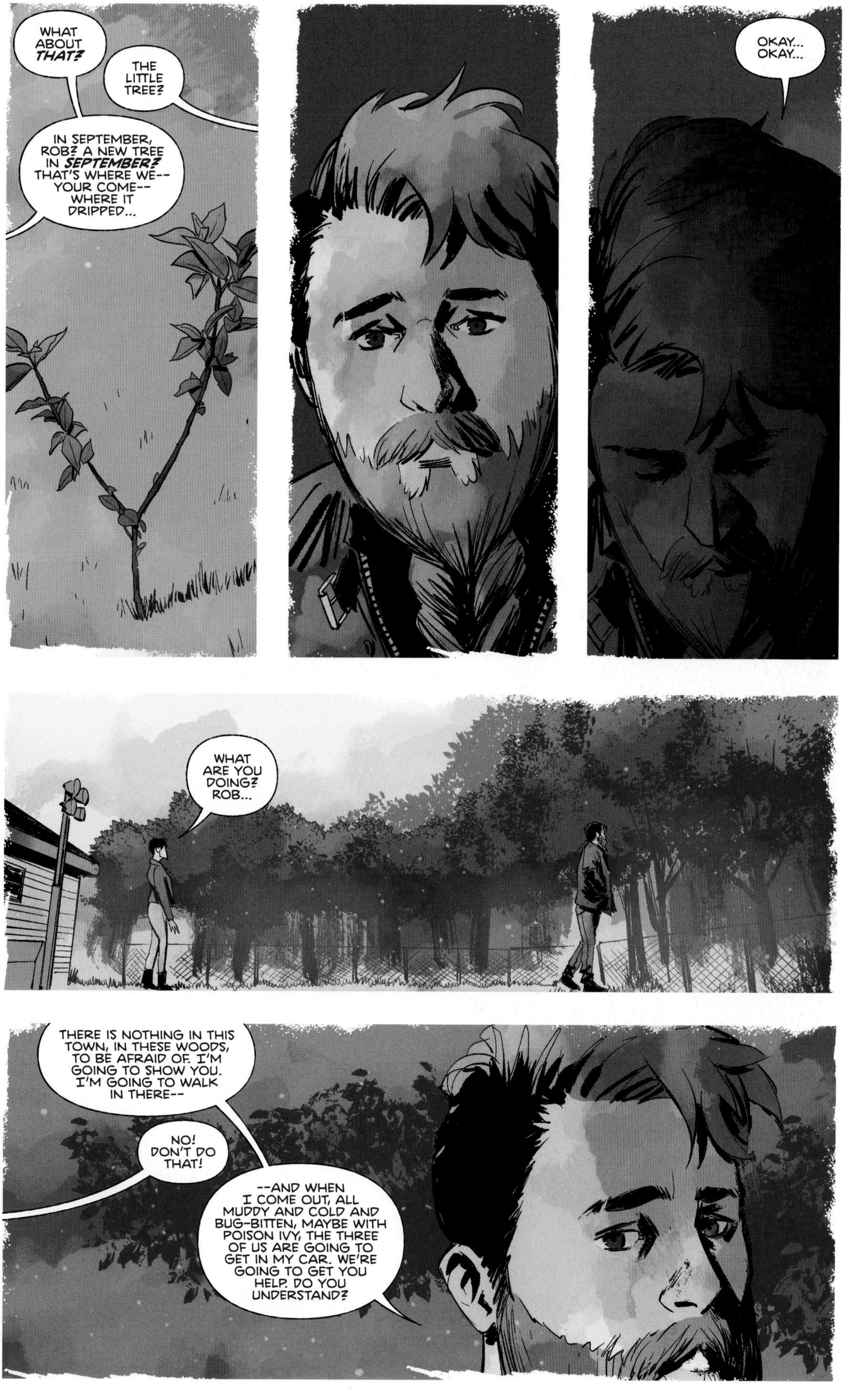
WHAT ABOUT *THAT?*
THE LITTLE TREE?
IN SEPTEMBER, ROB? A NEW TREE IN *SEPTEMBER?* THAT'S WHERE WE-- YOUR COME-- WHERE IT DRIPPED...
OKAY... OKAY...
WHAT ARE YOU DOING? ROB...
THERE IS NOTHING IN THIS TOWN, IN THESE WOODS, TO BE AFRAID OF. I'M GOING TO SHOW YOU. I'M GOING TO WALK IN THERE--
NO! DON'T DO THAT!
--AND WHEN I COME OUT, ALL MUDDY AND COLD AND BUG-BITTEN, MAYBE WITH POISON IVY, THE THREE OF US ARE GOING TO GET IN MY CAR. WE'RE GOING TO GET YOU HELP. DO YOU UNDERSTAND?

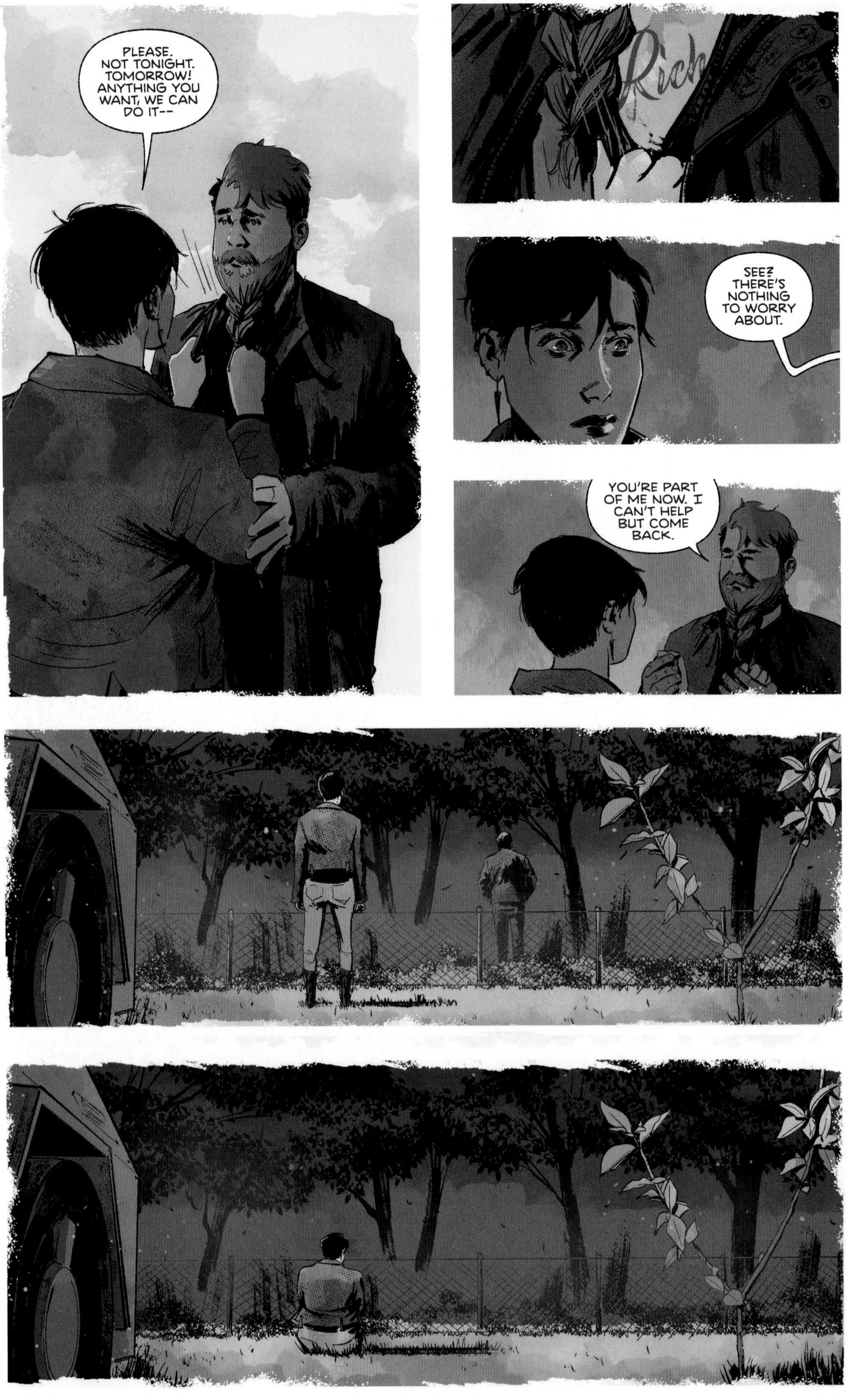
PLEASE. NOT TONIGHT. TOMORROW! ANYTHING YOU WANT, WE CAN DO IT--
SEE? THERE'S NOTHING TO WORRY ABOUT.
YOU'RE PART OF ME NOW. I CAN'T HELP BUT COME BACK.

HOOOOOOOOOOOOOOO

MAMA, WHY'S THE WIND SO LOUD?

PHONE WON'T WORK. HAS TO BE THE WIND.

IS ROB STUCK IN THE HURRICANE?

HE'S FINE, BABY.

WHAP! SLAP!

FUCK!

HOOOOODDOOOO

HOOOOOOO

THAT'S IT. WE'RE GOING FOR HELP. GET YOUR COAT.

BUT YOU SAID WE HAD TO STAY INSIDE, YOU SAID IT WAS A CONTEST TO SEE--

SYBIL! GRAB YOUR GODDAMN COAT!

LISTEN TO ME, SYB. WHEN WE GET OUT THERE, HOLD MY HAND AND DON'T LET GO. YOU GOT THAT?

DO NOT LET GO.

HOOOOOOO

I WANT TO STAY HERE, MAMA...THE MUD MEN...

ON THREE. YOU READY? ONE... TWO...

CHICAGO

HOOOOOOOOOOOOOO

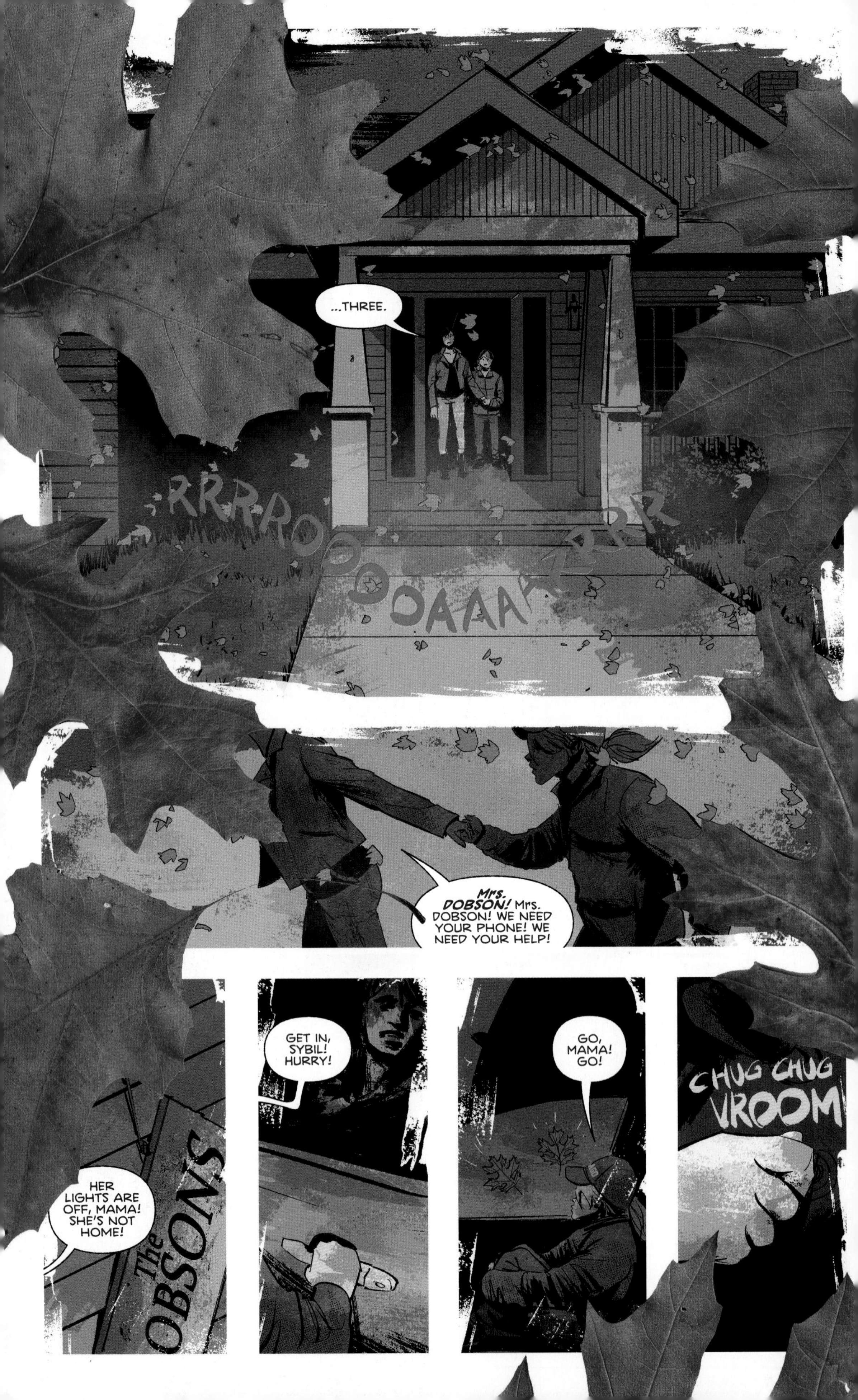
...THREE.
RRRROOOAAARRR
MRS. DOBSON! Mrs. DOBSON! WE NEED YOUR PHONE! WE NEED YOUR HELP!
HER LIGHTS ARE OFF, MAMA! SHE'S NOT HOME!
The OBSONS
GET IN, SYBIL! HURRY!
GO, MAMA! GO!
CHUG CHUG VROOM

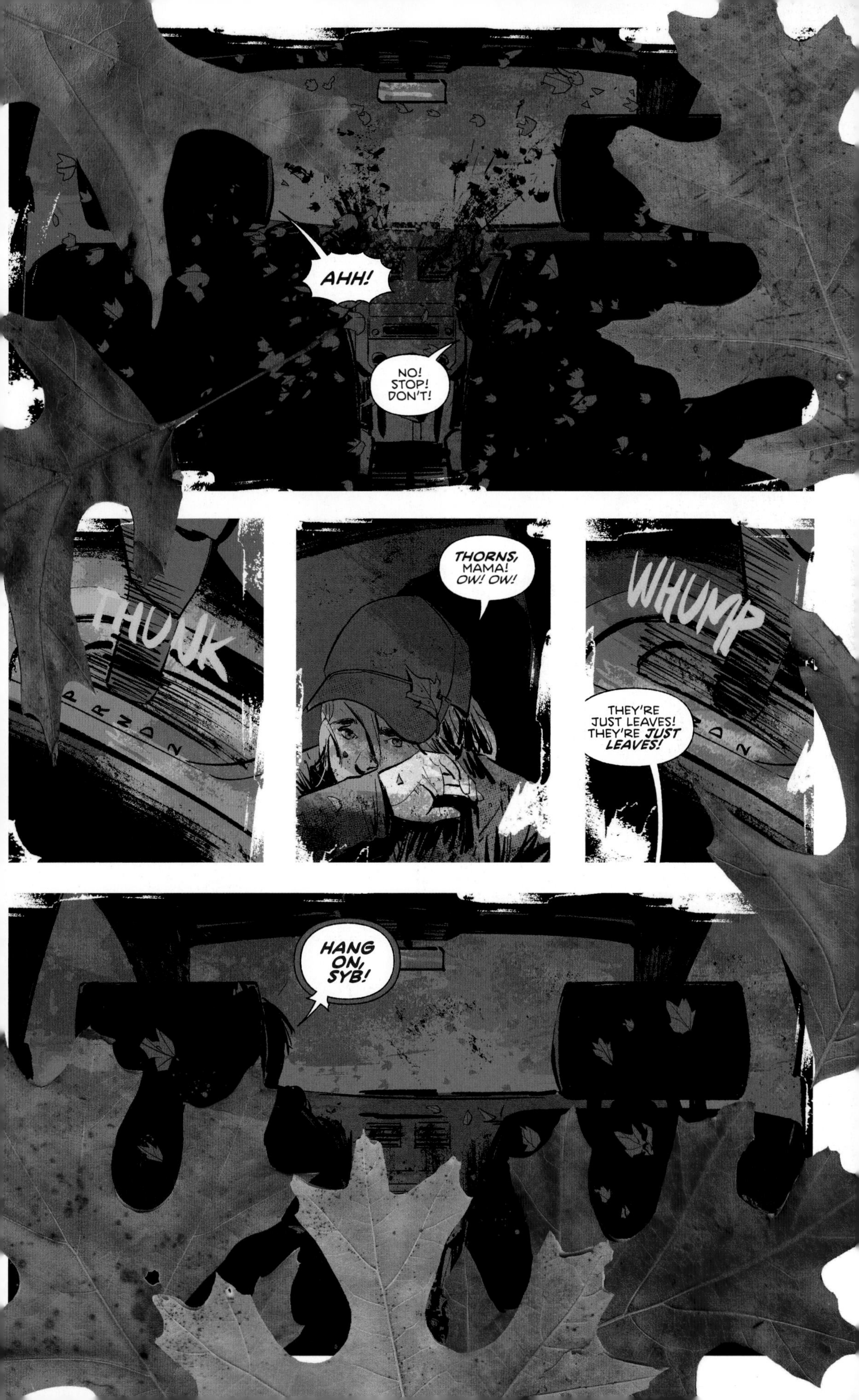
AHH!
NO! STOP! DON'T!
THUNK
THORNS, MAMA! OW! OW!
WHUMP
THEY'RE JUST LEAVES! THEY'RE JUST LEAVES!
HANG ON, SYB!

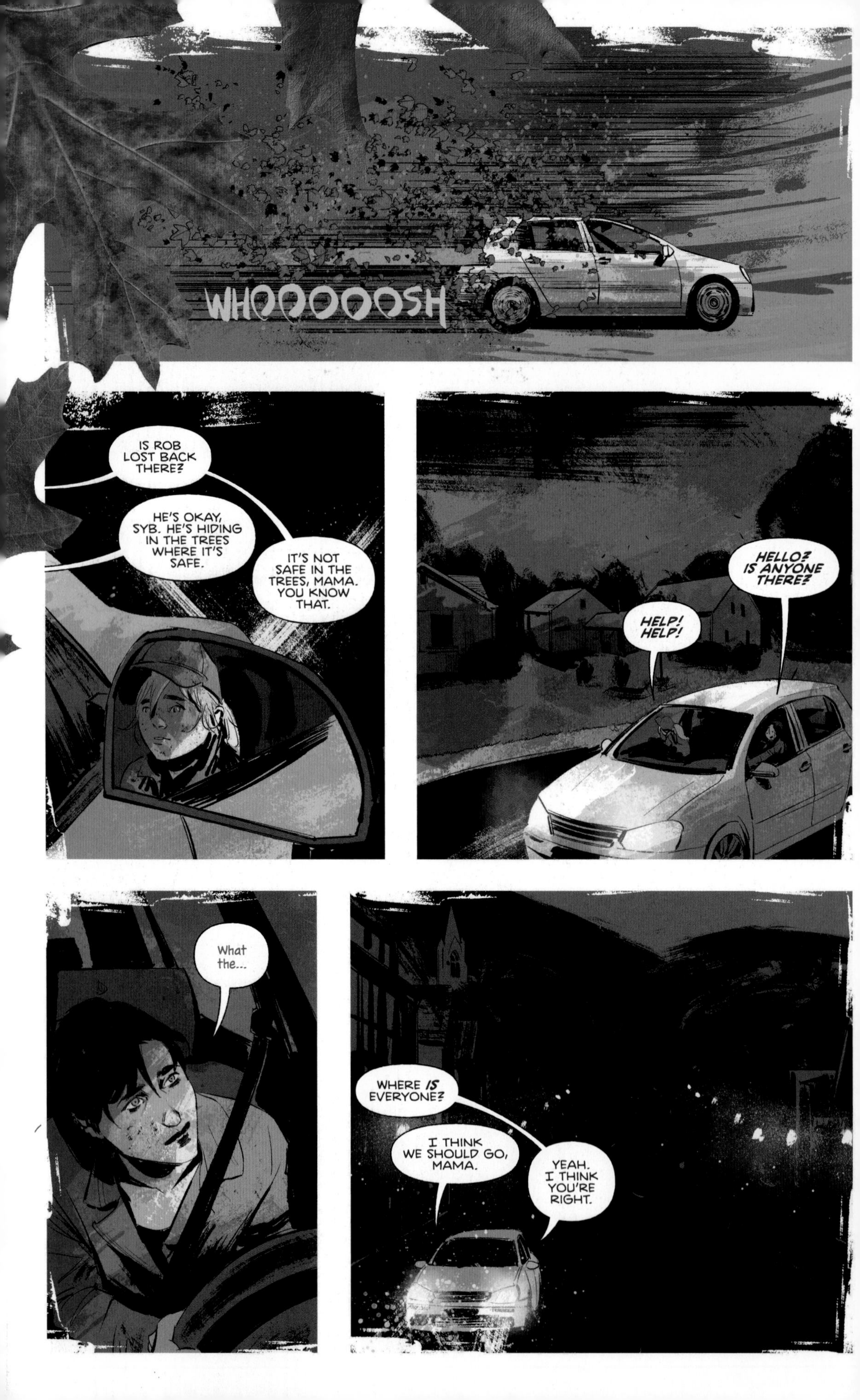
WHOOOOOSH
IS ROB LOST BACK THERE?
HE'S OKAY, SYB. HE'S HIDING IN THE TREES WHERE IT'S SAFE.
IT'S NOT SAFE IN THE TREES, MAMA. YOU KNOW THAT.
HELP! HELP!
HELLO? IS ANYONE THERE?
What the...
WHERE *IS* EVERYONE?
I THINK WE SHOULD GO, MAMA.
YEAH. I THINK YOU'RE RIGHT.

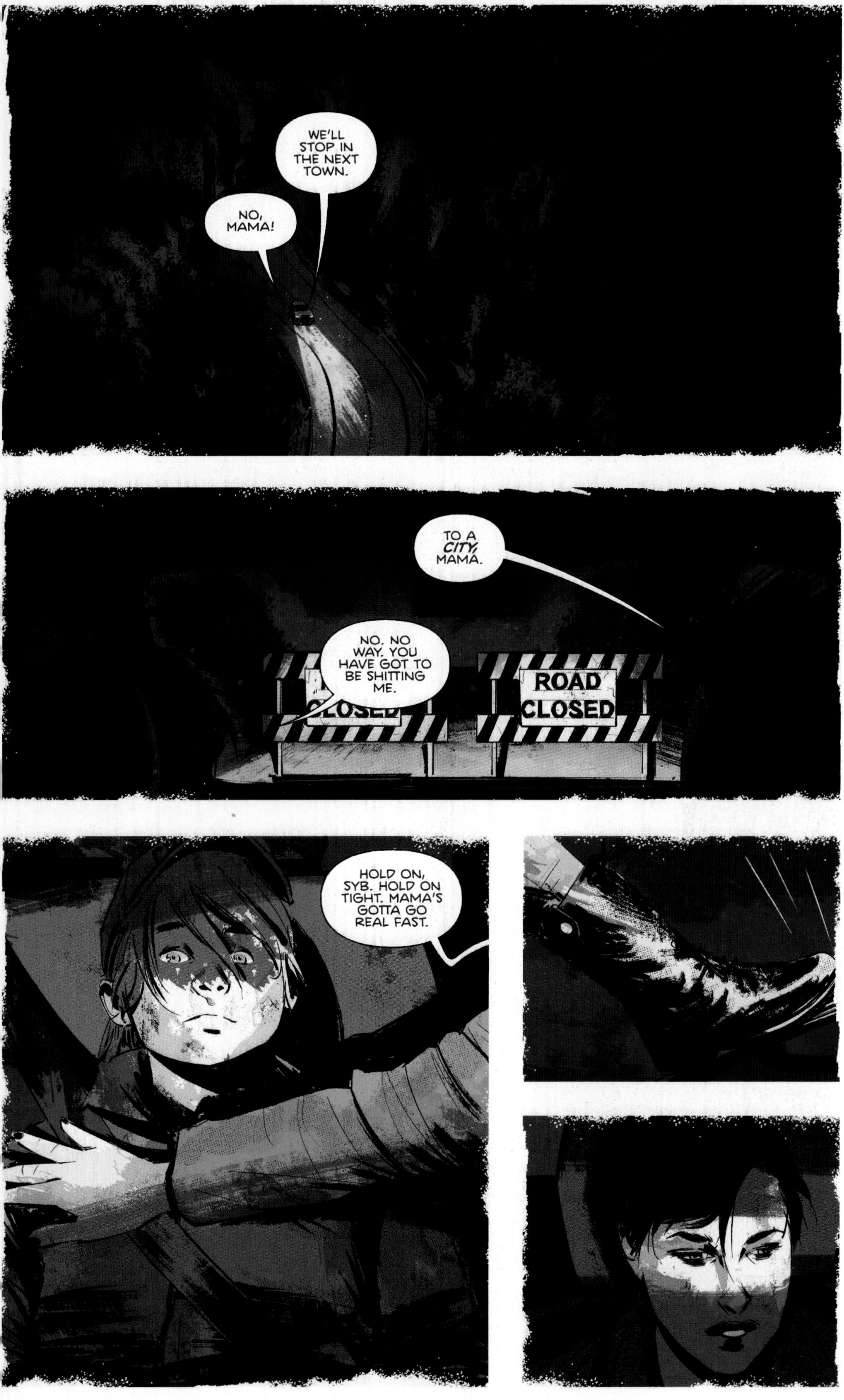
WE'LL STOP IN THE NEXT TOWN.
NO, MAMA!
TO A CITY, MAMA.
NO. NO WAY. YOU HAVE GOT TO BE SHITTING ME.
ROAD CLOSED
CLOSED
HOLD ON, SYB. HOLD ON TIGHT. MAMA'S GOTTA GO REAL FAST.

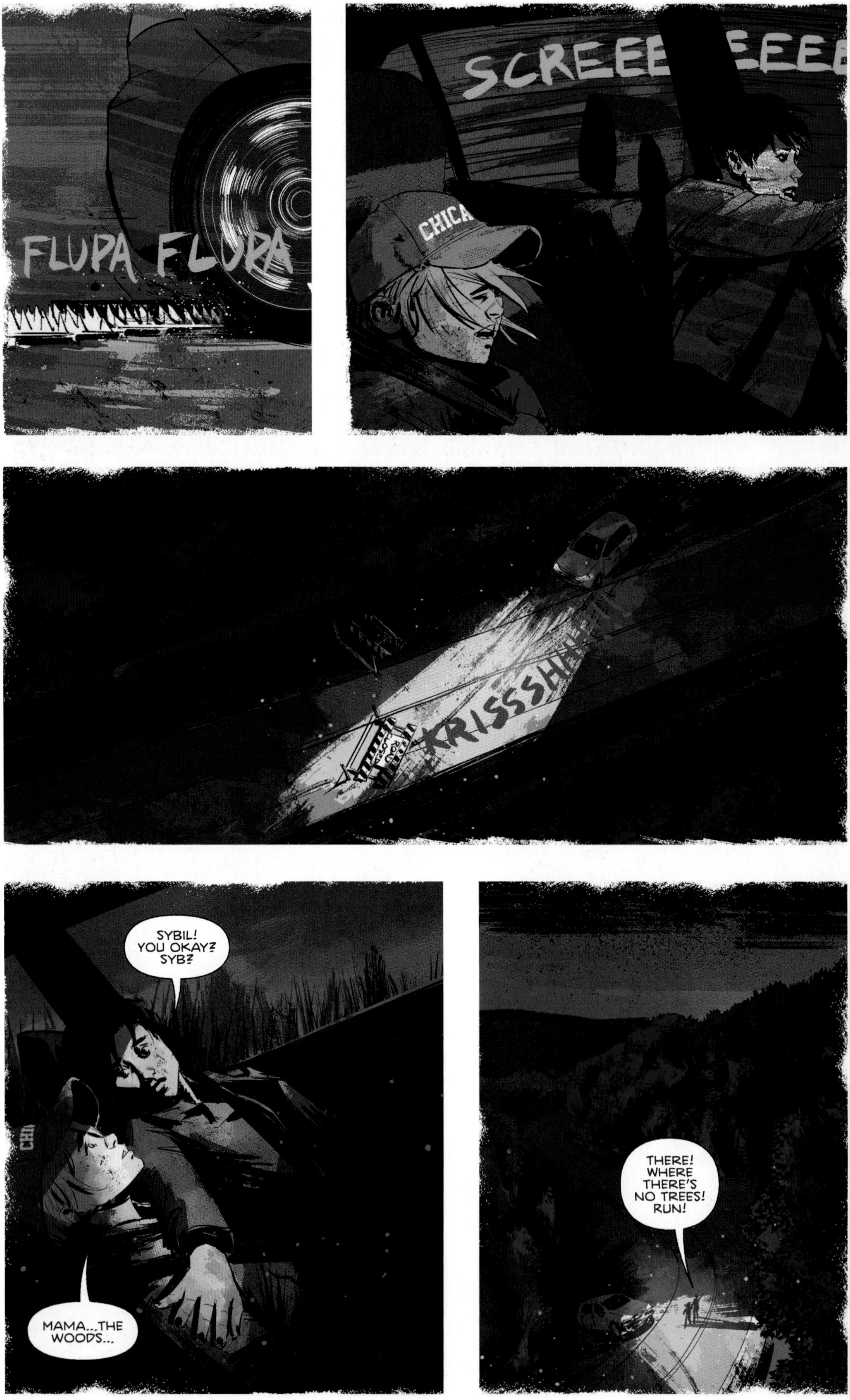
FLUPA FLUPA
SCREEEEEEE
CHICA
KRISSSH
SYBIL! YOU OKAY? SYB?
MAMA... THE WOODS...
THERE! WHERE THERE'S NO TREES! RUN!

COMFORT NOTCH
MEMORIAL PARK CEMETERY
KEEP GOING!
MAMA! NO! LET'S GO!
Oh GOD. *Oh* GOD.
SYBIL SOMERVILLE

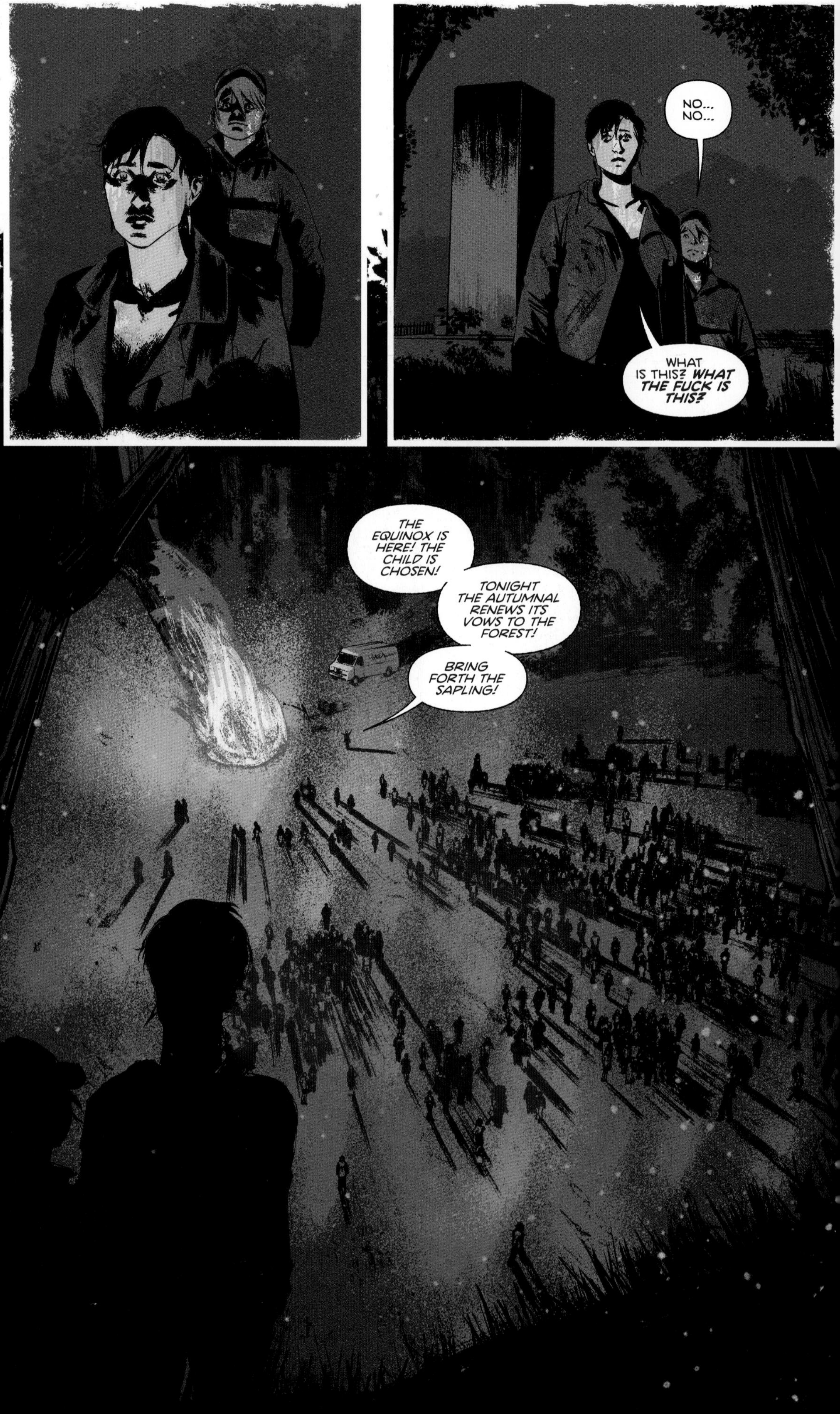
NO... NO...
WHAT IS THIS? WHAT THE FUCK IS THIS?
THE EQUINOX IS HERE! THE CHILD IS CHOSEN!
TONIGHT THE AUTUMNAL RENEWS ITS VOWS TO THE FOREST!
BRING FORTH THE SAPLING!

she

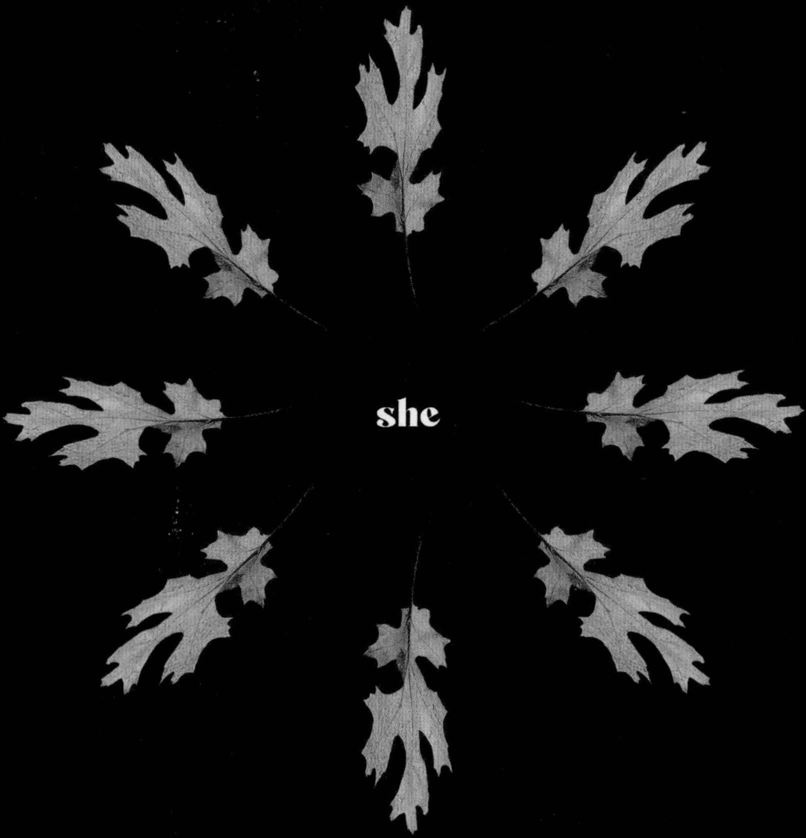

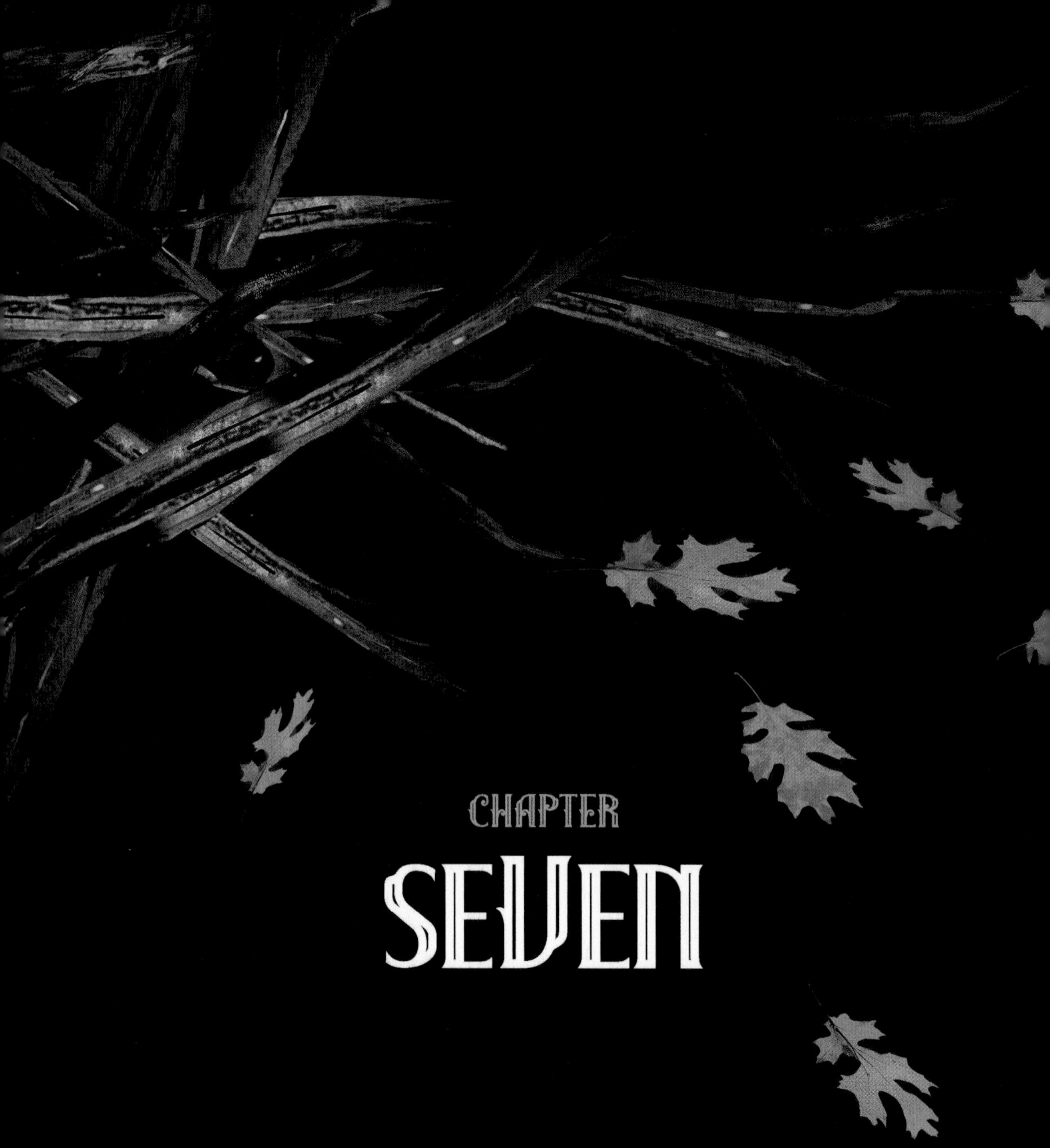

CHAPTER SEVEN

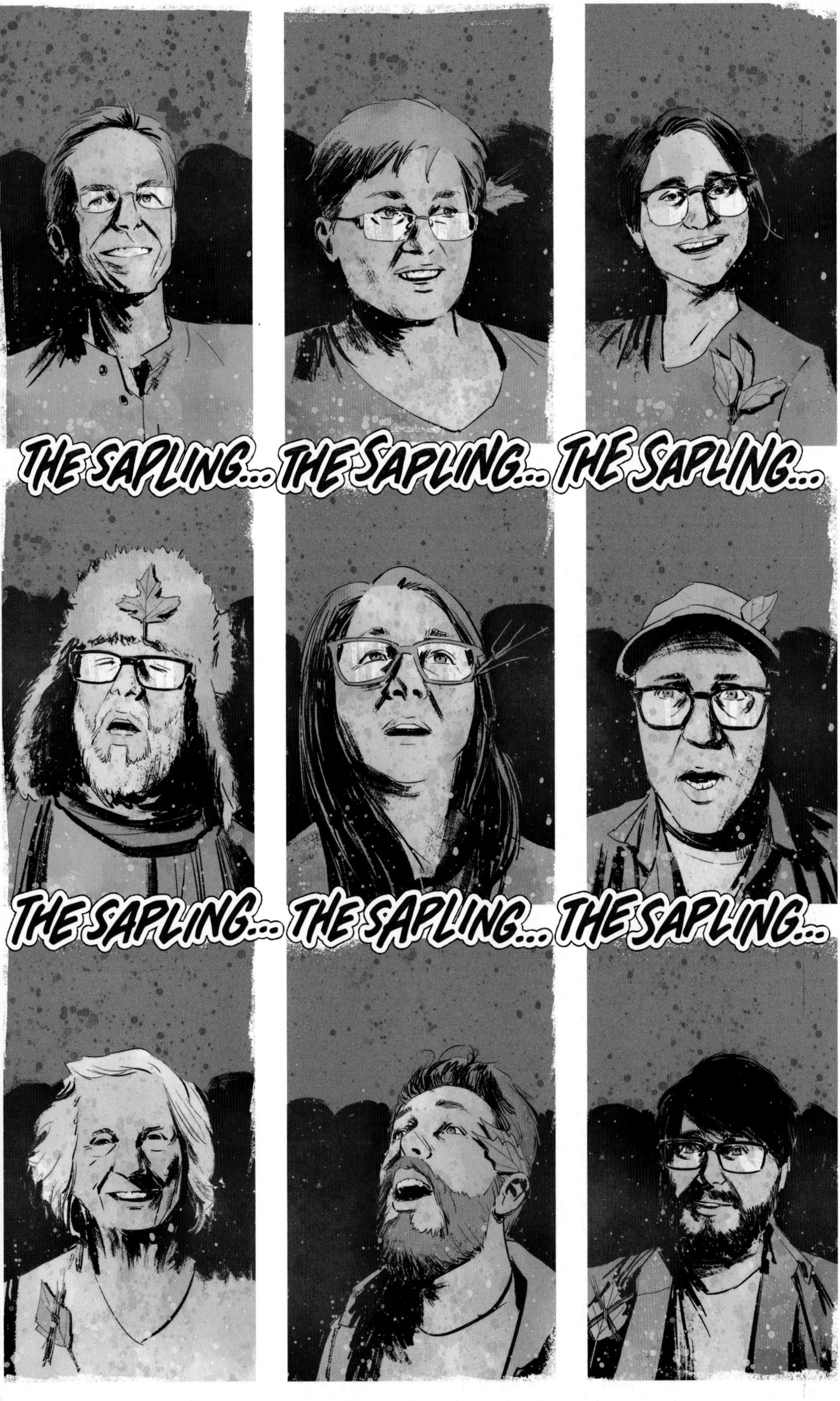
THE SAPLING...
THE SAPLING...
THE SAPLING...
THE SAPLING...
THE SAPLING...
THE SAPLING...

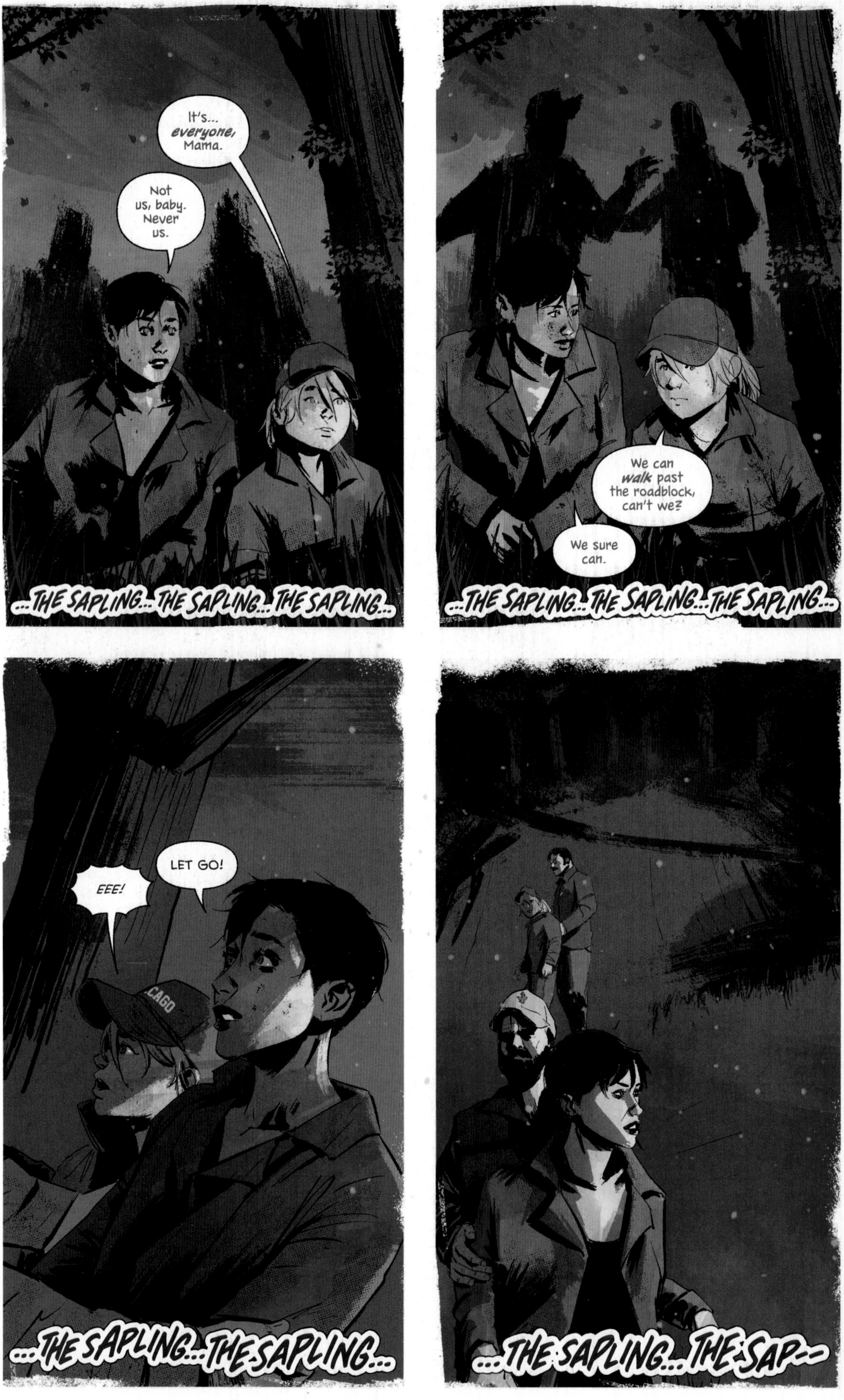
It's... *everyone,* Mama.
Not us, baby. Never us.
...THE SAPLING... THE SAPLING... THE SAPLING...
We can *walk* past the roadblock, can't we?
We sure can.
...THE SAPLING... THE SAPLING... THE SAPLING...
EEE!
LET GO!
CAGO
...THE SAPLING... THE SAPLING...
...THE SAPLING... THE SAP—

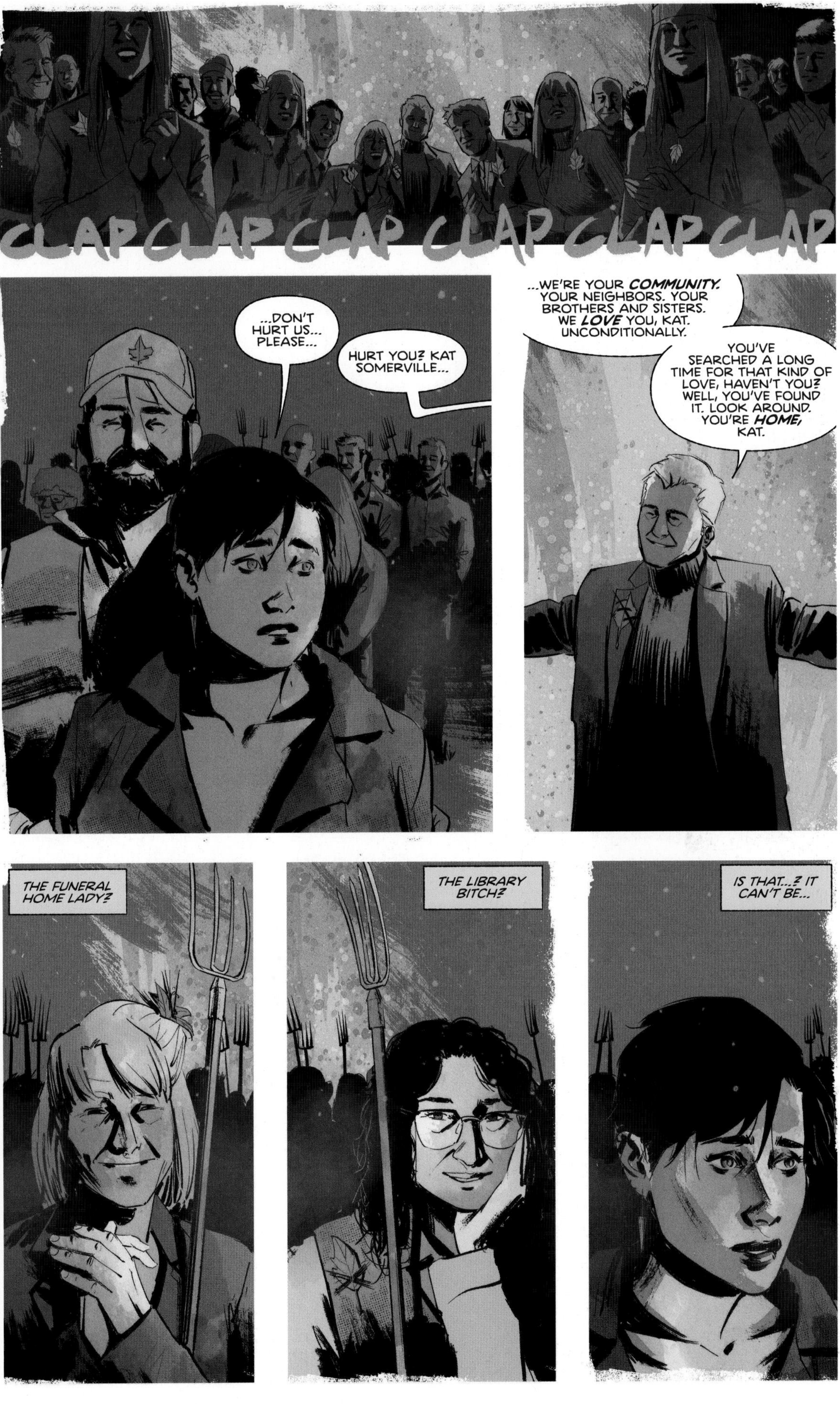
CLAP CLAP CLAP CLAP CLAP CLAP
...DON'T HURT US... PLEASE...
HURT YOU? KAT SOMERVILLE...
...WE'RE YOUR COMMUNITY. YOUR NEIGHBORS. YOUR BROTHERS AND SISTERS. WE LOVE YOU, KAT. UNCONDITIONALLY.
YOU'VE SEARCHED A LONG TIME FOR THAT KIND OF LOVE, HAVEN'T YOU? WELL, YOU'VE FOUND IT. LOOK AROUND. YOU'RE HOME, KAT.
THE FUNERAL HOME LADY?
THE LIBRARY BITCH?
IS THAT...? IT CAN'T BE...

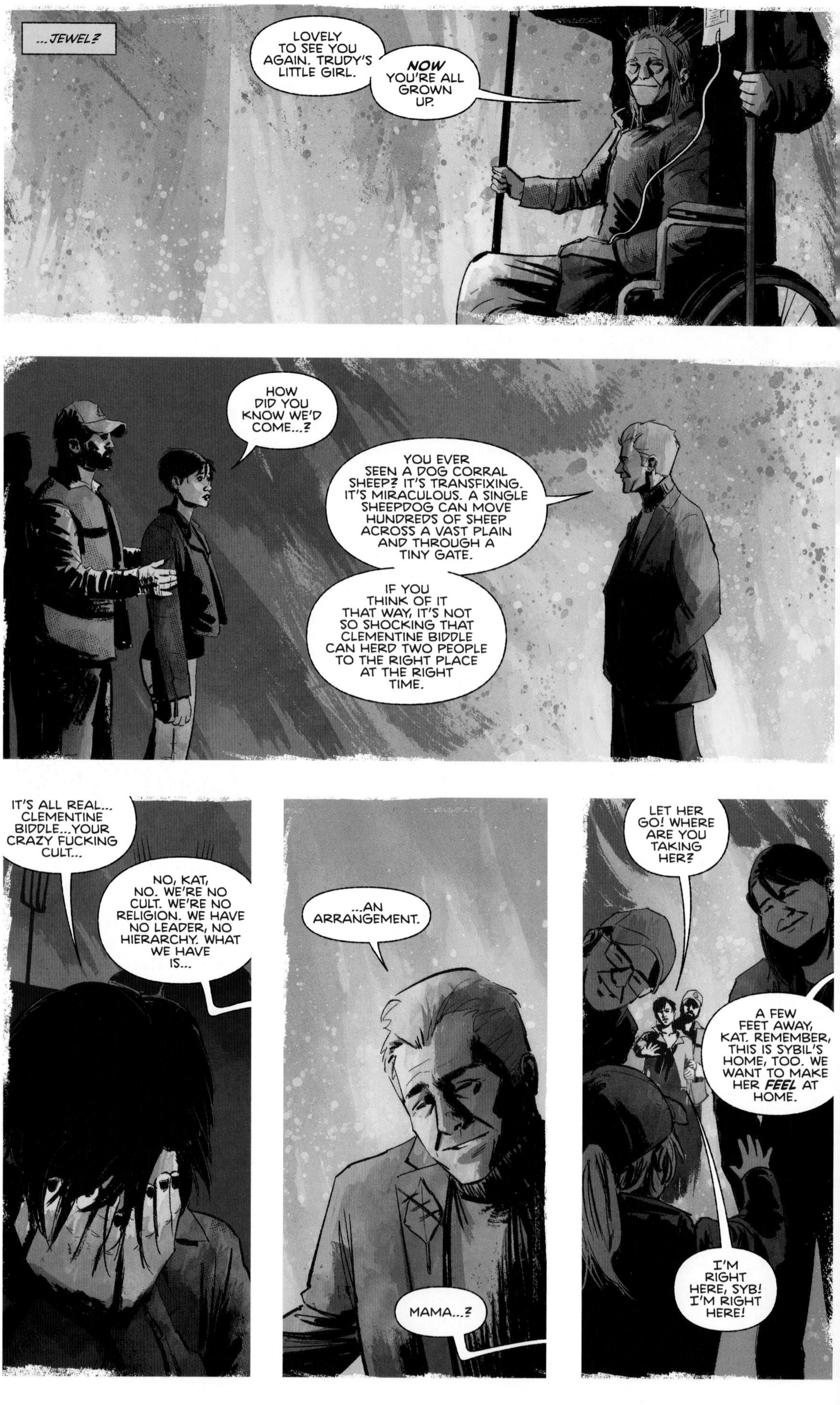
...JEWEL?
LOVELY TO SEE YOU AGAIN. TRUDY'S LITTLE GIRL.
NOW YOU'RE ALL GROWN UP.
HOW DID YOU KNOW WE'D COME...?
YOU EVER SEEN A DOG CORRAL SHEEP? IT'S TRANSFIXING. IT'S MIRACULOUS. A SINGLE SHEEPDOG CAN MOVE HUNDREDS OF SHEEP ACROSS A VAST PLAIN AND THROUGH A TINY GATE.
IF YOU THINK OF IT THAT WAY, IT'S NOT SO SHOCKING THAT CLEMENTINE BIDDLE CAN HERD TWO PEOPLE TO THE RIGHT PLACE AT THE RIGHT TIME.
IT'S ALL REAL... CLEMENTINE BIDDLE...YOUR CRAZY FUCKING CULT...
NO, KAT, NO. WE'RE NO CULT. WE'RE NO RELIGION. WE HAVE NO LEADER, NO HIERARCHY. WHAT WE HAVE IS...
...AN ARRANGEMENT.
MAMA...?
LET HER GO! WHERE ARE YOU TAKING HER?
A FEW FEET AWAY, KAT. REMEMBER, THIS IS SYBIL'S HOME, TOO. WE WANT TO MAKE HER FEEL AT HOME.
I'M RIGHT HERE, SYB! I'M RIGHT HERE!

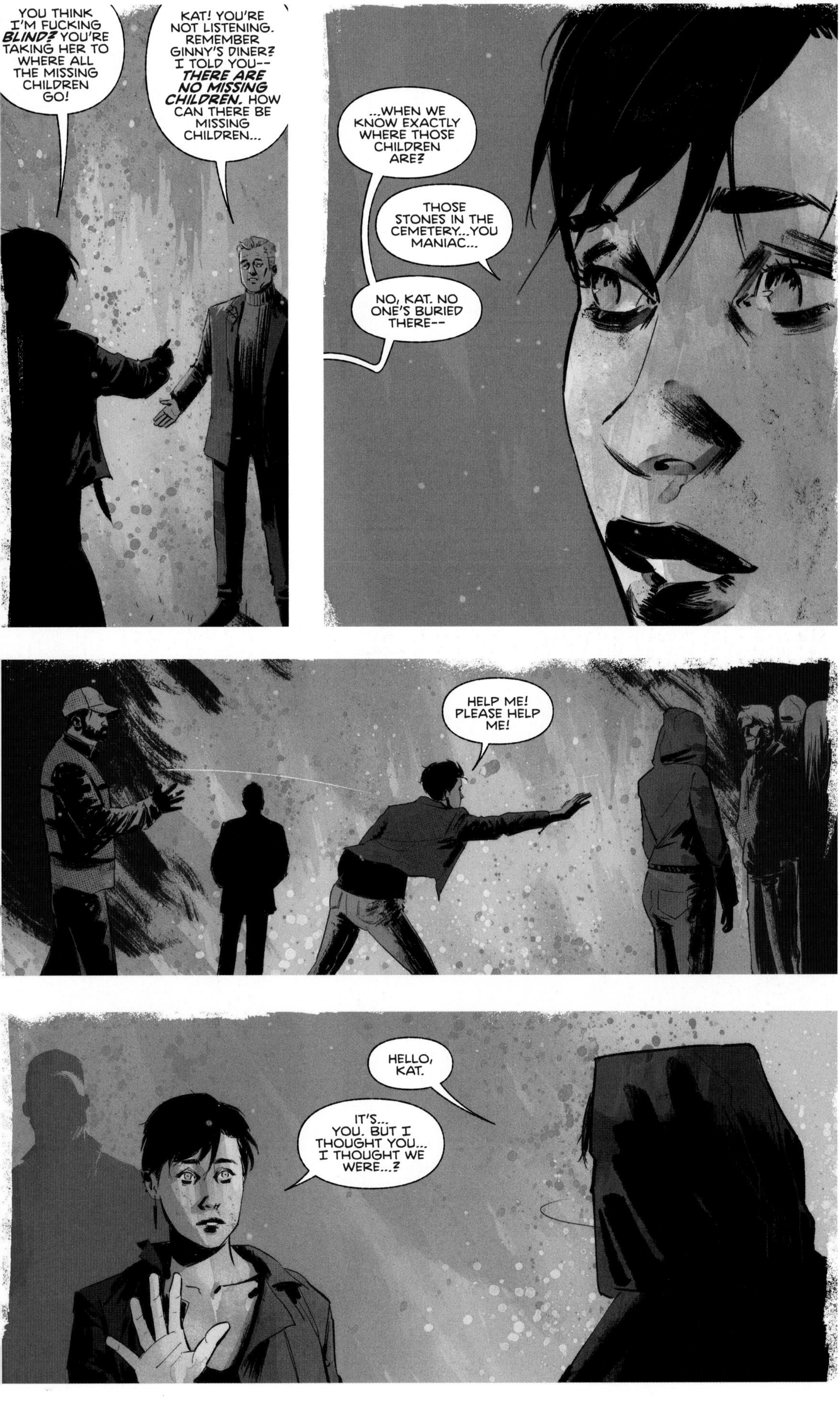
YOU THINK I'M FUCKING *BLIND?* YOU'RE TAKING HER TO WHERE ALL THE MISSING CHILDREN GO!
KAT! YOU'RE NOT LISTENING. REMEMBER GINNY'S DINER? I TOLD YOU-- *THERE ARE NO MISSING CHILDREN.* HOW CAN THERE BE MISSING CHILDREN...
...WHEN WE KNOW EXACTLY WHERE THOSE CHILDREN ARE?
THOSE STONES IN THE CEMETERY...YOU MANIAC...
NO, KAT. NO ONE'S BURIED THERE--
HELP ME! PLEASE HELP ME!
HELLO, KAT.
IT'S... YOU. BUT I THOUGHT YOU... I THOUGHT WE WERE...?

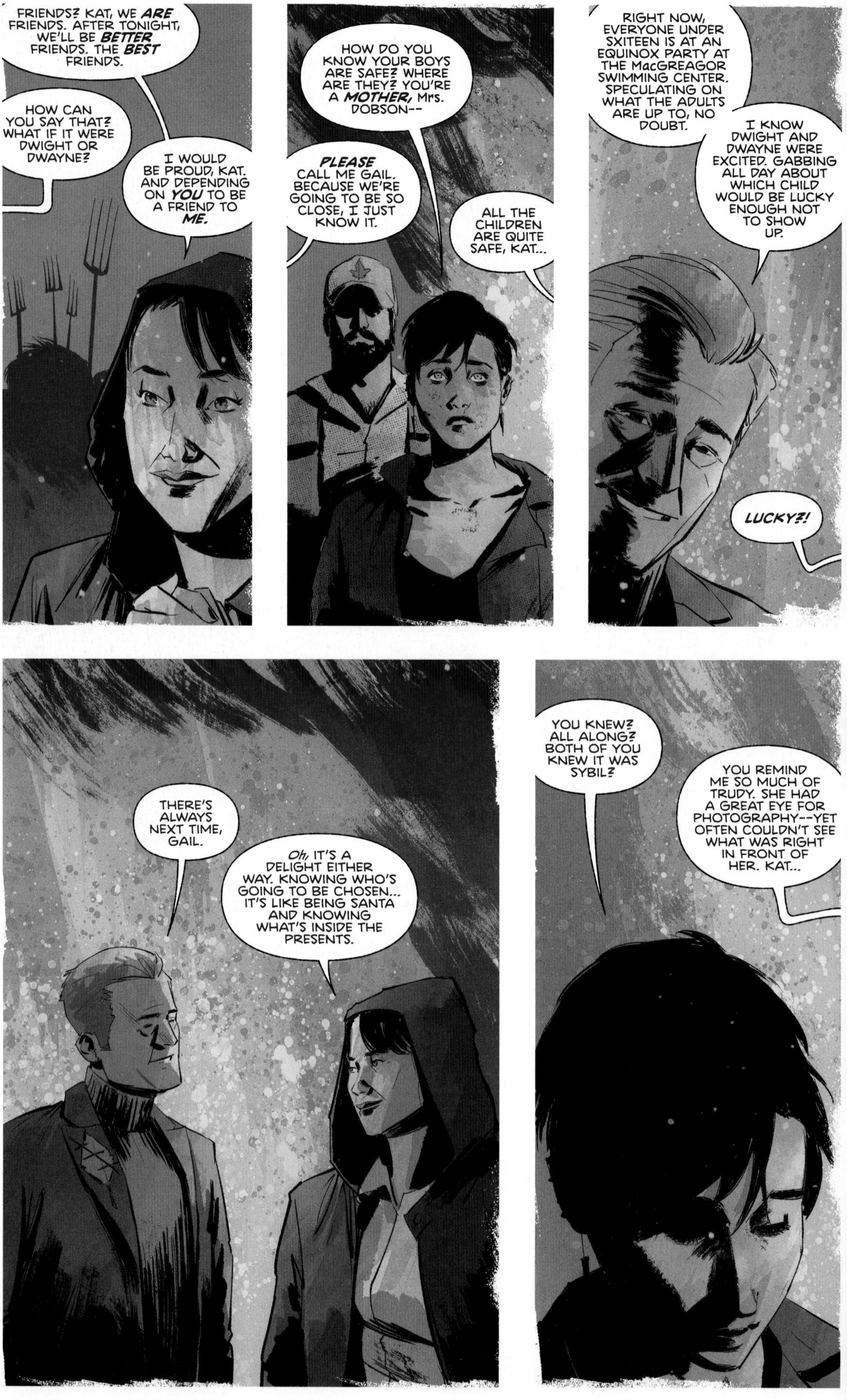
FRIENDS? KAT, WE ARE FRIENDS. AFTER TONIGHT, WE'LL BE BETTER FRIENDS. THE BEST FRIENDS.
HOW CAN YOU SAY THAT? WHAT IF IT WERE DWIGHT OR DWAYNE?
I WOULD BE PROUD, KAT. AND DEPENDING ON YOU TO BE A FRIEND TO ME.
HOW DO YOU KNOW YOUR BOYS ARE SAFE? WHERE ARE THEY? YOU'RE A MOTHER, Mrs. DOBSON--
PLEASE CALL ME GAIL. BECAUSE WE'RE GOING TO BE SO CLOSE, I JUST KNOW IT.
ALL THE CHILDREN ARE QUITE SAFE, KAT...
RIGHT NOW, EVERYONE UNDER SXITEEN IS AT AN EQUINOX PARTY AT THE MacGREAGOR SWIMMING CENTER. SPECULATING ON WHAT THE ADULTS ARE UP TO, NO DOUBT.
I KNOW DWIGHT AND DWAYNE WERE EXCITED. GABBING ALL DAY ABOUT WHICH CHILD WOULD BE LUCKY ENOUGH NOT TO SHOW UP.
LUCKY?!
THERE'S ALWAYS NEXT TIME, GAIL.
Oh, IT'S A DELIGHT EITHER WAY. KNOWING WHO'S GOING TO BE CHOSEN... IT'S LIKE BEING SANTA AND KNOWING WHAT'S INSIDE THE PRESENTS.
YOU KNEW? ALL ALONG? BOTH OF YOU KNEW IT WAS SYBIL?
YOU REMIND ME SO MUCH OF TRUDY. SHE HAD A GREAT EYE FOR PHOTOGRAPHY--YET OFTEN COULDN'T SEE WHAT WAS RIGHT IN FRONT OF HER. KAT...

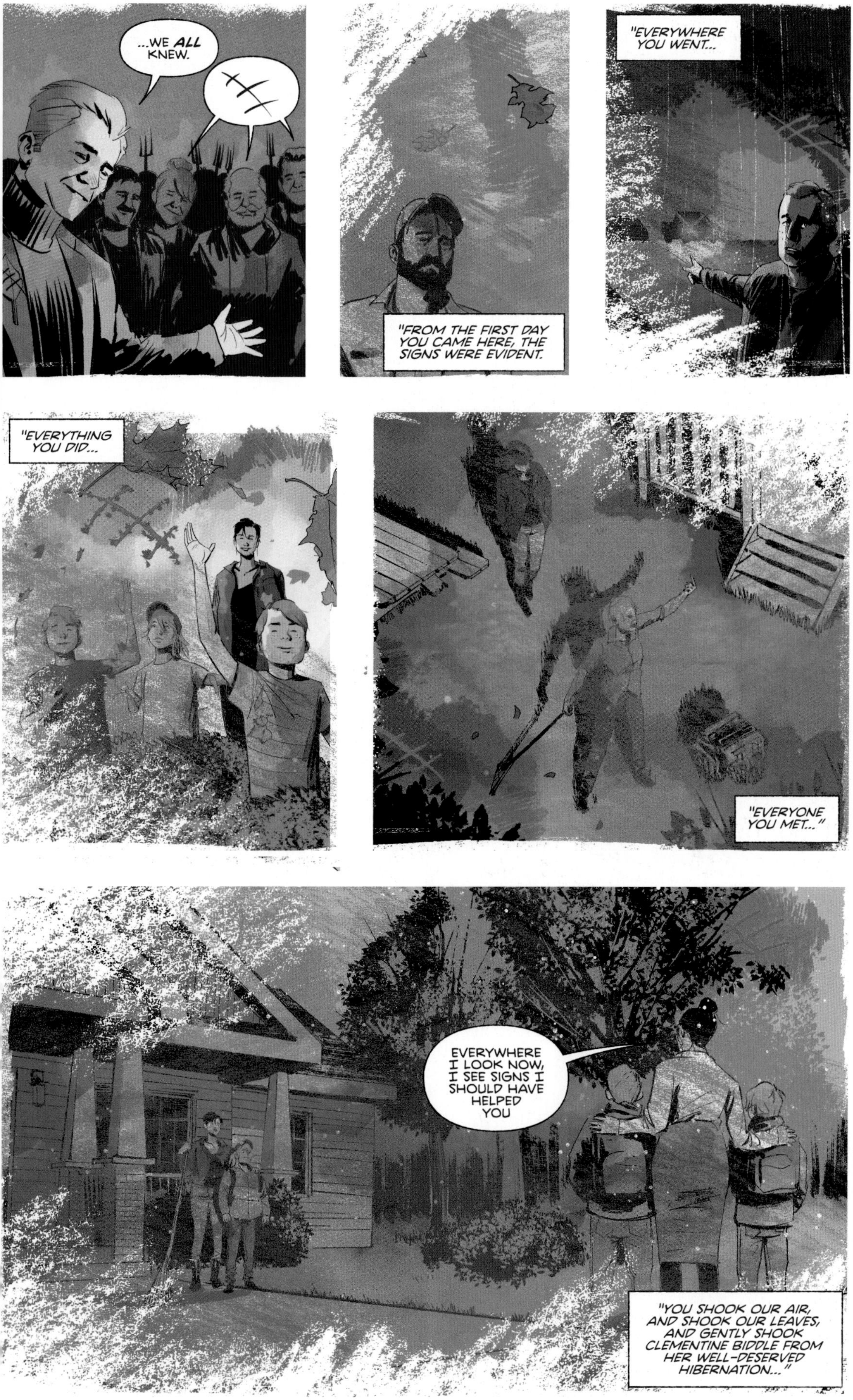
...WE ALL KNEW.
"FROM THE FIRST DAY YOU CAME HERE, THE SIGNS WERE EVIDENT.
"EVERYWHERE YOU WENT...
"EVERYTHING YOU DID...
"EVERYONE YOU MET..."
EVERYWHERE I LOOK NOW, I SEE SIGNS I SHOULD HAVE HELPED YOU
"YOU SHOOK OUR AIR, AND SHOOK OUR LEAVES, AND GENTLY SHOOK CLEMENTINE BIDDLE FROM HER WELL-DESERVED HIBERNATION..."

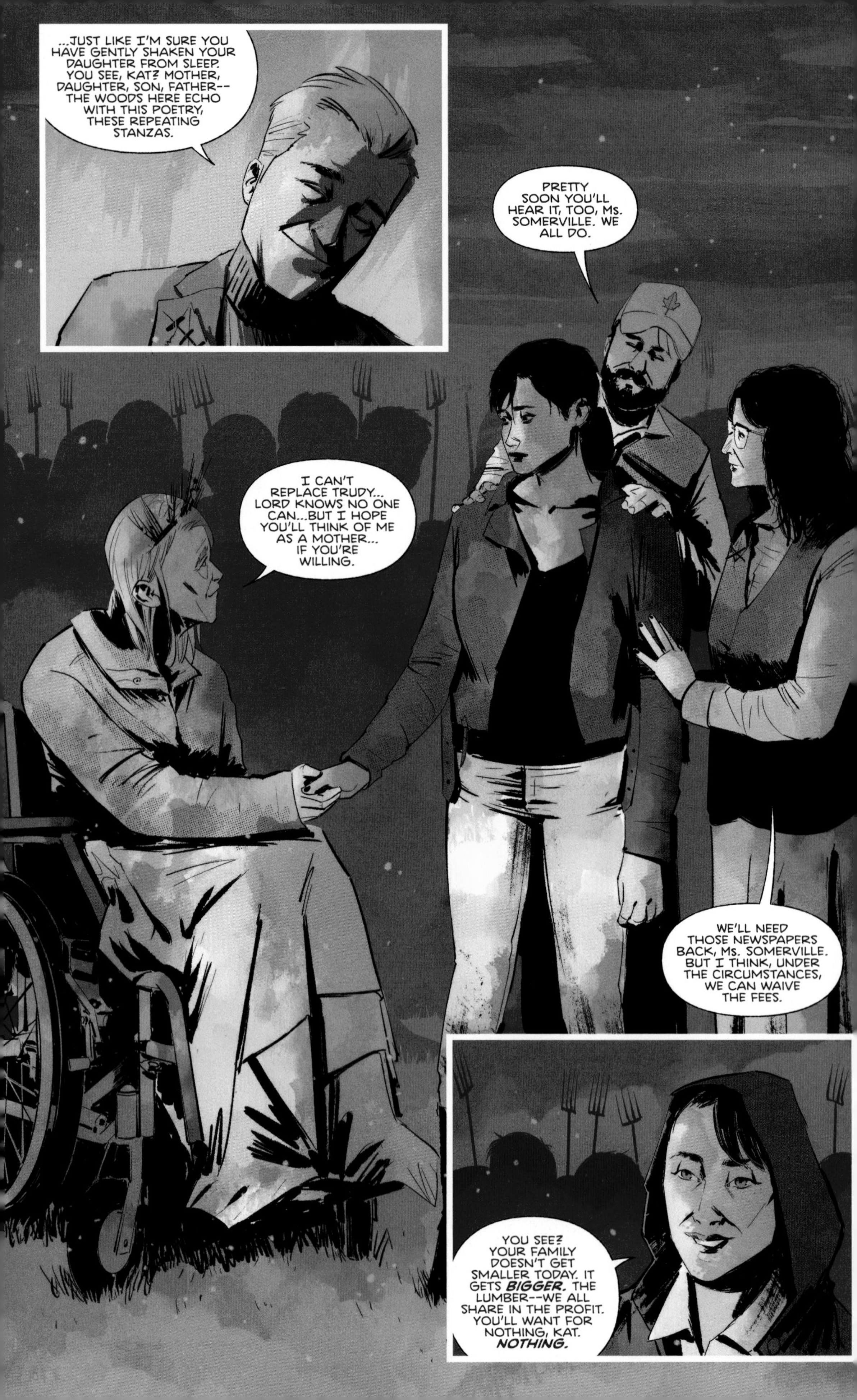
...JUST LIKE I'M SURE YOU HAVE GENTLY SHAKEN YOUR DAUGHTER FROM SLEEP. YOU SEE, KAT? MOTHER, DAUGHTER, SON, FATHER-- THE WOODS HERE ECHO WITH THIS POETRY, THESE REPEATING STANZAS.
PRETTY SOON YOU'LL HEAR IT, TOO, Ms. SOMERVILLE. WE ALL DO.
I CAN'T REPLACE TRUDY... LORD KNOWS NO ONE CAN...BUT I HOPE YOU'LL THINK OF ME AS A MOTHER... IF YOU'RE WILLING.
WE'LL NEED THOSE NEWSPAPERS BACK, Ms. SOMERVILLE. BUT I THINK, UNDER THE CIRCUMSTANCES, WE CAN WAIVE THE FEES.
YOU SEE? YOUR FAMILY DOESN'T GET SMALLER TODAY. IT GETS ***BIGGER.*** THE LUMBER--WE ALL SHARE IN THE PROFIT. YOU'LL WANT FOR NOTHING, KAT. ***NOTHING.***

BUT *YOUR* FAMILY... AUBREY...CLEMENTINE BIDDLE *KILLED* HIM. HOW CAN YOU POSSIBLY...?

NO, KAT. THAT'S NOT HOW IT WORKS.

WE LOVED AUBREY. BUT HE SAW THE SIGNS AS MUCH AS ANYONE. THAT CAR--IT WAS HIS ATTEMPT TO GET YOU TO DRIVE AWAY.

CAROL RAVINTZKY WAS MUCH THE SAME. SHE TOLD YOU TOO MUCH, TOO SOON.

AUBREY AND CAROL... *YOU* DID THAT? THESE *PEOPLE* DID THAT?

IT WAS...A *MESSIER EQUINOX* THAN WE'VE HAD IN A TIME. WE ALL REGRET WHAT HAD TO BE DONE.

BIDDLE, BIDDLE, SHREWD AND SLY... BEWITCH, SEDUCE, BEFUDDLE, AND LIE...

THE ORIGINAL VERSES. WELL DONE, KAT.

AT LONG LAST, LET ME HAND YOU THE MISSING PIECES.

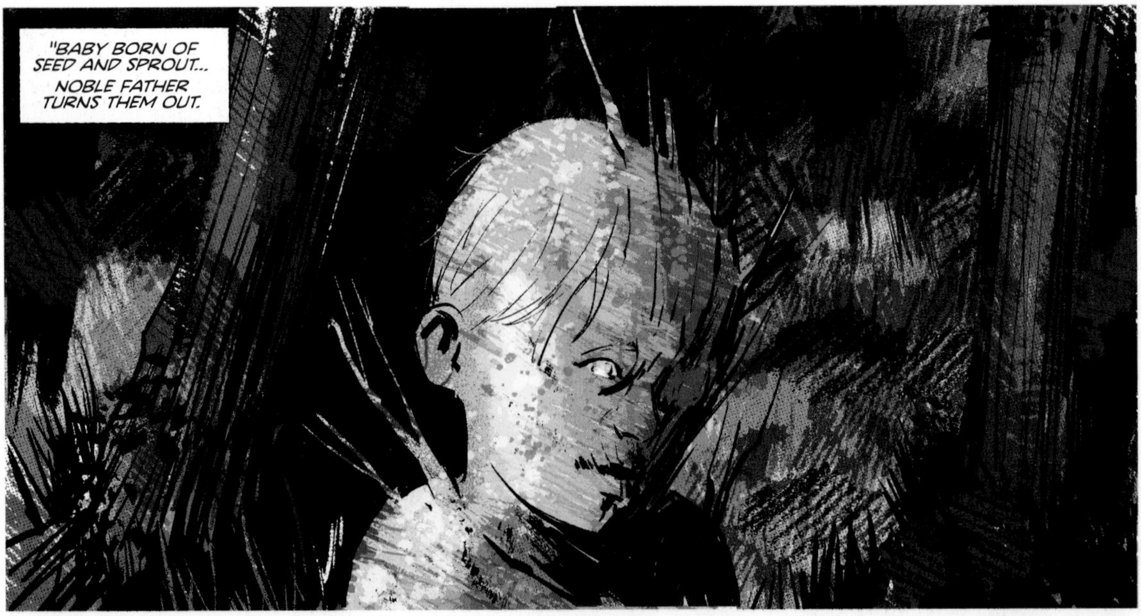
"BABY BORN OF SEED AND SPROUT...
NOBLE FATHER TURNS THEM OUT.

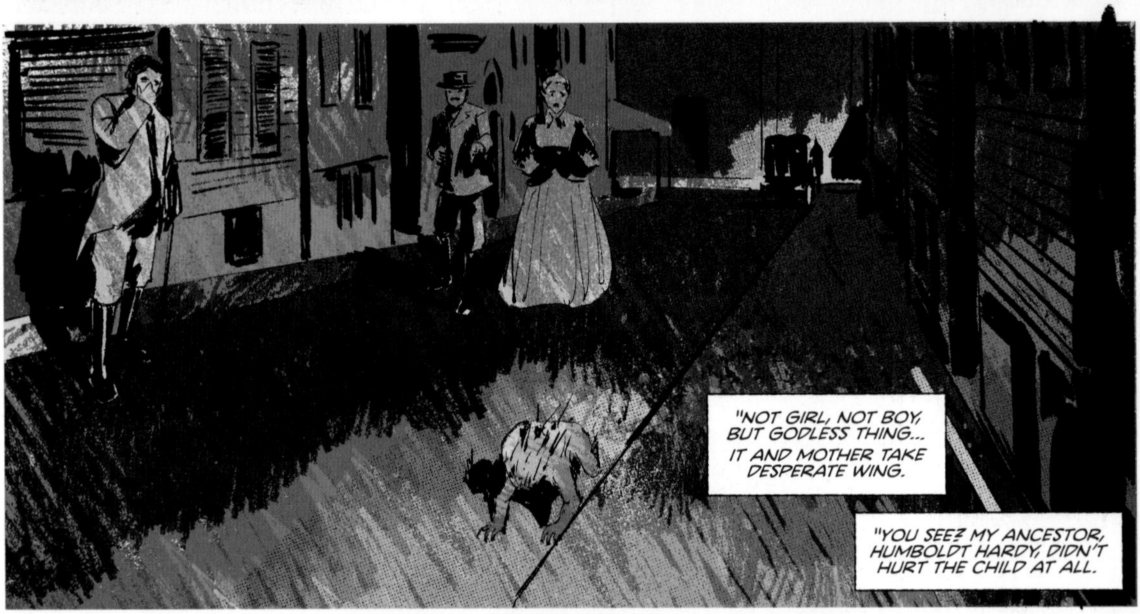
"NOT GIRL, NOT BOY, BUT GODLESS THING...
IT AND MOTHER TAKE DESPERATE WING.
"YOU SEE? MY ANCESTOR, HUMBOLDT HARDY, DIDN'T HURT THE CHILD AT ALL.

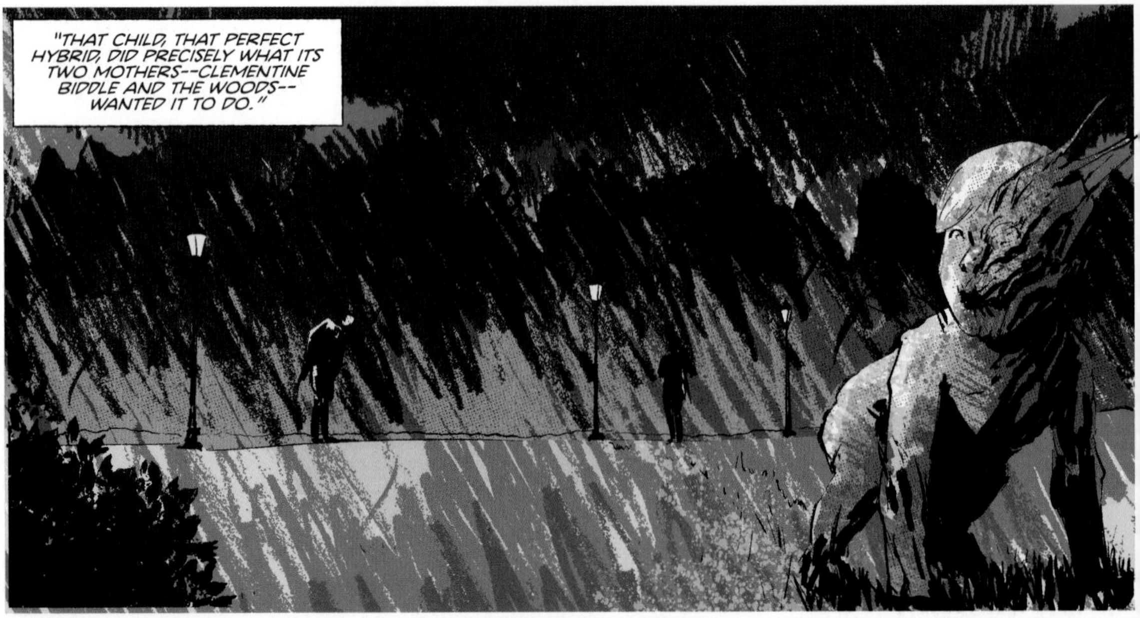
"THAT CHILD, THAT PERFECT HYBRID, DID PRECISELY WHAT ITS TWO MOTHERS--CLEMENTINE BIDDLE AND THE WOODS--WANTED IT TO DO."

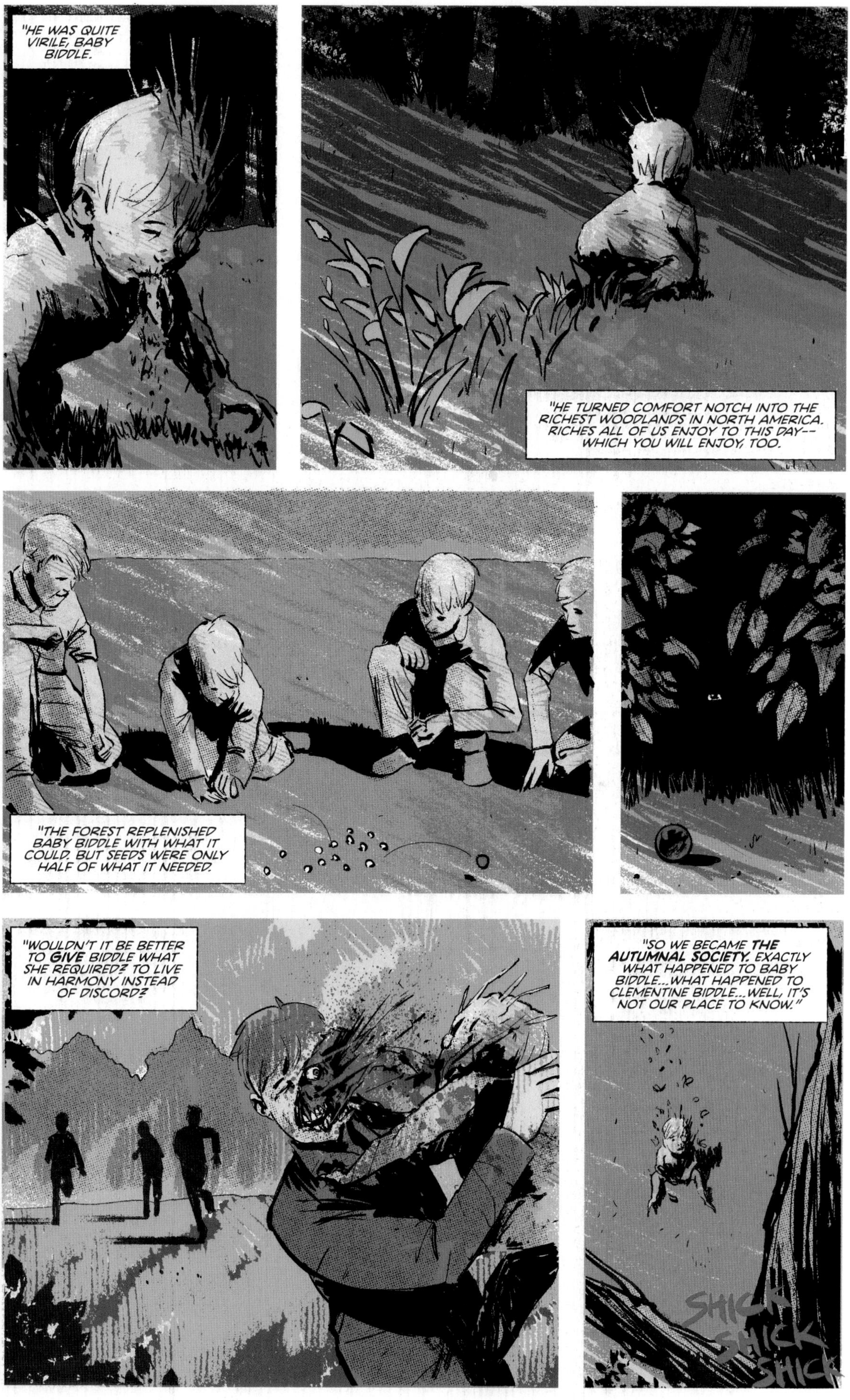
"HE WAS QUITE VIRILE, BABY BIDDLE.
"HE TURNED COMFORT NOTCH INTO THE RICHEST WOODLANDS IN NORTH AMERICA. RICHES ALL OF US ENJOY TO THIS DAY-- WHICH YOU WILL ENJOY, TOO.
"THE FOREST REPLENISHED BABY BIDDLE WITH WHAT IT COULD. BUT SEEDS WERE ONLY HALF OF WHAT IT NEEDED.
"WOULDN'T IT BE BETTER TO GIVE BIDDLE WHAT SHE REQUIRED? TO LIVE IN HARMONY INSTEAD OF DISCORD?
"SO WE BECAME THE AUTUMNAL SOCIETY. EXACTLY WHAT HAPPENED TO BABY BIDDLE...WHAT HAPPENED TO CLEMENTINE BIDDLE...WELL, IT'S NOT OUR PLACE TO KNOW."
SHICK
SHICK
SHICK

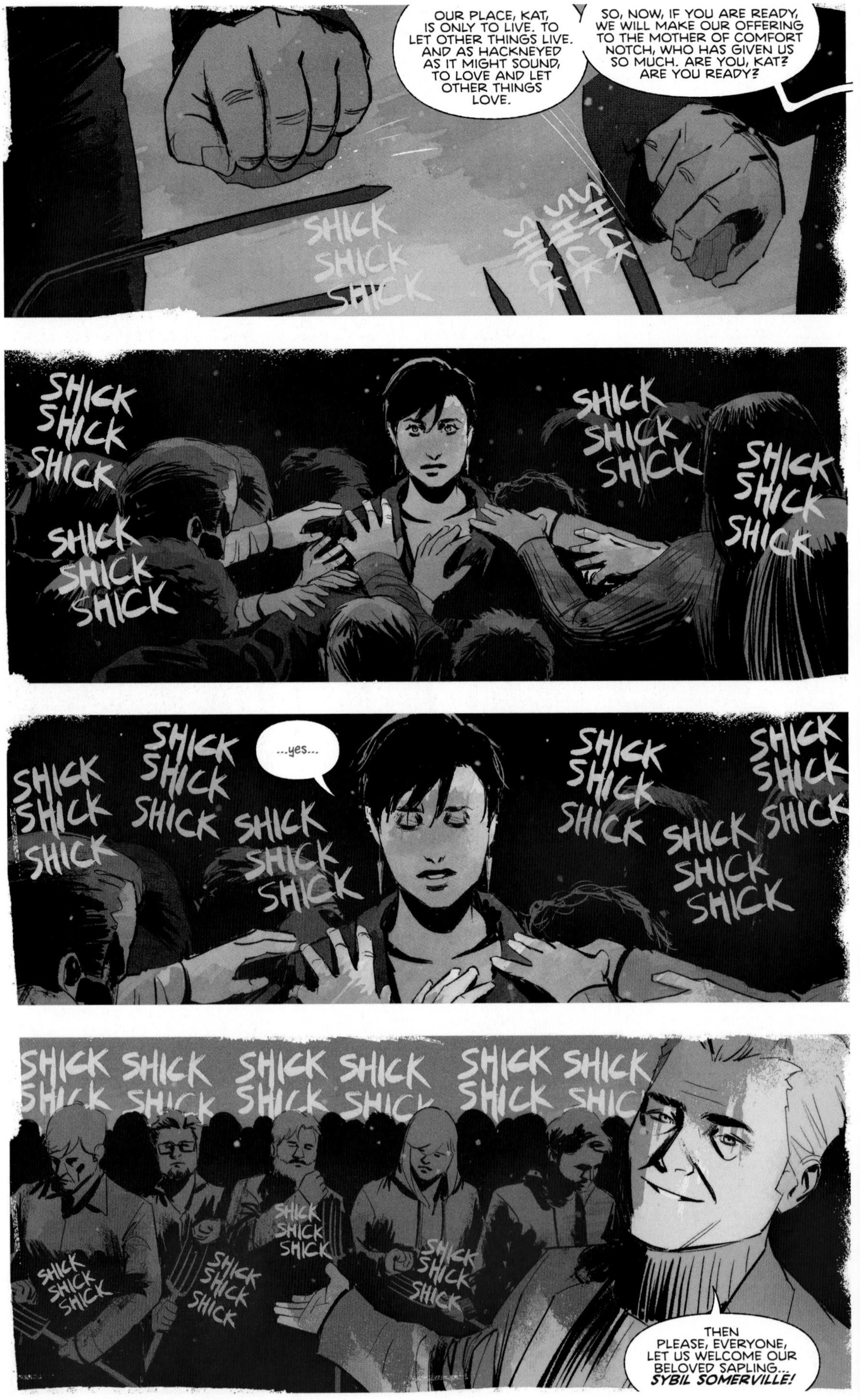

OUR PLACE, KAT, IS ONLY TO LIVE. TO LET OTHER THINGS LIVE. AND AS HACKNEYED AS IT MIGHT SOUND, TO LOVE AND LET OTHER THINGS LOVE.
SO, NOW, IF YOU ARE READY, WE WILL MAKE OUR OFFERING TO THE MOTHER OF COMFORT NOTCH, WHO HAS GIVEN US SO MUCH. ARE YOU, KAT? ARE YOU READY?
SHICK SHICK SHICK
SHICK SHICK SHICK
SHICK SHICK SHICK
SHICK SHICK SHICK
SHICK SHICK SHICK
SHICK SHICK SHICK
...yes...
SHICK SHICK SHICK
SHICK SHICK SHICK
SHICK SHICK SHICK
SHICK SHICK SHICK
SHICK SHICK SHICK
SHICK SHICK SHICK
SHICK SHICK SHICK SHICK SHICK SHICK
SHICK SHICK SHICK SHICK SHICK SHICK
SHICK SHICK SHICK
SHICK SHICK SHICK
SHICK SHICK SHICK
SHICK SHICK SHICK
THEN PLEASE, EVERYONE, LET US WELCOME OUR BELOVED SAPLING... ***SYBIL SOMERVILLE!***

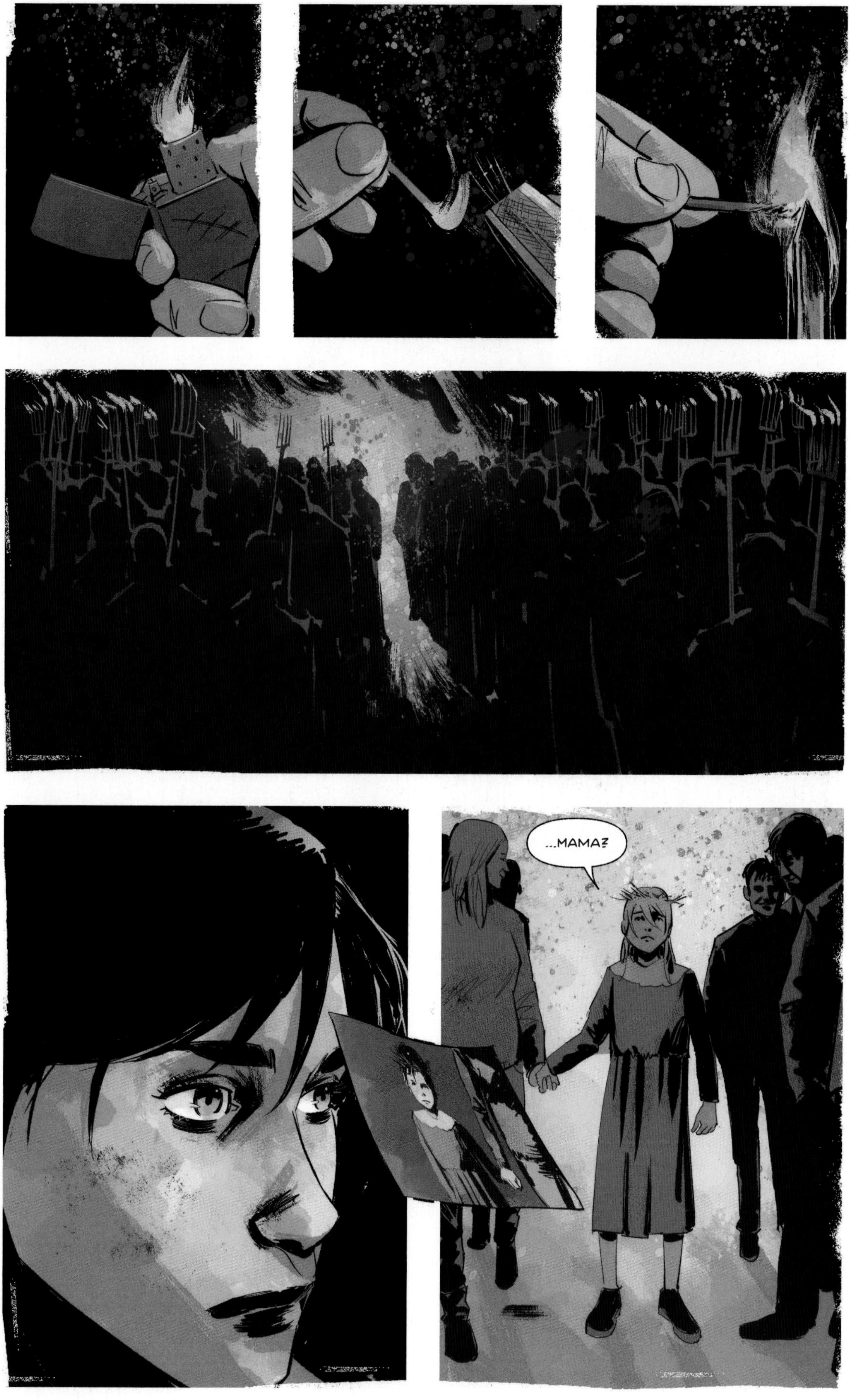
...MAMA?

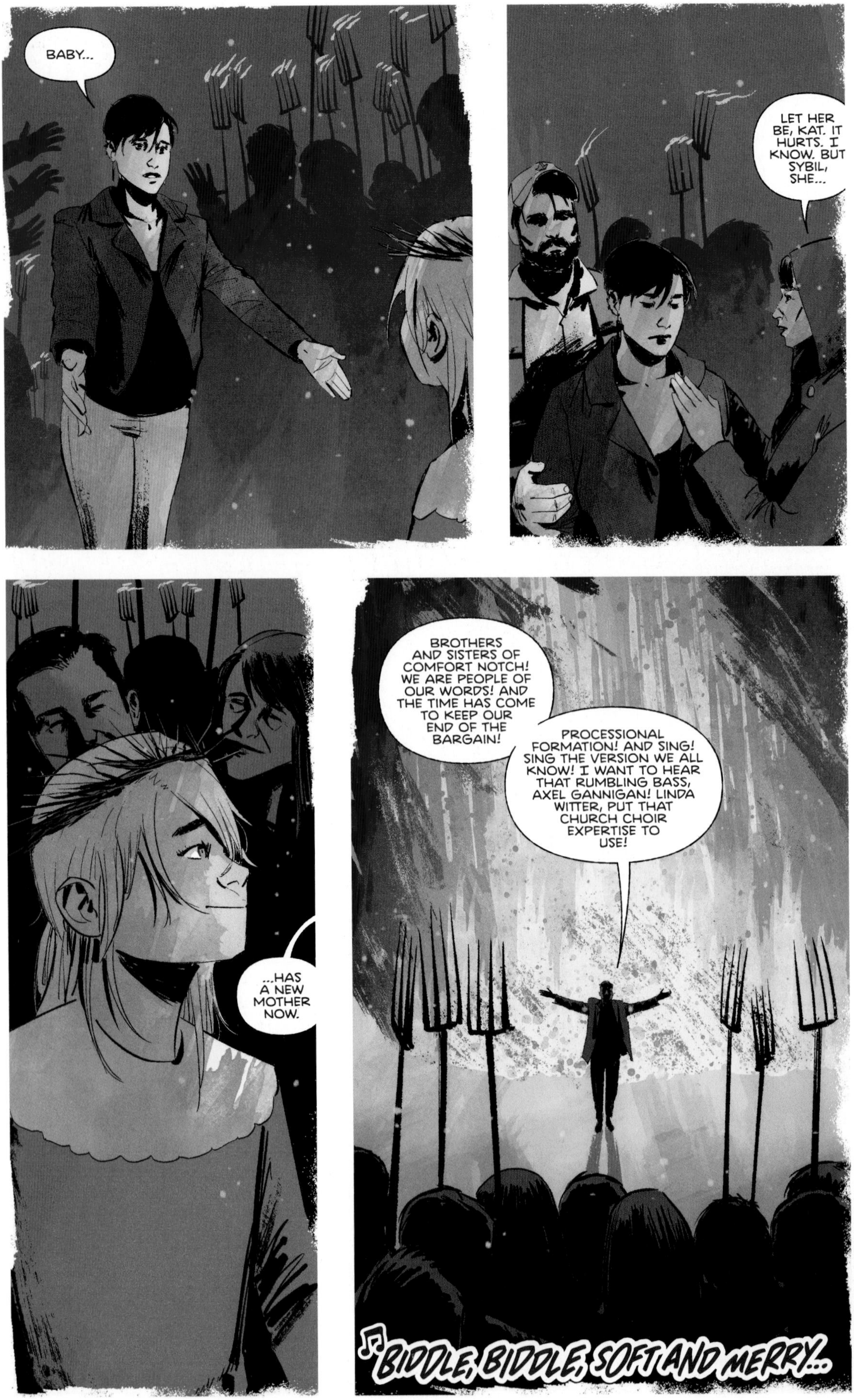
BABY...
LET HER BE, KAT. IT HURTS. I KNOW. BUT SYBIL, SHE...
...HAS A NEW MOTHER NOW.
BROTHERS AND SISTERS OF COMFORT NOTCH! WE ARE PEOPLE OF OUR WORDS! AND THE TIME HAS COME TO KEEP OUR END OF THE BARGAIN!
PROCESSIONAL FORMATION! AND SING! SING THE VERSION WE ALL KNOW! I WANT TO HEAR THAT RUMBLING BASS, AXEL GANNIGAN! LINDA WITTER, PUT THAT CHURCH CHOIR EXPERTISE TO USE!
♪ BIDDLE, BIDDLE, SOFT AND MERRY...

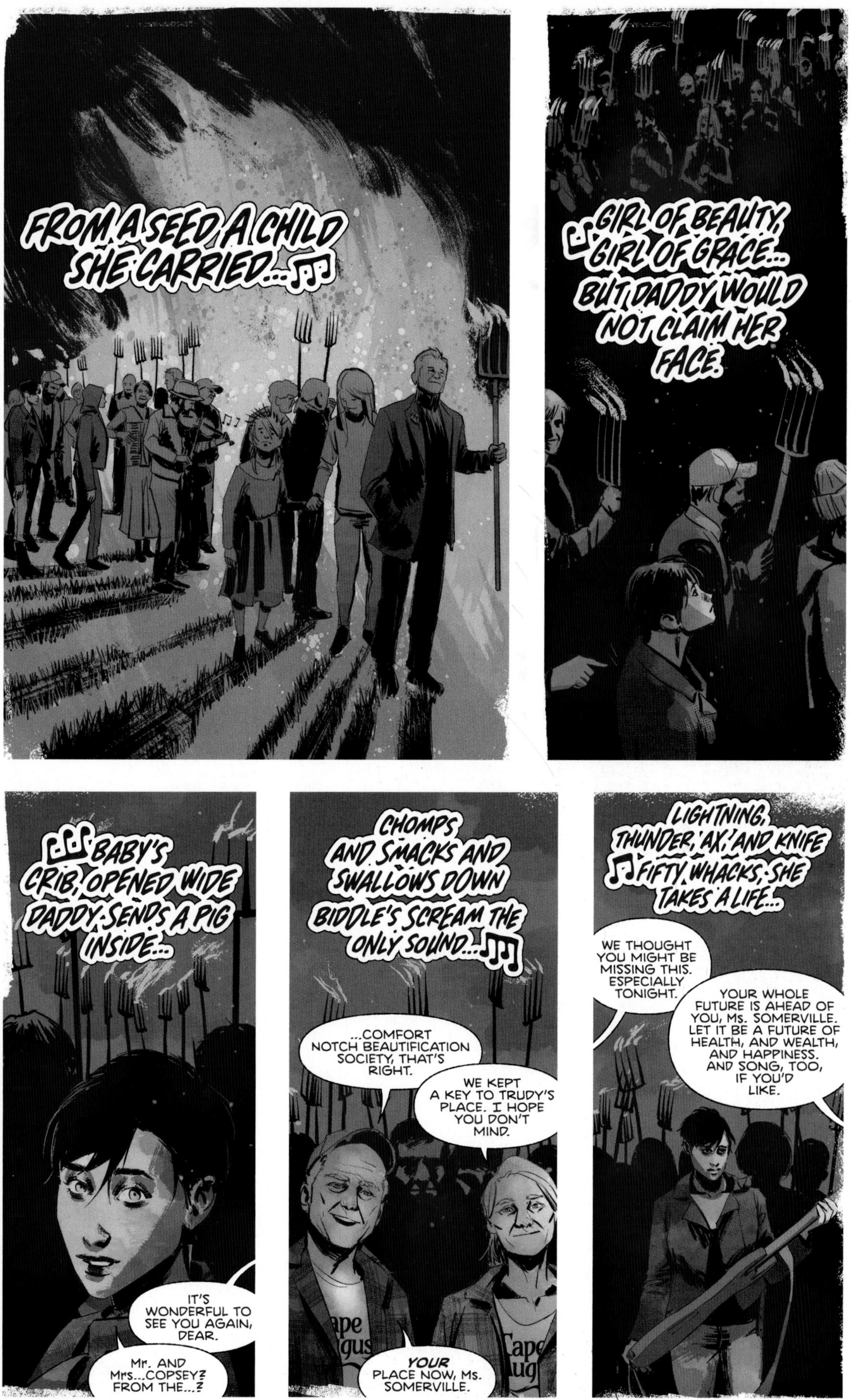

FROM A SEED A CHILD SHE CARRIED...
GIRL OF BEAUTY, GIRL OF GRACE... BUT DADDY WOULD NOT CLAIM HER FACE.
BABY'S CRIB, OPENED WIDE DADDY SENDS A PIG INSIDE...
IT'S WONDERFUL TO SEE YOU AGAIN, DEAR.
Mr. AND Mrs...COPSEY? FROM THE...?
CHOMPS AND SMACKS AND SWALLOWS DOWN BIDDLE'S SCREAM THE ONLY SOUND...
...COMFORT NOTCH BEAUTIFICATION SOCIETY, THAT'S RIGHT.
WE KEPT A KEY TO TRUDY'S PLACE. I HOPE YOU DON'T MIND.
YOUR PLACE NOW, MS. SOMERVILLE.
LIGHTNING, THUNDER, AX, AND KNIFE FIFTY WHACKS, SHE TAKES A LIFE...
WE THOUGHT YOU MIGHT BE MISSING THIS. ESPECIALLY TONIGHT.
YOUR WHOLE FUTURE IS AHEAD OF YOU, MS. SOMERVILLE. LET IT BE A FUTURE OF HEALTH, AND WEALTH, AND HAPPINESS. AND SONG, TOO, IF YOU'D LIKE.

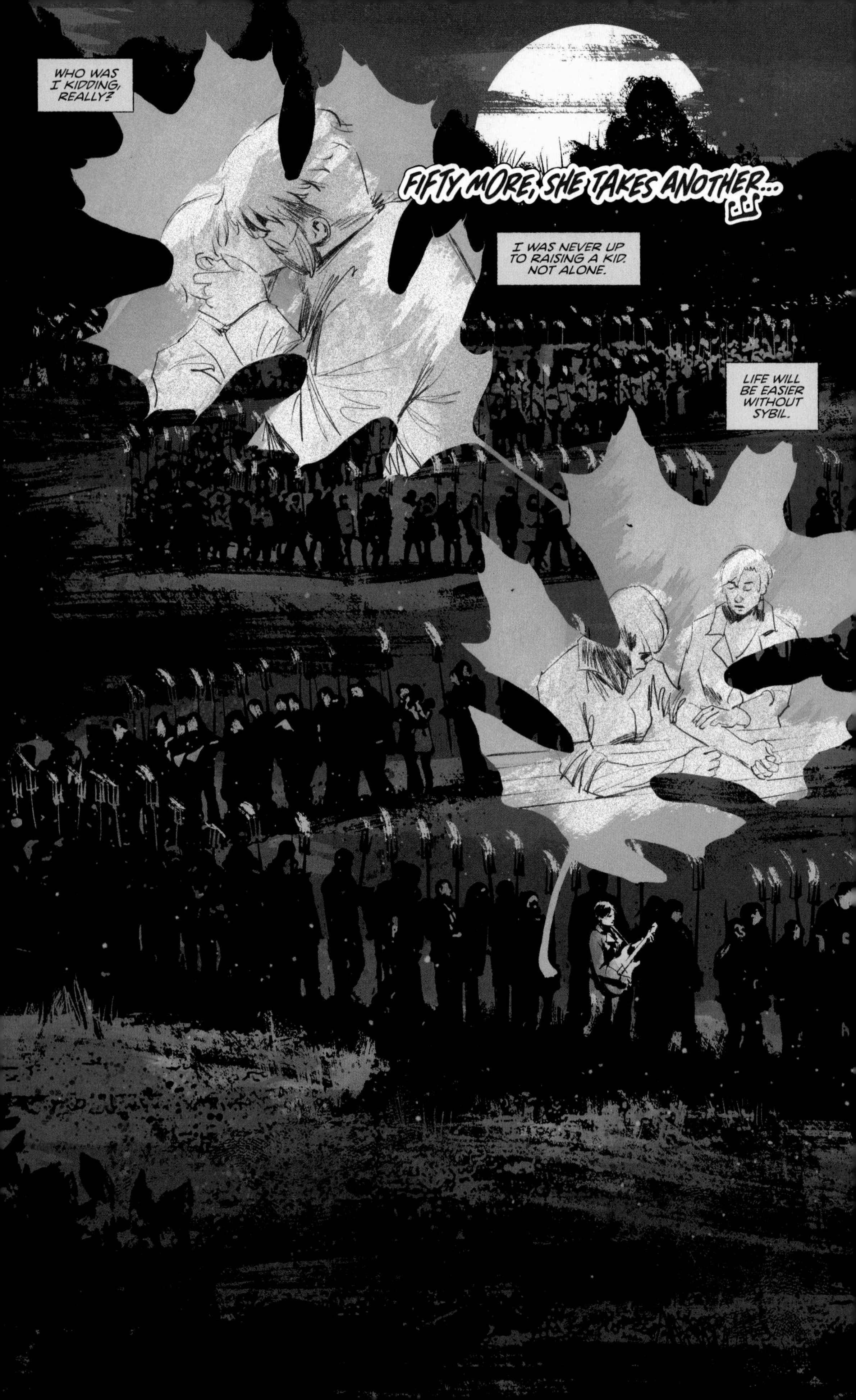
WHO WAS I KIDDING, REALLY?
FIFTY MORE, SHE TAKES ANOTHER...
I WAS NEVER UP TO RAISING A KID. NOT ALONE.
LIFE WILL BE EASIER WITHOUT SYBIL.

MURDERESS NOW INSTEAD OF MOTHER.
HEAD AND HAIR AND BONE AND BLOOD...
SHE'D ONLY REMIND ME OF THE PAST I HAVE TO FORGET.
TURN STONE AND LEAF, AND TREE AND MUD.
ONE DAY, WHEN I'M READY, I CAN TRY AGAIN.
WATCH YOUR FEET NOW, WATCH YOUR NOSE...
BIDDLE, BIDDLE...
WITH THIS FAMILY AROUND ME, I'LL DO BETTER.

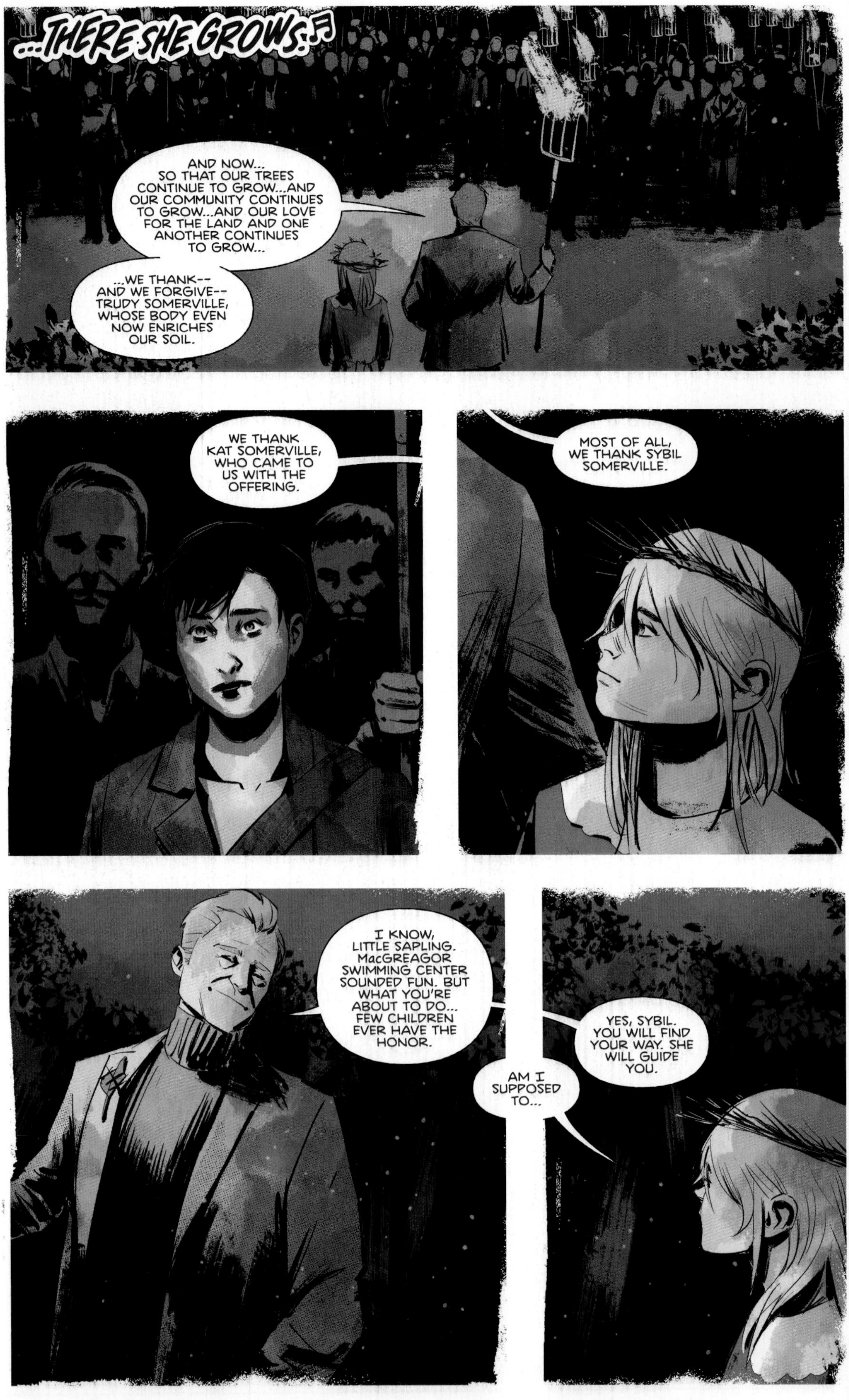
...THERE SHE GROWS.
AND NOW... SO THAT OUR TREES CONTINUE TO GROW...AND OUR COMMUNITY CONTINUES TO GROW...AND OUR LOVE FOR THE LAND AND ONE ANOTHER CONTINUES TO GROW...
...WE THANK-- AND WE FORGIVE-- TRUDY SOMERVILLE, WHOSE BODY EVEN NOW ENRICHES OUR SOIL.
WE THANK KAT SOMERVILLE, WHO CAME TO US WITH THE OFFERING.
MOST OF ALL, WE THANK SYBIL SOMERVILLE.
I KNOW, LITTLE SAPLING. MacGREAGOR SWIMMING CENTER SOUNDED FUN. BUT WHAT YOU'RE ABOUT TO DO... FEW CHILDREN EVER HAVE THE HONOR.
AM I SUPPOSED TO...
YES, SYBIL. YOU WILL FIND YOUR WAY. SHE WILL GUIDE YOU.

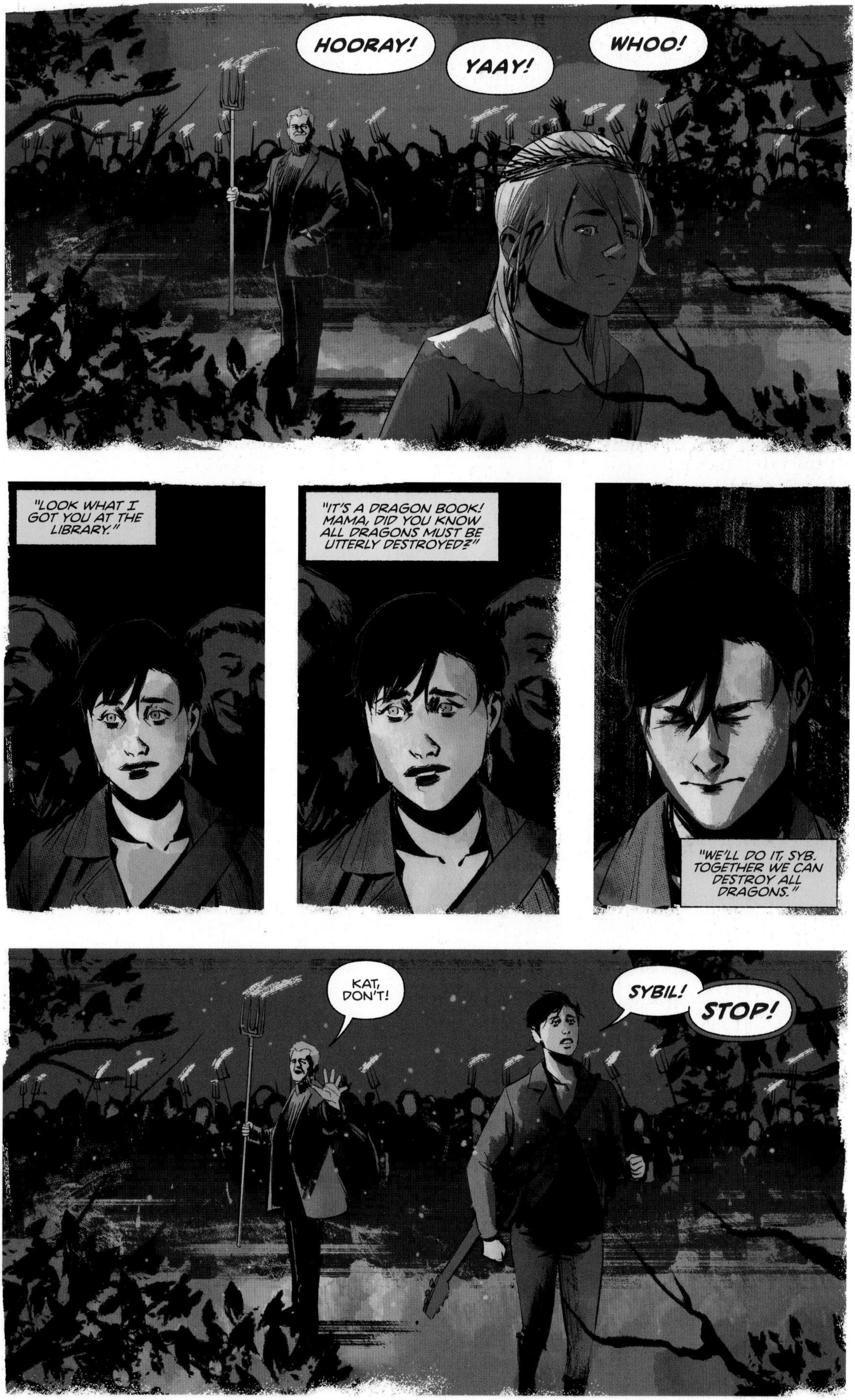
HOORAY!
YAAY!
WHOO!
"LOOK WHAT I GOT YOU AT THE LIBRARY."
"IT'S A DRAGON BOOK! MAMA, DID YOU KNOW ALL DRAGONS MUST BE UTTERLY DESTROYED?"
"WE'LL DO IT, SYB. TOGETHER WE CAN DESTROY ALL DRAGONS."
KAT, DON'T!
SYBIL!
STOP!

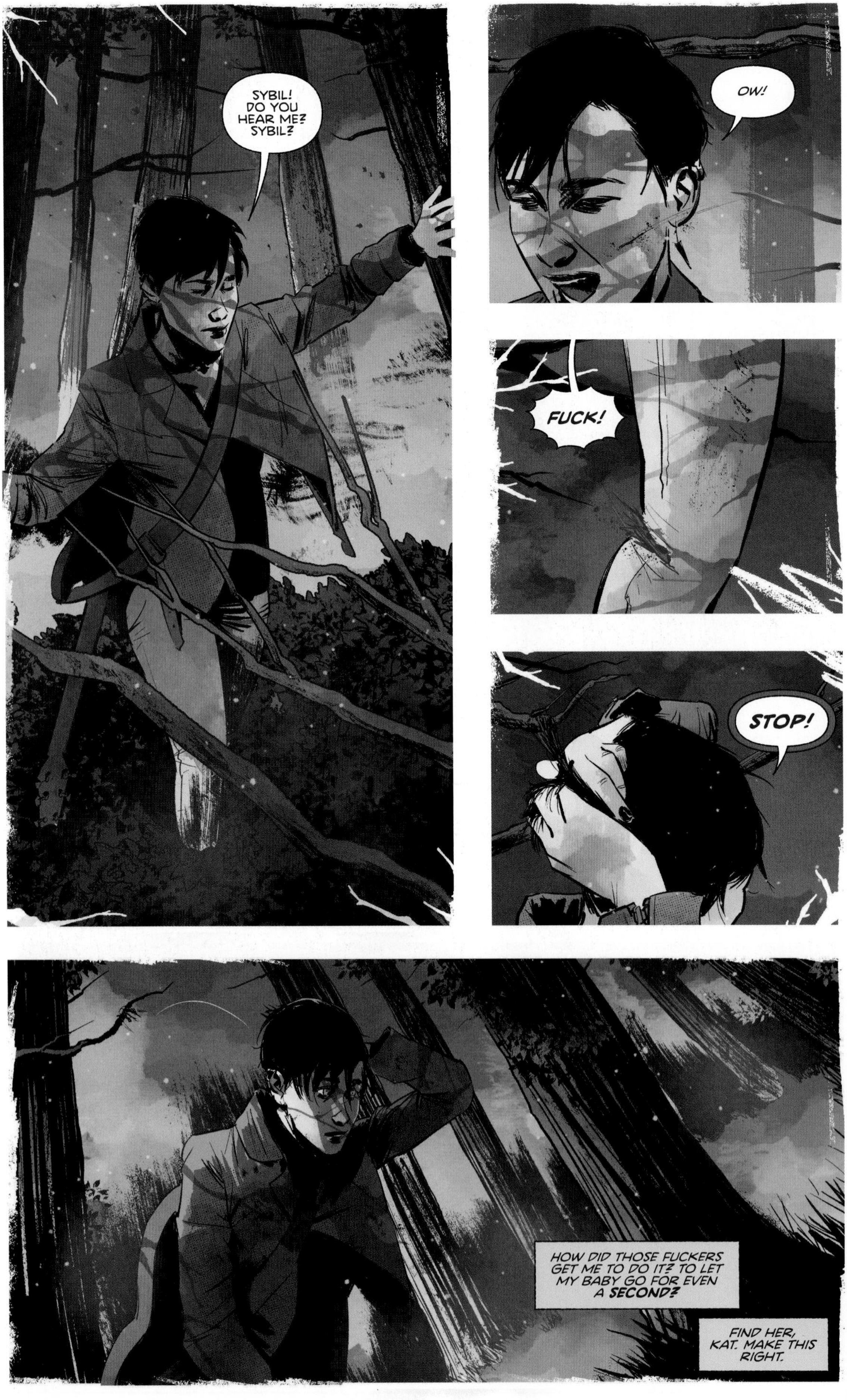
SYBIL! DO YOU HEAR ME? SYBIL?
OW!
FUCK!
STOP!
HOW DID THOSE FUCKERS GET ME TO DO IT? TO LET MY BABY GO FOR EVEN A SECOND?
FIND HER, KAT. MAKE THIS RIGHT.

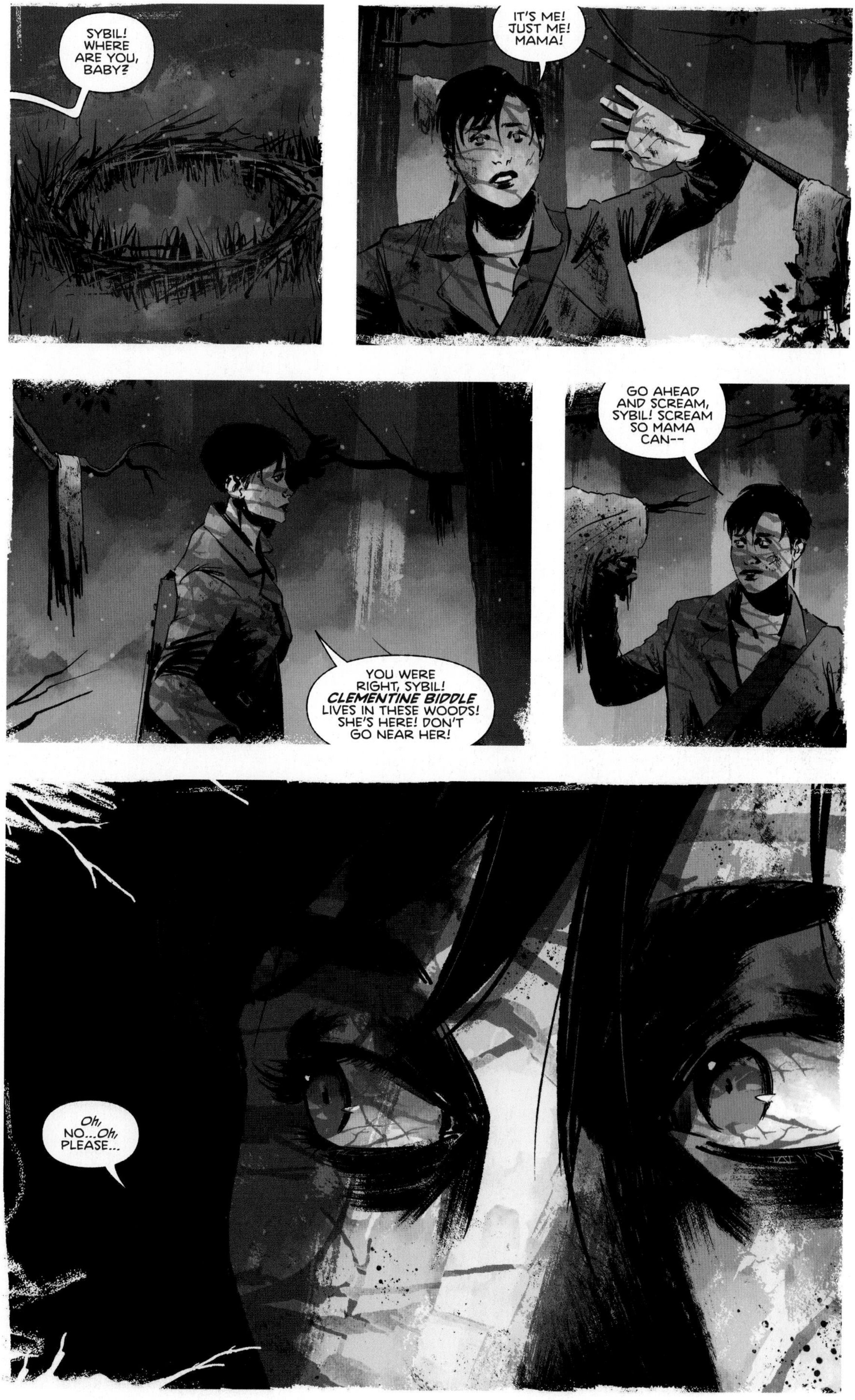
SYBIL! WHERE ARE YOU, BABY?
IT'S ME! JUST ME! MAMA!
YOU WERE RIGHT, SYBIL! CLEMENTINE BIDDLE LIVES IN THESE WOODS! SHE'S HERE! DON'T GO NEAR HER!
GO AHEAD AND SCREAM, SYBIL! SCREAM SO MAMA CAN--
Oh, NO...Oh, PLEASE...

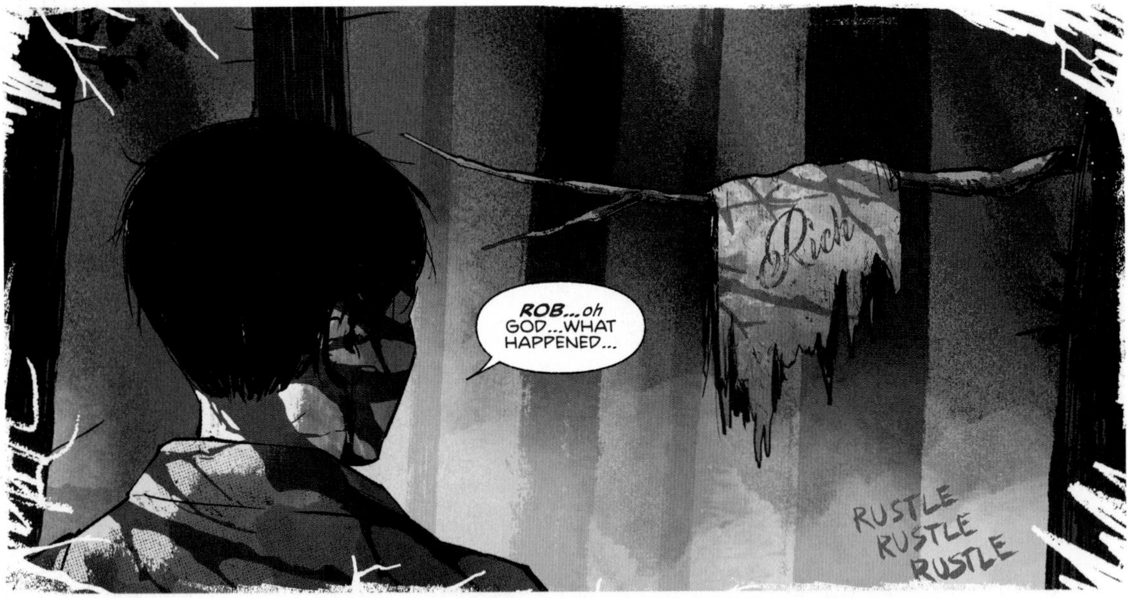
ROB...oh GOD...WHAT HAPPENED...
Rich
RUSTLE RUSTLE RUSTLE

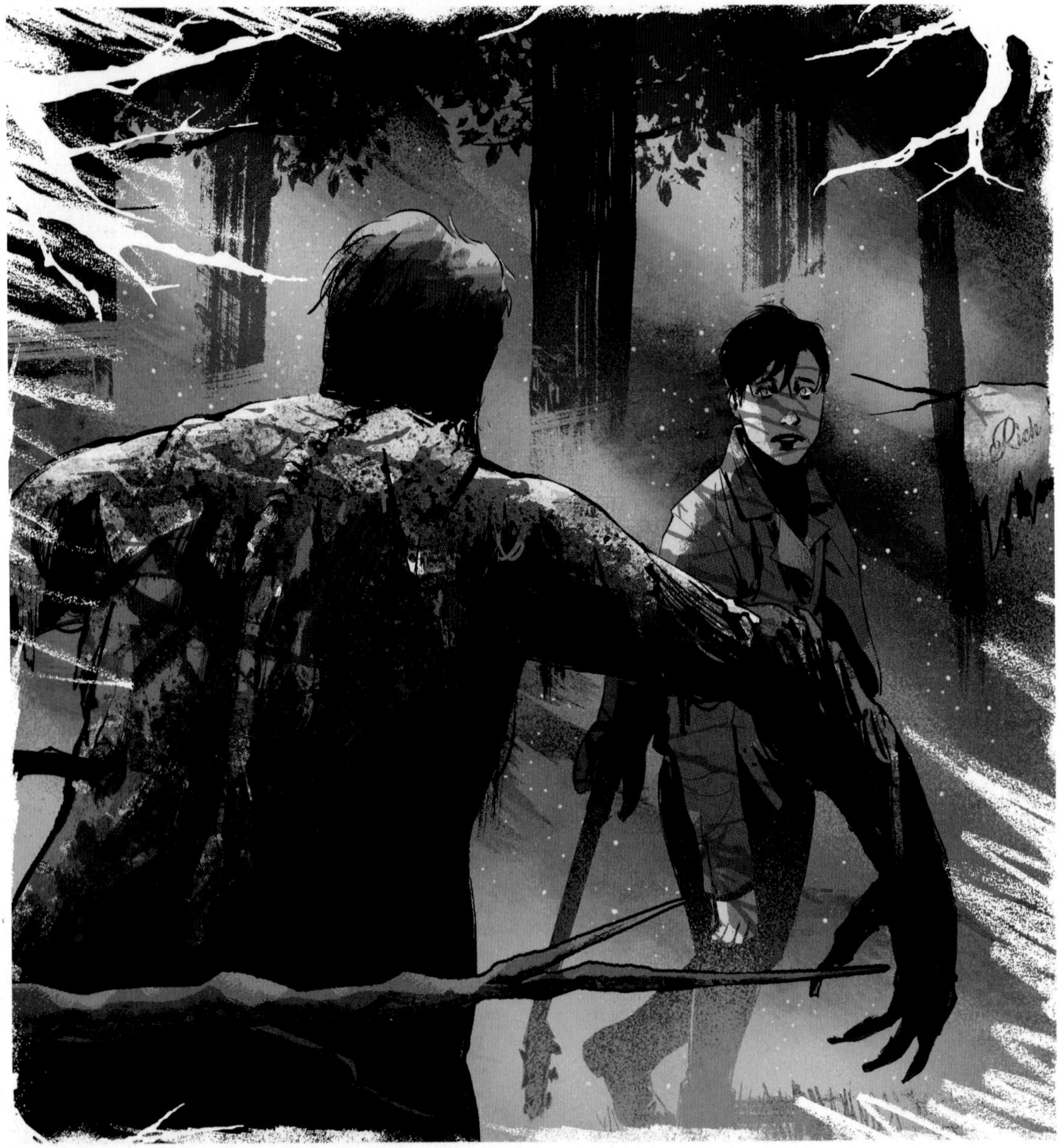
Rich

grows.

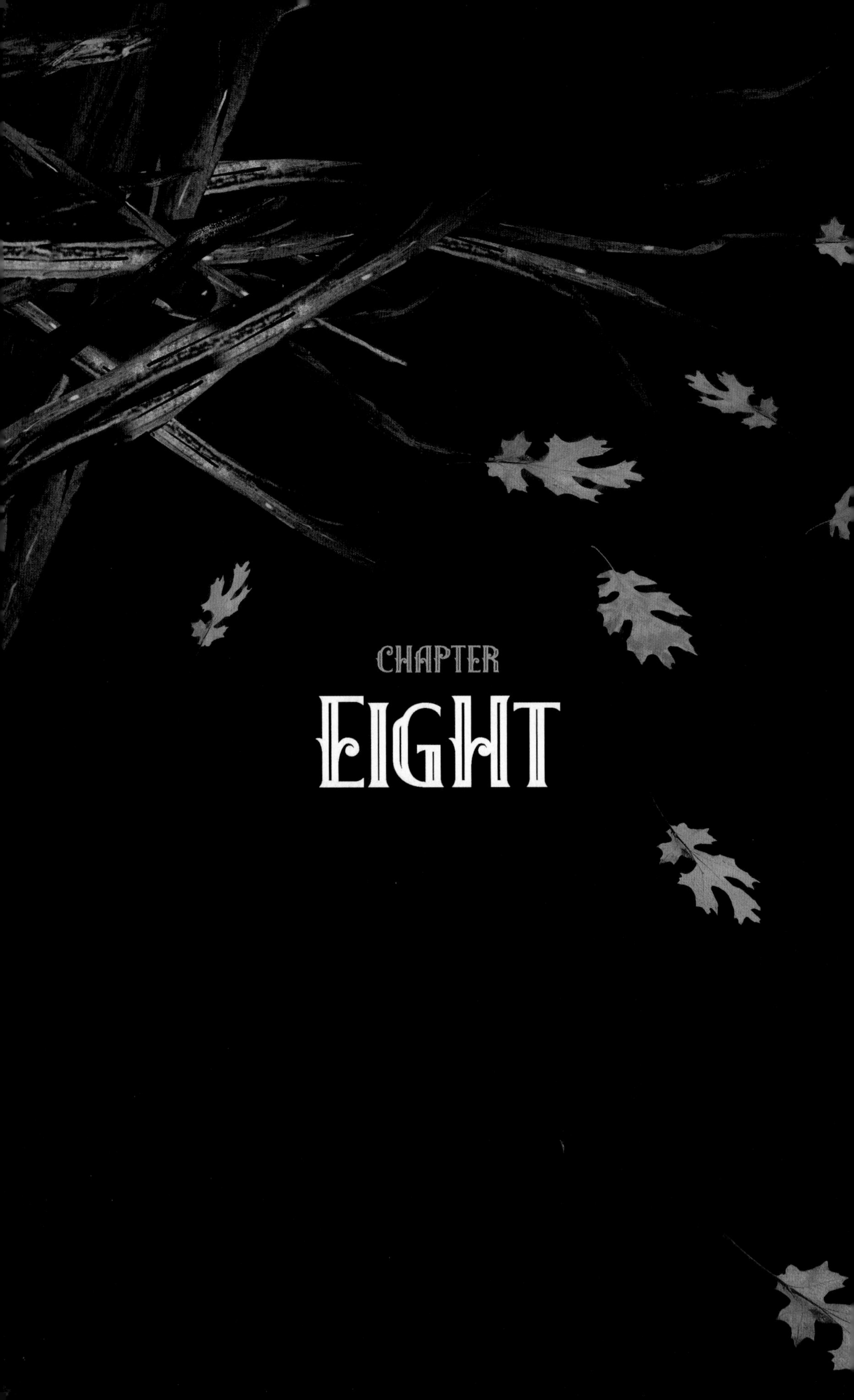

CHAPTER EIGHT

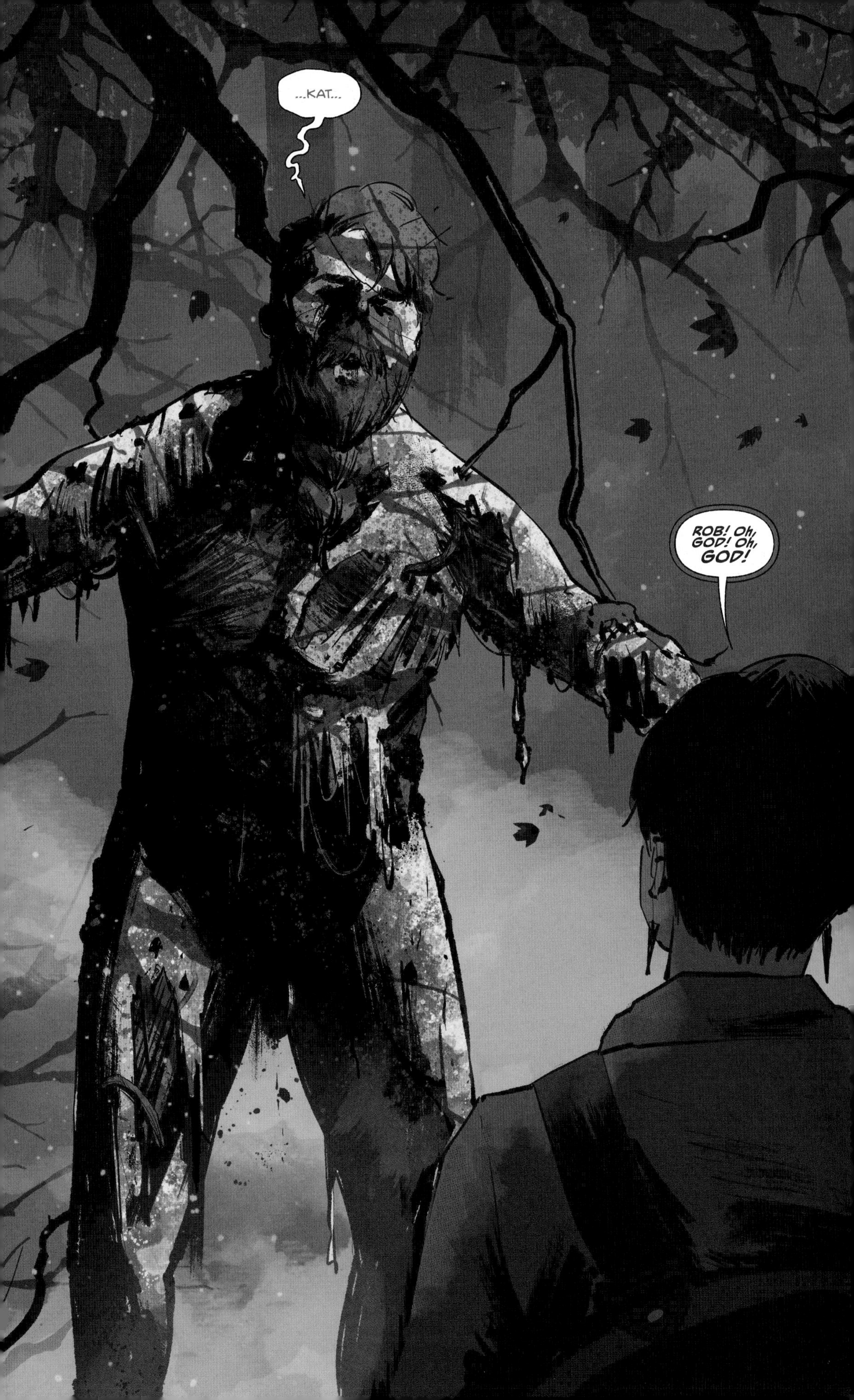
...KAT...
ROB! OH, GOD! OH, GOD!

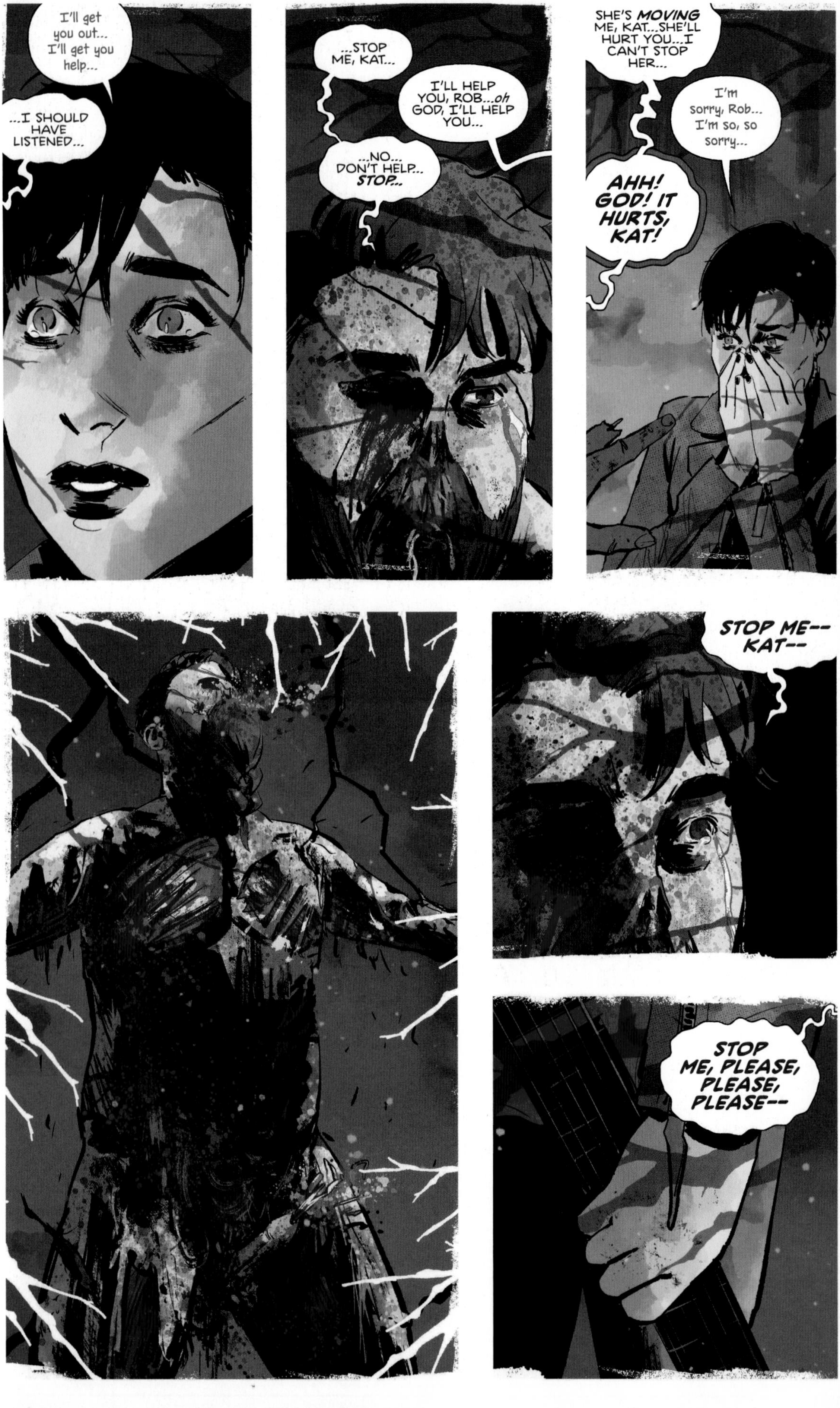
I'll get you out... I'll get you help...
...I SHOULD HAVE LISTENED...
...STOP ME, KAT...
I'LL HELP YOU, ROB...oh GOD, I'LL HELP YOU...
...NO... DON'T HELP... STOP...
SHE'S MOVING ME, KAT...SHE'LL HURT YOU...I CAN'T STOP HER...
I'm sorry, Rob... I'm so, so sorry...
AHH! GOD! IT HURTS, KAT!
STOP ME-- KAT--
STOP ME, PLEASE, PLEASE, PLEASE--

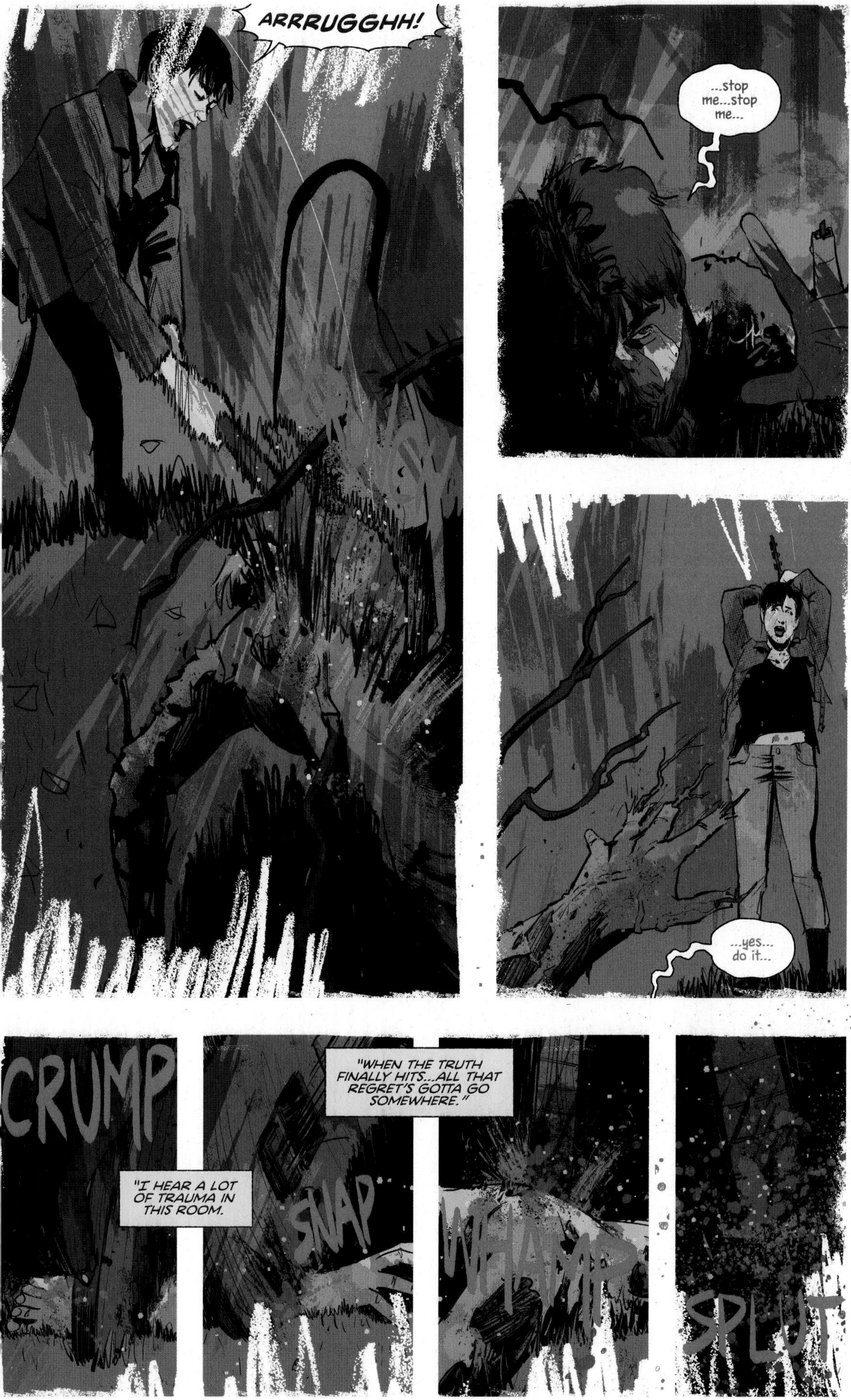
ARRRUGGHH!
...stop me...stop me...
...yes... do it...
CRUMP
"I HEAR A LOT OF TRAUMA IN THIS ROOM.
"WHEN THE TRUTH FINALLY HITS...ALL THAT REGRET'S GOTTA GO SOMEWHERE."
SNAP
WHAMP
SPLUT

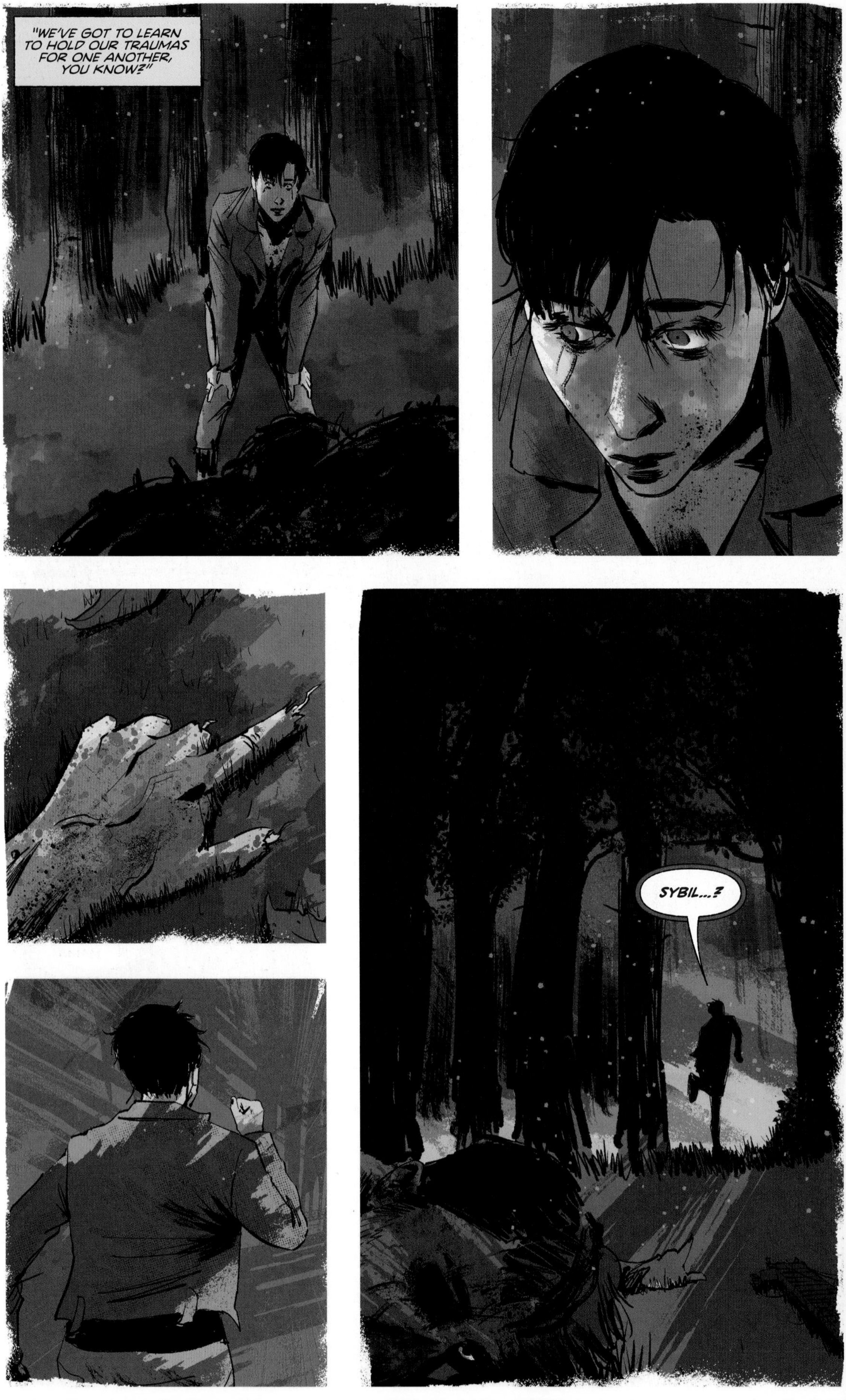
"WE'VE GOT TO LEARN TO HOLD OUR TRAUMAS FOR ONE ANOTHER, YOU KNOW?"
SYBIL...?

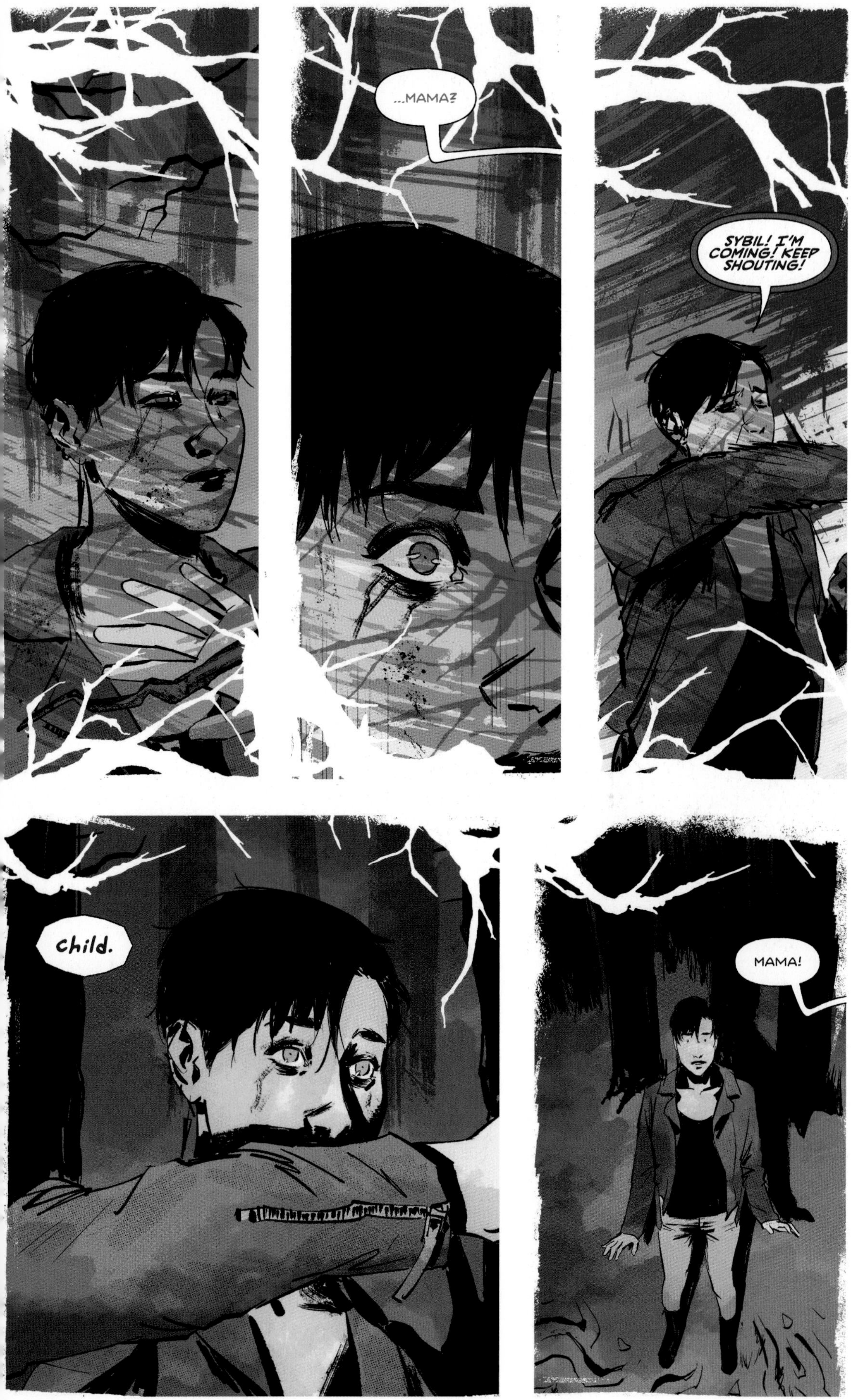
...MAMA?
SYBIL! I'M COMING! KEEP SHOUTING!
child.
MAMA!

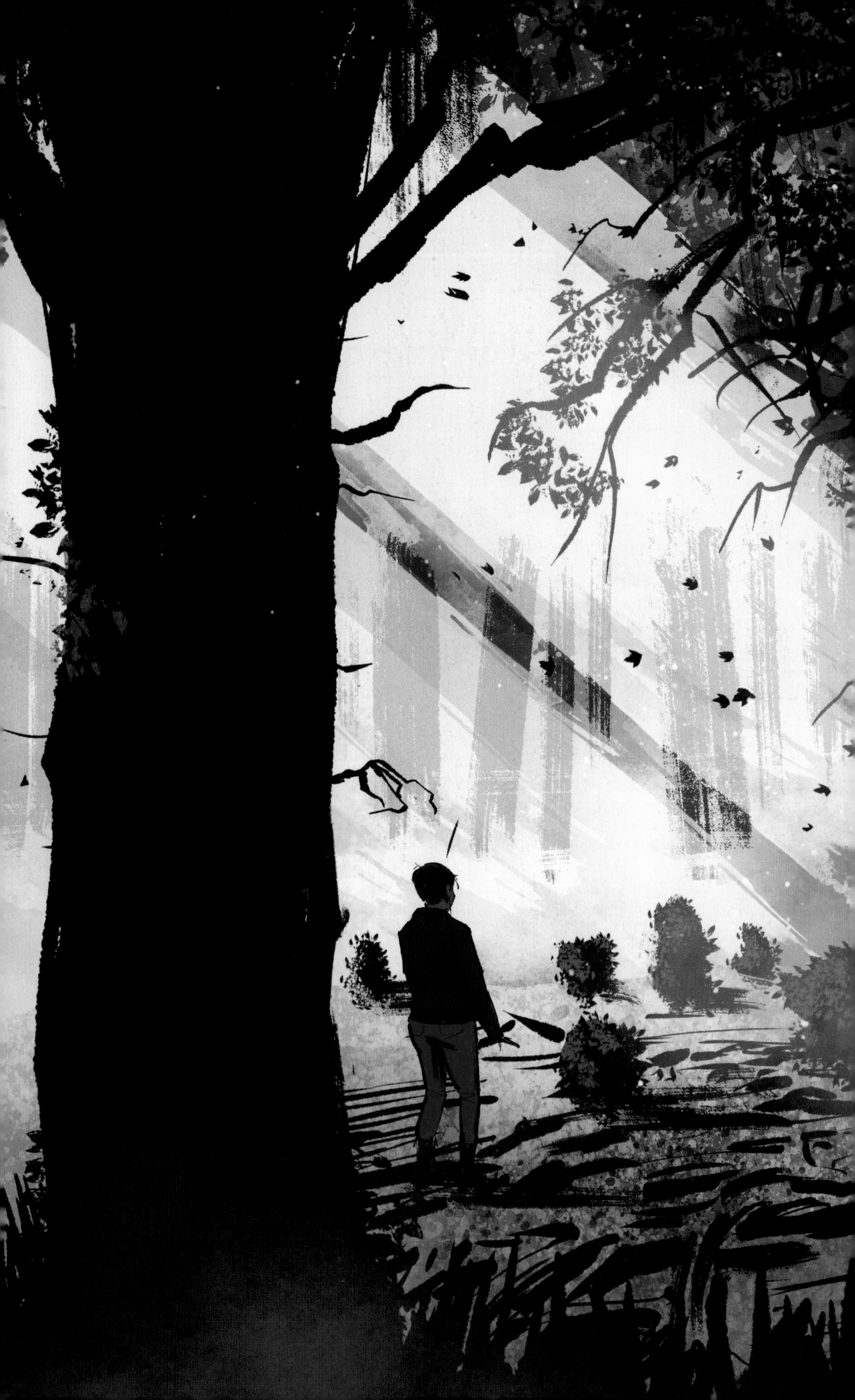

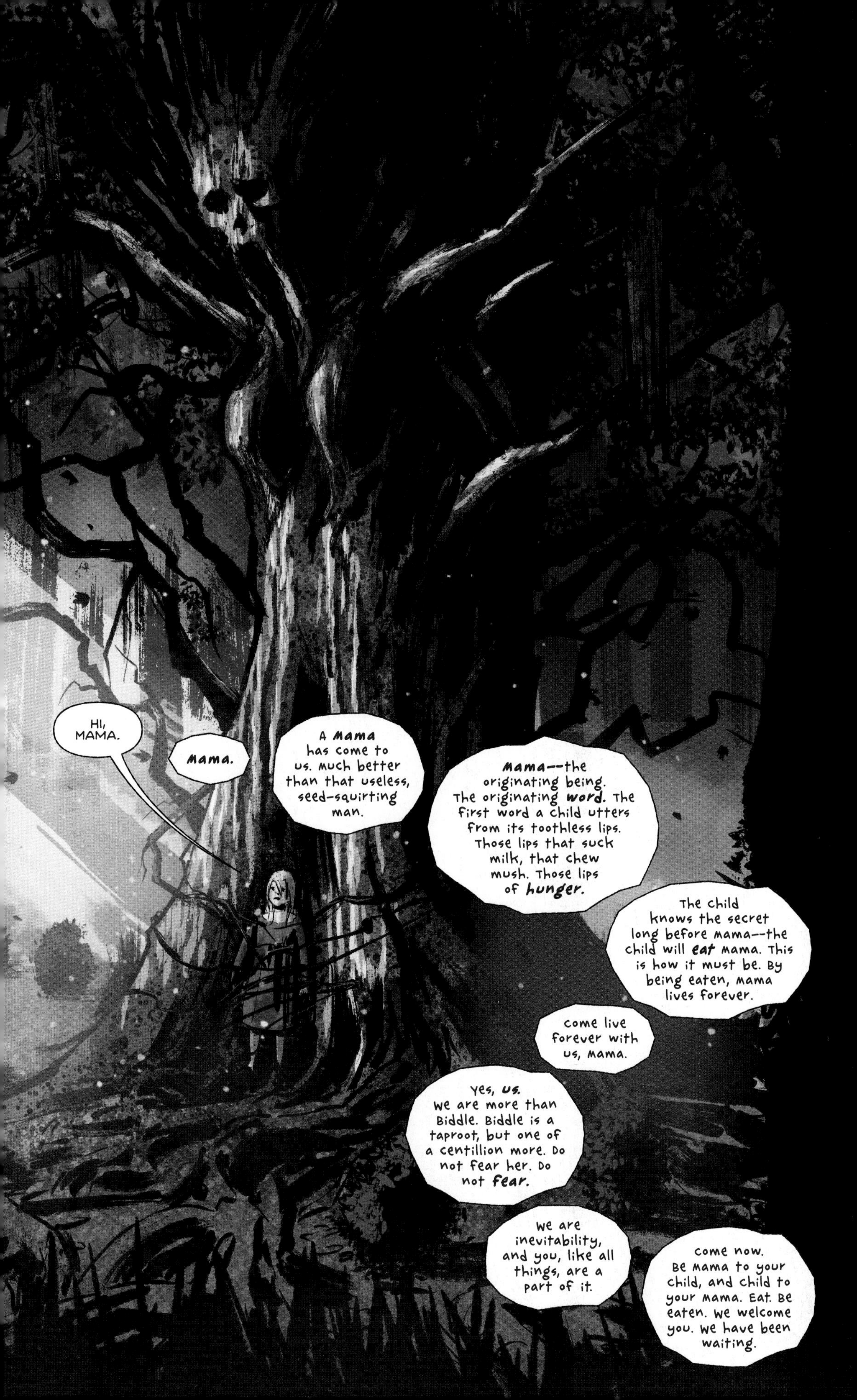
HI, MAMA.
Mama.
A Mama has come to us. much better than that useless, seed-squirting man.
Mama--the originating being. The originating word. The first word a child utters from its toothless lips. Those lips that suck milk, that chew mush. Those lips of hunger.
The child knows the secret long before mama--the child will eat mama. This is how it must be. By being eaten, mama lives forever.
come live forever with us, mama.
Yes, us. we are more than Biddle. Biddle is a taproot, but one of a centillion more. Do not fear her. Do not fear.
we are inevitability, and you, like all things, are a part of it.
come now. Be mama to your child, and child to your mama. Eat. Be eaten. we welcome you. we have been waiting.

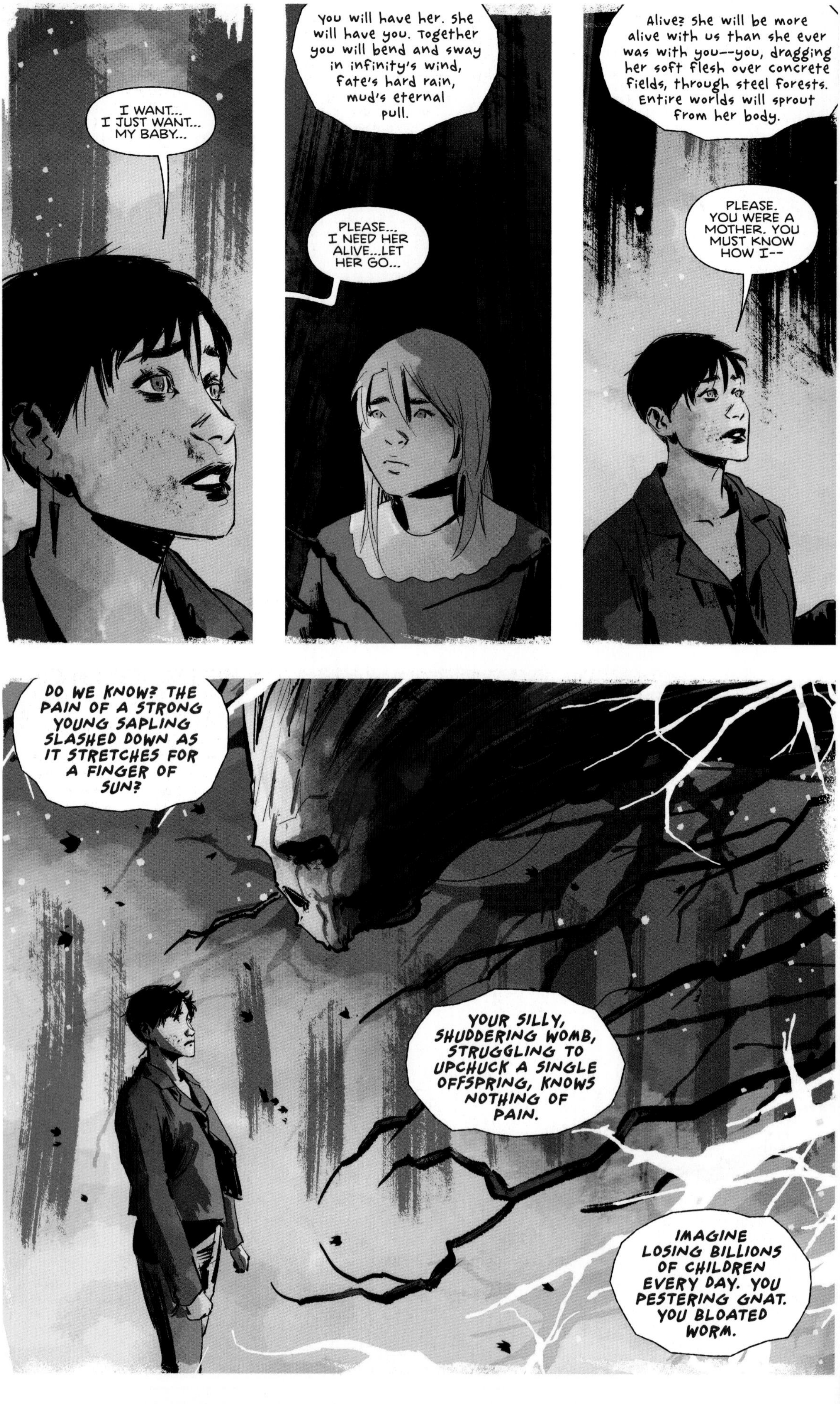
I WANT... I JUST WANT... MY BABY...
You will have her. She will have you. Together you will bend and sway in infinity's wind, fate's hard rain, mud's eternal pull.
PLEASE... I NEED HER ALIVE...LET HER GO...
Alive? She will be more alive with us than she ever was with you--you, dragging her soft flesh over concrete fields, through steel forests. Entire worlds will sprout from her body.
PLEASE. YOU WERE A MOTHER. YOU MUST KNOW HOW I--
DO WE KNOW? THE PAIN OF A STRONG YOUNG SAPLING SLASHED DOWN AS IT STRETCHES FOR A FINGER OF SUN?
YOUR SILLY, SHUDDERING WOMB, STRUGGLING TO UPCHUCK A SINGLE OFFSPRING, KNOWS NOTHING OF PAIN.
IMAGINE LOSING BILLIONS OF CHILDREN EVERY DAY. YOU PESTERING GNAT. YOU BLOATED WORM.

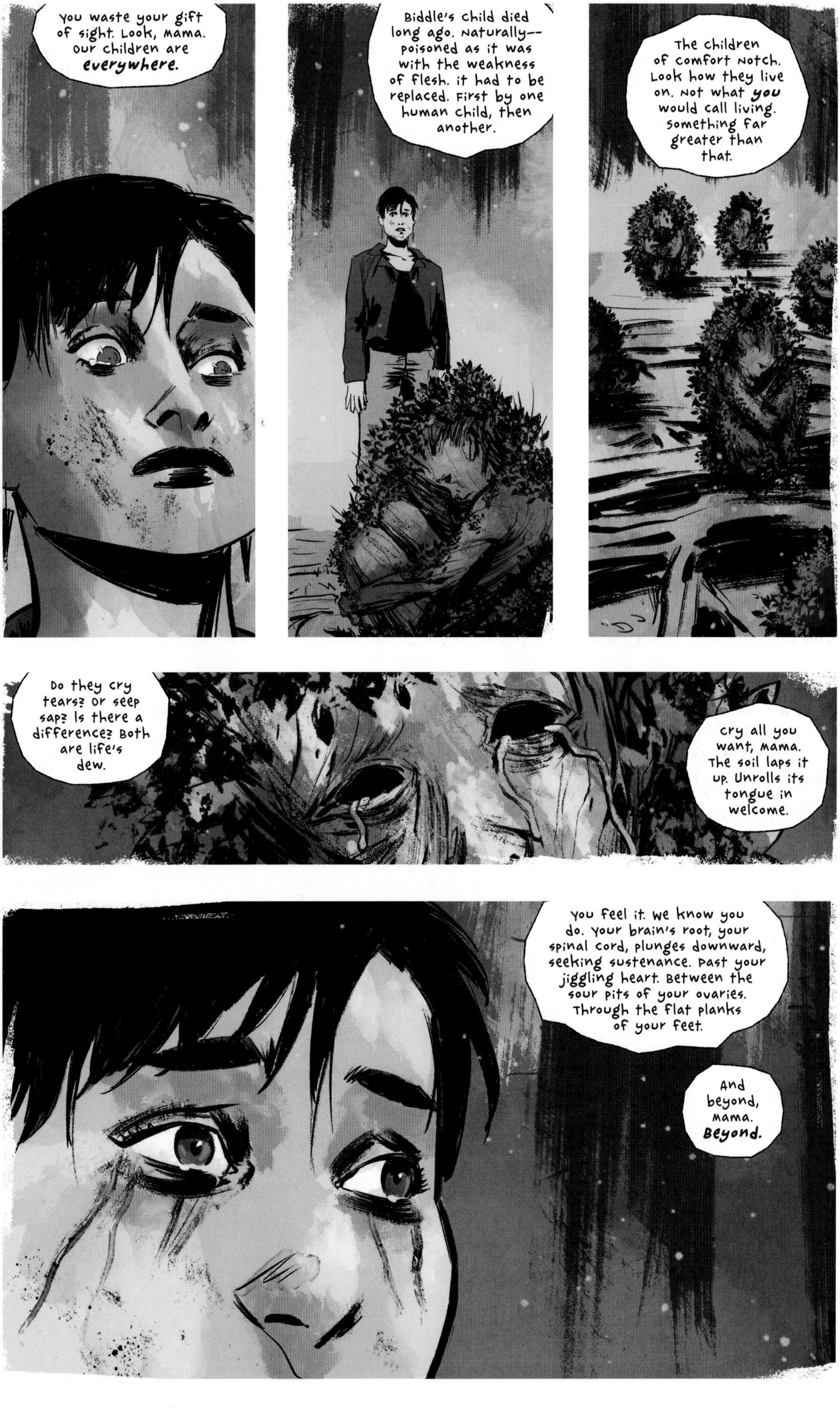
You waste your gift of sight. Look, mama. Our children are **everywhere.**
Biddle's child died long ago. Naturally-- poisoned as it was with the weakness of flesh. It had to be replaced. First by one human child, then another.
The children of Comfort Notch. Look how they live on. Not what **you** would call living. Something far greater than that.
Do they cry tears? Or seep sap? Is there a difference? Both are life's dew.
Cry all you want, mama. The soil laps it up. Unrolls its tongue in welcome.
You feel it. We know you do. Your brain's root, your spinal cord, plunges downward, seeking sustenance. Past your jiggling heart. Between the sour pits of your ovaries. Through the flat planks of your feet.
And beyond, mama. **Beyond.**

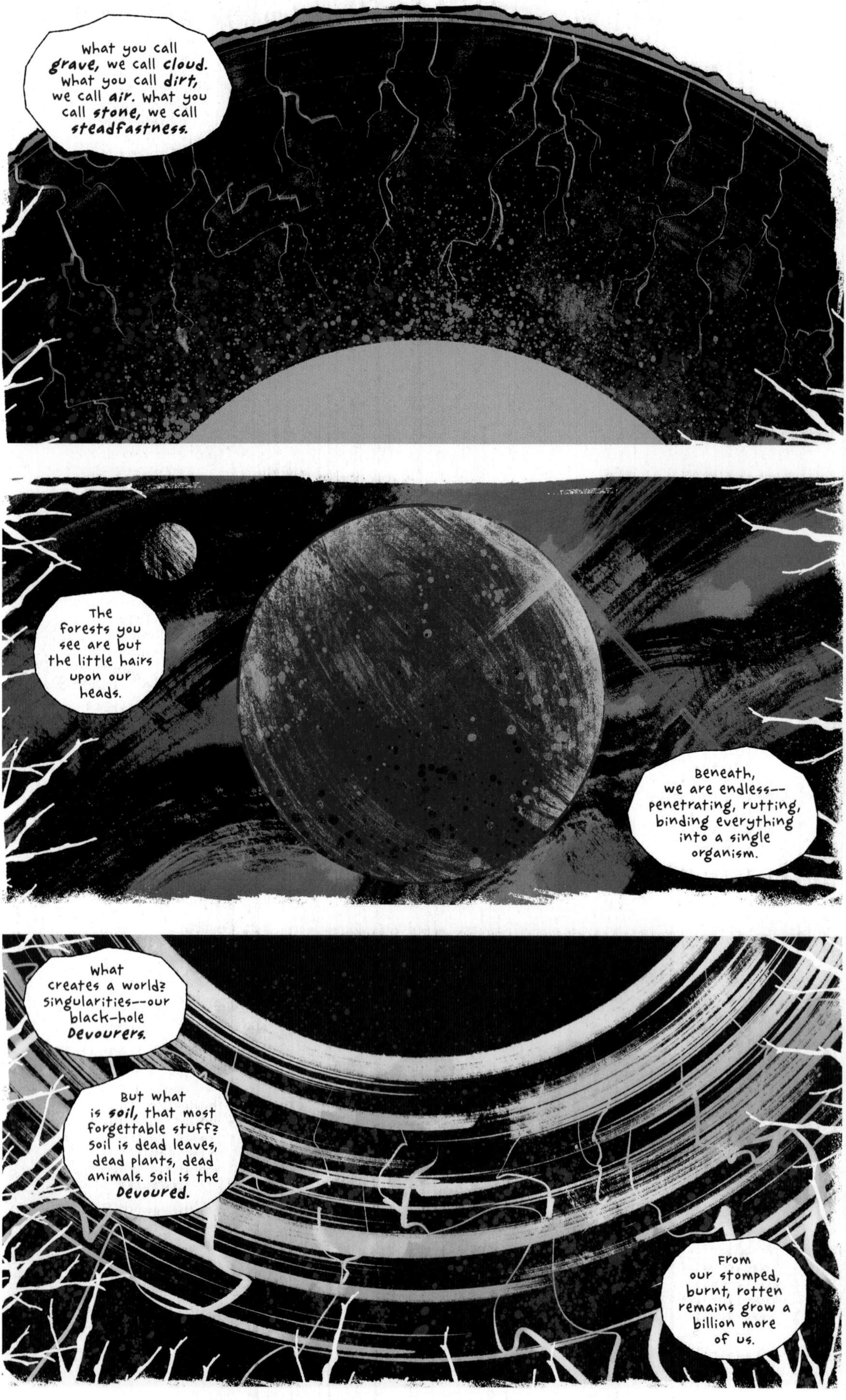
What you call grave, we call cloud. What you call dirt, we call air. What you call stone, we call steadfastness.
The forests you see are but the little hairs upon our heads.
Beneath, we are endless--penetrating, rutting, binding everything into a single organism.
What creates a world? Singularities--our black-hole Devourers.
But what is soil, that most forgettable stuff? Soil is dead leaves, dead plants, dead animals. Soil is the Devoured.
From our stomped, burnt, rotten remains grow a billion more of us.

It is impossible to dig a hole into dirt. only circles, rings, infinitudes.

Your pain is pleasure. Because your **death** is **life.**

How long did you live? How rich was your life? All that matters is that you *die* and *decompose*, become the soil, the tree, the everything.

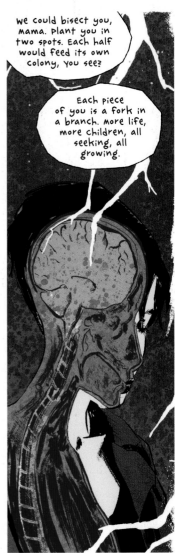

we could bisect you, Mama. Plant you in two spots. Each half would feed its own colony, You see?

Each piece of you is a fork in a branch. More life, more children, all seeking, all growing.

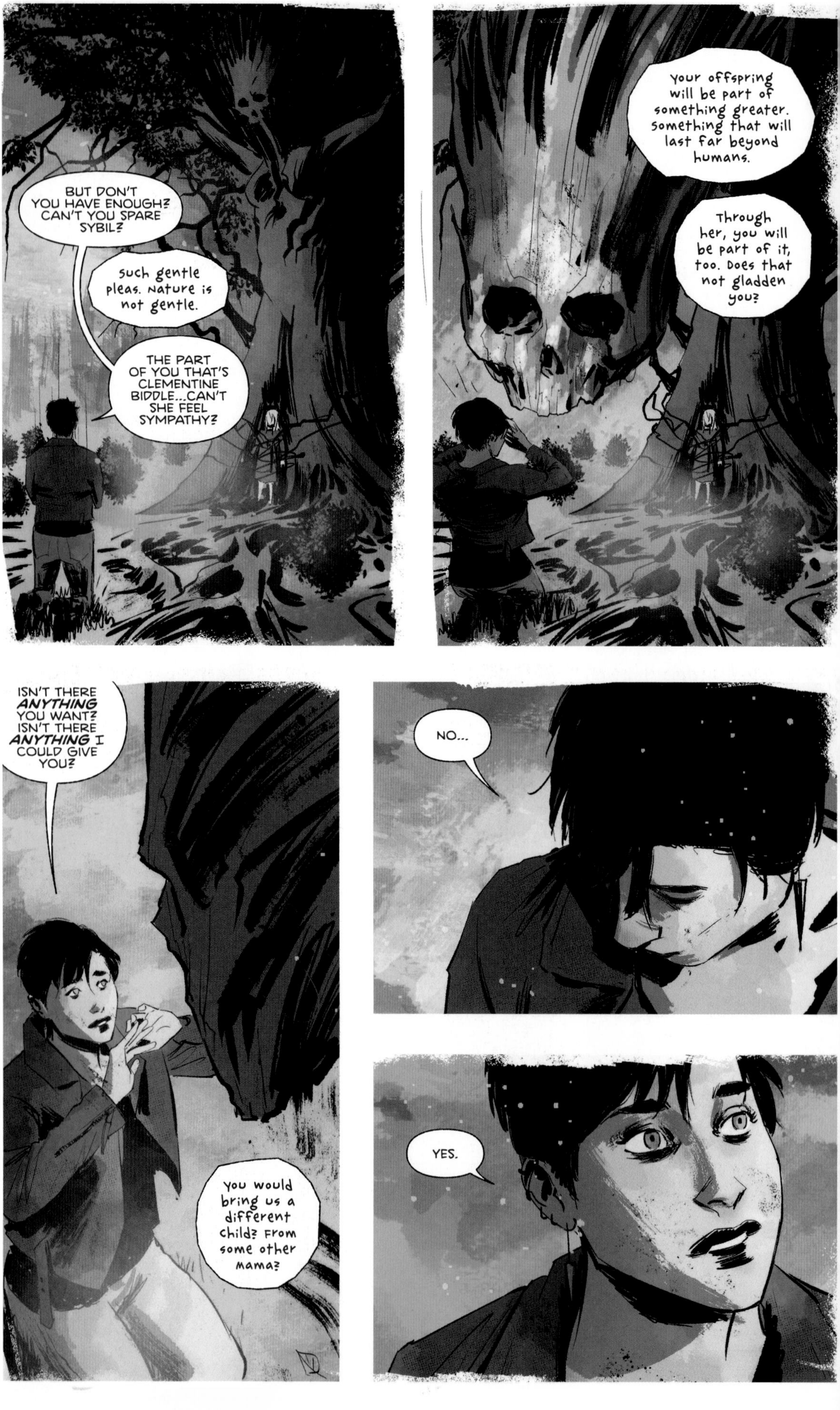
BUT DON'T YOU HAVE ENOUGH? CAN'T YOU SPARE SYBIL?
Such gentle pleas. Nature is not gentle.
THE PART OF YOU THAT'S CLEMENTINE BIDDLE...CAN'T SHE FEEL SYMPATHY?
Your offspring will be part of something greater. Something that will last far beyond humans.
Through her, you will be part of it, too. Does that not gladden you?
ISN'T THERE ANYTHING YOU WANT? ISN'T THERE ANYTHING I COULD GIVE YOU?
You would bring us a different child? From some other mama?
NO...
YES.

ME. TAKE ME.
Taking you does nothing to make others obey.
NOT TO REPLACE SYBIL. TO REPLACE YOU.
...ME?
TWO HUNDRED YEARS. CLEMENTINE, YOU'RE TIRED. AREN'T YOU TIRED? IF YOU LET SYBIL GO, I'LL...I'LL TAKE YOUR PLACE... I'LL BE A PART OF...THIS.
It won't matter if I stop. The trees...the leaves...they'll keep on going...
I DON'T CARE. IT'S MY PROBLEM NOW. JUST LET MY SYBIL GO FREE.
No one has ever...no has one ever asked...

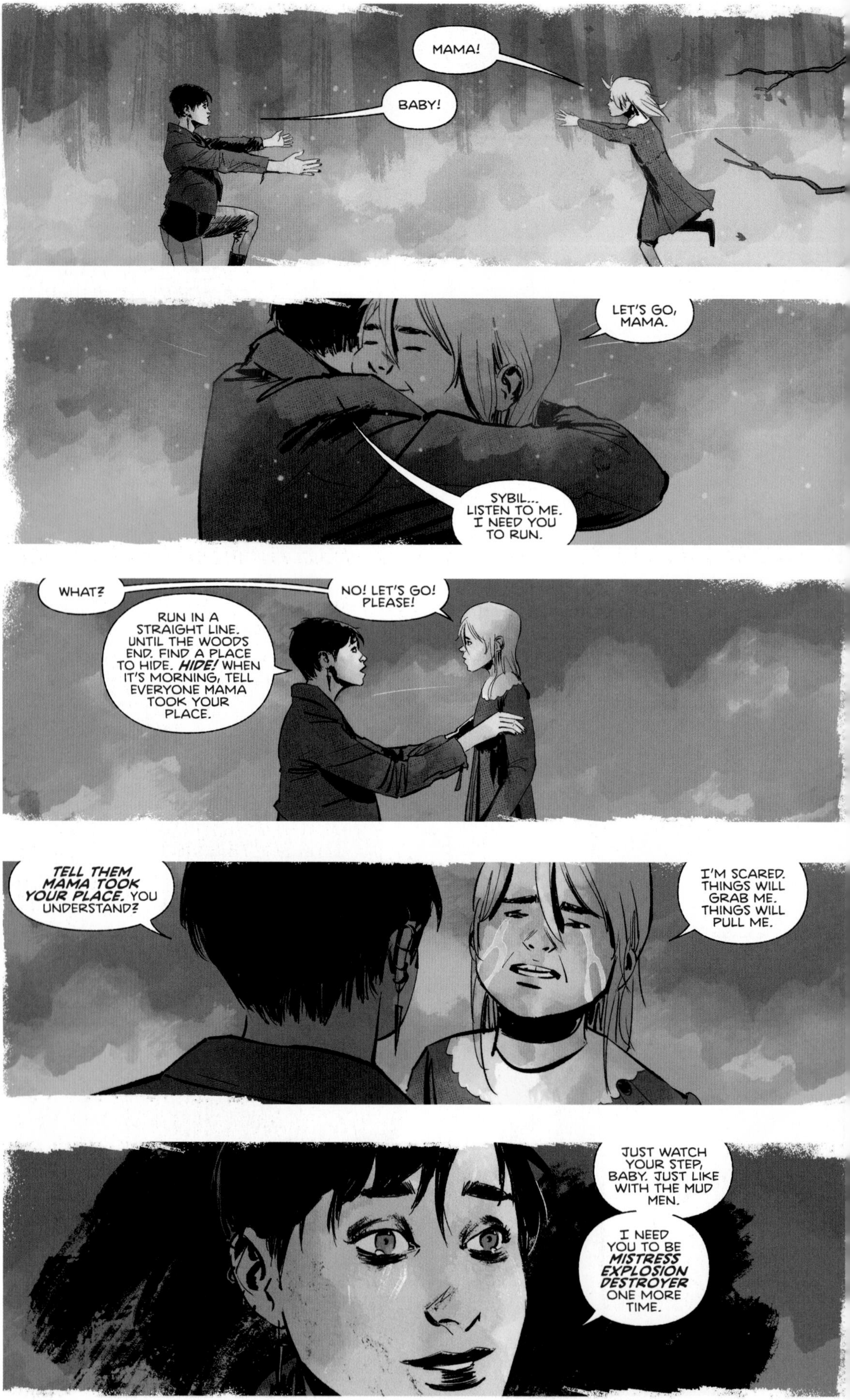
MAMA!
BABY!
LET'S GO, MAMA.
SYBIL... LISTEN TO ME. I NEED YOU TO RUN.
WHAT?
NO! LET'S GO! PLEASE!
RUN IN A STRAIGHT LINE. UNTIL THE WOODS END. FIND A PLACE TO HIDE. HIDE! WHEN IT'S MORNING, TELL EVERYONE MAMA TOOK YOUR PLACE.
TELL THEM MAMA TOOK YOUR PLACE. YOU UNDERSTAND?
I'M SCARED. THINGS WILL GRAB ME. THINGS WILL PULL ME.
JUST WATCH YOUR STEP, BABY. JUST LIKE WITH THE MUD MEN.
I NEED YOU TO BE MISTRESS EXPLOSION DESTROYER ONE MORE TIME.

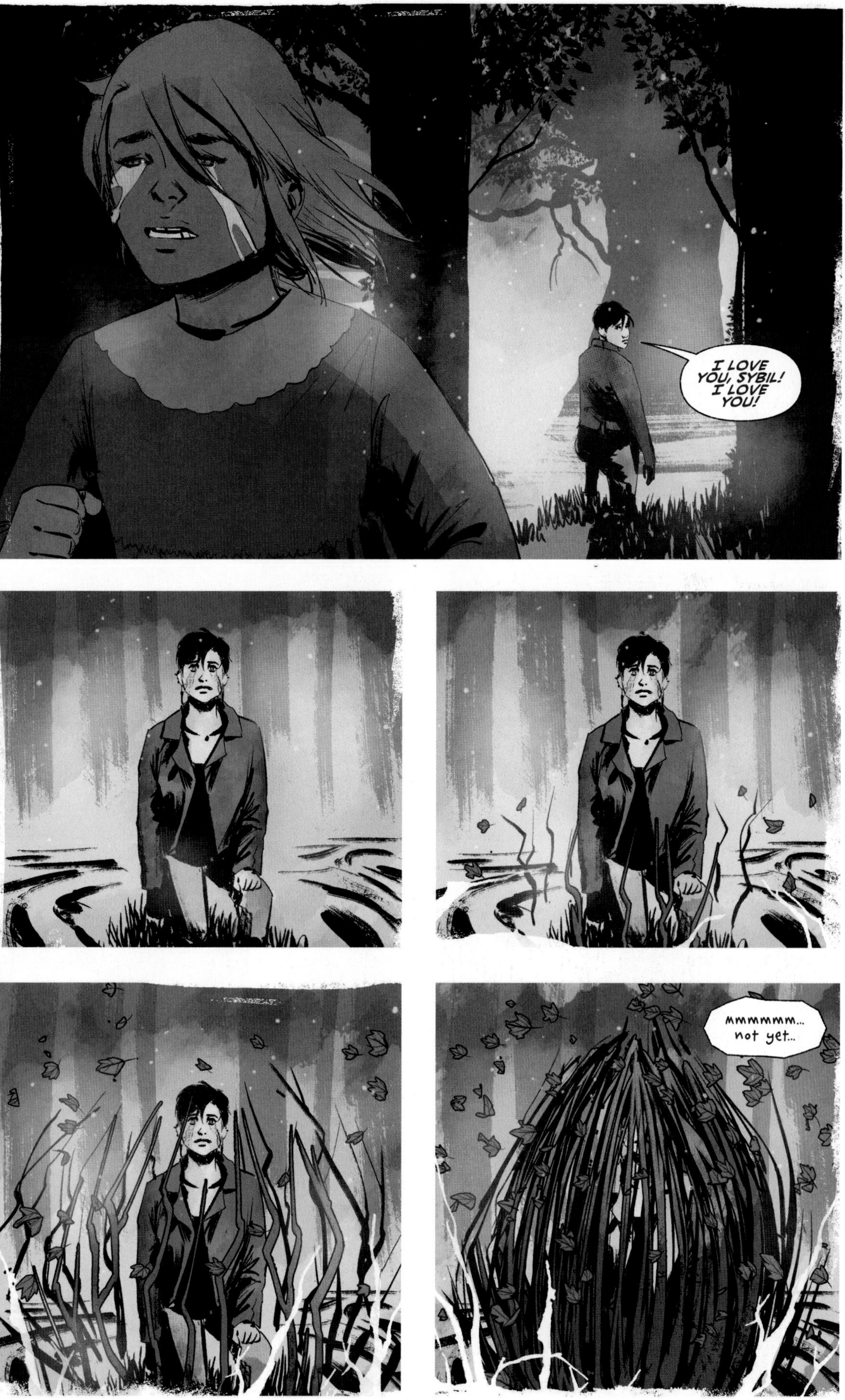
I LOVE YOU, SYBIL! I LOVE YOU!
mmmmmm... not yet...

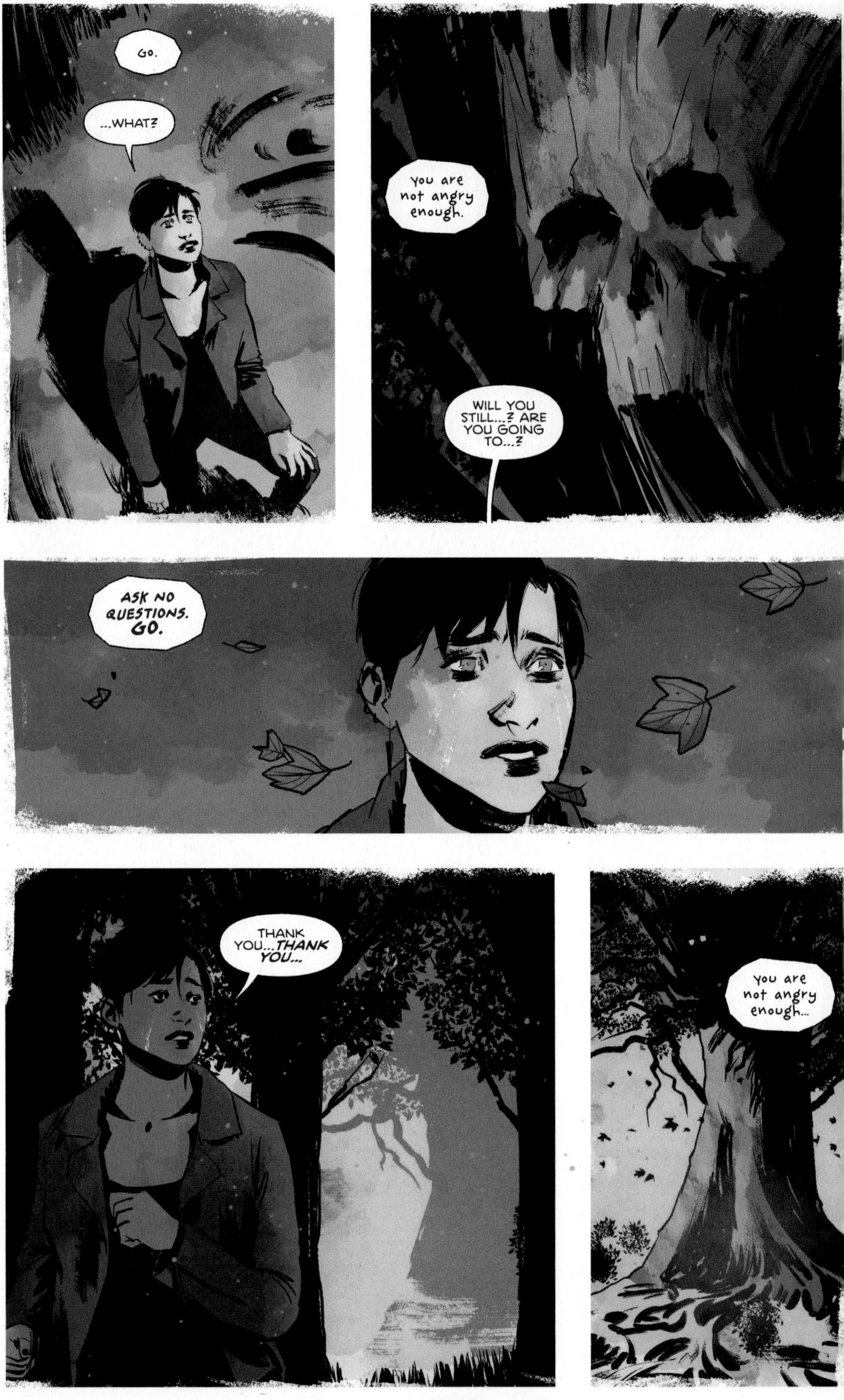
GO.
...WHAT?
you are not angry enough.
WILL YOU STILL...? ARE YOU GOING TO...?
ASK NO QUESTIONS. GO.
THANK YOU...THANK YOU...
you are not angry enough...

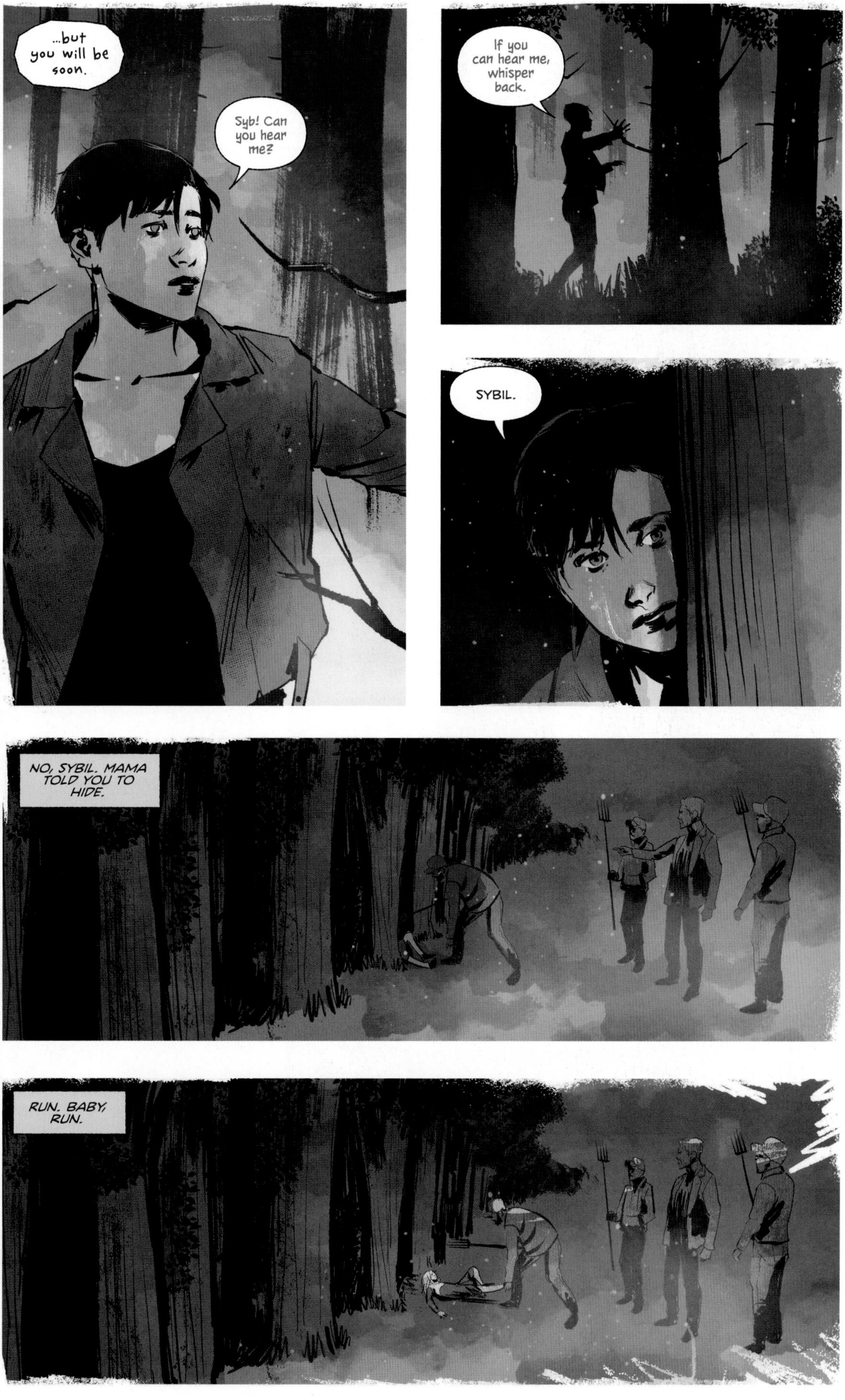
...but you will be soon.
Syb! Can you hear me?
If you can hear me, whisper back.
SYBIL.
NO, SYBIL. MAMA TOLD YOU TO HIDE.
RUN. BABY, RUN.

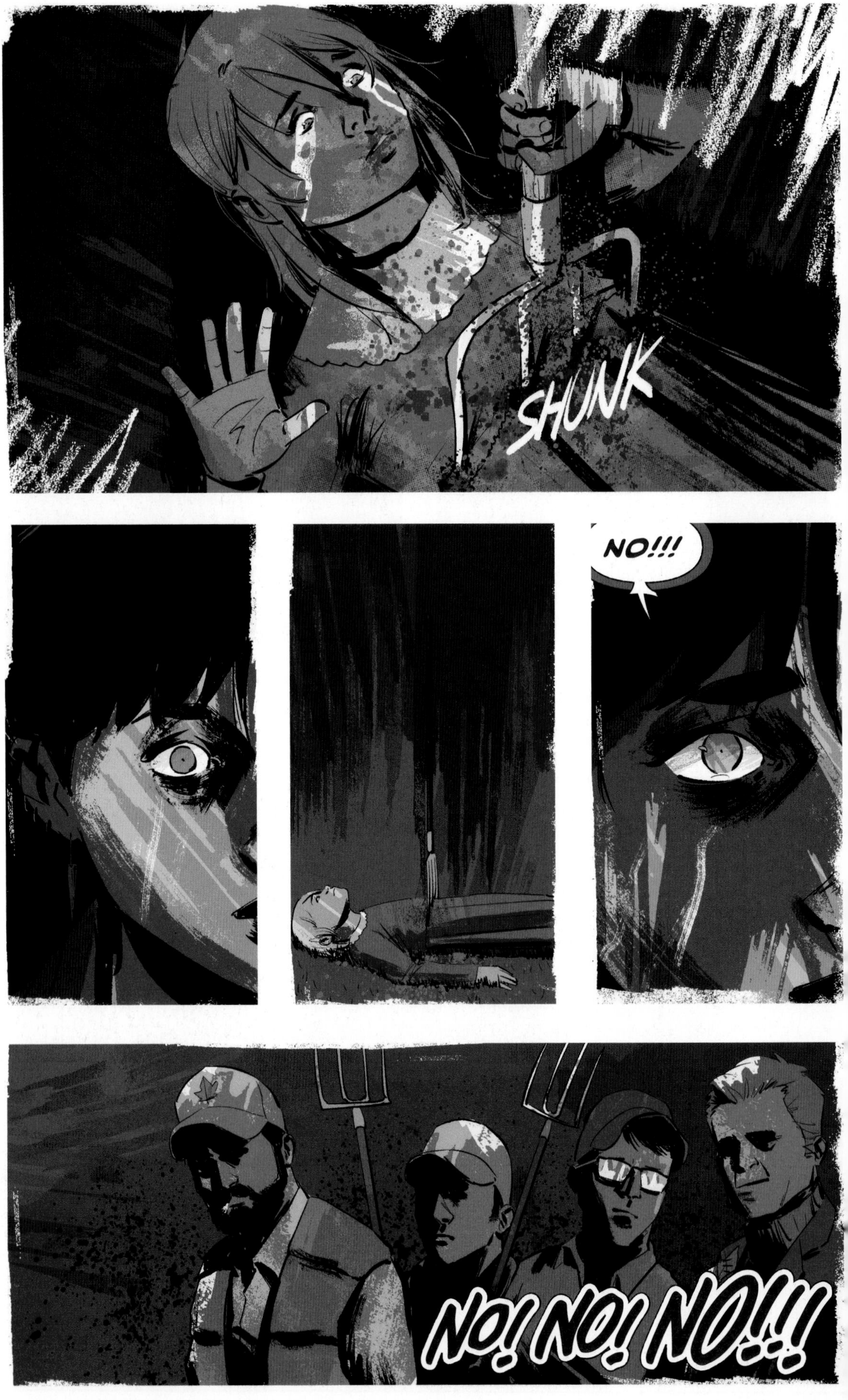
SHUNK
NO!!!
NO! NO! NO!!!

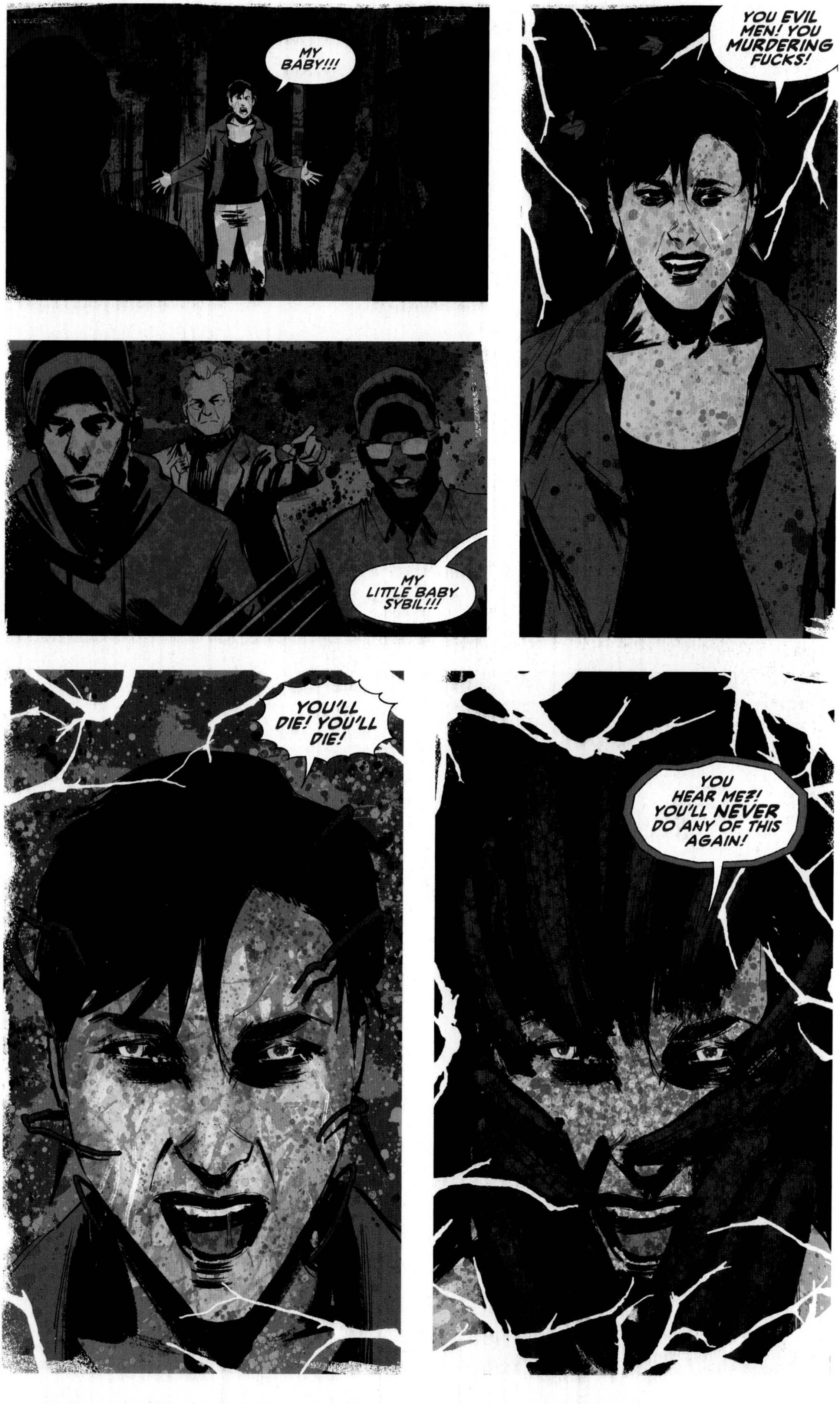
MY BABY!!!
MY LITTLE BABY SYBIL!!!
YOU EVIL MEN! YOU MURDERING FUCKS!
YOU'LL DIE! YOU'LL DIE!
YOU HEAR ME?! YOU'LL NEVER DO ANY OF THIS AGAIN!

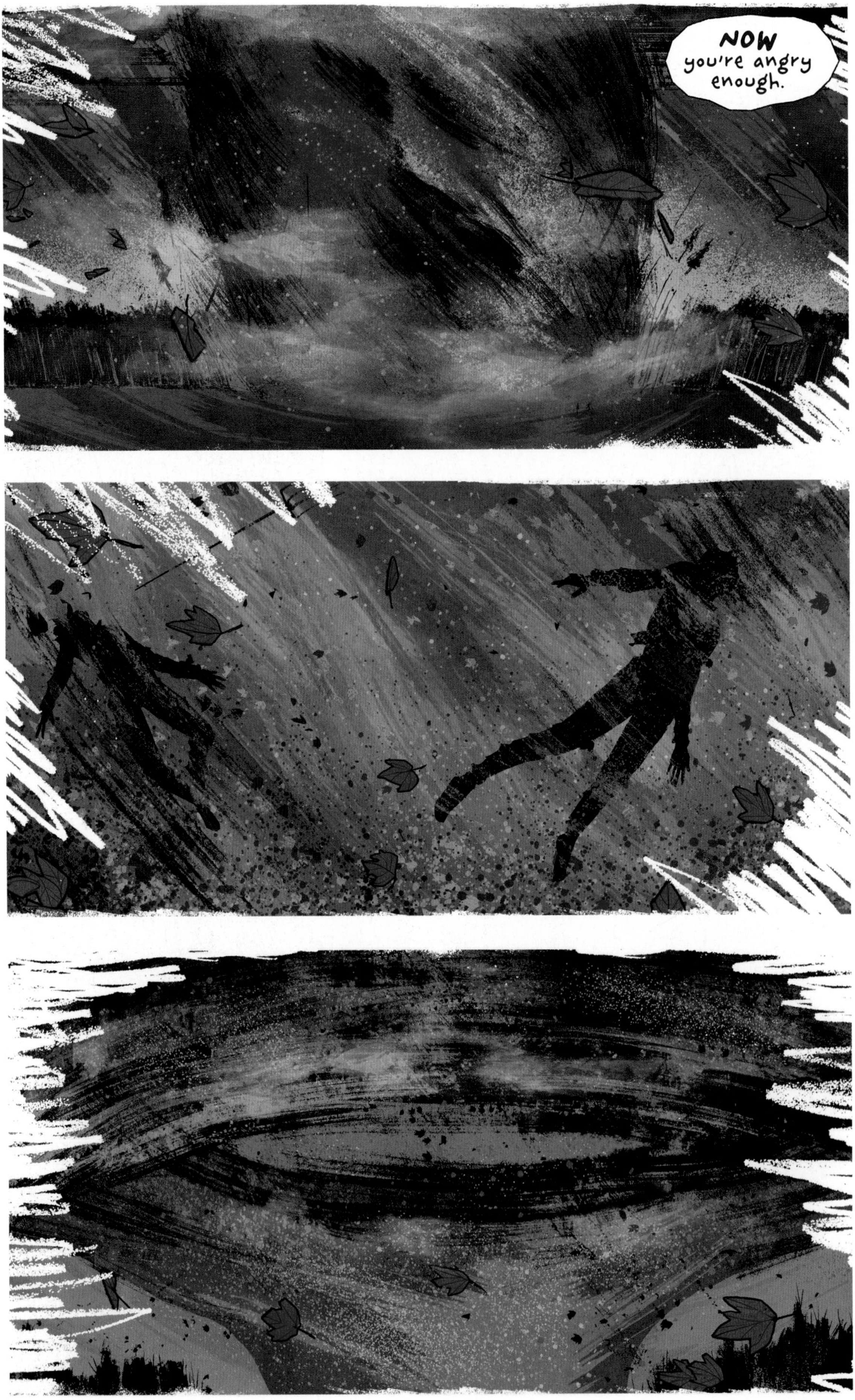
NOW you're angry enough.

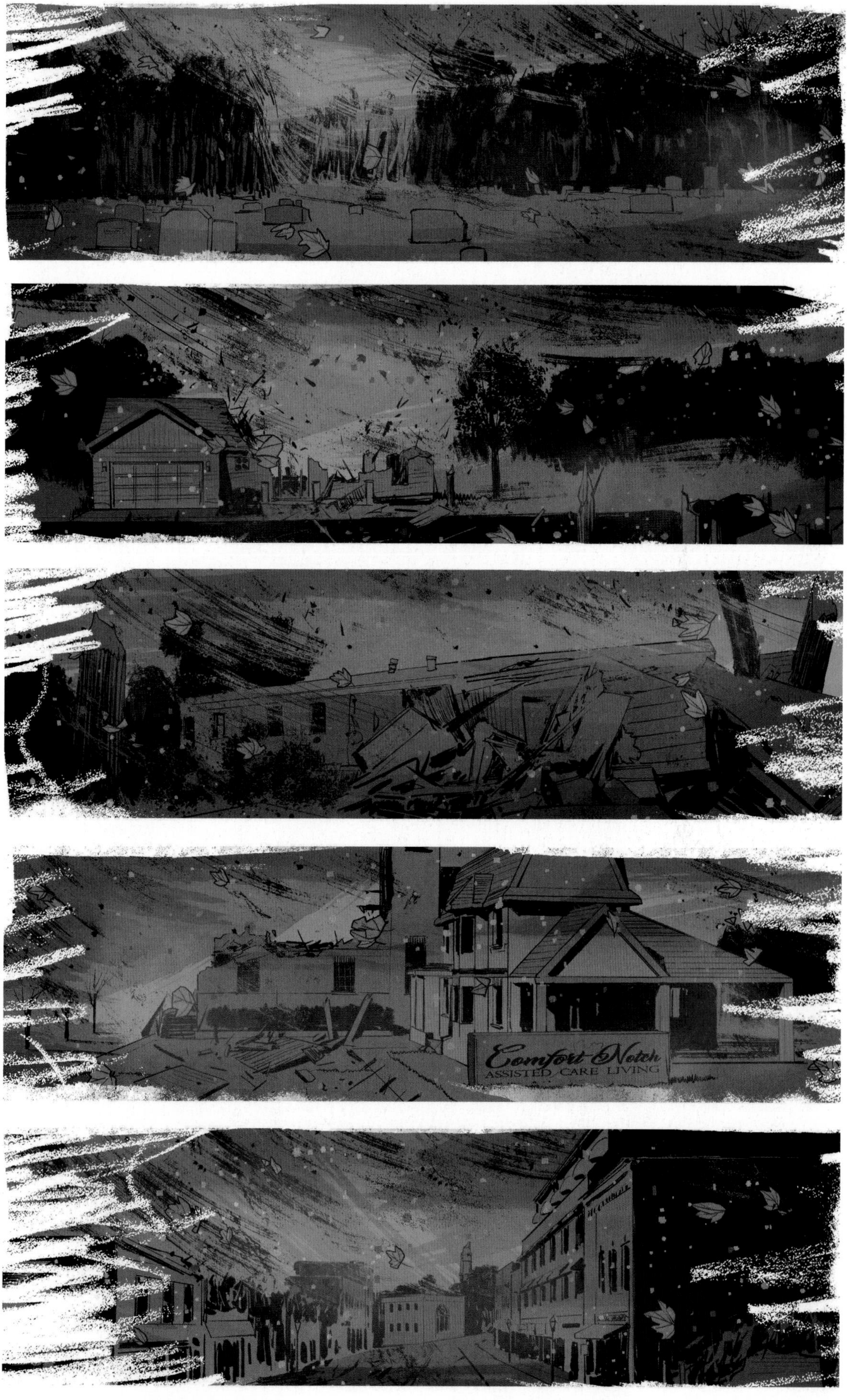
Comfort Notch
ASSISTED CARE LIVING

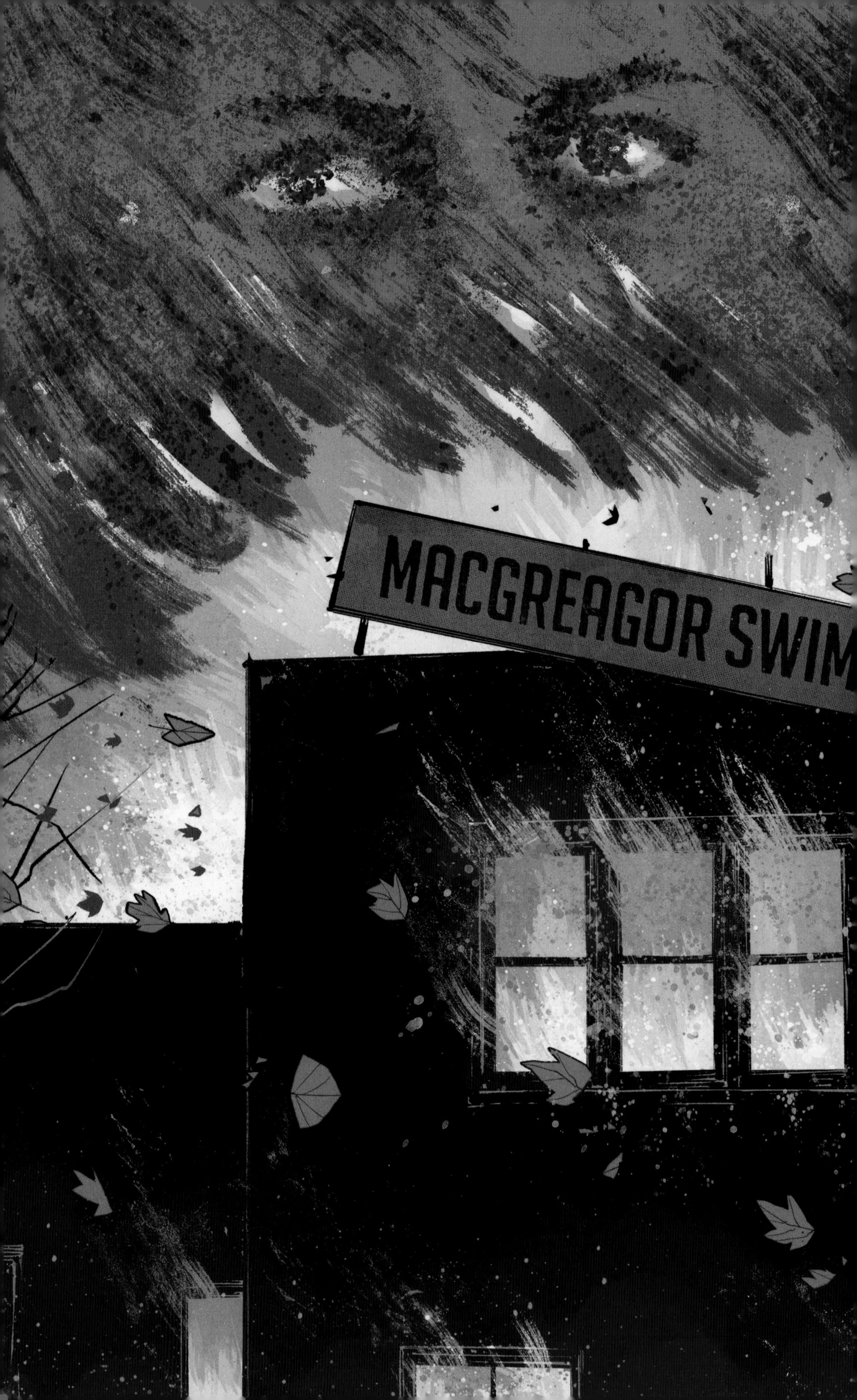
MACGREAGOR SWIM

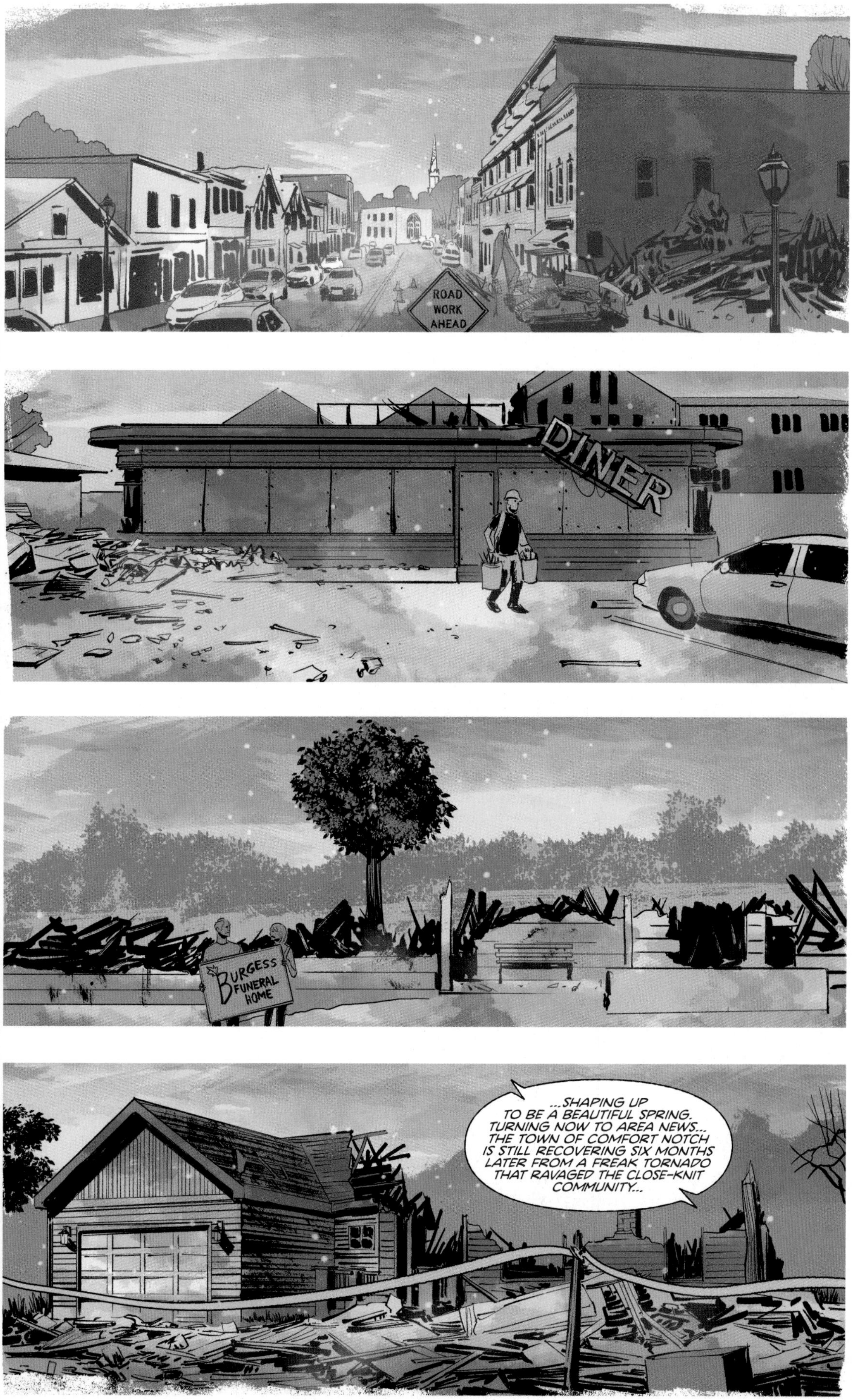
ROAD WORK AHEAD
DINER
BURGESS FUNERAL HOME
...SHAPING UP TO BE A BEAUTIFUL SPRING. TURNING NOW TO AREA NEWS... THE TOWN OF COMFORT NOTCH IS STILL RECOVERING SIX MONTHS LATER FROM A FREAK TORNADO THAT RAVAGED THE CLOSE-KNIT COMMUNITY...

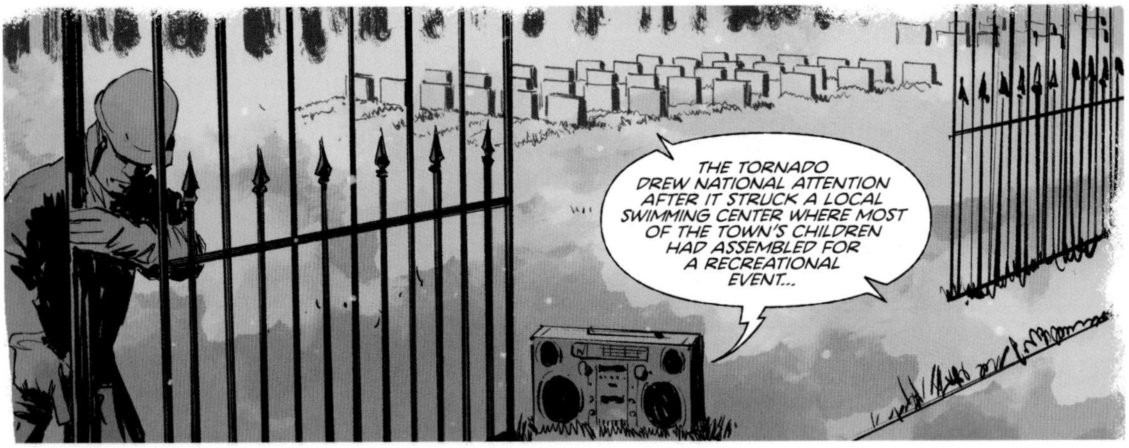
THE TORNADO DREW NATIONAL ATTENTION AFTER IT STRUCK A LOCAL SWIMMING CENTER WHERE MOST OF THE TOWN'S CHILDREN HAD ASSEMBLED FOR A RECREATIONAL EVENT...

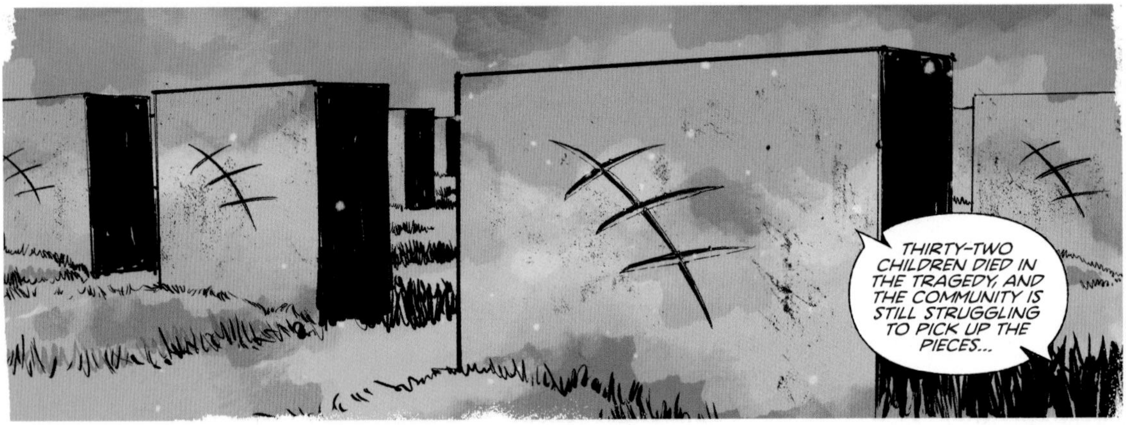
THIRTY-TWO CHILDREN DIED IN THE TRAGEDY, AND THE COMMUNITY IS STILL STRUGGLING TO PICK UP THE PIECES...

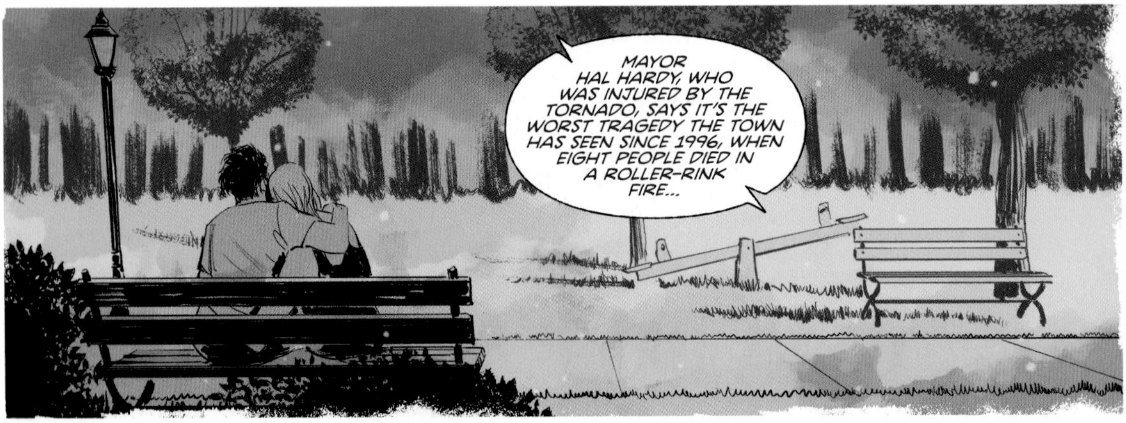
MAYOR HAL HARDY, WHO WAS INJURED BY THE TORNADO, SAYS IT'S THE WORST TRAGEDY THE TOWN HAS SEEN SINCE 1996, WHEN EIGHT PEOPLE DIED IN A ROLLER-RINK FIRE...

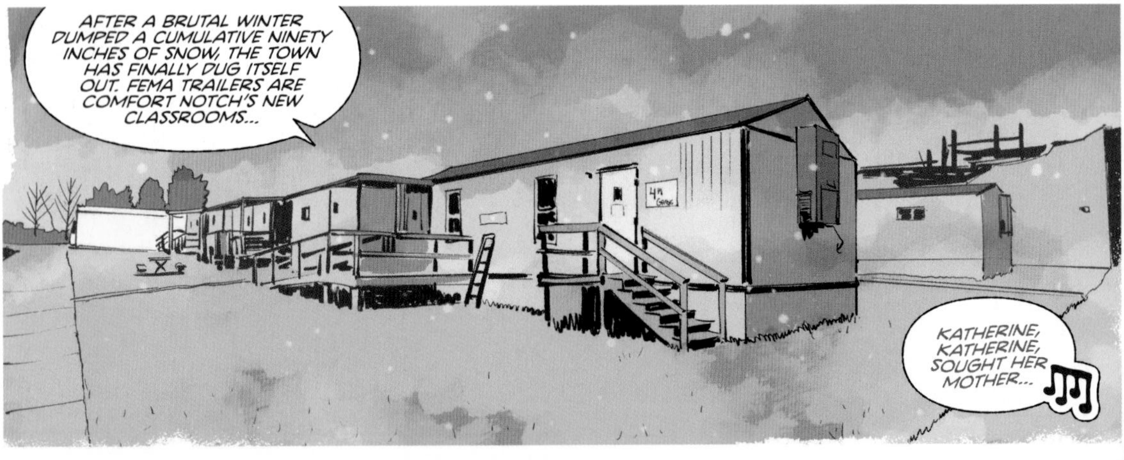
AFTER A BRUTAL WINTER DUMPED A CUMULATIVE NINETY INCHES OF SNOW, THE TOWN HAS FINALLY DUG ITSELF OUT. FEMA TRAILERS ARE COMFORT NOTCH'S NEW CLASSROOMS...
KATHERINE, KATHERINE, SOUGHT HER MOTHER...

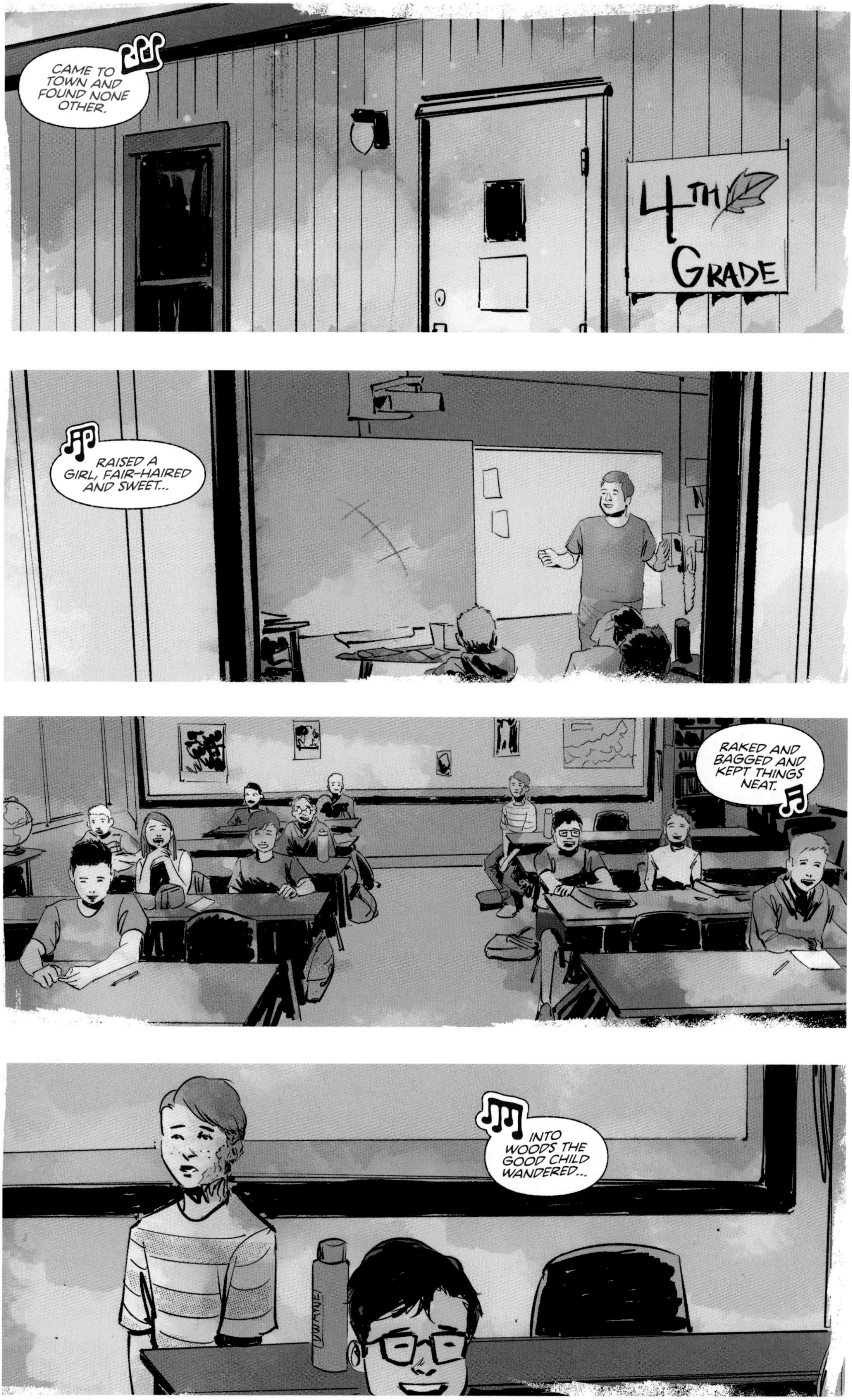
CAME TO TOWN AND FOUND NONE OTHER.
4TH GRADE
RAISED A GIRL, FAIR-HAIRED AND SWEET...
RAKED AND BAGGED AND KEPT THINGS NEAT.
INTO WOODS THE GOOD CHILD WANDERED...

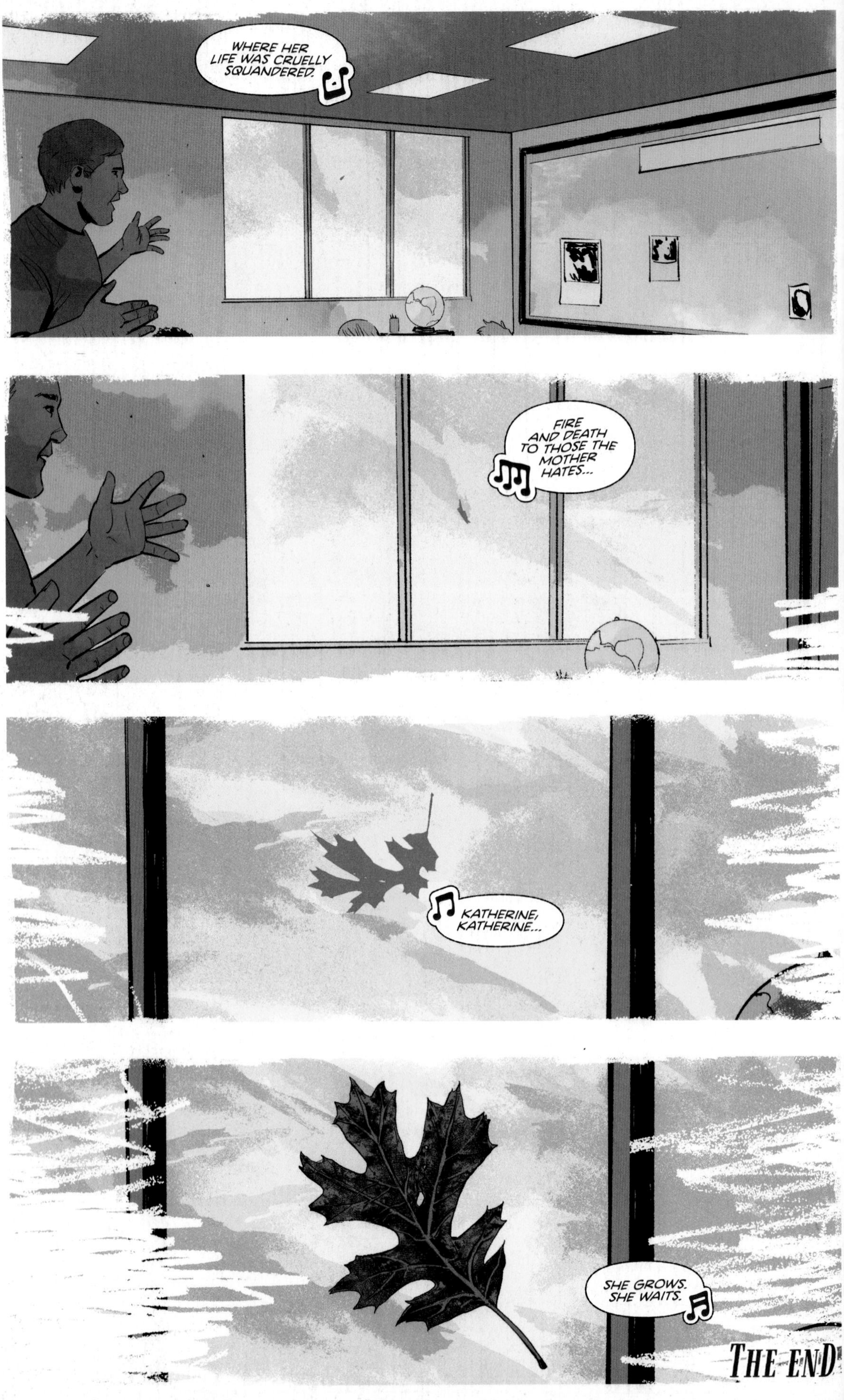
WHERE HER LIFE WAS CRUELLY SQUANDERED.
FIRE AND DEATH TO THOSE THE MOTHER HATES...
KATHERINE, KATHERINE...
SHE GROWS. SHE WAITS.
THE END

ART OF THE
AUTUMNAL

Pen and brush,
charcoal,
and
tablet—

Featuring

CHRIS SHEHAN

NATHAN GOODEN

MARTIN SIMMONDS

JASON WORDIE

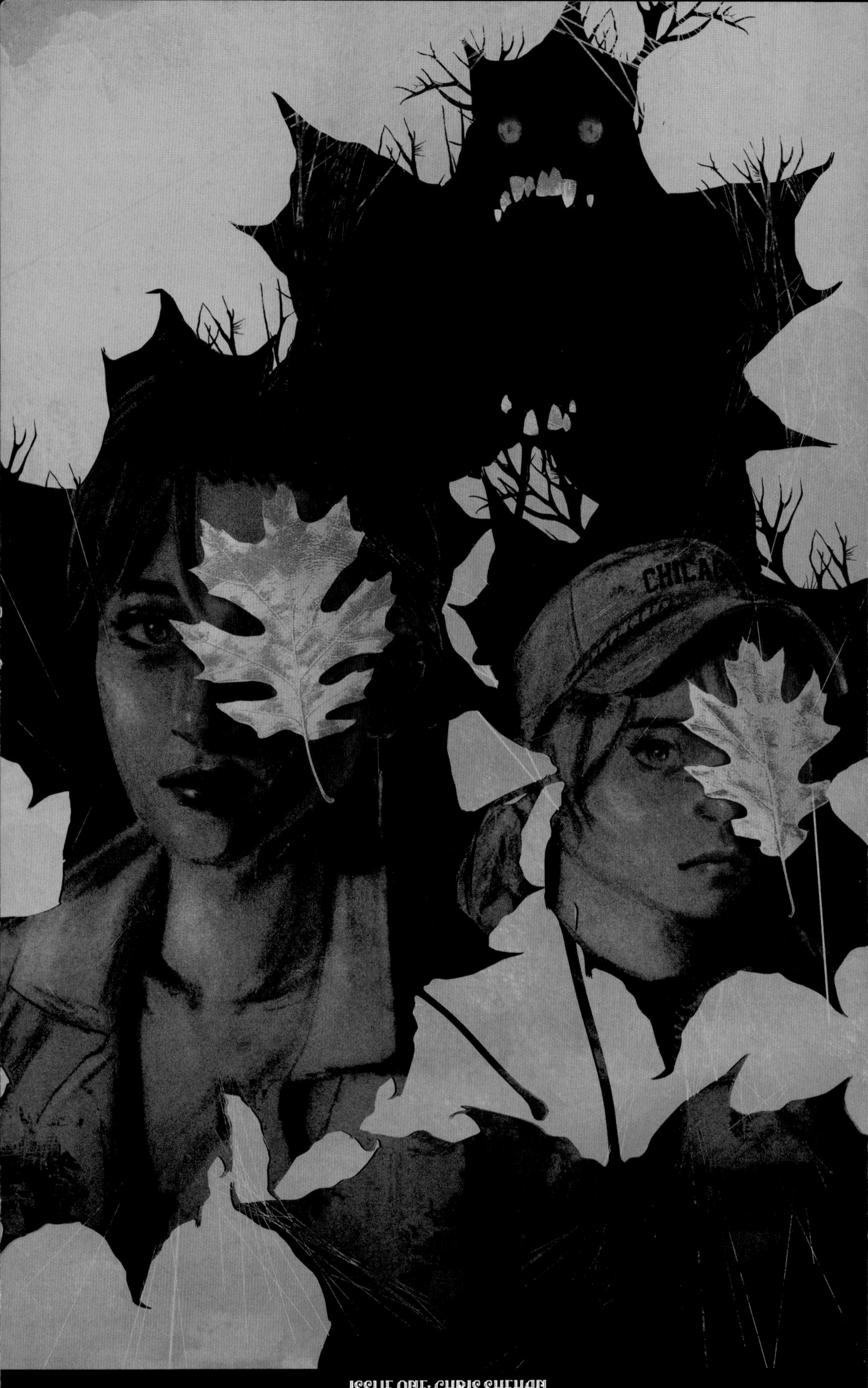
CHICAG

ISSUE ONE: CHRIS SHEHAN

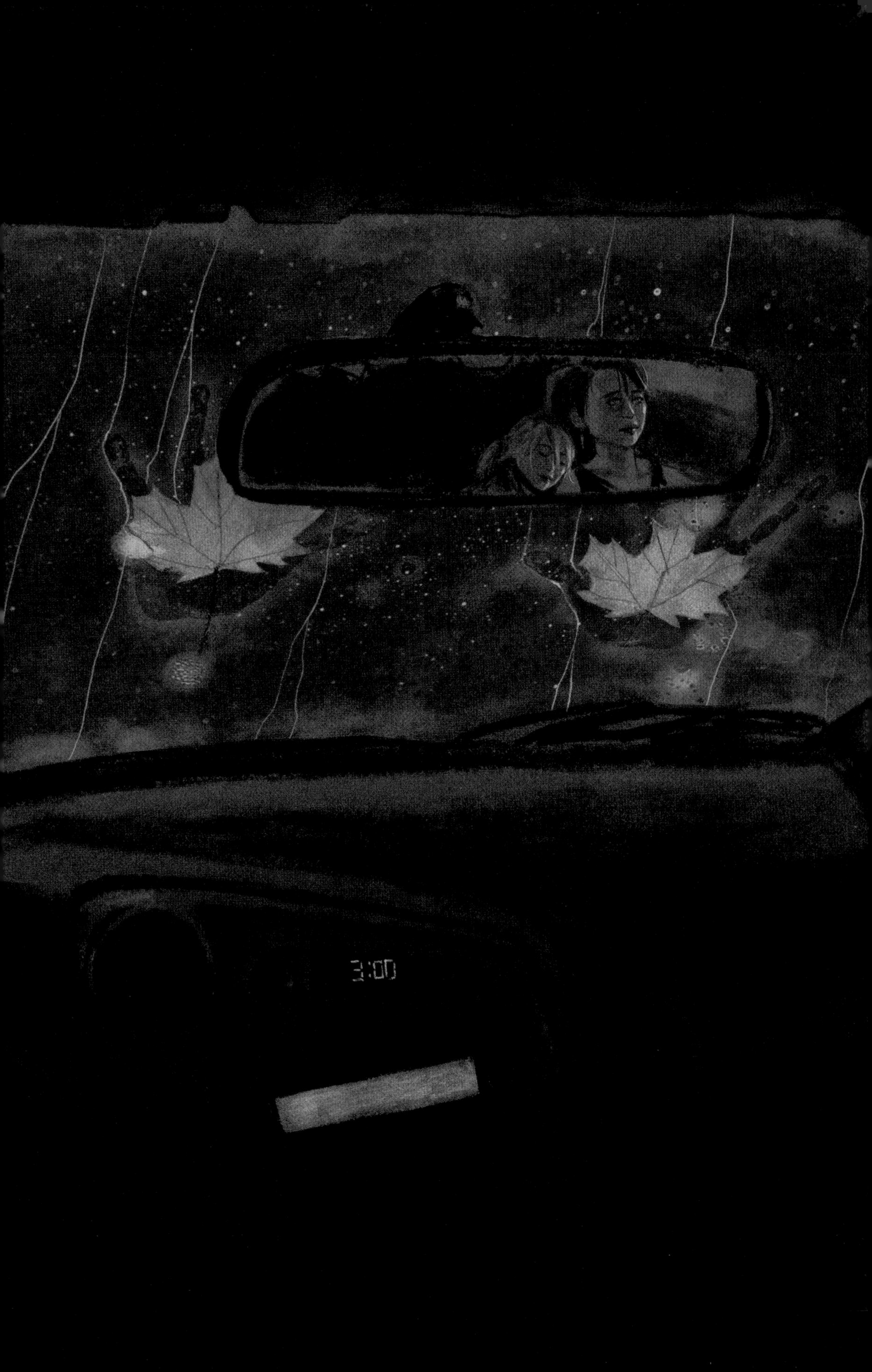
3:00

ISSUE TWO: CHRIS SHEHAN

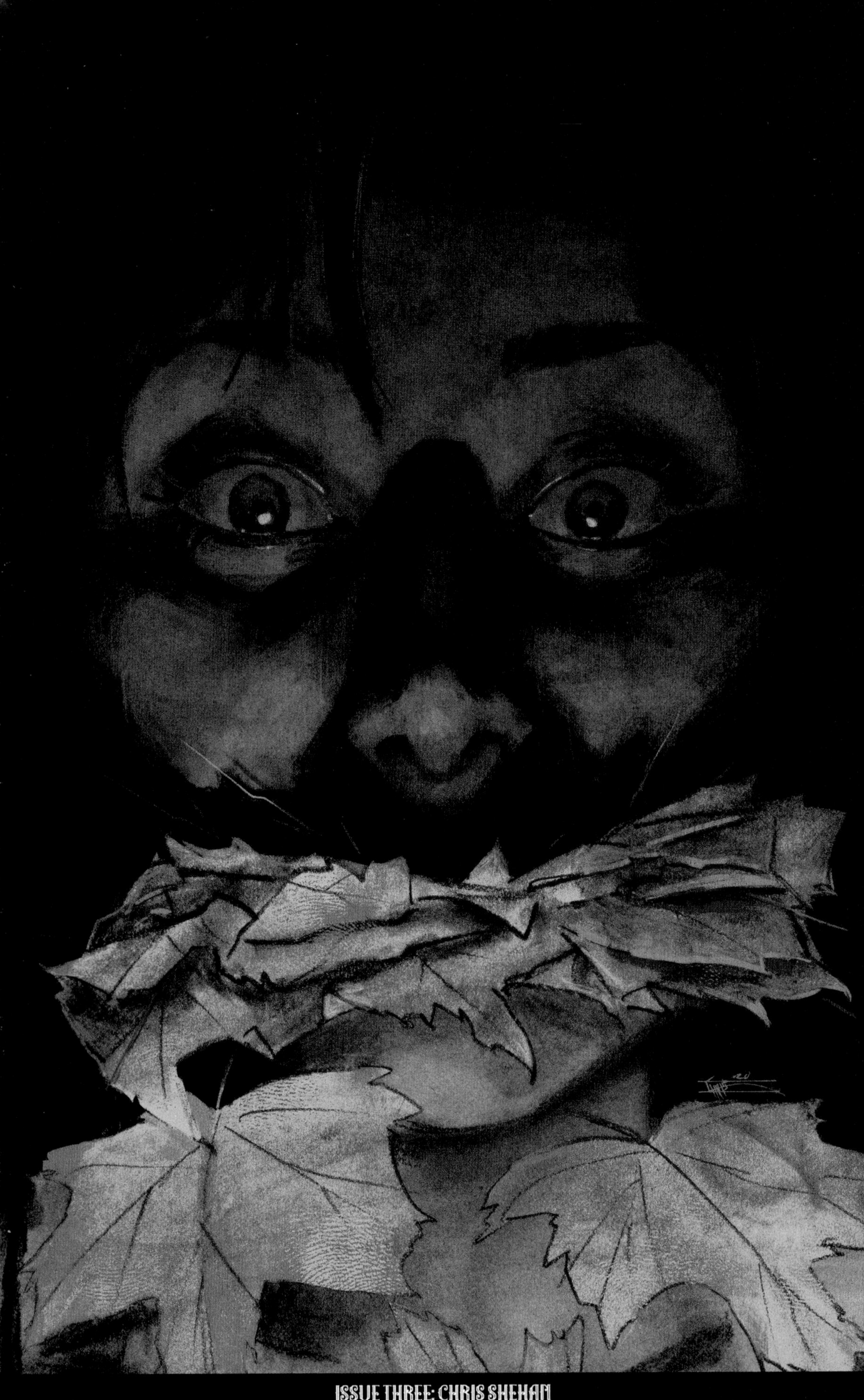

ISSUE THREE: CHRIS SHEHAN

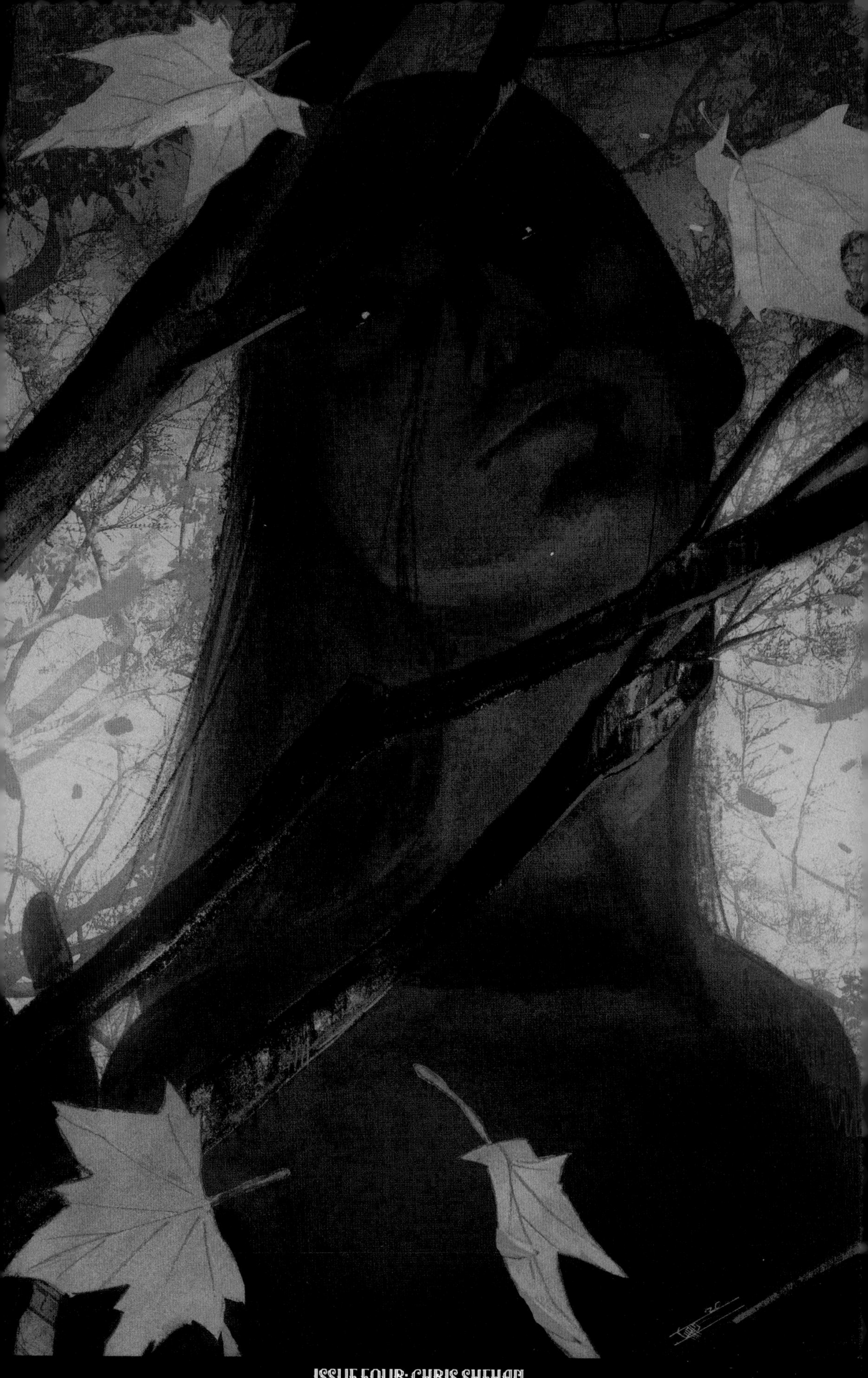

ISSUE FOUR: CHRIS SHEHAN

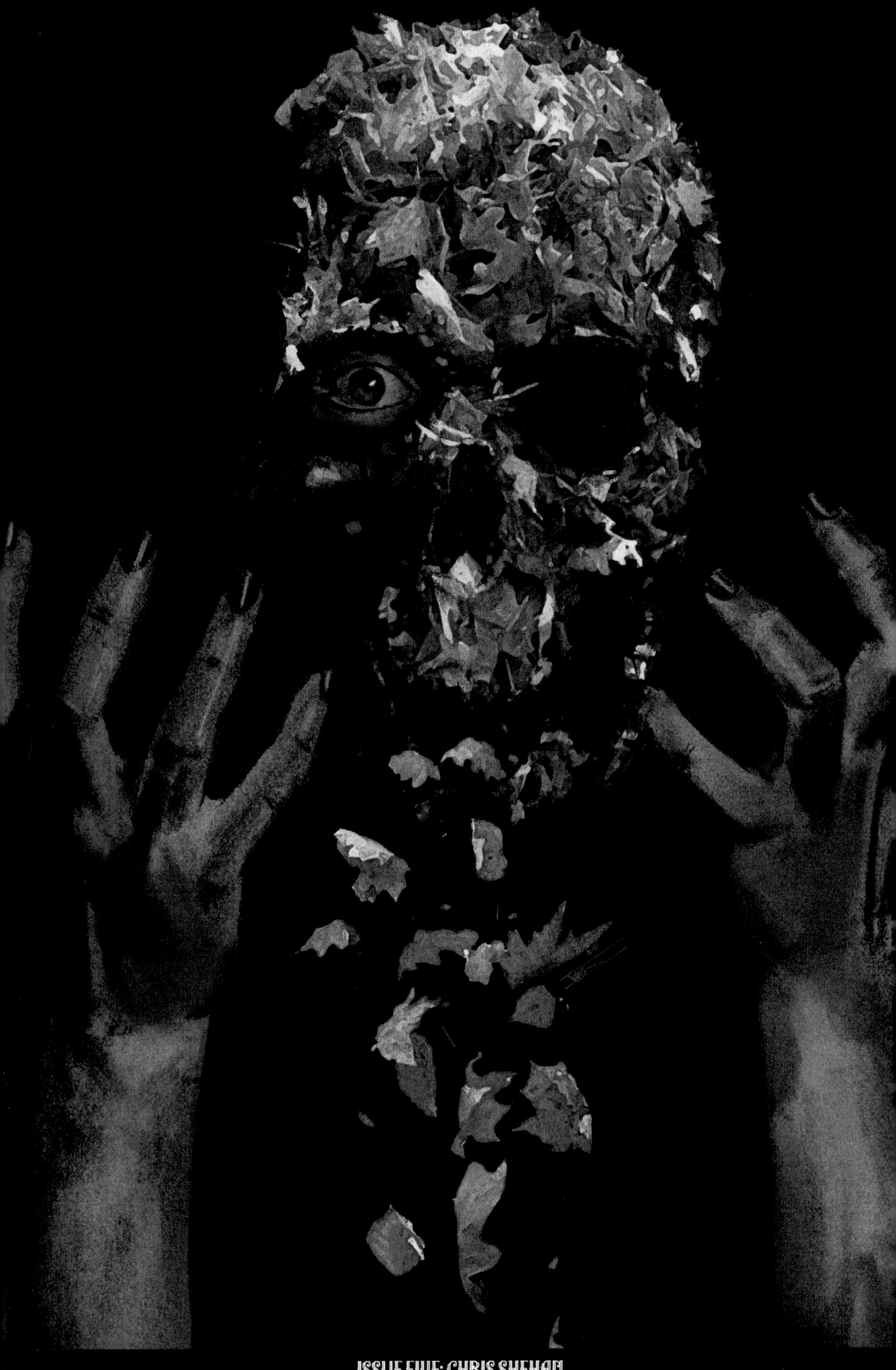

ISSUE FIVE: CHRIS SHEHAN

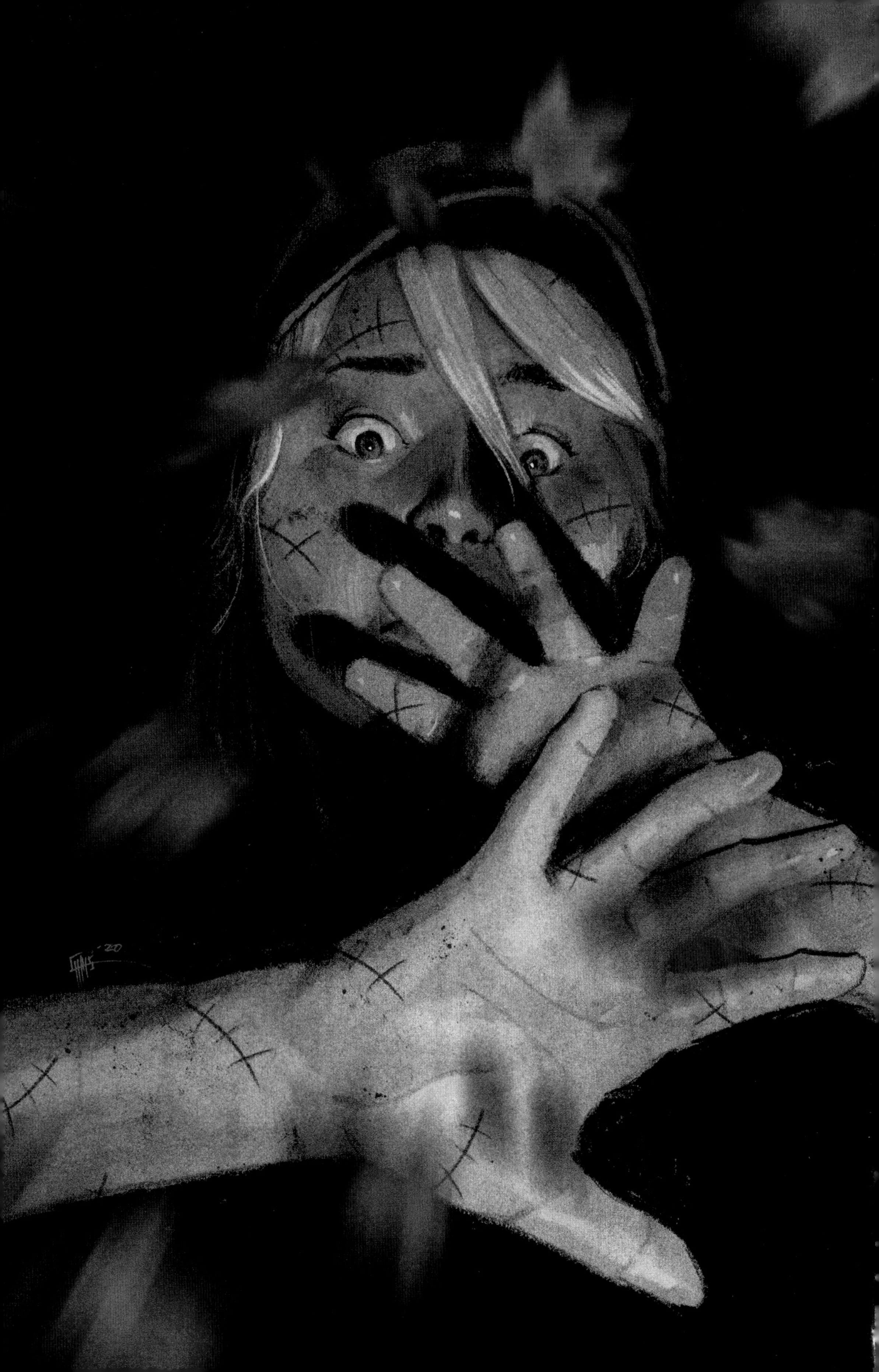

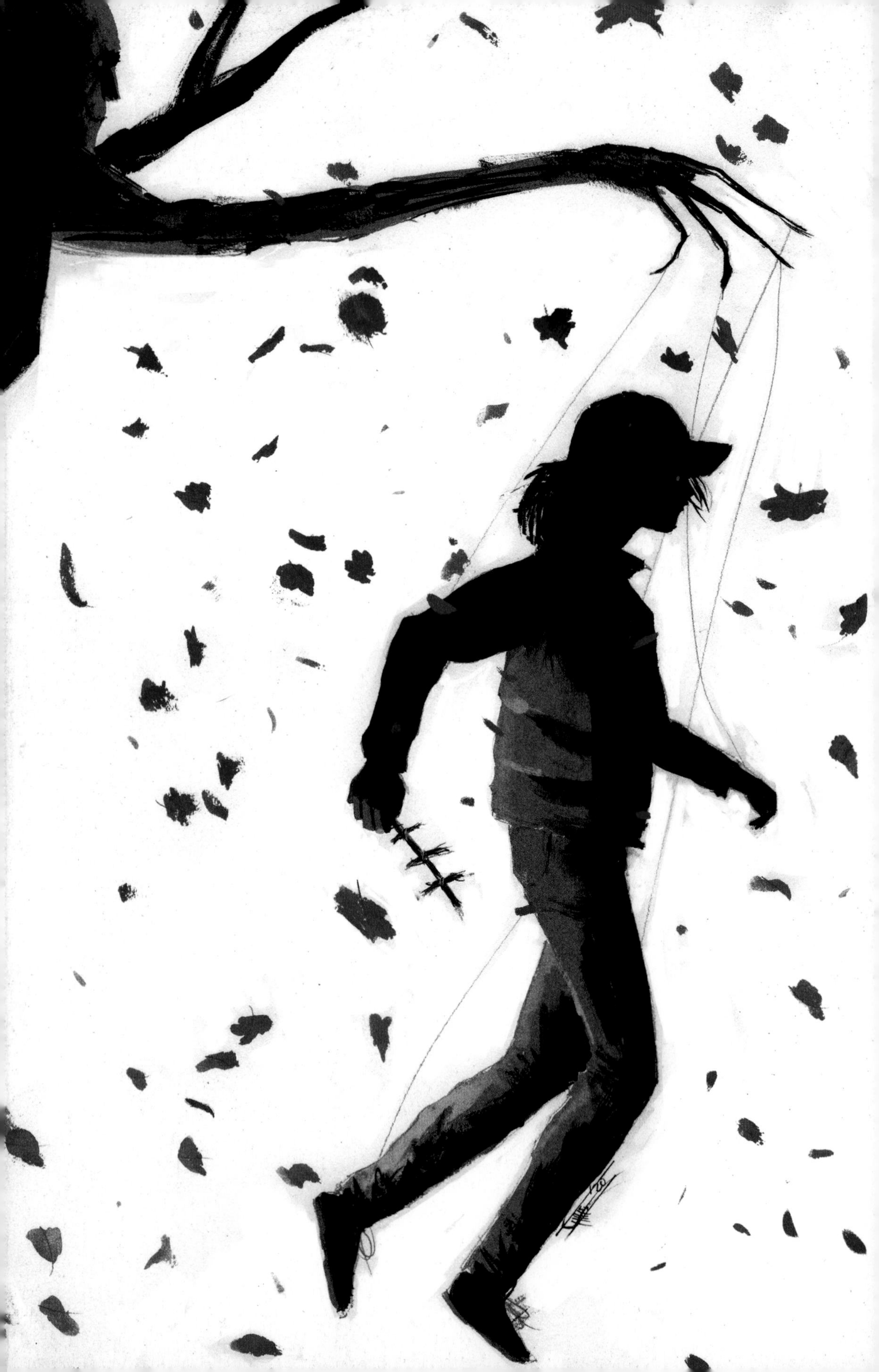

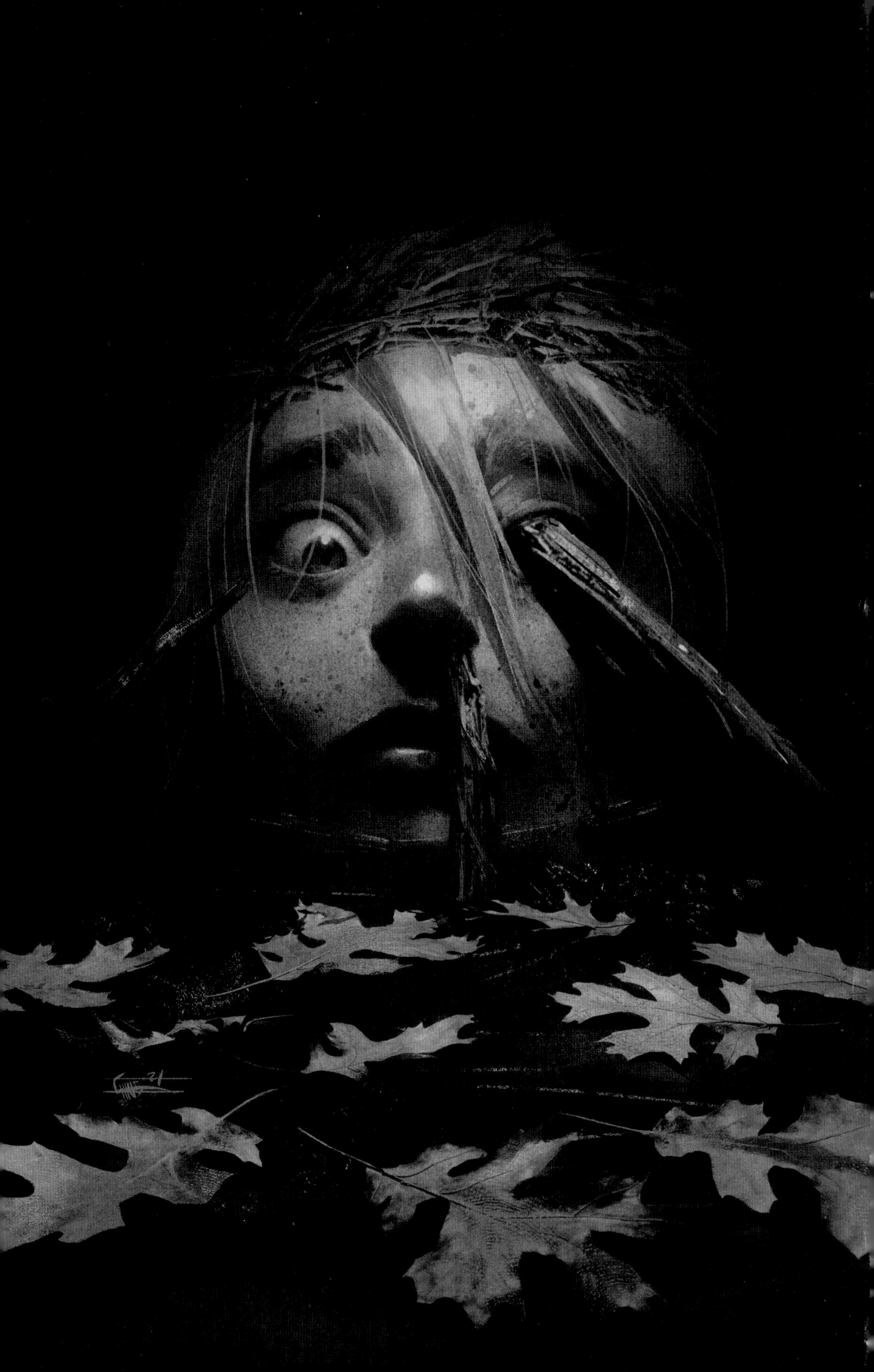

ISSUE EIGHT: CHRIS SHEHAN

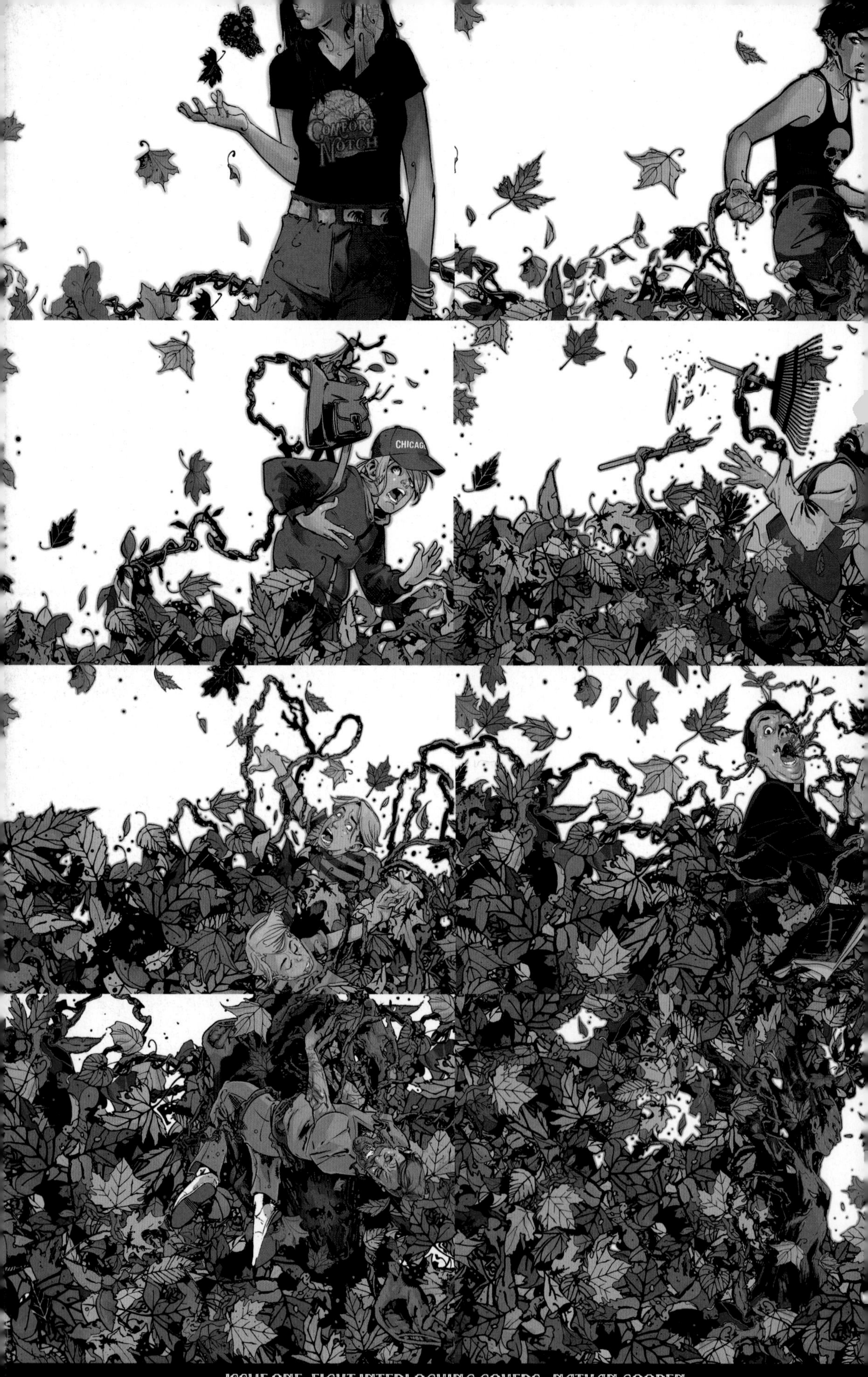
COMFORT NOTCH
CHICAG

ISSUE ONE–EIGHT INTERLOCKING COVERS - NATHAN COOPER

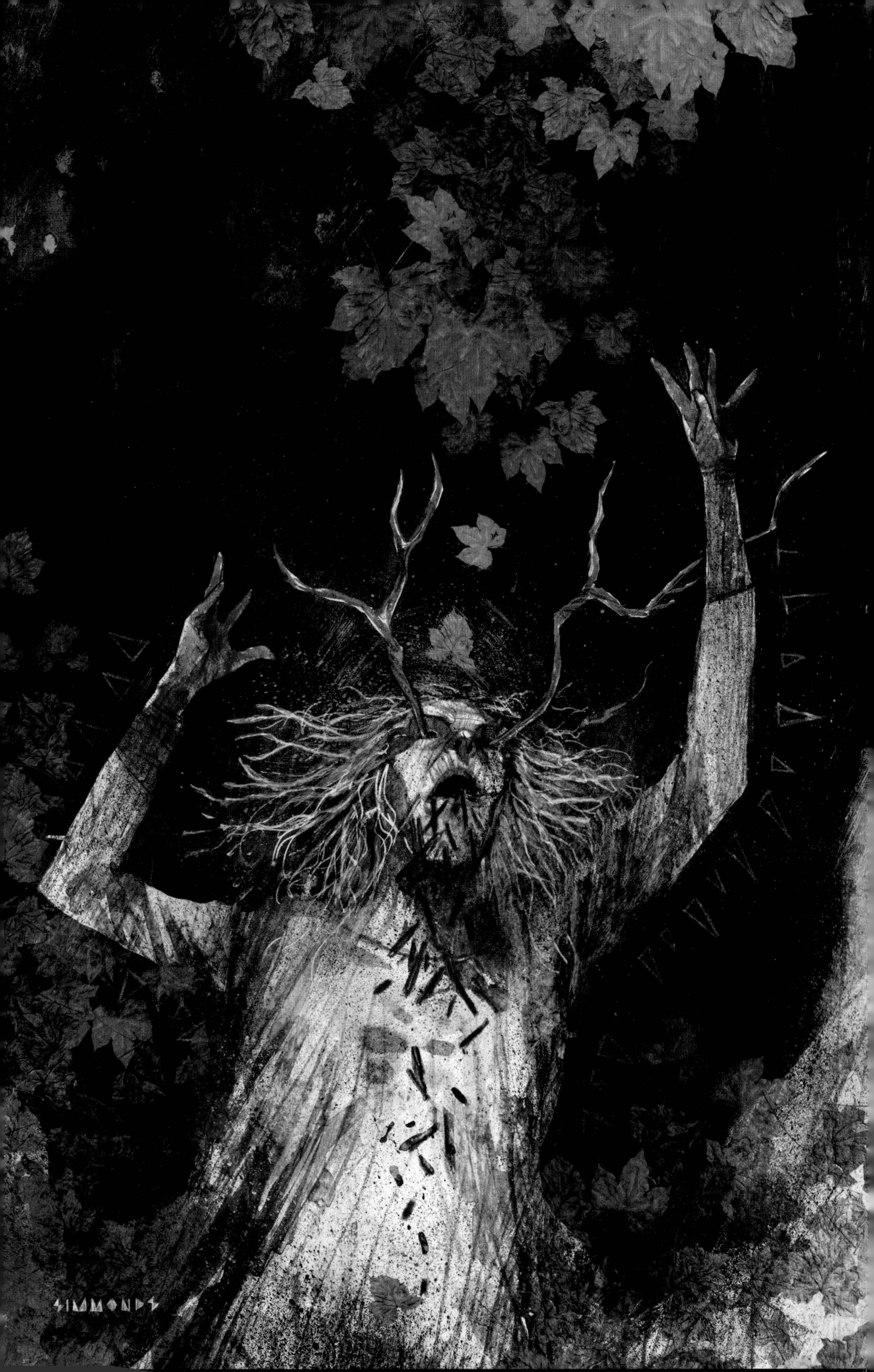
SIMMONDS

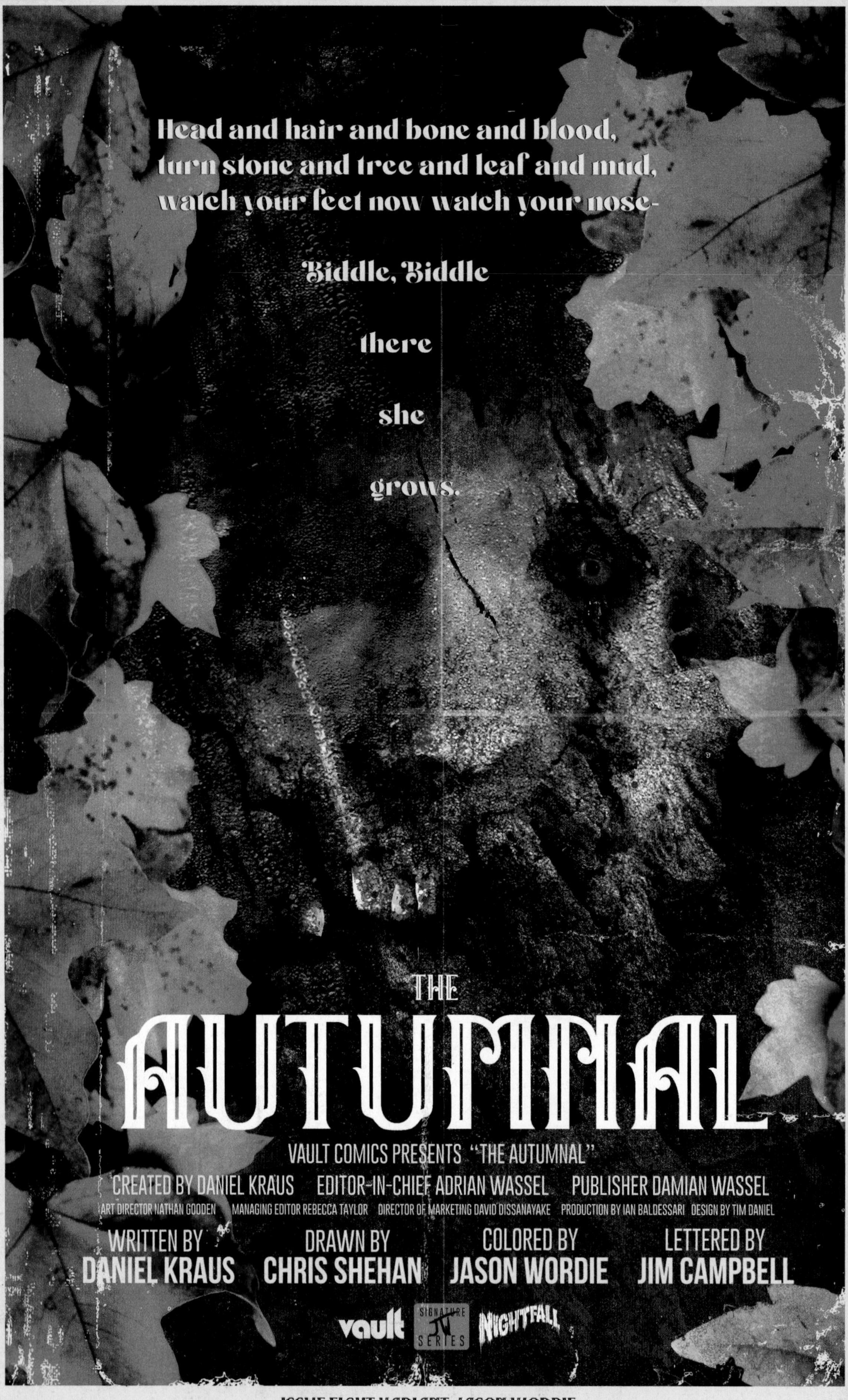

Head and hair and bone and blood,
turn stone and tree and leaf and mud,
watch your feet now watch your nose-
Biddle, Biddle
there
she
grows.
THE
AUTUMNAL
VAULT COMICS PRESENTS "THE AUTUMNAL"
CREATED BY DANIEL KRAUS EDITOR-IN-CHIEF ADRIAN WASSEL PUBLISHER DAMIAN WASSEL
ART DIRECTOR NATHAN GOODEN MANAGING EDITOR REBECCA TAYLOR DIRECTOR OF MARKETING DAVID DISSANAYAKE PRODUCTION BY IAN BALDESSARI DESIGN BY TIM DANIEL
WRITTEN BY DANIEL KRAUS
DRAWN BY CHRIS SHEHAN
COLORED BY JASON WORDIE
LETTERED BY JIM CAMPBELL
vault
SIGNATURE SERIES
NIGHTFALL

ISSUE EIGHT VARIANT: JASON WORDIE